Robert Charles.
July 1991
Fletcher School of
Law and Diplomacy.

THE LIMITS OF ALLIANCE

Psychology and Deterrence

Edited by Robert Jervis, Richard Ned Lebow,
and Janice Gross Stein

Getting to the Table:
The Processes of International Prenegotiation

Edited by Janice Gross Stein

The Limits of Alliance

NATO OUT-OF-AREA PROBLEMS SINCE 1949

Douglas Stuart · William Tow

THE JOHNS HOPKINS UNIVERSITY PRESS

BALTIMORE AND LONDON

Printed in the United States of America

The Johns Hopkins University Press
701 West 40th Street
Baltimore, Maryland 21211
The Johns Hopkins Press Ltd., London

The paper used in this publication meets the minimum requirements of
American National Standard for Information Sciences—Permanence of
Paper for Printed Library Materials, ANSI Z39.48–1984.

Library of Congress Cataloging-in-Publication Data

Stuart, Douglas T.
The limits of alliance.

(Perspectives on security)
Includes bibliographical references.
1. North Atlantic Treaty Organization.   2. World
politics—1945–   .   3. United States—Military policy.
4. Great Britain—Military policy.   5. France—Military
policy.   I. Tow, William T.   II. Title.   III. Series.
UA646.3.S795   1990   355′.031′091821   90-4407
ISBN 0-8018-3808-8 (alk. paper)

CONTENTS

CONTENTS

PART III
FRANCE

PART IV
THE OTHER NATO MEMBERS

CONTENTS

ACKNOWLEDGMENTS

THIS BOOK represents a seven-year research effort by the authors, begun in 1982 and completed at the end of 1988. During that period we drew upon the talents and generosity of a large number of people. We would like to thank those individuals without whose help we could not have completed the project.

Much of the initial research (archival work and interviews) was made possible by the support of the NATO Information Service and the Fulbright Commission under the auspices of the NATO International Fellows Program. Members of the NATO staff were also extremely helpful in answering our questions and directing us to European officials and institutions involved in out-of-area issues. Special thanks go to Ambassador Henning Wegener (Assistant Secretary General for Political Affairs), Ms. Elaine McDevitt, Dr. Giuseppe Stano, and Dr. Ferdinand Welter of the NATO Information Service, and Dr. Rainer Rupp of the NATO Economics Directorate.

Among the colleagues who assisted us with research advice were Georges Delcoigne, Jim Digby, Michael Fry, Peter Foot, Brigadier Kenneth Hunt, Larry Kaplan, Uwe Nerlich, Robert O'Neill, Elizabeth Sherwood, Geoffrey Warner, and Cees Wiebes. Richard Ned Lebow, consulting editor of the Johns Hopkins Perspectives on Security series, was especially helpful at every stage in the process.

We owe a special debt of gratitude to our research assistants: Philip Brick, Roberto Domeison, Philip Frayne, Chris Griffin, Amin Kahn, Heinz Kern, Marzenna Kowalik, Ryo Shimuzu, and Ishtiaque Zaman. Essential typing and logistical support was provided by Mary Baitinger, Linda Dugan, Carol Gustin, Vickie Kuhn, and Kathy Matthes.

Gerald Bender, chairman of the USC School of International Relations, and Sylvester Whitaker, dean of the USC Social Science Division, demonstrated a keen interest in the project and were instrumental in providing timely financial support to see it through. We are very grateful for their help. We would also like to acknowledge USC's Center for International Studies and its director, Thomas Biersteker, and associate director, Cecilia Cicchinelli.

The Johns Hopkins University Press was patient and extremely helpful

ACKNOWLEDGMENTS

throughout the project. Special thanks go to our editor, Carol Ehrlich, and to JHUP's executive editor, Henry Tom.

Finally, and most importantly, we thank our families: our wives, Carol and Leslie, and our daughters, Laura and Shannon. Without their abiding support and encouragement we would be much less fulfilled as scholars and persons.

THE LIMITS OF ALLIANCE

INTRODUCTION

During the 1980s, NATO out-of-area cooperation became a subject of intense interest among Western academics and policy makers. In less than a decade, a substantial scholarly literature developed relating to the problems of coordinating political, economic, and military responses to problems arising outside of the established NATO boundaries.[1] Most of the articles, books, and reports are policy-oriented and prescriptive, and many treat the NATO out-of-area issue as a recent phenomenon. Indeed, some of these works give the impression that the problem of determining when and where NATO should become involved in events occurring beyond the treaty area was created in 1979 by the Soviet intervention in Afghanistan.[2]

The fact that there is still no comprehensive analysis of the historical antecedents of the out-of-area debate is curious, because out-of-area issues have been a source of intra-alliance dispute since NATO was established. Such issues as Suez (1956) and Indochina (1949–54) are well known, but other out-of-area disputes over the last forty years—in Indonesia, Tunisia, and Portuguese Africa, to name a few—deserve more attention than they have received. The ahistorical nature of the recent out-of-area literature is also misleading, since it encourages readers to assume without question that NATO faced unique and unprecedented out-of-area threats in the 1980s, and to accept as a first premise that the NATO boundaries established in 1949 are inappropriate to the challenges of today.

The Need for a Historical Perspective

The purpose of this book is to place the out-of-area debate in the context of NATO's history since 1949. We intend to compare and contrast out-of-area crises—how they began, how they were handled, and how they affected the alliance as a whole. We will survey the out-of-area issue on a country-by-country basis, in order to highlight our basic theme: the difficulty of maintaining a regionally demarcated multilateral alliance comprising nations that recognize important security interests beyond the alliance's perimeters.

In the process of surveying the history of NATO out-of-area disputes, we hope to be able to say something about the nature of alliances in general, and about the uses of influence in any alliance relationship. We begin by observing that the phrase *unconditional alliance* has no place in the international relations lexicon except as a diplomatic nicety for an imperial relationship. All alliances involve a complex interplay of identical, complementary, and competing national interests. Traditionally, nations have sought to build both offensive and defensive alliances upon clearly articulated common interests, while leaving potential sources of intra-alliance dispute for resolution at some later date. Often, however, divergent national interests that are initially suppressed by alliance members in the face of a common threat or in pursuit of a common gain become increasingly disruptive over time, leading ultimately to the alliance's collapse. Thus, Talleyrand's observation that "treason is a matter of dates" applies nicely to the politics of alliance creation and dissolution throughout history.

Unrealistic expectations tend to exacerbate problems of conditional cooperation. Robert Jervis has noted that an alliance leader will often overestimate the degree to which its distinct national security interests are shared by the junior members of an alliance.[3] The history of NATO provides ample support for this theory (American involvement in Korea and Vietnam, Washington's arguments regarding the vulnerability of Persian Gulf oil supplies, etc.). But our study will provide several illustrations of false expectations by junior allies as well. In the case of the Belgian Congo, for example, Brussels was encouraged by the rhetoric of "common security interests" enshrined in the NATO Treaty to hope that other allies, including the alliance leader, would be sympathetic and supportive. The same was true of France in Indochina and, of course, Suez.

Glenn Snyder has made a special contribution to our understanding of the dynamics of alliance formation and maintenance by his distinction between "general" and "particular" interests. General interests, according to Snyder, "stem from the anarchic structure of the system and the geographic position of the state."[4] Throughout history, the general interest that has most often led states to seek alliance is the perceived need to balance a common threat.[5] But states also bring particular interests with them when they enter alliances. These interests reflect the unique historical, ideological, and geostrategic circumstances of each ally, and they are often in competition with the particular interests of other alliance members. Snyder tells us that "such conflicts and alignments of interest and ideology establish the background of relationships against which the overt alliance bargaining process takes place."[6]

Snyder argues that the most important determinant of cohesion in an alliance is the nature of the international system which has shaped the general interest of the allies. Thus, in a tight bipolar arrangement—characterized by clearly delineated blocs, two overwhelmingly large alliance leaders, and a visible common threat—conflicting particular interests are not likely to lead to the alliance's collapse. The allies simply have nowhere else to go. Conversely, in a multipolar system in which "high mutual dependence coexists with plausible realignment options," incompatible particular interests are more likely to lead to the alliance's collapse.

Bipolarity and multipolarity also have interesting implications for the kinds of intra-alliance bargaining which are the central focus of this study. For example, to the extent that members of a bipolar alliance recognize that none of the members realistically has the option of abandoning the alliance, there is very little incentive to restrain the rhetoric of intra-alliance disputes over particular interests—such as out-of-area commitments. Each ally will seek to utilize the alliance to solicit support for its particular out-of-area concerns and will complain bitterly when such support is not forthcoming. In the end, however, the *demandeur* will not be able to manipulate the threat of defection in order to get its way. On the other hand, persistent demands for support for out-of-area interests cannot be stifled by threats of expulsion from the alliance. By contrast, in a multipolar system in which "an ally's defection is a calamity, yet distinctly possible," all parties must be cautious about intra-alliance disputes over out-of-area interests. The demands upon intra-alliance diplomacy are much greater in this situation, because both the opportunities for manipulating another ally and the risks associated with mismanagement are greater.[7]

NATO

To place NATO in the context of this theoretical discussion, we would observe that it is a defensive alliance, established during an era of tight bipolarity to balance a commonly perceived threat.[8] By 1948, the United States and the key Western European governments had recognized a mutual interest in the creation of a collective security arrangement to deter Soviet aggression. As Hans Morgenthau describes it, the alliance "sprang naturally and almost inevitably from a common concern with a common heritage that had a chance to survive only through common support."[9]

But there was nothing "natural" or "inevitable" about the form that this security arrangement ultimately took. Indeed, even a cursory review of the discussions between and within the allied governments prior to 1949 provides a bewildering collection of alternative schemes for collective defense. There were, for example, a number of different proposals involving "concentric circles" and "gradations" of global alliance membership and treaty obligation.[10] And some Western European colonial governments expressed interest in an Atlantic alliance that could be stretched to cover contingencies among the overseas territories as events required.

These diverse and competing schemes reflect the multiplicity of particular interests of key Western governments in the late 1940s. While all signatories to the NATO Treaty agreed that Moscow constituted the greatest potential threat to Western security, each member brought other concerns and interests to the alliance as well. Paris, for example, considered domestic unrest and the escalating conflict in Indochina to be its most immediate security problems at the time, and still viewed Germany (particularly a reunified Germany) as a serious long-term security threat. Britain, meanwhile, hoped to use NATO as a means toward a more general foreign policy goal of fostering a "special relationship" with the United States and, in the process, preserving the benefits of empire. Italy sought NATO membership as a means of acquiring status and influence in the Western community. And virtually all of America's new allies saw NATO as an instrument for gaining access to U.S. Military Assistance Program (MAP) funds.

As the alliance leader, the United States faced the problem of transforming these multiple interests and perspectives into a collective security arrangement focused on the Soviet threat. As the Washington Preparatory Talks (for an Atlantic alliance) progressed, all participants came to agree that the treaty area would have to be clearly delineated, and that with the possible exception of Algeria, alliance membership would have to be limited to North America and Western Europe. This left considerable room for disagreement, however, regarding *which* European countries should be granted membership. The participants in the talks summarized the problem in a joint memorandum to their respective governments:

> A North Atlantic security system composed exclusively of the United States, Canada and the present parties to the Brussels Treaty [France, Britain and the Benelux states] would not be fully effective. On the other hand, even the combined military resources of these nations would be inadequate to warrant their assuming hard and fast commitments for the security of a large number of geographically scattered countries. A line must be drawn somewhere.[11]

Ultimately, as a result of several political compromises, the line was drawn around twelve countries. French acceptance of the Scandinavian states was understood as a quid pro quo for Anglo-Saxon accession to French demands for the inclusion of Algeria and Italy. Spain was kept out because of its authoritarian government, but the authoritarian Salazar regime in Portugal (with its important base facilities in the Azores) was invited in. Greece and Turkey were noticeably absent, which in retrospect appears anomalous, since the NATO Treaty represented the military extension of the Truman Doctrine, which had been formulated in response to events in the Eastern Mediterranean. But the participants in the Washington Preparatory Talks agreed that extension of the alliance into the Eastern Mediterranean would blur the regional identity of the pact and risk the kind of overcommitment that U.S. Undersecretary of State Robert Lovett described as "spreading the butter so thin that it would not feed anyone."[12]

Yet key NATO members still feared that the establishment of the Atlantic

Alliance, with its narrowly defined regional identity, would encourage Moscow to threaten the security of those countries that had been excluded from the alliance. This concern led Washington and London to enter into discussions about the possibility of creating a southern counterpart to NATO—a Middle East Defense Organization (MEDO)—which might include Greece and Turkey and be linked in some way to the North Atlantic Treaty. MEDO was envisioned both as a means of dealing with indigenous security problems in the Eastern Mediterranean and Middle East region and as a means of coping with the Soviet threat, which was understood by all of the NATO signatory governments to be *global* in nature.

Concern about the global nature of the Soviet threat also contributed to the decision by the signatory governments to include in the final treaty a clause that would permit consultation on out-of-area issues as required. The compromise nature of the final document is reflected in the tension between Article 6 of the treaty, which clearly stipulates the geographic boundaries of the alliance, and Article 4, which commits the signatory governments to consultation whenever "the territorial integrity, political independence, or security of any of the parties is threatened." All parties understood that Article 4 had the potential of being used by members of the alliance to meddle in each other's global affairs or to attempt to draw allies into a signatory's out-of-area problems. But it was also assumed that some flexibility might be required in order to adjust the regional alliance to the wider world. It was left to future diplomats to manage the contradictions between the two articles on a case-by-case basis.

During the 1950s, various European allies tested the extent to which NATO membership could be manipulated in support of their particular extraregional interests. France was arguably the most successful in this regard. From 1950 to 1954, Washington covered 80 percent of the costs of the Indochina war effort. Furthermore, in 1952 France succeeded in obtaining the first official NATO sanction for an out-of-area operation, when the North Atlantic Council issued a public statement of "wholehearted admiration" and "continued support" for French actions against the Vietminh.[13] The limits of American and allied support were nonetheless made clear to Paris at Dien Bien Phu.

Successive French governments were often angered by the conditional nature of NATO's support and by American interference in colonial affairs. In general, however, this anger was tempered by the fact that France did not really expect any better treatment in a postwar international system over which it had very limited control. Britain, on the other hand, had staked its foreign policy on America's willingness to accord it a special status within the Western security community. In view of these much higher expectations, Britain was usually frustrated, both within the NATO alliance and in its efforts to solicit support for its initiatives beyond the treaty area. London's conspicuous absence from the 1951 alliance among the United States, Australia, and New Zealand (ANZUS), as well as its failure to influence U.S. policy regarding the establishment of

MEDO, are symptomatic of the problems that Britain faced in its efforts to coordinate global security policy with the United States on anything but Washington's terms during the 1950s.

For both Britain and France, the Suez crisis was the most important test of the extent to which the concept of "common security interests" could be stretched to support their particular out-of-area interests during the cold war era. Suez was a unique, and a uniquely disruptive, event for NATO because of the incompatible national interests that were engaged, because of the personalities involved, and above all because of the fundamentally incorrect expectations that all of the key actors brought to the crisis.

Suez also highlights the point made earlier about intra-alliance conflict in a situation of tight bipolarity. The level of intra-alliance recrimination was very high during and after the Suez crisis (as was true in the cases of French Indochina, Tunisia, the 1973 Arab-Israeli conflict, and Afghanistan). But since both France and Britain had no choice but to remain in the U.S.-sponsored Western security system in the mid-1950s, there were strict limits on how far they could go in defending their particular extra-European interests in the face of concerted American opposition. On the other hand, Washington was ready and willing to use its considerable political and economic power to compel obedience from its junior allies. In the end, however, the United States had no choice but to forgive (if not forget) the misbehavior of France and Britain.

The Suez crisis had a chastening effect on all of the members of the NATO alliance. It helped to dispel many of the misperceptions which had characterized intra-alliance relations during the early 1950s. In France, it reinforced a growing mood of dissatisfaction with the politics of bipolarity and a growing desire to find a way to manipulate the bipolar system to French advantage. Suez also represented a milestone in the history of postwar European decolonization. It hastened the process of European global retrenchment and thereby helped to eliminate the principal source of intra-alliance dispute during the first two decades of NATO's history. By the late 1960s, however, other types of out-of-area disagreements had come to the fore, compounded by new misunderstandings and misperceptions.

FIVE TYPES OF OUT-OF-AREA DISPUTES

The intra-alliance disputes that surfaced during the 1950s set the pattern for subsequent out-of-area challenges to NATO cohesion. Most American and European problems in the Third World have, by common consent, been kept outside of the NATO forum. In some cases, however, out-of-area problems have created intense conflicts within the alliance. Our study will focus upon five types of out-of-area situations which have periodically spilled over into the NATO forum.

1. Situations in which NATO members have been concerned about the possibility of "guilt by association" with the out-of-area policies of another ally.
2. Situations in which one NATO member has seen another member's out-of-area actions as an infringement upon its *domaine réservé* in the Third World.
3. Situations in which a NATO member involved in an out-of-area campaign has solicited the direct or indirect support of other alliance members and has been rebuffed.
4. Situations in which the out-of-area preoccupations of a NATO member are criticized by other allies on the grounds that they are diverting attention, energies, or resources away from the alliance.
5. Situations that highlight fundamental differences of opinion among NATO allies regarding the nature or implications of threats to the alliance or beyond the alliance treaty area.

These five types of situations are not mutually exclusive. Indeed, some out-of-area disputes have been especially resistant to resolution precisely because they have involved aspects of three or more of these situations at once. The French Indochina situation, for example, exhibited characteristics of all five types of situations.

Guilt-by-Association Disputes

Concern about "guilt by association" with European colonialism was a consistent theme in internal American discussions throughout the cold war era. During the Suez crisis, for example, President Dwight D. Eisenhower complained that the allies were forcing him to choose between "following in the footsteps of Anglo-French colonialism in Asia and Africa or splitting our course away from their course."[14] The Eisenhower administration was subsequently criticized by John F. Kennedy for not going far enough or fast enough in splitting its course from the European colonialists. Once in office, Kennedy's own efforts to obtain support among Third World governments by pressuring Portugal and Belgium to alter their colonial policies precipitated a brief but intense confrontation within the alliance. A more recent example of concern about guilt by association was Spain's assertion only two days after joining NATO that membership in the alliance "in no way" implied Spanish support for Britain's policies during the Falklands dispute.[15] Guilt by association with the policies of NATO allies was subsequently picked up as a theme by those individuals and parties within Spain that campaigned against Spanish membership in the alliance.

Domaine Réservé Disputes

Out-of-area initiatives by one NATO member which are considered by another member to be an intrusion into its *domaine réservé* have precipitated some of the most intensely recriminatory debates during the alliance's forty-year history. All of the NATO allies have at one time or another agreed with de Gaulle's frequent complaint that NATO provided members with an institutional mechanism for interfering in another member's sovereign affairs. When the issue has involved colonial possessions, however, psychological factors of guilt and frustration have combined with this sense of resentment over outside meddling to make the resultant disputes hard to settle and hard to forget.

Domaine réservé disputes have frequently been the flip side of guilt-by-association disputes. In the case of NATO, the aforementioned attempt by John F. Kennedy to press Portugal and Belgium to change their colonial policies was a guilt-by-association issue from Washington's point of view, but a *domaine réservé* issue for Lisbon and Brussels. Kennedy's campaign ultimately failed, partly because the majority of NATO members accepted the Portuguese and Belgian definition of the situation.

These disputes have proven to be especially intractable when the parties involved have contested each other's claim to special responsibility or authority. The 1983 American invasion of Grenada had the potential of becoming a major crisis within the alliance precisely because it involved a country which two NATO allies considered to be within their *domaine réservé*. From the American perspective, the Grenada intervention represented a reaffirmation of the Monroe Doctrine. From Britain's point of view, however, Grenada was a Commonwealth concern.[16] According to one British commentator, "It was unthinkable—certainly unprecedented—for the US to intervene militarily in a Commonwealth state against the express wishes of HMG."[17] The reasons why Grenada did not become an intra-NATO crisis are discussed in Chapter 12.

Disputes over Solicitations of Support

Out-of-area policies by one alliance member can also become a source of intra-alliance dispute if the nation involved solicits direct or indirect support from other members. Direct support involves the provision of troops, arms, or logistical assistance, or the contribution of economic or diplomatic backing. Indirect support involves allied adjustments for a rapid or gradual reduction of one member's contribution to the alliance owing to its preoccupation with some military campaign outside of the treaty area. Solicitations of direct or indirect support have typically been justified by the argument that the ally involved in the out-of-area contingency was making a contribution to the common security interest by its military actions beyond the treaty area.

French defense experts and policy makers developed the most sophisticated version of this argument in the 1950s, in the form of the *guerre révolutionnaire* thesis. The thesis stressed the interdependence of Atlantic security and Third World stability, the global nature of the communist threat, and the unique contribution that France was both willing and able to make to preserving order in the Third World—if only it could count on the economic and diplomatic support of its NATO allies. More recently, American efforts to work out arrangements within NATO in support of the USCENTCOM (U.S. Central Command, formerly the Rapid Deployment Force, or RDF) have involved solicitations of both direct and indirect assistance and have used many of the same *guerre révolutionnaire* arguments employed by France in the 1950s.

Solicitations of direct or indirect support are likely to be rebuffed if some of the allies whose support is being solicited are critical of the out-of-area initiatives of the *demandeur* and concerned about guilt by association with the particular out-of-area event.

Burden-sharing Disputes

Closely related to solicitation of support disputes are intra-alliance debates that involve accusations by one ally that another alliance member is not carrying its fair share of the Atlantic defense burden because of its preoccupation with challenges beyond the treaty area. This fourth type of out-of-area dispute is analytically distinct from the third type in the sense that it does not involve any actual solicitation of help by the nation involved in the out-of-area situation. Portugal's involvement in Africa and America's involvement in Vietnam illustrate the kinds of long-term out-of-area situations which have come under criticism from time to time within NATO. U.S. proposals for double-counting many of its NATO-designated troops so that they are also earmarked for Middle East/Persian Gulf duty under USCENTCOM have also come under criticism from some allied governments as a potential degradation of the American contribution to the alliance.

Disputes Regarding the Nature and Identity of the Threat

The fifth and final type of out-of-area dispute has typically involved differences of interpretation by various NATO members in response to developments outside of the treaty area. Soviet actions beyond the treaty area have been the source of the most divisive out-of-area debates during the last decade, because they go to the heart of the alliance relationship and force each NATO member to reassess the threat that has served as the principal rationale for its participation in NATO. In the most serious cases, this process of reassessment has gone on in the midst of intense diplomatic activity, during a short time period, and in the full glare of public attention.

The Soviet invasion of Afghanistan triggered just such a dispute among the NATO allies. Coming as it did less than two months after the start of the Teheran hostage crisis, the Soviet invasion of Afghanistan confirmed many of the worst fears of an already extremely insecure American leadership. A consensus quickly formed in Washington around the proposition that the USSR had been encouraged by Western complacency to extend its power into Southwest Asia. There was also a general suspicion in Washington that this was only the first step in a much larger and more menacing Soviet campaign. From the American point of view, the relatively calm response of key European allies to the Soviet intervention in Afghanistan was evidence that these governments had become corrupted, perhaps irredeemably so, by the inducements of East-West détente.

The Afghanistan crisis not only highlighted fundamental differences between the United States and its NATO allies on the issue of détente, it also elevated the issue of out-of-area cooperation to the status of a high priority agenda item for all future NATO ministerial meetings.[18]

Changes in NATO Out-of-Area Disputes since 1949

Table 1 lists the five types of out-of-area disputes which we have introduced and relates the five types to all major extraregional events that have engaged the interest of two or more NATO allies since 1949.[19]

The most striking aspect of the table, which highlights the principal findings of our book, is the shift over time from *domaine réservé* issues as the major sources of intra-alliance dispute to burden-sharing and definition of threat issues as the primary sources of intra-NATO disagreement. The reasons for this trend are developed throughout this book, but can be summarized here.

First, most *domaine réservé* disputes occurred during the first two decades of NATO's history, when key European allies still had extensive, though dwindling, colonial ties. The central dynamic of this period was European attempts to retain the vestiges, or at least the perquisites, of empire in the face of American suspicion of European colonialism and the expansion of American global influence. Thus, American concerns about guilt by association with European colonialism confronted European resentments about U.S. interference in traditional *domaines réservés*. This confrontation was often played out within the NATO forum, with Europeans seeking to utilize the alliance to solicit U.S. backing for extraregional initiatives while resisting American efforts to interfere in these out-of-area situations. For its part, Washington generally took a strict constructionist position on the question of allied responsibilities beyond the NATO Treaty area—citing the alliance's regional identity as a means of refusing support. Washington also used the NATO forum to question or criticize particular European allies for their out-of-area activities.

TABLE 1

Five Types of Out-of-Area Disputes

Event/Date	Type 1 Guilt by Association	Type 2 Domaine Réservé	Type 3 Solicitation of Support	Type 4 Burden Sharing	Type 5 Definition of Threat	Participants	Behavior
Indonesia (1949)	x U.S. view	x Dutch view				U.S./Holland	Acrimonious but controlled
Middle East (MEDO) (1949–53)	xx U.S. view	xx U.K. view	x By U.K.			U.K./U.S.	Moderate/controlled dispute
Indochina (1949–54)	x U.S. view	xx FR view	x By France	xx U.S. view	x FR/U.S. disagree	FR/U.S./U.K.	Initially collaborative, then progressively recriminatory. Intense French recrimination after fall of Dien Bien Phu
Korean War (1950–53)			x By U.S.		x U.S./U.K. disagree	U.S./U.K./FR	Essentially collaborative, but actions reflected differing interests & concerns in region
ANZUS (1951–53)			x By U.K.			U.S./U.K.	Strong, but controlled U.K. resentment—U.K. uses NATO to seek access

Continued on next page

TABLE 1—Continued

Event/Date	Type 1 Guilt by Association	Type 2 Domaine Réservé	Type 3 Solicitation of Support	Type 4 Burden Sharing	Type 5 Definition of Threat	Participants	Behavior
Suez (1956)	xx U.S. view	xx U.K. & FR view	x By U.K. & FR; by allies in context of Hungarian crisis	x Allied view of U.K./FR action		U.S./U.K./FR/ Germany/ Belgium	Intense confrontation between U.S. and U.K./FR. Strong F.R.G. criticisms of U.K. & France
Lebanon/Jordan (1958)	x U.S. view	x U.K. view				U.S./U.K./ allies	Essentially collaborative, but actions reflected differing views of rights and interests in region. Some allies profide support (basing, etc.)
Tunisia (1958–61)	x Allied view	x French view				U.S./U.K./FR/ Scandinavian allies	Strong FR resentment of allied policies
Laos (1959–62)			x by U.S.			U.S./U.K./FR	U.S. uses SEATO forum to solicit support; U.K. & FR resist— some spillover to NATO
Kuwait (1961)	x U.S. concern	x U.K. view				U.S./U.K.	Moderate/controlled disagreement, with some allied aid to U.K.

	View (1)	View (2)	Secrecy	Coverage	Disagreement	Parties	Outcome
Brunei (1961)				x U.S. concern		U.S./U.K.	(use of F.R.G. bases, overflight of Turkey) Moderate U.S. concern for U.K. overextension—kept out of NATO forum
Belgian Congo (1961)	x U.S. view	x Belgian view				U.S./Belgium/other European allies	Strong but controlled disagreement
Portuguese Africa (1961–74)	x Initially U.S.; later, view of Scandinavian allies	xx Portuguese view	x By Portugal	x By U.S., then Scandinavian allies		U.S./Portugal	Periodic intense conflict
Vietnam (1961–75)			x By U.S.	xx Allied coverage	x U.S./allies disagree	U.S./various allies—FR in particular	Controlled—periodic U.S. requests for aid periodic allied complaints about U.S. Asian involvement, gradual drawdown of U.S. troops in NATO
Cuban Missile Crisis (1962)			x By U.S.			U.S./all allies	Essentially collaborative, but strong residual resentment by Turkey
Irian Jaya (1962)		x Dutch view				U.S./Holland	Controlled dispute (Holland also attempted

Continued on next page

TABLE 1—*Continued*

Event/Date	Type 1 Guilt by Association	Type 2 Domaine Réservé	Type 3 Solicitation of Support	Type 4 Burden Sharing	Type 5 Definition of Threat	Participants	Behavior
							to use SEATO to solicit support)
Six-Day War (1967)	x Allied view		x By U.S.			U.S./all allies	Controlled disputes over overflight rights and base use
Malaysia (1963–66)			x By U.K.	x U.S. concern		U.S./U.K.	U.K. uses SEATO to solicit support, U.S. resists—some spillover to NATO
Yom Kippur War (1973)	x Allied concern		x By U.S.			U.S./allies	Intense U.S. criticism of allied lack of support
Arab oil boycott (1973)			x By U.S., Holland		x U.S./allies disagree	U.S./all allies	Intense dispute, carried on in various forums—NATO summits, etc.
Zaire 2 (1978)		x Belgian concern	xx By France		x FR/Belgium disagree	FR/Belgium/ U.S.	Essentially collaborative, but actions reflect different interests and concerns
Afghanistan (1979)			x By U.S.		xx U.S./allies disagree	U.S./allies	Strong U.S. pressure for allied actions, including support for

Event	Subordinate view	Ally view	Instigated (U.S.)	Allied concern	U.S./allies disagree	Parties	Nature of dispute
							RDF. Intense disagreements
Yamal Pipeline (1979–83)			x By U.S.		x U.S./allies disagree	U.S./allies	Strong U.S. pressure for allied rejection of Soviet offer. Allies resist U.S. demands
Terrorism (1981–present)			x By U.S.		x U.S./allies disagree	U.S./allies	Periodic U.S./allied disagreements over means of response and significance of threat
Persian Gulf (1979–present)			xx By U.S.	x Allied concern	x U.S./allies disagree	U.S./allies	Initial disagreements, then essentially collaborative
Falklands (1982)	x Spanish view	x U.K. view				U.K./Spain/allies	Moderate criticism by Spain and certain allies
Chad (1982–84)		x French view				U.S./FR	U.S., Belgium assist; controlled FR resentment—kept out of NATO forum
Grenada (1983)		x U.K./U.S. disagree				U.S./U.K.	Strong but controlled dispute—kept out of NATO forum
Achille Lauro (1983)	x Italian view		x By U.S.			U.S./Italy	Intense but controlled dispute
Lebanon MLF			x		x	U.S./U.K./FR/	Essentially collabora-

Continued on next page

TABLE 1—Continued

Event/Date	Type 1 Guilt by Association	Type 2 Domaine Réservé	Type 3 Solicitation of Support	Type 4 Burden Sharing	Type 5 Definition of Threat	Participants	Behavior
(1982–84)		U.K./FR/Italy all claim special expertise	By U.S.			Italy	tive, but actions reflect some differing approaches to peacekeeping and different interests in Lebanon & Middle East
Libya (1985, 1986, 1989)	x Italian view		xx By U.S.		x U.S./Italy disagree	U.S./Italy/ other allies	Moderate U.S. pressure; strong Italian resentment. U.K. provides support for U.S. action in 1986

Notes: In cases where an out-of-area event exhibits characteristics of more than two types, two checks (xx) indicate our interpretation of the type(s) which most accurately describe the central issues under debate.

FR = France; F.R.G., Federal Republic of Germany

By the mid-1960s, however, the process of European retrenchment from former colonies was almost completed, while America had begun to feel the effects of global overextension. This led to a reversal of roles, with Washington increasingly calling upon its allies to assist it beyond the NATO Treaty boundary in the name of alliance solidarity. Not surprisingly, the European allies took pleasure from time to time in turning America's old strict constructionist arguments against the alliance leader now that they had been perforce relieved of their overseas responsibilities. Guilt by association continues to be a source of intra-alliance dispute, but since the late 1960s it has usually taken the form of European concerns about being tied implicitly or explicitly to U.S. interventionist initiatives in the Third World.[20]

But other important changes were occurring by the late 1960s as well. The relative decline in American power in the international system was just beginning to be evident in the form of the "Vietnam Syndrome" and challenges to the U.S.-sponsored Bretton Woods system. Since that time, various American administrations have looked at the Atlantic Alliance as a target for defense cuts in an era of economic stringency. NATO out-of-area disputes have become one component of a broader intra-alliance burden-sharing debate, which is discussed in Chapter 6.

The NATO burden-sharing issue has been complicated in recent years by the aforementioned disagreements between Washington and key European allies about the nature of the threat posed by Moscow and the meaning and importance of détente. Such disagreements are entirely understandable after four decades of peace and stability in central Europe. And we should not be surprised to find that NATO out-of-area disputes during the last decade have frequently taken the form of disagreements about the definition of the Soviet threat. The extent of U.S.-European disagreement on issues of détente and definition of threat is reflected in a report published by the U.S. Senate Committee on Foreign Relations in the wake of the Soviet intervention in Afghanistan. The report asserted that "since detente for the Europeans has always been a European matter, they found the implications of aggression in remote Afghanistan for continuing cooperation with the East in Europe disturbing, but not necessarily fatal." The report goes on to observe that in the United States, the reaction was entirely different. "The remains of detente went utterly stale" and resulted in "the end of lingering American hopes for a non-confrontational relationship with the U.S.S.R. in matters affecting the developing world."[21] At present, these differences of opinion on questions of East-West détente and the nature and degree of the Soviet threat represent the greatest potential challenges to NATO cohesion. Out-of-area issues are likely to continue to play an important role in forcing these issues to the surface.

Our study will focus upon the changes cited above, to illustrate how certain types of out-of-area disputes have replaced others over the last forty years. Since the United States, the United Kingdom, and France are the three alliance members that have been most involved in out-of-area situations since 1949, the bulk of our study (the first three parts) will concentrate on these nations. Part 4 will consider the out-of-area policies of the other NATO members: Belgian and Portuguese attempts to retain control, or at least influence, in Africa in the face of allied criticisms, Germany's efforts to keep the allies focused on the central front during the era of decolonization, Holland's efforts to preserve a foothold in Asia, and so forth.

At the core of our study is the persistent tension between what Glenn Snyder calls the general interest, which has been recognized by all allies since 1949 (in preserving NATO to deter Soviet aggression), and the particular extraregional interests that each ally has felt compelled to protect and advance. We will assess the efforts by each ally to balance these Atlantic and extraregional security commitments in the development of its overall defense posture.

In our Conclusion, we will consider the current state of the balance between general and particular interests within the NATO alliance, and will respond to some recent proposals for modifying NATO's boundaries, in light of the lessons learned from this historical survey.

PART I

THE UNITED STATES

INTRODUCTION TO PART I

DURING the early cold war era, there was a general consensus among U.S. defense experts that Western Europe represented American's paramount geostrategic interest outside of North America. But the *relative* weight that Washington would have to assign to Western Europe as a focal point of its overall postwar global containment strategy remained unclear. The need to establish geographic boundaries for the North Atlantic Alliance thus provided U.S. policy makers with one of the first opportunities for discussing the global requirements for a strategy of anti-Soviet containment.

Four decades after the American defense establishment first debated Europe's place in the *Pax Americana,* these fundamental questions remain unanswered. In recent years, however, the debate has intensified and become more focused, as U.S. security planners have become increasingly predisposed to frame the problem in terms of choices between NATO responsibilities and commitments beyond the treaty area in an era of financial stringency.

Part 1 surveys the positions taken by American security planners on NATO out-of-region questions since 1949. Our discussion begins with an analysis of six competing views within the U.S. security establishment regarding Europe's place in the global containment scheme during the formative period of the cold war. We then discuss the impact of this architectonic debate on Washington's original policies toward Atlantic security and NATO. Attention is then directed toward those extra-European crises that have tested Washington's willingness to harmonize its out-of-region policies with its NATO allies. Finally, we discuss the place of NATO in America's global security calculations during the 1980s and into the 1990s as Washington has increasingly sought to reconcile its general and its particular alliance interests.

CHAPTER 1

SIX SCHOOLS OF THOUGHT
ON AMERICAN POSTWAR
SECURITY

Since about 1943, six distinct factions have taken part in debates regarding the priority that should be accorded to European security in U.S. global defense planning, and the appropriate means for assuring European security. During the Truman and Eisenhower administrations, preference for one school over another tended to be determined by one's opinion about five things:

1. The immediacy and seriousness of the Soviet military threat.
2. The extent to which one considered security in all areas of the world to be interdependent.
3. One's faith in the potential value of the United Nations as a source of world order.
4. The relative importance accorded to different regions of the world.
5. The extent to which one was preoccupied with the risks of American geopolitical and/or economic overextension.

The six factions were never exclusive clubs; many individuals reflected the arguments of two or three schools in their foreign policy views. Nor do we argue that an individual associated with one school of thought remained in that school throughout the entire cold war era. For example, Dean Acheson was a leading spokesman for the "Europe First" group in the late 1940s, but joined the ranks of the "NSC 68" faction in 1950. For each faction, we have identified individuals who were spokespersons at a particular time.

In this chapter the viewpoints and policy preferences of each of these factions will be outlined, and the relative influence of each faction will be considered. The reactions by Washington's allies to each of these factions will be dealt with intermittently throughout this book.

THE UNIVERSALIST/IDEALIST FACTION

The universalist/idealist faction tended to endorse many of the classical Wilsonian prescriptions for collective security and national self-determination in the postwar world order. A strong United Nations, forcefully administering the collective security system through a superpower-dominated Security Council, had a singular appeal to many Americans who had always found European balance-of-power politics distasteful. Many Americans also tended to assume that only the United States could ensure that the process of Third World development and decolonization would be managed in ways that would preserve Western interests in those areas.[1]

The vision of a globally active Security Council under the joint control of Washington and Moscow was viewed with concern by Britain and France for two reasons. First, Paris and London remembered the failures of the League of Nations' global collective security system during the interwar period. U.S. assurances that the new arrangement would be more effective (a "League with teeth") were questioned by many European political leaders, on the grounds that the two nations that were essential for providing the "teeth" were likely to have a great deal of difficulty in agreeing on how and where collective security action was to be taken. The British and French delegates to the San Francisco Conference (which established the United Nations) therefore pressed the U.S. delegation for assurances that a *regional* collective defense formula would be incorporated into the final version of the U.N. Charter as a fallback in the event that the global approach to peacekeeping failed.[2] The end result of the proceedings was Article 51, which represented a victory for the proponents of regionalism, at the expense of the collective security "purists."[3]

The second reason for British and French concern about the creation of a strong and globally active Security Council was the suspicion that Washington would use the organization to press for decolonization and undermine their *domaines réservés*. Clearly, to Franklin Roosevelt and the American electorate at large (which shared FDR's concern about "guilt by association" with European colonialism), the 1941 Atlantic Charter committed the British to back legitimate self-determination, rather than to attempt to preserve the "confetti of empire" from India to Hong Kong, when the war was over.[4] Indeed, Roosevelt's anticolonialism went beyond merely contesting British overseas interests. He likewise envisioned the dismantling of the French, Belgian, and Dutch colonial networks, and regarded international trusteeship arrangements as the best available mechanism for advancing the principle of self-determination in the postwar international system.[5]

It should be mentioned that FDR anticipated an *evolutionary* decolonization which, while meeting the United States' short-term desires for access to markets and strategic materials, would "preclude radical challenges to European control of dependent areas, thus preventing revolutionary elements from seizing power," in a replay of the Bolshevik victory after World War I.[6]

In addition, it was assumed by Washington that *managed* decolonization would enhance European economic recovery, thereby facilitating the United States' gradual decoupling from Western European security commitments.[7] The European allies, in turn, played up this theme of "managed" decolonization, warning that a too sudden dissolution of their overseas possessions would endanger their postwar economic reconstruction and undermine their influence in the postwar international system. They argued that an orderly process of decolonization had to be preceded by the establishment of durable political institutions in these regions, in order to withstand the challenges of emerging anti-Western forces, possibly backed by Soviet power.[8] Unless the domestic preconditions for decolonization were in place, the Europeans contended, the newly established Third World states could come under the sway of the Soviet Union, which was accustomed to governing others through the rule of force rather than through the assent of the governed.[9]

This went to the heart of the matter, since many U.S. policy makers believed that the Europeans had neither the desire, capability, nor skill required to "manage" the transition from colonialism to democracy in the Third World. Many Americans also harbored disdain for the French and British forces as a result of defeats suffered in Indochina and Singapore (respectively) at the hands of the Japanese in the Asian-Pacific theater, and at the hands of the Germans in British—and French-controlled African and Middle Eastern territories during the early stages of World War II.

Roosevelt's death in April 1945 left this transatlantic dispute unresolved. Within a very short time Cordell Hull, Edward Stettinius, and other major representatives of the universalist/idealist approach had left the government. The few who were left over from FDR's administration—such as Vice-President Henry Wallace and Cloyce K. Huston, chief of the State Department's Division of Southern European Affairs—were increasingly isolated in the Truman era, as Kennan, Acheson, and other containment advocates rose to prominence. After 1945, events in Eastern Europe and Southwest Asia made it easier for critics of the universalist/idealist faction to depict this group as being out of touch with postwar realities, in the face of either Soviet-backed or indigenous anti-Western revolutionary change.

Although the more idealistic aspects of the universalist/idealist approach had been abandoned by most influential U.S. policy makers before the end of 1946, one important element of Roosevelt's foreign policy was perpetuated by his successors. U.S. policy makers continued to exhibit a general suspicion of the colonialist policies of the major European allies. Moral arguments for decolonization were downplayed after FDR's death, but the United States continued to doubt the motives behind the colonialist policies of France, Britain, Holland, Belgium, and Portugal and, more importantly, continued to view most European colonialist initiatives as detrimental to overall Western security.

As Washington became preoccupied with what it perceived to be a worldwide communist threat, U.S. policy makers became somewhat more inclined to consider colonial territories as important elements in the global containment scheme. But this reassessment did not automatically lead U.S. policy makers to defer to the European colonial allies on security issues pertaining to the Third World. Instead, the United States responded to security threats in developing regions either by continuing to press the case for decolonization (in order to temper lingering feelings of "guilt by association," "get on the right side of change," and assure itself of basing privileges and strategic access rights when the European colonialists lost control to nationalist forces) or by actively seeking to supplant the Europeans in the Third World territory or region as the most direct means of ensuring that the global containment strategy was properly managed.

THE RESOURCE/GEOGRAPHIC CONSTRAINTS FACTION

The problem of assuring the United States of basing rights throughout the world preoccupied the Joint Chiefs of Staff (JCS) during and after World War II. American military planners began in 1943 to develop their postwar plans around the theme of "defense-in-depth," with the United States safeguarding the most important sea lines of communication (SLOCs) in both the Atlantic and Pacific oceans. A "defense-in-depth" strategy required the United States to retain control of the network of bases acquired during World War II. These bases stretched from America's West Coast along the peripheries of the Asian Pacific via the Aleutians, the Philippines, Okinawa, and Japan, and from its East Coast through the Azores into a "West African Zone" of forward defense.[10] This tendency to treat various territories in the Third World as staging areas or strategic assets brought the JCS into direct conflict with members of the universalist/idealist group from time to time.[11] On the other hand, the Joint Chiefs found common cause with the universalist/idealists in their opposition to proposals for supporting Western European colonial policies, out of a general disdain for the allies' military reliability and fear of overextending limited U.S. defense assets.

The Joint Chiefs also tended to play a cautionary and restrictive role in the negotiations that led to the creation of NATO. Soon after World War II, the JCS was directed to draw up a global strategic assessment, dividing the world into specific military regions and estimating the levels of U.S. military power required to respond to the threats and problems in each region. As William Kaufmann has since recalled, "[When] their estimates were added up, they proved too large for any conceivable budget."[12] Subsequent attempts by the JCS to stretch U.S. military capabilities to levels they felt were necessary for meeting American global security needs led the JCS to "relativize" the European dimension in their overall defense planning. For example, during the

March 1948 negotiations at the Washington Preparatory Talks, which laid the groundwork for the North Atlantic Treaty, both the JCS and (to a lesser extent) the staff of the National Security Council recommended to the American delegation that U.S. security guarantees toward Western Europe be limited to generalized, bilateral agreements with the separate Brussels Pact members.[13]

What is most significant about this early contingency planning is the reluctance of the JCS to consider a forward defense of Western Europe at the expense of a *global* U.S. military strategy. This outlook helped to shape U.S. thinking about subsequent burden-sharing issues within the alliance. A May 1948 Joint Strategic Survey Staff Report illustrated Washington's preoccupation with husbanding its resources. It urged caution regarding the Senate's pending Vandenberg Resolution, which authorized the president to enter into negotiations leading to an Atlantic security arrangement and challenged the direction that the Washington Preparatory Talks were taking:

> We should not be committed to any military plans that might unduly influence or even jeopardize optimum overall global strategy. . . . While the desirability of assistance [to Europe] is recognized, it is also clear that its extent must be limited by the necessity of avoiding both undue reduction of [U.S.] resources essential to our own national security and undue interference with our own military requirements, as well as the harmful influence on our global strategy that might result.[14]

As the Washington Preparatory Talks progressed, the JCS came to accept the need for a standing defense organization to guarantee the security of continental Europe. They nonetheless continued to express concern about the possibility that the new defense pact might prove to be an excessive drain on American military assets, particularly if it was used by America's allies to draw the United States into neocolonial conflicts in the Third World. A January 1949 JCS memorandum (1868/40) graphically reflected this viewpoint:

> While agreeing . . . with the idea of collective defense embodied in the proposed pact, the Joint Chiefs of Staff believes that its scope should not be such as to result in undue disparity between our commitments and our present or prospective strength. For this reason, it may be well to examine rather carefully the wording of Article 7 [of the proposed North Atlantic Treaty, which called for allies to "consult together whenever one's 'territorial integrity' was threatened or when a situation existed which constituted a threat or a 'breach of the peace'"]. . . . The word "territorial" . . . can be construed to include the colonies of all the signatories of the Pact . . . [and] consultation will be involved whenever there exists any situation *anywhere* which constitutes a threat or a breach of the peace. [This] . . . could constitute a very large order indeed and one that does not appear to be essential to the North Atlantic Pact.[15]

As the above quote illustrates, the JCS was strongly opposed to any policy that reduced U.S. sovereign control over decisions about war and peace. These arguments did, in fact, affect the American negotiating position during the 1948 Washington Preparatory Talks. Thus, while NATO formed five Regional Planning Groups, the United States formally affiliated itself only with the North Atlantic Ocean and the Canada-United States groups. Washington accepted only "auxiliary" status with the Northern Europe, Southern Europe-Western Mediterranean, and Western Europe committees, in accordance with the Joint Chiefs' warning that the alliance should go no farther than "prudential military cooperation, the parameters of which were determined by the need to retain a United States commitment to European security."[16]

In addition to wrestling with the North Atlantic Treaty's effect on its own plans for implementing a global defense-in-depth strategy, most members of the JCS were concerned that the initial incorporation of too many Southern European nations in the alliance would place an unnecessary strain on America's military assistance program.[17] Some representatives of the JCS disagreed with this argument, however, and contended that the failure to include such countries as Italy, Greece, and Turkey in NATO could be misinterpreted by the Soviet Union as a lack of U.S. resolve, thereby placing the extended containment strategy at risk. In the case of Italy, JCS chairman General Omar Bradley also expressed a concern in early 1949 that if Rome were excluded from the Atlantic security treaty it could "lose heart" and succumb to communism. It was this concern, rather than any JCS calculation about Italy's role in supporting the Sixth Fleet, that finally persuaded U.S. military planners to support Rome's application for membership in NATO.[18]

Following the actual signing of the North Atlantic Treaty, the JCS moved to revise its war planning in accordance with America's new European defense commitment. During the early 1950s, the Joint Strategic Plans Committee issued a series of studies of where NATO fit within the United States' global defense commitments. The committee also proposed a number of new command structures to integrate the North Atlantic Treaty area more smoothly into the U.S. global security network.[19] The JCS nonetheless continued to act as a restraining voice in discussions of U.S.-European defense cooperation outside of the NATO border during the cold war era.

THE "EUROPE FIRST" SCHOOL

Dean Acheson and other members of the "Europe First" faction in Washington shared the Joint Chiefs' concern for rationing America's limited military resources in the postwar system. They diverged from the U.S. military establishment, however, in the importance that they accorded to Western Europe in their calculations of how and where U.S. military assets should be spent. Acheson did share the Joint Chiefs' preference for a strict constructionist approach to NATO's out-of-area role, as well as a limited and conditional U.S. treaty obligation. He nonetheless argued forcefully to Congress that Western Europe had to be accorded priority status in America's global containment strategy. In advocating NATO's ratification before the Senate Foreign Relations Committee during May 1950, he asserted that "if anything happens in Western Europe, the whole business goes to pieces and therefore our principal effort must be building up the defenses . . . of Western Europe, and, as far as Asia is concerned, treating that as a holding operation."[20]

In arguing for the North Atlantic Treaty's ratification, the secretary of state also claimed that NATO qualified as a regional collective security instrument under UN guidelines, thus partially deferring to the concerns of the universalist/idealist group. Specifically, Acheson contended that NATO members agreed to differentiate between "regional collective defense" and "enforcement action" in conformity to Article 51 of the United Nations Charter. Regional collective defense could be undertaken independent of Security Council approval. Enforcement action, by contrast, involved the use of military force for intervention against hostile insurgent elements or for other reasons than self-defense. This type of action could not be initiated by Western governments independent of Security Council approval.

Accordingly, the language of the North Atlantic pact was modified during negotiations leading to its creation so that any American commitment to respond to an Atlantic crisis would have to be in a *regional* context and would allow both the president and the Senate to exercise their constitutional prerogatives for approving the dispatch of U.S. military forces.[21]

Acheson's formula for determining the scope of NATO membership was to include a northern and southern flank component sufficient to reinforce Central European defense efforts, but to avoid making the alliance so large that it lost its "Atlantic" identity and risked being seen as a competitor to the United Nations itself. Acheson summarized this outlook in a memorandum written after conversations with Turkish officials about possible NATO membership for their country:

> In undertaking the creation of regional security arrangements, we had to start somewhere. We had been confronted in the beginning with two main alternatives: to attempt an all-embracing security arrangement which would include all the countries in the world except the Soviet bloc, or to begin with a smaller group such as the North Atlantic area. The all-embracing idea simply presented too many difficulties.[22]

Acheson also skirted the difficult question of how the Canadian Arctic and the French Algerian directorates could be considered to be in the same collective defense "region." He feared that if he publicly addressed the ambiguities inherent in this situation, the delicate security consensus then developing between the United States and Western Europe could be jeopardized. Instead, he emphasized Western Europe's importance to American security as an integral part of Atlantic sector protection of the United States.[23] From this point of view, any Atlantic security arrangement was a legitimate regional defense concern for both Americans and Europeans. But this argument did little to clarify the issue of how large NATO's legitimate regional purview really was, or should be.

Acheson's campaign in support of a Eurocentric containment policy appeared to backfire within one month of his testimony before the Senate. In June 1950, North Korean forces invaded South Korea, frustrating any hopes that America would be left free to concentrate its military power and energies predominantly on the Atlantic region. By the end of 1950, the United States could deploy only 110,000 troops in South Korea as opposed to China's 256,000 and North Korea's 100,000. General Douglas T. MacArthur's stymied offensive at the Yalu River and the massive intervention of Chinese troops on Pyongyang's behalf during late November 1950 dashed hopes raised at a joint meeting of the State and Defense departments on November 21 that additional U.S. ground forces could be sent to Europe.[24]

Ironically, however, Korea ultimately served to bolster the influence of the Europe-first group in Washington. Indeed, Lawrence Kaplan has argued that the Korean War had a more direct and immediate impact on U.S. security policy in Europe than in Asia.[25] The Korean War provided the necessary impetus for Truman and, subsequently, Eisenhower, to obtain congressional support for the remilitarization of Germany and the deployment of U.S. troops to Europe. In answering Senate Foreign Relations Committee inquiries submitted during 1951 about the mobile reserve capabilities of NATO armies, George C. Marshall, in his new capacity as secretary of defense (having relinquished the secretary of state position to Acheson), reiterated the European priority in U.S. force planning. He stipulated that the development of a U.S. mobile reserve deployable to extraperipheral crisis points in Asia or in other developing regions could only be considered *after* the two U.S. combat divisions then stationed in Europe were adequately supplemented with four additional ones.[26] Acheson likewise advised Congress that the West would not have been in nearly as good a situation as it had been in Korea in 1950 if the communists had decided to invade Greece, where "we don't have any troops within a thousand miles."[27]

THE "GLOBAL STRONGPOINTS" FACTION

George Kennan, director of the State Department's Policy Planning Staff from 1947 till the end of 1949, originally opposed U.S. participation in a North Atlantic alliance on the grounds that the Brussels Pact of 1948 should be allowed to stand on its own merits and develop its own military organization.

When his opposition to NATO was overruled by the Truman administration, Kennan subsequently advocated a limited and conditional U.S. role within the alliance. As he later recalled in his *Memoirs,*

> I favored what was sometimes referred to as the "dumbbell" concept; the combination, that is, of a unit at the European end based on the Brussels Pact, and another unit at the North American end. . . . I was prepared to see us accept such an arrangement if this was the only way the Europeans could be given the reassurance necessary for them to proceed confidently with the task of economic and domestic-political recovery.[28]

Kennan believed that the principal arena of Soviet-Western rivalry lay in the realm of politico-economic competition. Accordingly, he was more concerned with resuscitating the economies of key Eurasian countries and encouraging loyalty and a sense of confidence among Eurasian publics than in pursuing a costly military arms race with the USSR. Identifying "vital" defense interests, according to Kennan, would help the Americans avoid the trap of overextension.

Kennan thus shared the JCS's concerns about America's ability to sustain an open-ended and global security commitment. He went beyond the Joint Chiefs' comparatively narrow interpretation of a postwar military containment system, however. More than U.S. military planners, he understood the imperative for the United States, as the de facto leader of Western defense efforts, to demonstrate reasonable levels of sensibility toward the diverse international security concerns of its prospective North Atlantic Treaty partners. In addition to the global system of bases envisioned by the JCS, he thus sought to identify geopolitical "strongpoints" beyond the Western Hemisphere where Washington's containment efforts were likely to be most successful: "a concentration on the defense of particular regions, and means of access to them, rather than on the defense of fixed lines."[29]

When pressed for specifics, however, Kennan tended to confuse his listeners. During the Washington Preparatory Talks, for example, Kennan painted a very vague picture of an Atlantic pact comprising three separate "tiers" of membership.[30] "Full voting members" would constitute those countries whose homeland or insular territories "are washed by the waters of the North Atlantic or which form part of a close union of states (e.g., the Benelux states)." The Brussels Treaty powers, Norway and Denmark, as well as Canada and the United States on the North American side, were identified by Kennan for "full, voting membership." In addition to the full members, Kennan proposed an "associate member" category, consisting of nations primarily interested in a military guarantee in exchange for base rights. Kennan argued that the chiefs of staff representing such associate countries should not attend regular military planning sessions conducted by the core group. Portugal and Sweden were two of the nations discussed as candidates for "associate" status. Kennan also proposed a third, "affiliate member" category. Various British Common-wealth nations or other Third World states that had been assured of military protection by former colonial powers or that were deemed eligible by virtue of their strategic location were included in this grouping.

By proposing the affiliate classification, Kennan and the Policy Planning Staff demonstrated their acceptance of the need to incorporate some type of global dimension into NATO's outlook and strategy. They also demonstrated a recognition of how difficult it would be for the allies to argue that certain Third World territories should be designated as "key pro-Western actors beyond Europe" meriting a full and unmistakable NATO military commitment. In fact, Kennan acknowledged that "the admission of any single country beyond the North Atlantic area would be taken by others as constituting a precedent, and would almost certainly lead to a series of demands from states still further afield that they be similarly treated."[31] On the other hand, Kennan feared that failure to include such countries would invite Soviet aggression. In the face of this contradiction, Kennan favored Third World "affiliation" with the alliance in the hopes that the concept would appear to be sufficiently binding to deter Moscow while remaining sufficiently vague so as not to impose unmanageable demands on U.S. troops or treasure.

Kennan's recognition that some Third World territories that were still under European control might, under certain circumstances, constitute "vital" de-fense interests for Washington was viewed by the European colonial allies as a very positive development. London and Paris were still coping with the residual influence of FDR's universalist/idealist group in Washington, as well as with the Joint Chiefs' general opposition to the incorporation of European colonial interests into its Wartime Emergency Plans. Kennan's notion of NATO mem-bership gradations attracted more than passing interest in the British Foreign Office, which invited him to visit London for further discussions and to explore how the Atlantic Community could be extended "so as to embrace to some degree . . . the Middle Eastern countries, India, Southeast Asia, and Aus-tralia."[32]

In the end, however, the idea of an Atlantic alliance based on a system of "resident members, non-resident members and summer privileges" (Robert Lovett's description of Kennan's plan) was never weighed seriously by the participants in the Washington Preparatory Talks.[33] Kennan himself seems to have abandoned the idea shortly after proposing it, as he notes in his memoirs that "the only sound standard for membership . . . was indeed the geographic one; this was the only one that was without ambiguity and could clearly be shown to have only defensive connotations."[34] The logic of confining NATO's purview to confronting the Soviet threat directed against Western Europe pre-vailed.

Kennan's effort to articulate a containment system built around selected strongpoints was commendable insofar as it attempted to formulate guidelines for the *discriminate* allocation of Western defense assets across the globe. But he never succeeded in getting rid of the "ambiguities" inherent in his theory of alliance membership, or, for that matter, in his concept of global containment based on a network of strongpoints.

In summarizing our discussion of Kennan's vision, it is worth mentioning that some commentators have since argued that if a three-tiered membership formula had been properly worked out and adopted by NATO's architects in 1949, the alliance might not be criticized to the extent that it has in recent years as becoming outdated and irrelevant to contemporary security problems. Historian Alan Henrikson has advanced this "missed opportunity" argument:

> Had such concentric rings of decision and liability been deemed feasible, the present-day, somewhat artificial separation of NATO members' North Atlantic roles and non-North Atlantic roles and the absence of Alliance ties with much of the Third World might to a degree have been avoided. In strictly and narrowly conceiving the membership—in the interest of speed, unity, and secrecy—the partners may have lost a chance for a flexible, worldwide security grouping in the future, having a major North-South dimension.[35]

In the concluding chapter, we will take issue with Henrikson's interpretation of missed opportunities and will discuss why Kennan's vision was a prescription for institutional disaster.

THE NSC 68 GROUP

NSC 68 was a hastily prepared document—requested by President Harry S Truman on January 31, 1950, and completed nine weeks later. Its purpose was to reassess the nature and scope of the Soviet threat and to offer recommendations for U.S. defense policy. The sense that a fundamental reassessment was necessary was shared by most members of the American foreign policy community. They believed that the international system was moving rapidly, and perhaps permanently, toward a condition of tight bipolarity.

Indeed, a great deal had changed in a short time, and most of the changes were considered to be for the worse. The two most significant setbacks from the point of view of most people in Washington were the August 1949 Soviet explosion of a nuclear device and the establishment of the People's Republic of China (PRC) two months later.[36] The victory of the forces of Mao Zedong did not represent an immediate and direct threat to U.S. security in the eyes of American defense planners. It is arguable, however, that it had an even greater impact than the Soviet A-bomb test in shaping the alarmist mood of Washington policy makers. Prior to October 1949, geostrategic thinking about containment tended to reflect the arguments of Nicholas Spykman. Spykman's theories about the maintenance of a postwar *Pax Americana* underscored the importance of unchallenged U.S. access to—if not direct hegemony over—

both peninsular Europe and the coastal Far East. Spykman claimed that postwar America's security could be best ensured with the cooperation of key rimland maritime powers and a strong foothold on *both* sides of the Eurasian land-mass.[37] With the "fall of China," however, the largest of these footholds was seen as not only collapsing, but actually being acquired by Moscow.

Under the circumstances, the White House felt compelled to reconsider the security not only of the United States and NATO but also of the entire free world. The result was NSC 68, which introduced an entirely new element into the internal U.S. debate about security priorities. In contrast to the other groups evaluated in this chapter, all of which pressed their case for certain priorities at the expense of others, the NSC 68 group said in effect that everything mattered enormously, and all modalities of defense needed to be improved. This faction, then, called for what John Gaddis has insightfully described as a "symmetrical" containment posture, in which American strength was to be brought to bear in any theater, against all forms of incremental or large-scale aggression, using a wide array of weapons.[38]

Because Truman had been committed since 1948 to holding down defense spending, he was understandably concerned about the budgetary implications of globalized containment. But before he was forced to choose between his campaign commitments and his concern about the Soviet threat, North Korea invaded the South, and the whole picture changed. Truman's previous qualms about defense budgets disappeared in the face of the emergency, and congressional critics of defense spending fell into line. The U.S. defense budget was increased by 257 percent in a year.[39]

As already stated, the Korean War did nothing to undermine the importance of Europe in the eyes of most U.S. policy makers. For these individuals, in fact, Korea was seen as the opening volley, or perhaps even a feint, in a cold war that was rapidly heating up, with the ultimate target being Western Europe. Lest anyone question this interpretation of events, an influential group of citizens under the leadership of Tracey Voorhees (formerly undersecretary of defense) and James Conant (president of Harvard) engaged in a campaign to convince the U.S. public and U.S. leaders of the dangers of "a 'Korea' in Western Europe" unless substantial improvements were made in NATO's defense posture as soon as possible.[40] Likewise within the government, a November 1950 national intelligence estimate by the Central Intelligence Agency warned that "the fighting in Korea and throughout Southeast Asia . . . can be exploited . . . *to create conflict between the U.S. and its Western European allies over the diversion of U.S. strength to the Far East.*[41]

The principal deficiency that U.S. intelligence analysts and independent observers identified in NATO was the absence of a substantial American troop presence in Europe. The ineffectiveness of nuclear bomber forces in deterring North Korea during the early stages of the Korean War gave weight to the argument that NATO needed "balanced collective forces" with improved conventional *and* nuclear capabilities. Less than a month after the outbreak of fighting in Korea, the Joint Chiefs of Staff had concluded that modern-day battlefield conditions "would probably not come about normally" by Western forces' tactical manuevers. Selection of appropriate military targets for nuclear strikes without unacceptable damage to civilian populations, moreover, would be highly difficult in densely populated areas such as Korea or Western Europe.[42] This argument temporarily undermined the position advanced by a "nuclear reliance school" in Washington, which was competing with the NSC 68 group for predominance in U.S. strategic thinking at the time. As we shall see, however, the setback was only temporary.

By September 1950 Truman had decided to dispatch additional U.S. land forces—between four and six U.S. Army divisions—to NATO Europe in support of the goal of balanced collective forces. Acheson had the primary responsibility for selling the idea to Congress, in a series of discussions which cold war historians would later refer to as the "Great Debate." Acheson and Truman were assisted in their campaign to sell the troop deployment plan to Congress by Dwight D. Eisenhower, who was to become NATO's first Supreme Commander. Eisenhower was particularly effective in responding to those critics of the U.S. troop deployment plan who argued that the Europeans should make the necessary adjustments in manpower themselves. He argued that a U.S. troop commitment was necessary in order to encourage the Europeans to pursue their own rearmament programs with more vigor than had been the case up to that time. These arguments were reinforced by George Marshall, who by then had replaced Louis Johnson as secretary of defense. Marshall assured Congress that six U.S. divisions, combined with thirty-four European division equivalents, would be sufficient to guarantee the security of "rather significant portions" of Western Europe.[43]

Still arrayed against the Truman administration were a small cadre of neo-isolationists in Congress and members of the Joint Chiefs who held to the "resource/geographic constraints perspective" and feared a U.S. overcommitment to manipulative European allies. In order to obtain the reluctant support of these critics, the administration promised to incorporate the West German Bundeswehr into NATO as soon as possible, notwithstanding British and French fears over the ramifications of this move. Truman and his advisers also assured their critics that the U.S. troop deployments were a temporary corrective measure, that the European allies would be pressed to deploy their own troops so that the U.S. divisions could return home, and that in the interim the NATO allies could be relied upon at least to fulfill established troop contribution commitments. Truman and his successor were to discover, however, that the commitment to bring the American troops home, and the commitment to press the other NATO allies to make good on their manpower contributions, were impossible to fulfill—in large part because of the preoccupation of key European allies with their individual out-of-area security problems.

Of course, by this time the Truman administration had also come to reevaluate the importance of the United States' own defense commitments beyond the NATO Treaty area. During his Senate testimony in support of U.S. troop deployments to Europe, Acheson sought to communicate the administration's new assessment of the global nature of the Soviet threat and the strategic interdependence of various theaters:

> The Russians [have] any number of bets. If they [win] any of them, they [win] all. . . . If they dominate Italy, where Communist pressures are increasing, they could probably take Greece, Turkey, and the Middle East. Their aim is control of the Eastern Mediterranean and the Middle East. From there the possibilities for penetration of South Asia and Africa [are] limitless.[44]

This "successive loss" argument, later to be characterized as the "domino theory," was subsequently developed by other administration spokesmen, including representatives of the CIA and the JCS.[45] There was still a "Europe First" component in these arguments, in the sense that they continued to express the belief that the ultimate prize in the East-West struggle was control of Western Europe. What was progressively abandoned, however, was the assumption that priorities necessitated choices—either in terms of budgets or in terms of the commitment of American military power.

THE "NUCLEAR RELIANCE" SCHOOL

Concurrent with the development of the JCS, Kennan, and Acheson positions, an alternative faction began to develop within American defense planning circles. Its proponents sought to limit U.S. defense spending while at the same time enhancing U.S. politico-military influence worldwide by recourse to nuclear weapons. This group regarded a "tripod," composed of nuclear weapons, strategic bombers, and forward base deployments, as the most cost-effective Western response to the global threat represented by the Soviet Union.

Early postwar nuclear reliance proponents included Secretary of the Navy James Forrestal (subsequently appointed the first secretary of defense), General Curtis E. LeMay (commander of the Strategic Air Command), and, most notably, John Foster Dulles (special consultant to Truman and Acheson, and later Eisenhower's secretary of state). One of the earliest and most important postwar policy statements by the nuclear reliance group was the "Clifford Memorandum," which was prepared at President Truman's request and submitted to him in September 1946 by Clark M. Clifford, his special counsel.

Clifford relied heavily on the opinions of White House Chief of Staff William P. Leahy and Forrestal in his formulation of successive drafts of the memorandum. The final draft stressed the global nature of the Soviet threat and the futility of any attempt to cope with that threat on a region-by-region basis. It is striking for its alarmism and the stridency of its rhetoric—especially given that it came a full three and one-half years prior to the submission of NSC 68. Its most important conclusion was that future U.S. containment efforts directed against Moscow and its communist allies would be successful only if Washington were prepared to fight a nuclear war of global proportions.[46] The president subsequently elected not to distribute the document throughout official Washington despite his general agreement with its conclusions. Truman felt that there was already "too much loose talk about the Russian situation" and no need to contribute to the problem.[47]

Notwithstanding the president's cautious response, "preventive war" thinking about the Soviet threat continued to gain support from both American and European adherents. Even Kennan speculated about what would happen to the U.S. ability to deter war on Western Europe's behalf when the Soviets were able to build a large nuclear weapons stockpile, and the U.S. Air Force adopted nuclear preemption as its prevailing strategic philosophy during the late 1940s and early 1950s. In Europe, British opposition leader Winston Churchill urged the Americans to apply nuclear coercion against Moscow throughout 1948 to force a Soviet withdrawal from East Germany.[48] This type of reasoning soon became a minority position, however, as the Atlee government demonstrated with its strong opposition to the American use of nuclear weapons in the Korean War and with Churchill's letter rejecting the nuclear option in Indochina during mid-1954.

The Soviet Union's first nuclear weapons test, conducted in August 1949, lent a new urgency to the Clifford Memorandum's argument, yet simultaneously instilled a greater sense of restraint in U.S. policy circles about testing Moscow's resolve. Toward the end of President Truman's tenure in office and following the establishment of a formal command structure for the Atlantic Alliance, a policy of caution gradually evolved among the advocates of nuclear risk.

In December 1949, the Joint Chiefs of Staff approved a warfighting strategy for implementing the OFFTACKLE Emergency War Plan (JCS 2056), which involved the use of some 292 atomic bombs against Soviet targets throughout Eurasia. The attack was to be conducted from SAC airfields in the United Kingdom, Iceland, Newfoundland, Alaska, Guam, and Okinawa. B-29, B-36, and B-50 medium range nuclear-capable bombers were stationed at these sites, as well as B-36 intercontinental bombers at airfields located in the continental United States (CONUS).[49] Indeed, the perceived growing vulnerability of SAC centers, particularly in NATO Europe, led LeMay and other nuclear reliance advocates to press for the development of new strategic bases in other regions of the world as well. Washington asked the U.K. to grant it additional basing rights in Libya (then a UN trusteeship divided between Britain and France), while Paris was approached with a request for similar access to bases in Morocco and in other parts of North Africa. The United States also asked Denmark to allow it to conduct nuclear operations from Thule in Greenland.[50]

The nuclear reliance group actively resisted requests by the NATO allies for the deployment of U.S. ground forces to continental Europe. They also questioned the development of costly U.S. military forces for fighting a sustained conventional war beyond the European theater. Secretary of Defense Johnson's cancellation (summer 1949) of a new aircraft carrier, which the navy had justified as a major conventional warfighting element, was a victory for the nuclear reliance school within the Truman administration.

One year later, however, the nuclear reliance group lost some of its influence in Washington as a result of the Korean War and the formulation of NSC 68. By the fall of 1950, even the air force's chief of staff, Hoyt S. Vandenberg, one of those who continued to view preventive war favorably, conceded that NATO had been relying too heavily on the deterrent value of the Strategic Air Command bomber force.[51] Until Korea, the predominant JCS view was that the United States could endure a Soviet first strike using nuclear fission warheads and survive to fight a protracted global war. Yet recent archival research by David Allan Rosenberg, Marc Trachtenberg, and other historians has shown that the aforementioned Emergency War Plans were far too optimistic in their estimates of both the American nuclear arsenal's size (the Pentagon could rely only upon a stockpile of approximately 133 atomic bombs to destroy some seventy designated Soviet targets in 1949) and its capability for slowing a Russian military advance in Western Europe, the Middle East, or the Far East.[52]

The previously mentioned "Great Debate" then ensued in the form of highly charged congressional hearings and in public speeches closely followed by the American media and the public at large. At this point, the major postwar U.S. security factions pressed their respective cases before the American electorate. As already mentioned, George Marshall and Dean Acheson argued for stationing six U.S. divisions in Europe. But the nuclear reliance faction, led by John Foster Dulles, generated a strong rebuttal. Speaking in New York on December 29, 1950, Dulles offered what were later to become the stock cost-effectiveness arguments adopted by the Eisenhower administration after Communist Chinese forces began to tie down the UN troops in Korea. The future secretary of state observed that "with 20,000 miles of iron curtain" confronting the free world's defense perimeters, it would not be possible for the United States and its NATO allies to build up or sustain "static defense forces" that could make each of them "impregnable" to a future Russian attack.[53]

The nuclear reliance school finally came to dominate American strategic thought after the arrival of the Eisenhower administration in 1953. Reliance upon nuclear weapons became the cornerstone of the Eisenhower-Dulles team's efforts to hold down defense spending.[54] Neither the Suez crisis of 1956 nor the subsequent intervention of U.S. Marine and Army units in Lebanon during the July–August crisis of 1958 significantly altered Eisenhower's views on the need to rely primarily on nuclear weapons for global defense. The president subsequently reaffirmed his determination not to "fight on the enemy's terms and to be limited to his choice of weapons" if the West were to become simultaneously involved in several Third World conflicts.[55] Likewise, in carrying out a defense of Western Europe, tactical and strategic nuclear weapons were expected to be introduced early in any Warsaw Pact-NATO confrontation. This nuclear emphasis was deemed appropriate for American fighting outside of Europe as well.

In recognition of the increased importance of a secure network of overseas bases for strategic bomber missions, cooperation with the colonial allies was accorded somewhat greater importance in Washington. But the limits of the new administration's support for the colonial allies were established by the still pervasive sense of suspicion among U.S. policy makers that the Europeans were not reliable guarantors of stability in the Third World. In general, the Europeans were expected primarily to assist the United States by accepting greater responsibility for maintaining their own continental land force capabilities, and were discouraged from pursuing military policies in the Middle East or in East Asia independent of American control.

CONCLUSION

The six groups discussed above do not represent a complete list of the factions which contributed to the debate about how and where the Soviet Union should be contained in the postwar era. Other themes surfaced from time to time. For example, Senator William Knowland and, later, General Douglas MacArthur were the principal spokesmen for a small "Asia First" group, which campaigned to convince members of the Truman administration that, in terms of U.S. strategic interests, the future was in Asia, not Europe, and that an effective strategy of global containment had to begin with an effective military posture in the Pacific. But even after the outbreak of the Korean War, the Asia First group had difficulty in persuading the American mass and elite publics to regard that continent with equal or greater concern than Europe. On July 9, 1950, the Joint Chiefs of Staff postponed deciding on MacArthur's request for doubling U.S. ground forces fighting in Korea and for deploying atomic weapons there (although nuclear bombers were transferred to Guam in April of the following year after U.S. intelligence detected evidence of a massive Chinese ground offensive about to commence south of the 38th parallel). As one analyst has since characterized the JCS decision, it "reflected doubts about MacArthur's judgment, unwillingness to allow Korea to disrupt Europe-first strategic priorities, and a hesitancy to use nuclear weapons in a manner that seemed less likely to be decisive."[56]

Asia was simply not comparable to Europe in the minds of most Americans; it lacked similar cultural and political claims on U.S. sympathies. Furthermore, from the point of view of practical defense planning, it was difficult to imagine what a vigorous, long-term containment posture would look like, and what it would cost, in the wake of China's "loss" to the West. As the fear of Soviet global expansionism increased and the cold war set in, U.S. policy makers concluded that they had to accord more importance to Asia—but still not at the expense of the European strategic priority.

Neo-isolationism represented another minor theme in U.S. foreign policy debates in the postwar era. The neo-isolationists differed from their traditional isolationist predecessors in the sense that they tended to acknowledge that it would be inappropriate, and in any event, impossible, for the United States completely to remove itself from world affairs after 1945. In fact, Senator Robert A. Taft, one of the principal spokespersons for the neo-isolationist group in Congress, rejected the term *isolationist* altogether in the postwar era: "nobody is an isolationist today."[57] For nearly a decade following V-E day, however, the neo-isolationists consistently argued against American overcommitment to the security of Europe. They questioned the need for a binding, contractual commitment to allied security and subsequently questioned the need for the United States to contribute a large standing force to Europe. Underlying this argument was a suspicion that the European allies would exploit the opportunities provided by NATO membership to drain the U.S. budget and to manipulate U.S. foreign policy in support of their own purposes in the Third World.

The neo-isolationists also questioned whether Europe should be accorded priority in American foreign and defense plans. Many of the most influential within their ranks, including Taft, were in fact allied with the Asia First group in their criticisms of U.S. defense priorities. They tended to favor a firm U.S. security posture directed toward Asia—including a heavy reliance upon airpower and seapower and active support for the forces of Chiang Kai-shek—in order (somehow) to overthrow Mao Zedong on the Chinese mainland. In light of this open-ended commitment to a vigorous U.S. policy in Asia, John Gaddis rejects such terms as *isolationist* or *neo-isolationist* and opts instead for the term *unilateralists* to describe this group. In any event, the group played only a minor complicating and restrictive role in the shaping of U.S. defense policy during this period, and ultimately lost all policy focus by about 1955.

Table 2 provides a list of the key spokesmen for the six factions introduced above. The table also presents the principal arguments of each faction and summarizes the contributions that each made to the development of U.S. policy on issues of NATO membership, scope, and extraregional responsibility.

The task of the historian is simplified in those cases where competition between factions or groups is resolved by a definitive victory of one side over the other. This, unfortunately, is not the case here. In the interaction between the six factions within the U.S. foreign policy community reviewed in this chapter, only the universalist/idealist faction had disappeared from positions of power in Washington by the time that NATO was established. All of the other

TABLE 2

Universalist/Idealist

KEY PROPONENTS

Franklin D. Roosevelt (president)

Henry Wallace (vice-president)

Cordell Hull (secretary of state)

Edward Stettinius (secretary of state)

Basic Arguments

The UN can become an effective collective security instrument for pursuing U.S. *and* European global strategic objectives during the postwar era. A strategic division of labor for guaranteeing the stability of specific regions can be defined and followed by the wartime Allied powers, thus replacing the traditional balance of power in international affairs.

Policy Outcomes

The universalist/idealist approach lost momentum and credibility in U.S. politics soon after Roosevelt's death. It nonetheless continued to influence U.S. thinking about Allied colonial policies—reinforcing a general sense of suspicion and disdain for European policies in the Third World. Not surprisingly, the universalist/idealist approach never gained credibility among the other Allied powers.

Resource/Geographic Constraints

KEY PROPONENTS

Joint Chiefs of Staff

Natonal Security Council

Basic Arguments

U.S. military resources are insufficient to support indiscriminate containment around the world. Atlantic and Pacific SLOC access to the Western Hemisphere should be the main American defense priority, which requires a global rather than a European-weighted defense strategy. Initially, a Western counterattack against Soviet forces invading Western Europe would be conducted from extra-European bases. The Mediterranean/Middle Eastern regions should be a separate defense problem from that of defending Western Europe.

TABLE 2—Continued

Policy Outcomes

This faction played a restraining role during the initial round of talks relating to the creation of NATO. Following NATO's formation, the JCS modified its position in order to emphasize defense of Europe. Forward defense and extended containment replaced the earlier JCS preoccupation with defending SLOC access to the Western Hemisphere. No separate Mediterranean/Middle Eastern defense commands were established in NATO. Even after the creation of NATO, however, the JCS continued to warn against U.S. overcommitment to the colonial campaigns of the European allies.

Global Strongpoints

KEY PROPONENTS

George Kennan (director, Policy Planning Staff, State Department)

Charles Bohlen (counselor, State Department)

Basic Arguments

The Europeans should be encouraged to build their economies and to become as self-sufficient in defense as possible. The United States should be concerned with defending vital areas along the entire Eurasian landmass. In the event an Atlantic security alliance were to be formed, its geographic scope should be sufficient to secure Western control over Central Europe and guarantee U.S. base access to flank/peripheral European locales. Extra-European "affiliate members" should be included within an Atlantic alliance in order to manage and coordinate the global interests of the alliance members.

Policy Outcomes

European economic and defense self-sufficiency became the rationale for the Marshall Plan and for U.S. military assistance programs extended to the European allies.

"Europe First"

KEY PROPONENTS

Harry S Truman (president)

Dean Acheson (secretary of state)

John Hickerson (chief, Office of European Affairs, State Department)

Theodore Achilles (director, Western European Affairs, State Department)

Arthur Vandenberg (R., chairman, Senate Foreign Relations Committee)

Continued on next page

TABLE 2—Continued

George C. Marshall (secretary of state)

Walter Lippmann (American journalist)

Basic Arguments

Washington must accord highest priority to European security in its global defense planning. Ideals of colonial emancipation and world order must be integrated into a more traditional Eurocentric balance-of-power arrangement in order to underwrite Western security interests. It is assumed, but not strongly advocated, that the Europeans will gradually and willingly divest themselves of colonial responsibilities. But the United States should not jeopardize ties to its Atlantic allies by a campaign of pressure for European decolonization.

Policy Outcomes

NATO Europe became the focal point of U.S. global security thinking. NATO allies received most of the Mutual Defense Assistance Program (MDAP) funds from the United States. The United States agreed to station four additional divisions in Europe. Events beyond the NATO treaty area (Korea, Cuba) were frequently viewed as diversionary actions, with the real Soviet target being Western Europe.

NSC 68 School of Thought

KEY PROPONENTS

Paul Nitze (director, Policy Planning Staff, State Department, after 1948)

Dean Acheson (after 1949)

Robert Lovett (undersecretary of state)

Basic Arguments

Soviet nuclear capability undermined the value of a U.S. global containment strategy based almost entirely on nuclear threat; a significant conventional defense build-up would have to be undertaken as well. The United States should continue to attempt to establish geographic priorities, but strategic competition with the USSR is global in scope, and a political-strategic loss anywhere would be a serious setback for the West.

Policy Outcomes

Implemented with the advent of the Korean War, NSC 68 led to the formation of NATO's military command structure and increased U.S. military deployments in Eu-

TABLE 2—Continued

rope. NSC 68 also reinforced the importance of escalation control in crises in the Third World.

Nuclear Reliance

KEY PROPONENTS

John Foster Dulles (secretary of state)

General Curtis LeMay (commander, Strategic Air Command)

Clark M. Clifford (special counsel to President Truman)

James Forrestal (secretary of defense)

Basic Arguments

Reliance on nuclear weapons would significantly reduce the high costs of implementing extended containment. The credibility of U.S. containment can only be achieved if the Soviets really believe the United States will be willing to *use* its nuclear weapons in both European and extra-European crises. Preventive nuclear strikes should be considered a rational strategic option. American access to extra-European bases is critical if a viable nuclear containment strategy is to be established. Airpower will be the primary component in any U.S. containment strategy.

Policy Outcomes

President Truman opted to deploy land forces as the primary symbol of American extended containment in Europe, thereby deemphasizing the role of airpower in NATO. President Eisenhower, however, reestablished the primacy of nuclear reliance in U.S. defense policy for both European and extra-European locales. The threat of nuclear weapons use nonetheless became less credible as Korea (1950), and other Third World crises were met with U.S. conventional forces and offshore military power rather than nuclear weapons.

---

groups continued to compete for influence in shaping U.S. strategy as the international system became increasingly bipolar with intensified superpower competition. They held fundamental differences on how to assess and respond to the emerging Soviet threat in Europe and beyond. In a situation in which the U.S. government could not reconcile these internal differences, Washington could hardly expect to reconcile divisions between itself and its allies following the outbreak of the Korean War.

Frequently, the result of policy competition between these American schools of thought was an uneasy and, at times, incoherent compromise in U.S. alliance policy that recognized the centrality of European security for the United States but took note of the importance of other regions as well; that accepted the need for both nuclear and conventional defense of Europe but failed to resolve questions of how and when each instrument should be relied upon; that was committed to decolonization but without going too far, too fast at the expense of America's European allies or the global containment network. In short, the United States pursued a "push me—pull you" policy that often moved in two different directions at the same time, with the result that it generally ended up somewhere in the middle. The contradictions inherent in this posture were often most visible in those cases that involved out-of-area disagreements within NATO itself.

CHAPTER 2

DEFINING THE ALLIANCE'S
FLANKS AND BALANCING
ITS CENTER

THE POSITIONS taken by the U.S. delegates to the Washington Preparatory Talks on the issue of NATO membership were based upon competition and compromise between the six factions introduced in Chapter 1. The United States originally favored limited alliance membership, both as a means of demonstrating faith in the UN to manage global security problems arising beyond Central Europe and in recognition of inherent constraints on U.S. resources. Most participants in the Washington Preparatory Talks initially thought in terms of a seven-nation alliance composed of the United States, Canada, and the five signatories to the 1948 Brussels Defense Pact (Britain, France, and the Benelux states). As the talks progressed, however, key U.S. policy makers came to recognize the need to lengthen the list of treaty signatories, in accordance with the demands of its own global strategy.

EUROPE'S NORTHERN FLANK
AND U.S. GLOBAL SECURITY INTERESTS

A particular concern among U.S. security planners was the Soviet defense treaty imposed upon Finland in 1948, and its implications for the security of Scandinavia and the northern approaches to the Atlantic.[1] The United States was especially interested in assuring itself of access to the critical "anchor points" in the North Atlantic such as Greenland, Iceland, and the Faroe Islands, which had played an essential role in linking Europe to the United States during World War II. What the Americans did not anticipate was the necessity to defer to the Scandinavians' own regionally based security concerns in the context of alliance-wide interests.

Concern about the status of continued U.S. operations at Danish-controlled air bases in Greenland—Thule, Sondre Stromfjord, and Narsarssuak—prompted Washington to request an extension of the April 1941 Greenland Defense Agreement, and subsequently to encourage Copenhagen to join NATO during early 1949. U.S. defense officials foresaw the need to retain Washington's access to Greenland's bases owing to developments in modern warfare such as the introduction of nuclear strike aircraft. The Danish electorate, however, was in no mood to have the country become a high profile affiliate of an offensive-oriented U.S. nuclear extended deterrence strategy. In contrast to actual U.S. strategic thinking at the time, American arguments for renewal of basing rights were presented to the Danes in terms of denial and defense missions rather than nuclear strike missions. In its eagerness to retain deployment rights at the Danish-controlled bases, the United States offered Copenhagen veto rights in the construction and utilization of U.S. or NATO facilities in Greenland. This gesture was destined to backfire on Washington in later years when Denmark adopted policies of not allowing nuclear weapons on Danish soil and of restricting American supply and support activities in Thule and elsewhere throughout Greenland. [2]

Just as it was obvious that Washington had to go through the Danes to gain access to Greenland, it was also clear that the United States would have to go through Oslo to convince an insecure and uncertain Denmark to join the alliance. In fact, the principal actor in moving the Nordic countries toward NATO membership was Norway's foreign minister, Halvard Lange. Lange met with considerable domestic political opposition in his first efforts to press the case for NATO membership. Over time, however, the fact that Norway had lost its Finnish territorial buffer with the signing of the 1948 Soviet-Finnish treaty outweighed continued Norwegian Labor party opposition to NATO and drove Oslo to reject a neutralist position. In the wake of events in Czechoslovakia during early 1948, Lange succeeded in convincing the Storting to support a more open affiliation with the Western bloc. Lange's job was made easier by American promises to provide Norway with military supplies on financial terms they would never have matched by remaining nonaligned. [3]

Norway's announcement of its intention to enter into the treaty effectively destroyed the alternative Swedish-sponsored option of a Scandinavian Defense Union, which had previously been discussed between Norwegian and Danish officials in meetings held at Karlstad, Sweden, in 1949. [4] Without Norwegian membership in such a union, none of Sweden's political parties viewed a bilateral Swedish-Danish security arrangement as credible. Nor could Denmark afford the level of defense expenditures any such arrangement would inevitably have entailed. Denmark soon followed Norway into the Atlantic Alliance.

The Danish decision, in turn, encouraged Iceland to accept the invitation to join NATO. Thus, the 1951 bilateral U.S.-Iceland defense agreement (renegotiated in 1974) gave Washington responsibility for Iceland's defense within a NATO format.[5] The agreement permitted the United States to install defensive systems and conventional striking power close to key maritime access routes leading from the Greenland-Iceland-U.K.(GIUK) gap to North America. It was anticipated that installations in Iceland and Norway would constitute the essential northern edge of a global radar and communications network for distant early warning (DEW) and/or NATO Air Defense Ground Environment (NADGE) systems.

With the inclusion of three Nordic allies in NATO, Washington ensured the ability to maintain supply and reinforcement lines to Europe in the event of a Soviet invasion. American interest in establishing a flank defense in Scandinavia at the time of NATO's formation reflected JCS chairman General Omar Bradley's concern about the need to shore up "egress points" from Western Europe into the North Atlantic as part of a viable U.S. *global* defense posture. In congressional testimony soon after NATO's founding, Bradley related that the flank countries' membership in NATO constituted the most cost-effective means of assuring the security of the Western Hemisphere itself.[6] Internal JCS documents stressed that NATO's forward defense enhanced the North American continent's overall security and that, consistent with their concern for the management of scarce U.S. resources, American military forces were best deployed from peripheral positions around the European continent in the event of out-of-area crises.[7]

Expanding NATO's Southern Flank

Similar concerns about access to strategic "stepping stone" islands in other parts of the Atlantic led U.S. defense planners to invite Portugal, which controlled the Azores and Madeira archipelagos, to join the alliance. Indeed, at the time of NATO's formation, Portugal and its offshore islands were regarded not only as key points of departure for U.S. and allied offshore power to move in and out of Europe but also as a central element in U.S. defense planning for South America, Western and Southern Africa, the Persian Gulf, and the Near East. Offsetting such strategic considerations, however, were considerable feelings of "guilt by association" shared among U.S. policy makers and the U.S. public at large over having to deal with Portuguese leader Antonio Salazar—an unapologetic defender of Portuguese colonialism in Africa and a clear opponent of democracy in his own country.

Salazar recognized that he had considerable negotiating leverage as a result of his country's offshore facilities, and he made the United States come to him on the issue of NATO membership. This was something of a personal victory for the Portuguese leader, who had distrusted the United States since World War II, when Washington had considered fomenting a revolt among the inhabitants of the Azores as a means of acquiring access to a base there.[8] In order to convince a suspicious Congress of the appropriateness of Salazar's participation in an alliance "founded on the principles of democracy," the Truman administration pressed the distinction between Lisbon's "authoritarian" regime, which "the people freely voted for," and a "totalitarian" system.[9] The Truman administration also backed up its political argument with a reassurance that "Portugal's financial situation is sound; its budget has been balanced for the past fifteen years and the *escudo* is one of the firmest currencies in Europe. Portugal is participating in the ERP [European Recovery Program] but is receiving no financial assistance."[10] These rationales helped to salve the consciences of American legislators and to pave the way for Portuguese admission into the alliance as a founding member in 1949.

Having accepted the utility of adding a northern flank to the alliance and having convinced themselves of the necessity, if not the complete propriety, of Portuguese membership, U.S. defense planners next addressed the issue of Southeast European security. In describing the implications of the ongoing Greek civil war between communist and nationalist factions (in the aftermath of the withdrawal of British military assistance from pro-Western forces in Greece), the U.S. ambassador asserted that the security of the entire Near East, as well as North Africa, was at stake in the Balkans.[11] This theme of "interdependent security" surfaced again one month later as part of the rationale for the Truman Doctrine, and it was used to facilitate congressional acceptance of the Atlantic Alliance two years later.[12]

In view of the central role of Greece and Turkey in the formulation of American cold war policy, it is interesting that the Eastern Mediterranean was not included in the treaty area in 1949. During the Washington Preparatory Talks, both Athens and Ankara had communicated their interest in becoming signatory members of the alliance, but the United States blocked their requests on the grounds that extending the alliance into the Eastern Mediterranean would undermine its "North Atlantic" character. For the next eighteen months, Greece and Turkey complained that they had been singled out for exclusion by Washington and London (an argument that was strengthened by the inclusion of Italy as a signatory member). Athens and Ankara played upon the interdependent security argument, warning that their continued exclusion from NATO increased the risk of Soviet subversion, or even direct military action, in the Eastern Mediterranean. Washington's defense planners were not insensitive to these warnings, but the risks of "spreading the butter too thin" by overextending the alliance were given more credence.

Following the submission of NSC 68 and the outbreak of the Korean War, however, the Truman administration abandoned its opposition to Greek and Turkish membership in NATO, both as a means of reinforcing the deterrent threat to the Soviet Union in the southern region of the alliance and in order to take advantage of the twenty-five divisions that Athens and Ankara were prepared to contribute to NATO.

The Middle East as a Source
of Anglo-American Dispute

Having brought Turkey and Greece under the NATO umbrella, American and British military planners turned their attention to alternative formulas for securing their respective strategic interests in the Middle East. Specifically contemplated was the formation of a Middle East Command (1950–52) and, later, a Middle East Defense Organization (MEDO) (January 1952-July 1953). Any such grouping would have included its own Military Representatives Committee and Military Planning Group.[13] At various times in these discussions, the participants considered a direct link between NATO and MEDO, while at other times the emphasis was upon separate Atlantic and Middle East alliances, but with some overlapping membership.

Of most importance to our analysis, however, is that MEDO represented one of the first post-NATO out-of-area policy disputes between two of its major participants: Britain and the United States. The British felt that their experience in Middle Eastern security affairs ranging back well into the previous century gave them every right to view that region as their *domaine réservé* for purposes of Western defense planning. The Americans strongly believed that it was just this type of British thinking that could ultimately alienate a new breed of nationalist leaders, then coming to power in Egypt and other Middle Eastern locales, from Western strategic interests and affiliation.

Washington nevertheless gradually accepted the need to work closely with London to establish a comprehensive security arrangement in the region. Previously, the State Department's Office of Near Eastern Affairs had taken the lead in defining U.S. policy on an undeniable problem—that the Middle East lacked a "power center" necessary for implementing a comprehensive and credible pro-Western defense arrangement there.[14] NSC 47/5 (March 17, 1951) directed that, in view of the Iranian nationalist threat to British oil fields at Abadan and Egyptian president Nasser's criticisms of continued U.K. control of the Suez Canal base, Washington would have to support London's commitment to preserve Western access to the Suez Canal and to other Middle Eastern facilities. At the same time, however, the U.S. military establishment recommended that the United States seek to restrain Britain from taking unilateral military action against the Egyptians.[15] It is interesting that this same logic of "support-plus-restraint" also reflected the British approach regarding U.S./U.K. relations in the Middle East. Each government saw itself as more reasonable and realistic than the other on matters relating to Middle East security, and both assumed that the other would only accept advice and counsel if it was confident of the reliability and commitment of its partner.

The MEC/MEDO idea foundered on issues of membership and questions of command and responsibility—all symptoms of more fundamental policy differences between Washington and London. As noted above, the MEDO talks were complicated by the growth of Arab nationalism. This was particularly true in the case of Nasser's rise to prominence within the Third World's fledgling nonaligned movement. Nasser explicitly opposed the creation of a MEDO— either as an independent defense arrangement or as an adjunct to NATO—on the grounds that any such alliance would ultimately be used by Washington and London to reinforce colonial controls, pit Arab against Arab, and build up the West's basing system in the region.

When the Eisenhower administration came to power in 1953, it reassessed the MEDO idea in light of the growth of Arab nationalism. In July 1953, Eisenhower's secretary of state, John Foster Dulles, intimated to his British counterpart, Lord Salisbury, that it would be better to establish a Western military command structure in the Northern Tier instead of in the Middle East, since the Arab states "are preoccupied with problems other than the Soviet threat."[16] He also communicated the Eisenhower administration's opposition to NATO's assuming an explicit Middle Eastern security role, much to London's chagrin.

In 1955, the Baghdad Pact was established as a compromise arrangement. It was composed of traditional Northern Tier states—Turkey, Iraq, Iran, and Pakistan—along with Great Britain as the external power historically involved in the region. Without U.S. sponsorship, the pact would never have been created, yet the Americans were conspicuously absent from its membership. Washington provided the bulk of the military assistance to the Baghdad Pact members in the 1950s and 1960s.[17] But the United States was reticent to associate itself more explicitly with the organization, primarily because of its traditional interest in preserving its freedom of choice on issues of war and peace. The administration put the matter in blunt terms during Senator H. Alexander Smith's discussions with Assistant Secretary of State George V. Allen in Senate Foreign Relations Committee hearings (May 1956):

SENATOR SMITH: Didn't we inspire the idea of the Baghdad Pact after we got SEATO . . . and NATO? . . . Didn't we think the Baghdad Pact was a complementary collective security group in the middle?
ALLEN: That is right, Senator, but it came about a little differently . . . let's be quite honest with ourselves. The British are almost in the swim. They are in the cold water, and they are unhappy at the possibility that war might break out in that area and they would already be committed by treaty . . . to go in immediately, and we would wait awhile. They want us to be right in there from the word go at the time they get involved. I do not blame them at all, but we do not have quite the same position in the area, so we are reluctant on the Baghdad Pact.[18]

The United States also had two more specific reasons for not signing as a member of the pact. First, the pact was the target of intense criticism by various Arab leaders, most notably Nasser. From Washington's point of view, formal affiliation with the pact would have invited these Arab governments to focus their attacks on the United States, rather than on their traditional target, Britain. Second, as Dulles explained to Eden at this time, it was "politically impossible for the United States to join the Pact until we were able to offer a comparable security arrangement for Israel."[19] In the absence of formal U.S. membership, however, Norman Graebner's 1956 assessment of both SEATO and Baghdad was accurate: "Neither . . . add much material strength to the West, and it is doubtful if even the signatories have any interest in them except as they open an interesting wedge to the United States Treasury."[20]

If the United States had agreed to become an active member of the Baghdad Pact in 1955, it would have provided London and Washington with one more institutional forum for the discussion of Middle Eastern security issues. It is extremely unlikely, however, that the existence of another forum for consultation would have helped at all to divert Washington and London from the paths that led them toward the Suez crisis one year later. Their differences, based upon "guilt by association" and *domaine réservé* concerns, respectively, were probably insurmountable prior to Suez.

BALANCED COLLECTIVE FORCES AND THE ISSUE OF GERMAN MEMBERSHIP IN THE ALLIANCE

At the same time that U.S. policy makers were debating the issue of Greek and Turkish membership in the alliance and considering ways of linking NATO to some kind of MEDO, a more intense and divisive debate was beginning within and between allied governments on the question of German rearmament and Germany's proper role within the Western alliance. Ironically, this debate and the ultimate solution that was arrived at in 1955 were significantly influenced by developments *outside* the NATO Treaty area during the first half of the 1950s.

In January 1950, the North Atlantic Council met in Washington to address the question of how to distribute NATO's military assets among national and alliance security priorities. During these proceedings, Secretary of State Dean Acheson pressed the case for "balanced collective forces" designed to achieve "a pattern of area defense based on individual national specialization" within the NATO Treaty area. Under the balanced collective forces concept, the Europeans were expected to provide most of the ground forces and tactical air support needed to defend their own region, while Britain and the United States would accept primary responsibility for conducting strategic bombing operations and securing vital Atlantic sea and air lines of communication.[21]

Left unanswered was how a doctrine of balanced collective forces in Europe could be reconciled with the desire of London and Paris, in particular, to sustain balanced *national* forces for the defense of what they felt were still vital national defense interests beyond the treaty area. Indeed, prior to Suez, a balanced national forces approach was recognized by the U.K. and France as more essential to their overall defense interests than the more restricted "division of labor" arrangement preferred by the United States. According to Peter Foot,

> The Dutch might be persuaded that there was no need to rebuild their Navy. However, the Netherlands was a minor power. France and Britain could not be similarly dealt with. Both were determined to maintain their respective global perspectives. France, upon whose land forces much would depend in any war in Europe, kept her elite troops in Indochina; Britain, always reluctant about a "continental commitment," still cherished a post-Imperial role.[22]

French and British resistance to the balanced collective forces idea gradually fueled the suspicion among American politicians that the United States was being exploited by its NATO allies. The Truman administration assured the American public that U.S. troop contributions to NATO were "based on the expectation that our efforts will be met with similar action on their [the Europeans'] part."[23] In fact, however, Truman's advisers had little reason to expect that the U.S. manpower contribution would encourage the principal European allies to make significant increases in their separate national contributions to the alliance in the near term. Extraregional commitments precluded many NATO members from even contemplating anything resembling a balanced collective force within Europe. As Richard Barnet has since noted,

> Major French military forces were already bogged down in Indochina. The Dutch were absorbed in preserving the last tatters of their once fabulous Empire in the East Indies. The British were policing the remnants of theirs. The Portuguese were far more concerned to hold on to Mozambique, Angola, and Guinea-Bissau than to defend the Pyrenees, which they did not see as under imminent threat.[24]

The Europe-first school within the Truman administration saw the U.S. troop deployments in the NATO theater as a necessary accommodation to the fact that its principal NATO allies were still overcommitted abroad. But it was felt that the U.S. forces could not be maintained indefinitely in Europe; that to take the pressure off Washington, the European allies would have to settle their problems in the Third World expeditiously, so that they could take up their "fair share" of the NATO defense burden. In the interim, however, new sources for NATO manpower had to be found, and West Germany appeared to be the most logical answer.

In the face of Washington's determination to prod its European allies into greater self-sufficiency in defense, West German chancellor Konrad Adenauer moved on his own during the late 1940s and early 1950s to convince NATO governments of the indispensability of Germany to the long-term security of Western Europe. The German chancellor correctly calculated that the European defense issue could be used to help move West Germany from its postwar situation as an occupied territory toward his goal of sovereign equality. Adenauer was aided in this campaign by the galvanizing effect in the United States of the outbreak of the Korean War. Norbert Wiggershaus has since recalled that "within the Pentagon, the issue of German (and Japanese) rearmament was brought up less than forty-eight hours after the outbreak of hostilities [in Korea]."[25] Adenauer found that not only American policy elites, but at least some European leaders as well, were sensitive to his warning that "Stalin has the same plan for Europe as for Korea." As one Italian journalist expressed the problem at the time, "a 38th parallel runs through Berlin."[26]

By August 1950, the Consultative Assembly of the Council of Europe, meeting in Strasbourg, voted to support a proposal initially and dramatically raised by British representative Winston Churchill—and actively supported by Adenauer himself—to move toward the creation of a unified European army incorporating German personnel.

THE PLEVEN PLAN AND THE ATTEMPT AT AN EDC

In the months following the outbreak of the Korean War, Paris had intensified its efforts to block the remilitarization of Germany. But France's influence within the alliance was severely diminished by its overextension in Indochina and the general weakness of successive Fourth Republic governments. The French argument that it was carrying more than its fair share of NATO responsibilities by its resistance to the forces of communism in Asia was generating more sympathy by this time (in the wake of NSC 68, the North Korean invasion, and the "fall" of China). But this sympathy did not translate into political leverage for France within the NATO community.

The Pleven Plan was subsequently proposed by Paris on October 24, 1950, as the best arrangement that France could expect under the circumstances. The plan would have incorporated West German manpower into a European Defense Community (EDC) managed by a non-German defense minister (presumably French) appointed by and accountable to the Council of Europe and the signatories of the 1948 Brussels Treaty. Much to the chagrin of Washington, however, the transatlantic debate over the Pleven Plan languished for the next four years, as successive Fourth Republic governments rose and fell at a rapid pace and as French attention remained fixed upon Indochina. In the wake of the catastrophe of Dien Bien Phu and in the face of increasing U.S. pressure for a vote in favor of the EDC, the French government finally asked the National Assembly in August of 1954 to decide whether France should participate in the arrangement that Paris had initially sponsored. It seems clear that the government, led by Pierre Mendès-France, had no illusions about the prospects for such a vote. In fact, the opposition to the EDC within the assembly was so overwhelming that, by a vote of 319 to 264, the assembly decided not even to take up discussion of the treaty.[27]

Since most of the cold war historiography tends to assign all or most of the blame for the failure of the EDC to France, it is well to point out that one of the major reasons for the four-year delay in a French vote on the EDC was Paris' inability to convince the British to participate in the arrangement. France was concerned that *any* European defense arrangement that did not include Britain would inevitably become dominated by Germany. Britain, for its part, was reluctant to join an exclusively European defense pact because it still aspired to the dual roles of Commonwealth leader and American partner beyond the narrow confines of Europe.

The threat of a U.S. troop pullout from Europe, combined with intimations from the U.S. Joint Chiefs of Staff that Washington might conclude its own bilateral defense understandings with the Germans in the event that the European allies were unable to create an alternative to EDC, nonetheless drove Eden to organize the Nine-Power Conference, held in London at the end of September. Participants included (among others) Dulles, Eden, Mendès-France, P. H. Spaak, Lester Pearson, and Adenauer. The deliberations went more smoothly than many observers had first expected, primarily because of the British decision to reverse the position it had held during the EDC debates. Anthony Eden announced Britain's willingness to maintain four divisions and the U.K.'s Tactical Air Force in continental Europe "for so long as the Brussels Powers desired it" in support of a successor arrangement to the EDC. "From this point on," Eden tells us, "the Conference moved rapidly forward."[28] The 1948 Brussels Treaty arrangement was renamed the Western European Union (WEU) and placed under the auspices of NATO. Germany was integrated into NATO through the WEU in May of 1955.

The out-of-area issue surfaced at several points during the London discussions and played an important role in determining both the NATO military command structure and the size and composition of Germany's contribution to the alliance. Specifically:

1. Remembering German military offensives against North Africa in World War II, France and the lowland countries insisted that among the Federal Republic of Germany's (F.R.G.) weapons production limitations would be stipulations forbidding Bonn to build capital warships and long-range bombers.
2. Selected naval forces were exempted from the joint command in order to assure the principal NATO governments of their independence in the event of out-of-area responsibilities.
3. Perhaps most significant for this study, the French insisted that overseas forces could not be counted within NATO/WEU force totals on the principle that management of overseas territories was still a national rather than an alliance-wide responsibility.[29]

Predictably, the U.S. Joint Chiefs of Staff had argued that the issue of a German defense contribution to Western security could not be treated separately from an overall global strategy, which needed to be developed by the

United States and the other NATO powers. A credible German army deployed in Europe was expected to allow for more effective defense of Europe's perimeters while at the same time permitting America (and to a lesser extent, Britain) to improve its retaliatory striking power deployed in offshore positions. In a situation in which Britain and France were still preoccupied with problems overseas, however, Washington was not able to redeploy its European-based forces.

CONCLUSION

The inclusion of German, Greek, and Turkish military units in NATO during the first half of the 1950s tended to mask the disputes between Washington and the major European allies concerning the competing demands of Continental and colonial defense. Washington's position that it was entitled to define the context of alliance burden-sharing was predicated upon the reality that it alone could provide the type of credible guarantee of extended deterrence needed by both Britain and France to neutralize the Soviet threat in Europe, allowing them to pursue largely *national* security interests beyond their own continent. The Truman administration thus viewed British and French resistance to U.S. burden-sharing proposals within NATO as indicating a lack of appreciation for American efforts on their behalf. Disagreements about NATO versus out-of-area responsibilities were nonetheless mitigated by the fact that alternative sources of NATO manpower were found. The result was a brief breathing space for the alliance leaders, until the Suez crisis forced all involved governments to reassess the validity of NATO in a global context.

CHAPTER 3

THE SUEZ CRISIS

MUCH of the literature dealing with the Suez crisis has focused on the interpersonal misunderstandings that complicated efforts at consultation and policy coordination between France and Britain on the one hand and the United States on the other, during the period leading up to the November 1956 Anglo/French military operation. Suez does in fact provide students of foreign policy decision making with a fascinating case study of all manner of decisional errors, including defensive avoidance, attributional error, premature closure, wishful thinking, incorrect historical analogizing, and "groupthink."[1]

It is essential to note at the outset, however, that in some important respects there was no misunderstanding. For example, each of the three key actors had a clear sense of the others' basic opinions and concerns regarding Nasser and the nationalization of the Suez Canal. The United States understood why the other two felt compelled to take the actions that they did. Paris and London, moreover, understood why Washington opted to take a different tack in its dealings with the Middle East in general and with Nasser in particular. What none of the three major NATO allies understood, however, was the *priority* that the others accorded to Suez in the broader scheme of things, or the expectations that each brought to the crisis as a result of their shared membership in the alliance.

From London's vantage point, Egypt's nationalization of the canal was viewed against the backdrop of the gradual unraveling of British influence in the Middle East-Mediterranean region. By 1956, the signs of policy disintegration seemed to be everywhere. London had failed in its efforts to sponsor a MEDO and had had to settle for the Baghdad Pact—in the Northern Tier rather than the Middle East, and without U.S. participation. Riots in Aden and a full-blown separatist revolt in Cyprus threatened the stability of two other traditional imperial strongpoints. King Hussein's decision to remove the pro-British Glubb Pasha from his post as chief of staff of the Jordanian armed forces was viewed from Whitehall as a serious setback in a country whose regional cooperation and backing was considered to be essential. Finally, during the spring of

1956, the Soviet Union signed a treaty of friendship with Yemen and warned Britain not to attempt to interfere with Yemeni oil prospecting. All of these developments led London to treat the canal issue as the ultimate test of its ability to retain *any* influence in the Middle East.

French concerns were more focused, and more extreme. Nasser was linked in the minds of French policy makers with the ongoing crisis in Algeria. By this time, the National Liberation Front (FLN) was tying down between 160,000 and 170,000 French troops, and Paris was in the process of withdrawing two divisions from the NATO central front and additional forces from North Africa at the urging of the beleaguered military commanders in Algeria.[2] French leaders had convinced themselves that if they could cut off regional support for the rebels, the separatist movement could be contained and ultimately crushed. But Egypt was cooperating with Morocco and Tunisia to keep the FLN armed and trained and committed to the overthrow of French influence.

Washington, meanwhile, saw the nationalization of the canal in a different light. The United States was primarily concerned that the dispute over Suez not be permitted to undermine Washington's influence with key nations in the Third World (such as India), with important Third World participants in the global containment network (such as Pakistan), with influential Middle Eastern regional actors (such as Saudi Arabia), within the United Nations, and within NATO itself. Washington had been impressed a year earlier by Nasser's success during the Asian-African Conference, convened at Bandung, Indonesia. The Egyptian leader had returned home as a national hero and had established himself as the spokesman for Arab nationalism and as an indispensable player in any future attempts at Arab-Israeli conciliation. Egypt was also recognized as potentially the widest gate through which the Soviets could eventually enter the Middle East.

Each of the three allies had communicated its overriding concerns about Nasser and the Middle East to the others on numerous occasions prior to the nationalization of the canal, in an effort either to obtain their support or to discourage them from interfering in their *domaine réservé*. And each at various times had expressed sympathy for the other's point of view. Eisenhower, for example, notes in his memoirs that in view of the growing *Enosis* movement on Cyprus, Britain's decision to leave its Suez base in 1954, and the general "end-of-empire" feeling in England, London was in no mood to accommodate Nasser.[3] Washington was nonetheless anxious to convince London of the importance of drawing Nasser and other prominent Third World nationalists into the Western camp. In an address delivered to NATO's Ministerial Council on May 4, 1956, Dulles emphasized the West's vulnerability to Soviet exploitation of anticolonial resentments beyond the treaty area. His concerns were echoed by then-Belgian foreign minister Paul-Henri Spaak, who decried a lack of coordinated NATO policy planning toward the Third World.[4] Dulles also argued that there was no prima facie case for the Anglo-French contention that any action taken by Nasser to nationalize the canal would be illegal, and he called for multilateral negotiations, involving a representative sampling of the international community, to resolve the outstanding Anglo/French-Egyptian disputes. Finally, in response to the British and French warnings about Western oil cutoffs, Dulles claimed that the United States and others could make up the difference for the NATO allies in the event of a temporary closing of the canal. He also expressed his belief that within a short time supertankers would replace the smaller vessels, and that this change would ultimately make the Southern Cape route more cost-effective than the canal.[5]

From the British and French perspective, Egypt's nationalization of the canal was a straightforward act of aggression with serious implications for European access to oil, and even more serious implications for European relations with overseas dependencies. If Britain and France could be summarily kicked out of Suez by Nasser, their bases and properties in all of the other colonial territories would be fair game. Eden ridiculed Dulles for treating the crisis as "fundamentally a business dispute over the control of an international public utility."[6] The growing frustration of both French and British policy makers was due in large part to the domestic political pressures that they were experiencing. The British press frequently criticized Eden during this period for deferring to Washington on the whole issue of dealing with the Third World. In April, the *Daily Mail* complained that "in sermons against colonialism [the Americans] have helped preach faithful allies out of invaluable bases. But they have not preached themselves out of Okinawa, Formosa or Puerto Rico."[7]

As the leader of the alliance, however, the United States was also impressed by the differing opinions and concerns of its other European security partners. In particular, Germany, Italy, and the Scandinavian nations were critical of Anglo-French handling of the Suez situation and pressed Washington not to give in to pressure from London and Paris in favor of a tough stand against Nasser.[8] Likewise, Spain, which had its own problems with Britain over Gibraltar and which by this time had developed close bilateral military ties with the United States, applauded the Egyptian move and accused Paris and London of "unbridled and dangerous attitudes" toward Nasser.[9] As events unfolded, Washington came increasingly to play the role of mediator between Britain and France, on one side, and the majority of Western, Commonwealth, and Third World nations that took a position on the Suez nationalization issue on the other.

The United States position was straightforward. It favored negotiation in good faith with Nasser, and no implicit or explicit threats of military retaliation. The British had in fact been hinting to Washington since March that a coordinated military response might be the best way to deal with Nasser. But Dulles and Eisenhower had been consistent and firm in their rejection of this line of argument. They were backed up by the aforementioned European allies and by Australia and Canada. Australian prime minister Robert Menzies sought to impress upon Whitehall that a military response to the nationalization of the canal would sacrifice "the whole work we have put into developing Asian goodwill . . . [and] destroy the Commonwealth."[10] Such arguments convinced Washington that it was actually serving the interests of its two major NATO partners—London in particular—by attempting to steer them away from a self-destructive course in the Suez situation.

As negotiations stalled, however, Britain and France became convinced that the only realistic course was military intervention. British and French planners had been considering the logistical aspects of an intervention since the spring. During joint military staff discussions (August 7–9), Lieutenant General Sir Hugh Stockwell, who commanded the British 1st Corps, advised his French counterparts that "there could be no question of using the facilities of NATO" in view of the circumstances. Thus, Cyprus was designated as the "operational base" if a Suez invasion were actually to take place. Stockwell also argued that, "as the British could fairly claim a 'special relationship' with the Americans, by which they would hope to maintain the neutrality of the United States in the period of operation, Britain was the obvious choice for leadership."[11]

This, of course, was the most fundamental misperception. It had been nurtured by most British policy makers throughout the early cold war period in spite of numerous rebuffs. British diplomatic setbacks were at least partly offset, however, by the rhetoric of the NATO Alliance, which stressed "common security interests" and shared Atlantic values. Even French policy makers, who were still bitter about the "betrayal" at Dien Bien Phu, convinced themselves that Washington would be forced by the priority that it accorded to NATO and to the "special relationship" with Britain to offer no more than restrained criticism of an Anglo-French intervention in Egypt.

Thus, neither European ally was prepared for the forceful American response to the Anglo-French intervention, which began on October 31. The invasion took place under the guise of a peacekeeping initiative in the wake of the Israeli invasion of Egypt, which had begun two days earlier. In fact, the Israeli invasion had been secretly coordinated with Paris and London during the last two weeks of October. In a situation in which Eisenhower felt that he had been personally betrayed by two major allies, he authorized a multifaceted campaign of pressure—with London as the principal target. Britain was advised that previously discussed arrangements for the supply of American oil in the event of a closure of the canal did not apply in view of the circumstances. This action forced Britain to begin rationing gasoline. Washington also threatened economic punishment if the Anglo-French operation was not halted.

The seriousness of the crisis, and the confused nature of the events, is illustrated by the allied military situation in the Mediterranean. Eisenhower had deployed the Sixth Fleet to the Eastern Mediterranean to evacuate about two thousand Americans prior to the Anglo-French invasion. With the arrival of British and French vessels on November 4, the American fleet was pulled back to avoid a confrontation. Richard Rosecrance has argued, however, that "the U.S. fleet was presumably under orders to offer peaceful obstruction to the invasion force." He based this conclusion on a number of incidents involving U.S. and British ships and aircraft in the region. Rosecrance notes that "U.S. airplanes tested British carrier defenses" and that "unidentified submarines were detected on the floor of the Mediterranean." He concludes his account by noting that "the British naval commander had finally to ask his American counterpart to bring them [submarines] to the surface for fear of sinking an American vessel."[12] For its part, the American navy was unsure of who the "enemy" actually was, as reflected in Chief of Naval Operations Admiral Arleigh Burke's reported assurance to the State Department at the time, that in the event of a confrontation at sea, "the British, the French, and the Egyptians and the Israelis, the whole goddamn works of them we can knock off. But . . . you've got to be ready to shoot. . . . that's the only way we can do it."[13]

In the face of the unexpectedly intense American reaction, Eden felt that he had no choice but to back down. His decision to call off the British intervention without first coordinating such action with Paris convinced many Frenchmen that de Gaulle was right in his postwar arguments about the unreliability of *both* Anglo-Saxon powers. Having been abandoned by their purported British allies, the French contingent was forced to call off the invasion one day later. Alistair Horne has since related that some French troops subsequently turned over their weapons to anti-British Ethniki Organosi Kyprion Agoniston (EOKA) forces on Cyprus on their way back home from Suez.[14]

Other allies shared the American point of view regarding who had betrayed whom. Many NATO members had been feeling extremely exposed and vulnerable since October 25, when massive anticommunist rioting in Budapest had triggered a Soviet military invasion of Hungary. The situation in Eastern Europe was made more unpredictable by the concurrent upsurge of nationalist sentiments in Poland, which led many commentators to expect that Moscow would feel compelled to crack down on two satellite countries at the same time. To these allies, the Israeli/British/French operations in the Middle East, which began just four days after the uprising in Hungary, appeared to be an irresponsible exploitation of an explosive situation. They complained that the actions of Britain and France made it impossible for NATO to focus all of its attention on the Soviet threat in Eastern Europe and to develop a common NATO position in opposition to Moscow's behavior there. It was also contended that Britain and France had weakened the alliance's ability to respond militarily in the event that the chaos in Eastern Europe spilled across the central front. Even if the Anglo-French actions in Suez did not undermine NATO's ability to deter further Soviet actions, they made it impossible for the alliance to seize the moral high ground, since Soviet imperialism in Eastern Europe was considered by many nations (certainly most nations in the Third World) to be no more evil than Anglo-French imperialism in Suez. West Germany, as the most geostrategically exposed NATO country, was especially angered by the Middle East adventures. Student demonstrators in Hamburg carried signs that read, "Eden, Murderer of Budapest."[15]

Richard Neustadt's *Alliance Politics* is still the most insightful treatment of the misperceptions and mutual recriminations of Suez. He entitled his final chapter "The Limits of Influence," but it might better have been called "The Limits of Expectation." For the Suez crisis went to the heart of the question of what NATO allies could expect of each other outside of the treaty area. With particular reference to the Anglo-American component of the crisis, Neustadt speaks of the "hardship of transcending an accustomed frame of reference" and notes that "the lack of questions early and the paranoia later are both related to that frame of reference, 'friend.'"[16]

When viewed from the broader NATO context, the frame of reference that contributed to much of the misunderstanding and most of the claims of betrayal was, of course, "ally." A decade of inflated NATO rhetoric about "common security interests" had a seductive effect. It encouraged Britain to believe that if a *domaine réservé* out-of-area issue mattered enough to it, the other NATO members and, in particular, the alliance leader, would understand and defer—perhaps even lend a hand. This logic is clearly reflected in Eden's memoirs. "The course of the Suez Canal crisis was decided by the American attitude toward it. If the United States government had approached this issue in the spirit of an ally, they would have done everything in their power, short of the use of force, to support the nations whose economic security depended upon the freedom of passage through the Suez Canal."[17] Conversely, the Suez episode encouraged Washington, Bonn, and other members of the alliance to express outrage at what they believed was the British tendency to place the U.K.'s own national interests and commitments before those of the alliance. Much of that consternation was due to their embarrassment that two NATO members had defied international opinion in confronting a major nationalist figure in the Third World for what appeared to be misplaced reasons—bringing the "guilt by association" factor to the forefront on alliance deliberations during the crisis.

Interestingly, it was the French government, which had experienced the frustrations of grudging and very conditional allied support in Indochina and Algeria, which had the clearest sense of where alliance loyalties stopped and national responsibilities diverged. Prime Minister Guy Mollet's subsequent explanation for the decision not to inform the United States ahead of time of Anglo-French plans for an invasion is instructive in this regard. Unlike British explanations, which tended to stress the shortage of time and the operational requirements for secrecy, Mollet was straightforward. Washington was not informed in advance because "we were afraid that if we let you know you would have prevented us doing it—and that we could not agree to, you see."[18] Paris nonetheless convinced itself that if the Suez operation could be managed properly—as a *fait accompli* and with the collaboration of Britain—

Washington would grumble but adjust, and would then bring the other NATO members into line. France's error was its misjudgment of Eisenhower's response to a *fait accompli,* and its decision to go ahead with the intervention in the shadow of the Hungarian crisis.

The Americans and the British were guilty of more fundamental errors of perspective. Among the most interesting of the extensive historical surveys now emerging with the recent declassification of key British documents from the Suez period is Anthony Adamthwaite's thesis that if Britain had been more forceful in articulating and defending its own national interests in the Middle East during 1954–55, it could have averted the Suez confrontation and increased British leverage in Washington. Instead of benignly accepting its postwar "hemorrhage," Adamthwaite argues, the Churchill and Eden governments should have put less trust in the "special relationship" and more energy into pursuing what Permanent Secretary of Foreign Affairs Lord Strang later characterized as the French policy approach to alliance problems: "a self-regarding diplomacy conducted more purely for national ends."[19] To what extent an assertive British posture would have induced Washington to assume a more active role in Middle Eastern security politics in order to check residual British influence and power remains questionable. An independent British posture would have eliminated one of the principal sources of misunderstanding that fueled the Suez crisis. On the other hand, it would have made it easier for Washington to take even more punitive and recriminatory actions against Britain and France in response to the attack on Nasser.

AFTER SUEZ—AN EXPANDED NATO RECONSIDERED

NATO's secretary general, Lord Ismay, met in closed session with the permanent representatives of the Atlantic Council one week after the Anglo-French withdrawal from Suez, to discuss the issue of intra-alliance consultation on global, as well as regional, security.[20] These discussions were followed up by the well-known post-mortem analysis of the Suez crisis by the Committee of Three on Non-Military Cooperation (the "Three Wise Men"—Lester Pearson of Canada, Halvard Lange of Norway, and Gaetano Martino of Italy). This report focused on the failures of consultation within NATO during the period leading up to the Anglo-French intervention.[21] The committee recommended that discussions of common problems—including extraregional problems—be carried on "in the early stages of policy formation, and before national positions become fixed." The Wise Men further recommended that more extensive consultations take place "on items affecting [NATO] interests beyond the North Atlantic area."[22]

The British responded to this observation warily and with a tinge of bitterness. Foreign Minister Selwyn Lloyd noted at the December 1956 NATO Ministerial Meeting that "if consultation procedures meant that every member had a right to criticize and obstruct" all British policy decisions concerning its remaining global defense responsibilities, "not much will be accomplished."[23] French foreign minister Pineau adopted a more technocratic posture, noting that NATO's secretary general should be given clearer guidelines about when an extra-European crisis should be considered a matter for alliance consultation and when such consultation would be "inadvisable."[24]

Dulles presented the U.S. view on NATO's geographic scope and authority, which was similar to Lloyd's. He noted that the independence of each ally's national security interests had to be preserved, and that efforts to pool the sovereignty of the treaty members on global security issues could not be permitted to jeopardize that right. The United States, he explained, well understood the imperative of balancing national security interests with NATO responsibilities. Dulles observed that, after all, Washington had defense arrangements with forty-four countries—thirty of which were not affiliated with the Atlantic Alliance. Therefore, he argued, "matters of more direct concern to others cannot be put up for prior consultation in the North Atlantic Council. The U.S. cannot have a hierarchy of relationships among allies around the world."[25]

By November 1957, however, Washington was reportedly reconsidering this argument and was contemplating "some way of interlocking the various regional security organizations" in a more systematic fashion.[26] By doing so, the multiplicity of Western allied interests might be more easily managed under the U.S. extended deterrent. But General de Gaulle's proposal for a tripartite "directorate" appears to have distracted the attention of American policy makers at this time. As a result, no further action seems to have been taken by Washington regarding the general recommendations of the Three Wise Men for improving consultation on global security issues.

From the Eisenhower administration's standpoint, the credibility of the West's extended deterrence strategy had been badly shaken by Suez, and vigorous American efforts were required to correct the situation. The Eisenhower Doctrine, introduced by the president in early 1957, was designed, therefore, to reinforce the U.S. commitment to protect pro-Western Middle Eastern states from "international communism" without specifically designating the types of threats which would trigger an American response.[27] But the Eisenhower Doctrine, like the Carter Doctrine more than twenty years later, was announced before the United States had developed appropriate military instruments for carrying it out. Following the announcement of the Eisenhower Doctrine, a new emphasis was placed upon the U.S. Sixth Fleet in the Mediterranean, although the fleet had been developed as a "floating air force" rather than an interventionary instrument. Its principal assets were dual capable strike aircraft (the Skywarriors deployed on American carriers could bomb targets with either nuclear or conventional weapons along the Iranian-Soviet border some fourteen hundred miles east from selected points in the Mediterranean). For purposes of intervention, however, the Sixth Fleet could offer only an eighteen-hundred-strong Marine amphibious force. Without the 'raditional British force presence and basing facilities interspersed throughout the region to fall back upon, American strategic airpower alone was inadequate for responding to a truly major crisis in the world's most extensive oil-producing region.

By November of that year, in reaction to the further political gains of anti-Western nationalist factions in Syria and Iraq, U.S. military analysts recommended to the JCS that specific steps should be undertaken in support of the Eisenhower Doctrine: (1) initiating Sixth Fleet "good will visits" to Egyptian and Syrian ports; (2) implementing the "phased establishment" of a formal U.S. military command structure for the Middle East; (3) "full U.S. adherence to the Baghdad Pact . . . with [the] objectives of ultimate expansion of [the] Pact to include all Middle Eastern Countries"; and (4) "close coordination and concerted action by the U.S. and U.K." to deny the Soviet Union strategic access to the Northern Tier and the Middle East.[28]

CONCLUSION

If the Americans had succeeded in aligning their strategic interests in the Middle East more closely with those of France and/or Britain during the early and mid-1950s, precedents might have been established that would have made it easier for Washington to pursue the kinds of defense cooperation initiatives recommended in the Wise Men's report. But no such alignment of allied interests had been achieved. U.S. and U.K. defense planners had followed the avenue of nonchoice, diluting the idea of a MEDO by integrating it into the Baghdad Pact, with its focus on the Northern Tier rather than the Middle East. The process of nonchoice was completed in 1958, with the conversion of the Baghdad Pact (following Iraq's departure) to the largely ineffectual Central Treaty Organization (CENTO) and with the collapse of de Gaulle's proposal to "globalize" NATO under U.S.-U.K.-French tutelage.

CHAPTER 4

THE ISSUE OF DECOLONIZATION
FROM 1949 TO 1964

THE SUEZ CRISIS highlights two overriding preoccupations of U.S. policy makers regarding the out-of-area policies of NATO allies from 1949 through the mid-1960s: U.S. concern about "guilt by association" with European colonialism, and persistent American suspicion that the European colonial allies were seeking to exploit Washington within the NATO forum.

Limiting opportunities for European exploitation of the United States had been a priority for U.S. representatives at the 1948–49 Washington Preparatory Talks. American concerns about exploitation increased one day after the signing of the North Atlantic Treaty, when the allies submitted their requests for military and financial aid to Washington. The Truman administration had already assured the Europeans that it was prepared to press their case for military assistance in Congress, but U.S. diplomats also warned their NATO partners that excessive demands could precipitate an anti-European backlash. In particular, the allies were warned that the American public would react adversely if it appeared that they were pursuing independent military initiatives in the Third World at the expense of NATO or U.S. interests. By contrast, key European governments saw colonial affairs as a sensitive matter of sovereignty. Their concern was that the United States would use its economic influence, and its dominant position within the new alliance, to meddle in their *domaines réservés*.

Even prior to the signing of the treaty, the United States had demonstrated its willingness to intervene directly in the colonial policies of others. The Truman administration criticized Holland for its handling of Sukarno's revolutionary movement in Indonesia, for example, at the same time that the Dutch parliament was deciding whether or not to join NATO. In March of 1949, Dean Acheson warned that "in view of its obligations under the U.N. Charter," the administration might be compelled to refuse military assistance to Holland unless the Dutch government modified its colonial policies. In fact, Washington and London had been following a policy of arms embargo against the Netherlands since 1948 because of the Indonesian question.[1] Acting upon the recommendation of the Joint Chiefs of Staff, U.S. officials had also directed the U.S. ambassador to the Hague in November 1948 to encourage the Dutch to coordinate military plans with the United States regarding the Caribbean islands of Aruba and Curaçao (the Dutch West Indies) and to consider the possible coordination of West Indian military operations by the proposed NATO Defense Committee. The State Department subsequently reported that Holland rejected these requests "due to the resentment felt by the Netherlands over the part played by the United States in the Indonesian affair."[2]

Specific colonial policies pursued by key European allies during the 1950s tended to reinforce the suspicion held by many Americans that the allies were economically, politically, militarily, and even intellectually incapable of managing their affairs outside of the NATO Treaty area. Those policy makers who favored an active, globalist form of containment found common ground with factions concerned about rationing American resources in their criticisms of European colonial adventurism. The "Europeanists" in Washington nonetheless exercised a restraining influence on the Truman administration. They tended to stress two themes in defense of the European colonial allies: first, that the NATO Treaty implied a special responsibility to support the European allies, not only on issues of Atlantic security but in the Third World as well; second, that U.S. interference in the colonial policies of the allies could precipitate disputes within the alliance which would undermine the common defense. The case of the Netherlands notwithstanding, Truman and his advisers were generally sensitive to the arguments of the Europeanist faction—at least to the point of being willing to maintain a posture of "benign neglect" toward European colonial adventures whenever possible.

BROADENING CONTAINMENT: COUNTING THE DOMINOES IN ASIA

Britain and France temporarily benefited from America's response to developments in Asia during the late 1940s and early 1950s. Following as it did on the "loss" of China, the Korean War came to convince influential members of the Truman administration—including many people formerly affiliated with the "Europe first" group, such as Dean Acheson—that the United States would have to intensify its containment efforts outside the NATO Treaty area. The focus of the debate then shifted to the issue of how a more globally ambitious containment was to be achieved. One faction, guided by the logic of NSC 68, argued that the United States should draw upon its economic strengths to develop a much more comprehensive and "symmetrical" conventional force posture. They were challenged by the nuclear reliance faction, which favored the development of a secure forward-basing network for U.S. strategic assets as a more cost-effective solution. Both groups realized, however, that a globalized confrontation would require a greater reliance upon the residual out-of-area presence of the colonialist NATO allies.

As the Korean War dragged on, it forced U.S. planners to give more attention to Asia, both for its own sake and as the "first domino" in the intensifying East-West struggle. The problem was summarized in NSC 124/2 in June 1952:

> The loss of any of the countries of Southeast Asia to Communist control as a consequence of overt or covert Chinese Communist aggression would have critical psychological, political, and economic consequences. . . . an alignment with Communism of the rest of Southeast Asia and India, and in the longer term, of the Middle East . . . would in all probability progressively follow. Such widespread alignment would endanger the stability and security of Europe.[3]

As a result, Truman, and (initially) Eisenhower, increased U.S. support for the neocolonial policies of selected European allies in the Asian region during the early 1950s. American military planning documents began to place much greater emphasis upon the possibility of joint American, British, and French air and naval blockades against China in the event of Chinese aggression against Western military positions in Southeast Asia. U.S. defense experts also began to accord new geostrategic importance to the British deployments in the Malayan Peninsula and the French presence in Indochina, with the result that Washington grudgingly became more supportive of British and French military efforts to retain control of these territories.[4] By early 1954, the Eisenhower administration was seriously contemplating the need to broaden U.S. military intervention in Indochina through "united action" with its European and Asian allies. French forces in Indochina became the principal beneficiaries of this policy adjustment as reflected in the fact that between 1950 and 1954 the United States provided 80 percent of the funding for the cost of the war against the Vietminh.[5]

Over time, however, Eisenhower and, in particular, Dulles became more and more suspicious of the motives and capabilities of the colonial allies in the Third World, and more inclined to pursue a unilateralist course. The British and French opposed "united action" in Indochina during 1954 for different reasons (London wanted a diplomatic solution; Paris wanted quick and decisive U.S. military action to avoid military defeat). The 1956 Suez crisis also reinforced Washington's unilateralist predispositions and encouraged a greater willingness on the part of Eisenhower and Dulles to edge the colonial allies out of their remaining imperial territories in the name of world order and anti-Soviet containment.

KENNEDY'S EXPERIMENT WITH ANTICOLONIALISM

Domestic politics certainly played a part in moving Eisenhower away from his initial policy of support for European colonialism. Starting in 1957, the Eisenhower administration had to deal with partisan criticism of its hands-off approach to colonial issues in general, and its relations with France in particular. The most vociferous U.S. critic of Eisenhower's policies toward French colonialism was Senator John F. Kennedy, who explicitly called for Algerian independence in a Senate speech in July 1957 (see Chapter 16). Kennedy argued that France had proven itself to be incapable of dealing with, or even understanding, the independence movements that were "spreading like wildfire" throughout Africa.[6] The Eisenhower administration made it clear at the time that it rejected Kennedy's arguments and regretted the senator's interference in an issue of French domestic politics. But it became increasingly more difficult after this time for Eisenhower and Dulles to align themselves implicitly with French policies in Africa, or even to maintain a policy of noninterference.

In 1960, Kennedy campaigned for the presidency on a platform of America's global mission, leaving little doubt among European colonial powers that they would have difficulty in balancing their Atlantic relations with their colonial policies. One of JFK's principal advisers, George Ball, described the foreign policy approaches of Truman and Eisenhower as based upon "the assumption that the United States . . . was a status quo power. . . . If stability would be assured for a reasonable period through colonial structures, such as Portugal's, there was no reason for America to rock the boat." The Kennedy administration, according to Ball, "would frontally challenge this approach."[7] Kennedy promised that if he was elected he would "get things moving again" and, in particular, would adjust U.S. foreign policy to the realities of change in Africa and Asia.

Portugal was singled out for special attention by Kennedy and his "Africanist" advisers. The country was considered by the new administration to be politically as well as geographically on the margin of the NATO alliance and of limited value for U.S. or Western security, aside from the Azores base that it provided to the United States. Lisbon was therefore viewed as an easy target for a campaign of U.S. pressure that would send a new message to the Third World and the European allies.

The opportunity arose just two months after the Kennedy administration took office, in the form of a United Nations resolution calling for an inquiry into Portugal's management of its overseas "non self-governing territories." According to Arthur Schlesinger, the U.S. vote in support of this resolution represented a turning point in U.S. policy toward the Third World, which "liberated the United States from its position of systematic deference to the old colonial powers."[8] Schlesinger and others scored it as a major victory for the "Africanists" at the expense of the "Europeanists" within the administration.

One month later, at the NATO Ministerial Conference in Oslo, the United States again criticized Portugal for its policies in Angola. The United States also cut military assistance to Portugal in 1961 from a proposed figure of $24.75 million to $2.75 million and blocked U.S. commercial sales to Lisbon.[9]

The dispute precipitated by the U.S. vote in the United Nations is discussed in more detail in Chapter 23. At this point, it is enough to observe that Lisbon caught Washington by surprise with an impressive diplomatic counteroffensive within the NATO alliance during 1961. In his discussions with the colonial allies, Salazar skillfully depicted his dispute with Kennedy as a matter of principle—a *domaine réservé* issue—and as a precedent for future European relations with Washington on colonial issues. His arguments proved to be very influential among those allies that still controlled territory in the Third World.

In the end, however, it was the prospect of losing the Azores base which was the most important determinant of change in Washington's policy. The five-year basing agreement was due to expire at the beginning of 1962, and Kennedy was still extremely concerned about the risk of an East-West confrontation over Berlin. Furthermore, the new U.S.-sponsored strategies of "flexible response" and "forward defense" were expected to place an even greater premium on air transport of troops and materiel from the United States to Europe, and the JCS was not forthcoming with available, affordable, and politically reliable alternatives to the Lajes base in the Azores. By the end of 1962, the United States had completely abandoned its economic pressure campaign against Lisbon and had returned to its earlier policy of voting against U.N. resolutions critical of Portugal—in return for a (conditional) renewal by Lisbon of the Azores basing treaty.

During the first half of 1961, Belgium was the country within the alliance that was most sensitive to the precedents being set by the Kennedy administration in its initial forays against Portugal. Kennedy and his advisers were generally careful to distinguish between the Portuguese and the Belgian cases in their public statements, but many of the arguments that had been employed by the Africanists against Lisbon's policies in Angola implied a more active U.S. involvement in the Congo situation as well. Belgian suspicions were confirmed when the new administration proposed the "Stevenson Plan" in the UN in February of 1961. The plan called for the removal of all foreign military personnel from the Congo and explicitly condemned "those Belgians . . . providing military advice and assistance to the Congo."[10]

Brussels, responding as an ally of circumstance with Lisbon, reacted to this and subsequent initiatives by the United States in the UN by challenging Washington within the NATO community. Again, the Kennedy administration was caught off guard by the diplomatic opposition that Brussels was able to organize within NATO, and, as in the case of Portugal, Kennedy decided to back down. By the end of 1962, the United States had ceased taking positions in the UN that could be interpreted by Brussels as anti-Belgian. The United States was soon to be involved in a Third World conflict of its own in Southeast Asia, eventually prompting it quietly to solicit allied support for its defense of South Vietnam. The Belgian Congo proved to be the last postwar episode where American guilt by association with European colonialism clashed with the European sense of *domaine réservé*.

CONCLUSION

Kennedy's experiments in anticolonialism at the expense of first one, then another ally proved to be unsuccessful for precisely the reasons that the Europeanists in Washington had presented in the 1950s to warn Truman and Eisenhower against such initiatives: if serious confrontations arose between the United States and influential European colonial governments over decolonization issues, certain allies might be either unwilling or unable to back down, and the United States would be compelled to choose between NATO and the Third World. Under these circumstances, the Europeanists argued that it was better to avoid such confrontations whenever possible, by turning a blind eye to the neocolonial policies of the allies. By the time of Kennedy's death, the United States had also developed a greater sensitivity to the difficulties involved in Western-sponsored efforts to manage the processes of change in the Third World, as the United States itself became increasingly more involved in Vietnam.

CHAPTER 5

U.S. MILITARY INVOLVEMENT
IN ASIA: IMPLICATIONS
FOR NATO EXTRAREGIONAL
BURDEN SHARING

THE EXTENT to which the subsequent reversal of the American policy of conditional involvement in Asia, and America's entanglement in the Vietnam War, can be blamed on John F. Kennedy is still a point of debate in the scholarly community. What is beyond dispute, however, is that within a year of Lyndon Johnson's accession to the presidency, U.S. military involvement in Asia was transforming American security planners' views of the NATO out-of-area issue. But as the United States began to support a more global alliance, its European allies were forging policies that were moving in precisely the opposite direction.

The American military effort in Vietnam, far more than any other event, contributed to the fundamental reversal of roles between the United States and the European colonial allies on the fourth issue of out-of-area alliance politics: burden sharing. By the time that Vietnam had become the overriding preoccupation of U.S. policy makers, most of the European colonial allies had come, through hard experience, to appreciate the limits of their strategic reach. As a consequence, these allies were beginning to accept a strict constructionist interpretation of NATO's global responsibilities. U.S. defense planners, meanwhile, were increasingly inclined to argue that the world beyond NATO's borders had in fact become more dangerous since the early cold war era and that local containment in a limited geographic framework was no longer sufficient. In the words of Eugene Rostow at the time: "The only notion of equality among the nations [of NATO] which the times permit . . . [is] equality measured by the rule of proportionality. . . . the organization of the Alliance should take into account and indeed should anticipate the political changes which are taking place not merely in Europe but in the world as a whole.[1]

Secretary of State Dean Rusk became the most outspoken U.S. proponent of the global threat argument during the mid-1960s. Rusk claimed that both U.S. and European security interests were increasingly threatened in the Third World, and that Washington had an obligation to view its commitments and interests in Europe and Asia as well as in other regions as "part of the same fundamental world policy" of extended deterrence and defense.[2] A globalized threat required a collective response, according to Rusk. In return for increased allied support outside of NATO, he argued that Washington would be prepared to grant the Europeans more influence over Western security decisions within and beyond the Atlantic region.

In a series of influential articles written for the *New York Times* during January 1967, Cyrus L. Sulzberger summarized the changed U.S. perspective on the link between NATO security and Asian security. Sulzberger maintained that U.S. policy makers were now asking the NATO allies to endorse a "western flank" strategy for NATO in the Pacific, directed primarily against Communist China. He noted that as early as 1965, U.S. defense planners had urged British, French, and other NATO European governments to include the outermost Aleutians—but not Hawaii—in future alliance contingency planning. Sulzberger, along with many respected European strategists, concluded, however, that any American campaign to fuse Atlantic and Pacific defense planning would be no more successful in the Vietnam era than it had been in the earlier cold war era:

> NATO clearly understands our difficulty vis-a-vis Asia but, for it, the possible direct repercussions are two extremes: either Russia, frightened by Chinese surliness, might withdraw troops from Europe to Asia or seek a deal with America over NATO's head; or, obversely, Vietnam might lead to a Sino-American conflict from which Russia, for ideological reasons, felt it couldn't abstain.[3]

In either case, Sulzberger argued, the European allies could obtain little benefit, and would assume considerable risk, in agreeing to American "attempts to tie them through NATO to a 'forward strategy' in the Western Pacific."[4]

U.S. assertions that NATO security was inextricably linked to the stability and security of the Third World had a familiar ring to European colonial powers. France in particular had tried (for the most part, unsuccessfully) to interest Washington in its own national version of the *guerre révolutionnaire* thesis (discussed in Chapter 14) during the late 1940s and the 1950s. By the mid-1960s, however, the thesis had become essentially an American product for export to a European public that was neither willing nor able to buy it. Suddenly, it was the European allies who were being criticized by Washington for parochialism, rather than the other way around. Suddenly it was the Americans who were appealing to their allies to reject narrow Eurocentric arguments and to accept the "common security burden" along with the United States.

As American involvement in Vietnam developed during the fall of 1964, Undersecretary of State George W. Ball secured President Johnson's approval for sponsoring high-level consultations within NATO on problems arising outside of the treaty area. In December 1964, with the support of NATO Secretary General Manlio Brosio, the Americans suggested that four NATO meetings be held each year at the deputy foreign minister level or above to discuss world problems at large and to address any topic of extraregional concern to any of NATO's fifteen members.[5] While P.-H. Spaak (once more Belgium's foreign minister) and Dutch foreign minister Joseph Luns supported Ball's request, France moved to block the proposal, stating in effect that NATO was not an appropriate forum for considering extraregional security problems—a position startlingly in contrast with de Gaulle's earlier (post-Suez) support for a globalized NATO (see Chapter 17).[6]

It is interesting, especially given the aforementioned Dutch, Belgian, and Portuguese colonial policy disputes with the United States, that NATO's smaller countries were especially sympathetic toward Washington's problems in Southeast Asia. In a lecture delivered to American scholars in October 1966, for example, Spaak noted that Belgium's own history gave it a special appreciation of America's efforts to resist the tide of "Communist imperialism" in Asia. He concluded that the European governments "cannot, consequently, be astonished to see the United States prolong its effort" in Vietnam.[7]

The United States was also able to rely upon West German sympathy, and some diplomatic support, for its policies during the formative period of the Vietnam War. Indeed, Ball advised Johnson in July of 1965 that "Chancellor Erhard has told us privately that the people of Berlin would be concerned by a compromise settlement of South Vietnam." Ball, however, went on to offer the following perceptive caution:

> But . . . I suspect he was telling us what he believed we would like to hear. After all, the confidence of the West Berliners will depend more on what they see on the spot than on news or events halfway around the world. In my observation, the principal anxiety of our NATO allies is that we have become too preoccupied with an area that seems to them an irrelevance and may be tempted in [sic] neglect of our NATO responsibilities. Moreover, they have a vested interest [in an] easier relationship between Washington and Moscow. By and large, therefore, they will be inclined to regard a compromise solution in South Vietnam more as a new evidence in [sic] American maturity and judgement [than] of American loss of face.[8]

Ball's opinions about the European mood may have been formed, in part, by conversations with Willy Brandt, mayor of Berlin and, since February of 1964, chairman of the SPD opposition. Whether or not Brandt influenced Ball's thinking, the German party leader had by this time begun to press the thesis that

75

the continued presence of American troops in Europe would always be more important to Washington's allies than an American demonstration of resolve in Asia.[9]

At issue, of course, were the dual European concerns that Washington would press the allies to accept an active role in the Vietnam War effort or that America would reduce its own troop presence in Europe, or both. With reference to the first concern, members of the Johnson administration had begun to investigate ways of soliciting greater support from the United States' NATO partners (as well as Australia, New Zealand, the Philippines, and South Korea) in 1964. The president had communicated to his aides that he wanted to see some "new, dramatic, effective" forms of assistance from various U.S. defense associates. William Bundy subsequently pressed Britain and the ANZUS allies for some direct contribution to the war effort. He also advised representatives of the three Commonwealth governments that Johnson "wished to obtain assistance even from governments without strong Southeast Asian commitments, like Denmark, West Germany and India."[10] There was never any hope of a direct military contribution from the NATO allies, however, and when members of the Johnson administration intermittently felt compelled to put particular allies (such as Germany) on the spot, they were rebuffed.[11]

Many U.S. policy makers instinctively looked to Britain for understanding and support in this situation. Unfortunately, U.S. hopes that the "special relationship" could be used to obtain British military support for America's out-of-area problems proved to be unrealistic. By early 1968, Britain had already announced plans to end its military presence east of Suez in spite of U.S. (and, in particular, congressional) arguments that "a more prosperous Europe" must assume greater extraregional responsibilities in the future. A special subcommittee of the Armed Services Committee of the U.S. House of Representatives considered the conflict between U.S. and British policies in the 1960s:

> Termination of Great Britain's east of Suez role is most unwelcome to U.S. interests. It will increase pressure on the United States to assume the responsibility to fill the vacuum in the Persian Gulf area. It will add significantly to the destabilizing tendencies already prevailing in the Gulf and Southeast Asia. It will particularly erode an already weakened Commonwealth fabric. . . .
>
> . . . A change in government could reverse the more radical changes in British defense policies, resulting in the retention of British forces in Southeast Asia and the Gulf if regional countries so requested. . . .
>
> . . . The Subcommittee is hopeful that the Hong Kong garrison will be strengthened, that substantial U.K. military missions will function in Malaysia and Singapore and that some hardware support and training exercises will continue in the area. . . . The Subcommittee also hopes that the U.K. will see fit to maintain access to facilities in Masirah and possibly Bahrain to sustain a line of communication to the Far East.[12]

For the British, however, the timing of the American escalation in Vietnam was intensely problematic, given that its own recessional from points "east of Suez" was in full swing (see Chapter 11). Yet, as David Watt has observed, the "special relationship" remained surprisingly intact, given London's "refusal to send even a token British contingent to Vietnam."[13]

EUROPEAN COUNTERARGUMENTS:
A DIVERSION OF NATO's ATTENTION AND RESOURCES

By about 1967, all of Washington's NATO allies clearly understood that the wisest course for the alliance was to avoid recriminatory and unproductive discussions over burden sharing in Vietnam. But the European allies' polite silence did not solve the growing U.S. manpower problem caused by the Vietnam conflict's drain on American strategic resources. NATO Secretary General Brosio took note of European concerns about American defense commitments beyond Europe in an address to alliance parliamentarians delivered in late 1965:

> There are those who fear the expansion of the commitment and responsibilities of the United States in Asia, Latin America, and elsewhere. These critics hope that the United States will . . . withdraw from their existing commitments as soon as possible, in order to conserve their strength for the vital Atlantic and European sectors.[14]

The concerns of these "critics" appeared to be vindicated by the secretary of the army's annual report to Congress, submitted in early 1965, in which the secretary admitted that the overall strength of U.S. land forces in Europe had experienced a "temporary drawdown" to meet unit strength requirements in Southeast Asia.[15] Then, in May of 1967, the United States announced plans to remove thirty-five thousand troops from Germany, including two army brigades and four air force fighter-bomber squadrons. Washington explained that the troop cut was partly motivated by the need to offset growing foreign exchange costs attributable to the U.S. deployments in Europe (in spite of the Federal Republic of Germany's commitments to purchase more U.S. weapons systems and treasury bonds over the next few years). This initial action was followed six months later by an announcement that the United States could no longer guarantee that it would be able to send five divisions to Europe within sixty days after the outbreak of a major NATO/Warsaw Pact conflict, owing to the increased manpower requirements that the nation was facing elsewhere (525,000 in Southeast Asia by early 1969).[16]

Between 1964 and 1972, U.S. military personnel in West Germany decreased from 263,000 to 210,000; in what the Department of Defense termed "other Europe," from 119,000 to 62,000; and in the "Europe Afloat" category, from 54,000 to 26,000 (totaling an eight-year decrease from 436,000 to 298,000).[17] U.S. Army chief of staff William Westmoreland admitted during congressional testimony in 1970 that "the need to give an overriding priority to our troops in Vietnam has limited the support we have been able to give our forces elsewhere."[18] Likewise, former defense secretary James Schlesinger has written in *Foreign Affairs* that "the war in Vietnam became the preoccupation of the [Johnson] Administration. . . Gradually NATO became a secondary issue. It was increasingly neglected as the government's attention turned toward Southeast Asia."[19] It is worth mentioning, however, that progressive American troop cuts during the late 1960s did not encourage the European allies to attempt to make up the difference by increases in their troop contributions to NATO.

Conclusion

Allied skepticism over Washington's tendency to devote so much of its national security resources to Vietnam contributed to a blurring of NATO's own forward defense strategy. "Flexible response" was grudgingly accepted by the European allies in 1967 as NATO's official defense policy.[20] After this U.S. policy goal had been achieved, however, there followed a period of American nonpolicy—what Seyom Brown has since labeled "grandiose promises of conceptual innovation coupled with a confusing record of delivery"—which undermined serious efforts from either side of the Atlantic to coordinate global security problems within a NATO context.[21] Instead, the Europeans gradually became preoccupied with developing their own versions of détente and political reconciliation with the Soviet Union and Eastern Europe.[22] The mood of détente which had taken hold by the late 1960s made it easier for Washington to justify to its NATO allies its decision to redeploy troops to other theaters at a time when American preoccupation with Southeast Asia was growing. On the other hand, détente provided a new basis for the Europeans to question traditional U.S. containment postures and further complicated efforts to create the kind of intra-alliance "grand strategy" that had been envisioned by presidents Kennedy and Johnson.

CHAPTER 6

NATO AND GLOBAL BURDEN
SHARING: U.S. INITIATIVES
IN THE 1970S

BY 1969, American frustration with the seemingly unresolvable problem of Vietnam had encouraged a public mood in favor of global retrenchment. In recognition of this mood, and in light of the relative decline of American power according to most traditional standards, Richard Nixon and Henry Kissinger, upon their accession to office in 1969, opted to reduce America's worldwide security commitments. President Nixon emphasized that "our interests must shape our commitments rather than the other way around."[1] Washington communicated its intention to preserve American extended deterrence at the nuclear level and to retain its formal commitment to the NATO Treaty, while at the same time emphasizing that the European allies would be expected to assume a greater share of the West's overall defense burden.

THE TRANSATLANTIC BARGAIN AND
WASHINGTON'S REVISED GLOBAL STRATEGY

Henry Kissinger presented this new version of the transatlantic bargain as an essential component of his vision of a "stable structure of peace." What evolved, however, was an ambiguous form of forward defense that the Western Europeans could neither understand nor firmly support. In fact, the Nixon-Kissinger era proved to be an especially confusing period in U.S.-European relations.[2] Such conceptual ambiguity tended to encourage the inevitable concern among the European NATO allies that once the process of U.S. strategic retrenchment got under way, it would be hard to stop. Indeed, Kissinger's penchant for dramatic, architectonic change led him to consider several alternatives to NATO's military force structure in 1969. He considered options ranging from the maintenance of only a few U.S. bases in Europe (for preserving a minimal American nuclear tripwire) to the building up of a joint U.S.-Western European "total conventional defense."[3]

The Nixon administration raised European anxieties in 1969 and 1970 by announcing plans to reduce the total size of U.S. ground forces from $27^2/_3$ divisions to $17^1/_3$ divisions by the end of FY 1971 and by its abandonment of the "two-and-a-half-war" strategy observed by previous American postwar governments in favor of a "one-and-a-half-war" posture. Instead of planning to fight major conflicts in Europe and Asia simultaneously, as well as a limited, or "brushfire," war in the Middle East or in some other Third World setting, Washington was now committed to maintaining force capabilities for fighting only one general war in a single theater along with a single limited conflict at the same time. Most of the forces withdrawn from Vietnam (the maximum deployment there was 543,000 in early 1969) were to be deactivated, and Washington made no plans for redeploying significant portions of this force to NATO Europe.[4] Furthermore, while the Nixon Doctrine made no direct reference to reduced U.S. conventional force commitments in Europe itself, many NATO allies were sensitive to the possible precedent that was being set by the administration's warnings that Asian allies of the United States would have to become more responsible for their own conventional defense. An overall pattern of limiting U.S. capabilities for intervening in future extraregional contingencies was, however, clearly materializing. In 1972, for example, the U.S. Strike Command (STRIKCOM), specifically designed for intervention in conflicts outside of Europe, was dissolved. It was replaced by a more austere "Readiness Command," which was primarily a training unit designed to prepare forces for small-scale extra-European contingencies.

As the process of reducing American military power continued, the Nixon administration gradually refined its perspectives on the question of NATO out-of-area cooperation. As U.S. strategic assets in the Third World declined and U.S. public opinion pressure against *any* American interventionary initiatives in the Third World mounted, Washington came to the conclusion that Europe had to be asked to do more than ensure the security of the NATO central front. From now on, the Nixon administration emphasized, there would need to be "greater allied participation in decision-making issues likely to jeopardize regional or *global* security."[5]

Kissinger's response to the changed international situation in the early 1970s was summarized in an address on Atlantic relations in April 1973, in which he called for a "new Atlantic Charter":

> There have been complaints in America that Europe ignores its wider responsibilities in pursuing economic self interest too one-sidedly and that Europe is not carrying its fair share of the burden in common defense. . . . (NATO members) can no longer afford to pursue national or regional self interest without a unifying framework. . . . with burdens equitably shared.[6]

CHALLENGES IN THE MIDDLE EAST

For Kissinger, the critical test of the need for a "unifying framework" was the October 1973 Yom Kippur War and the subsequent Arab cutbacks in oil production for, and shipments to, NATO states. The secretary of state was the most outspoken critic of the Western European allies' failure to develop a common policy in the face of these related crises. In particular, he railed against the "stampede of dissociation" by America's NATO allies in response to U.S. requests for assistance in supplying Israeli forces during the Yom Kippur War. U.S. aircraft were denied base access and overflight rights by most European governments (the Netherlands and Portugal were the exceptions). This forced U.S. transport aircraft to travel an additional one thousand to two thousand miles, impeded the activities of the U.S. Sixth Fleet, and compromised America's overall power projection capability in the face of an impressive Soviet military presence in the region.[7]

Kissinger subsequently argued in his memoirs that

> the [European] legalistic argument was to the effect that obligations of the North Atlantic Treaty did not extend to the Middle East. But . . . our case for allied cohesion was based not on a legal claim, but on the imperatives of common interest. When close allies act toward one another like clever lawyers [and] if they exclude an area as crucial as the Middle East from their common concern, their association becomes vulnerable to fluctuating passion.[8]

Intra-alliance tension intensified when President Nixon called a worldwide military alert following Soviet threats to intervene against Israel on behalf of the warring Arab nations. Writing almost a decade after the 1973 Arab-Israeli War, Kissinger contended that the NATO allies "were really objecting not so much to timing as to the absence of opportunity to affect our decision. But imminent danger did not brook an exchange of views, and, to be frank, we could not have accepted a judgment different from our own."[9]

We assume that Kissinger recognized the inherent contradiction between his complaint about the failure of allied policy coordination and his admission that, "to be frank," the United States was going to pursue its own policies in the Middle East in any event. We further assume that since he could not resolve these contradictions, he chose to blur them in his memoirs by claiming that the Europeans really wanted the United States and the Soviet Union to solve their Middle East differences on a bilateral basis, so that they could pursue their own distinct European policies in the region without interference.

Kissinger's admission that consultation on an out-of-area issue is useless when one of the parties involved believes that it has no choice but to pursue an independent foreign policy goes to the heart of the problem addressed in this book. His comments also bear a striking resemblance to Mollet's candid explanation for not advising Washington of Anglo-French plans for the invasion of Suez: "we were afraid that if we had let you know, you would have prevented us."

In the wake of the 1973 events, all parties accepted the U.S. demand to discuss how to improve the procedures for NATO policy coordination in response to out-of-area crises. But there was considerable disagreement about the nature and scope of these improvements. Many Europeans recognized that attempts to use the European Economic Community (EEC) as the primary institutional framework for extraregional policy coordination had thus far only highlighted Europe's marginality in the international system. One commentator referred to it as "a schizoid posture, with the Europeans continuing to argue in EEC channels for an essentially 'neutral' policy while showing—in the NATO arena—greater sophistication in their understanding of the relevance of the Middle East to Alliance security interests."[10] While the United States was by now interested in pressing the allies to carry a greater share of the out-of-area burden, it was *not* yet prepared to accord the Europeans more influence over decisions relating to such tendentious issues as the Arab-Israeli dispute.

Under the circumstances, the June 1974 "Ottawa Declaration," with its theme of "rededication to NATO," was the best that could be achieved. It asserted that "the Allies are firmly resolved to keep each other fully informed . . . by all means which may be appropriate on matters relating to their common interests . . . bearing in mind that these interests can be affected by events in other areas of the world."[11]

By 1975, however, many defense experts were complaining that "rededication" was not enough. NATO consultative mechanisms had clearly not developed to the point where they could deal with the types of problems that had disrupted the alliance in 1973, or with a more globally active Soviet Union. As Sir Peter Hill-Norton, chairman of NATO's Military Committee, noted at the time,

The Soviets have no lines on their [fleet operations] maps at the Tropic of Cancer or anywhere else. As an organization, NATO is constrained to examine events within the NATO area and it is strangely reluctant to examine events outside . . . even though they may be of critical importance to NATO.

. . . The Supreme Allied Commander, Atlantic, has made within his own headquarters and without commitment by the other members of the Alliance, contingency plans. They are *not* laid before NATO for approval or even for notation. . . . There is a reluctance on the part of some allies to look outside the NATO area and I suspect the relevance stems as much from the fact that they are habitually unaccustomed to looking beyond continental Europe.[12]

By the mid–1970s, the debate about intra-alliance burden sharing—in defense of the NATO central front and in defense of common security interests beyond the treaty area—had become increasingly blurred and, at the same time, increasingly recriminatory, largely as a result of domestic political developments in the United States. As time passed, the European allies discovered that key American policy makers, as well as a significant portion of the elite and mass publics in the United States, harbored an intense, if rarely articulated, resentment against the NATO allies as a result of the Vietnam War experience. The U.S. failure in Vietnam contributed to a pervasive domestic political mood in favor of reassessing the entire alliance relationship, just as Dien Bien Phu had done in France two decades earlier.

THE BURDEN-SHARING DEBATE

During the first four years of President Nixon's tenure in office, domestic political pressures mounted for reducing the American military contribution to NATO. The campaign in Congress was led by Senate Majority Leader Mike Mansfield and Senator Stuart Symington, who were instrumental in authoring a succession of congressional resolutions designed to reduce U.S. military deployments abroad. Most noteworthy were H.R. 6531, an amendment to the Selective Service Bill which, if passed, would have mandated that U.S. troop deployments to Europe be cut back by 50 percent (150,000 men) by the end of 1971, and the Mansfield Amendment of September 1973 (narrowly defeated), which called for a 50 percent reduction over the ensuing three years.

A subsequent bill, the Jackson-Nunn Amendment, which *did* pass in late 1973, required contributions from NATO allies to offset that part of the U.S. balance of payments problem which was considered to result from U.S. troop commitments to NATO. The amendment called for reducing the number of U.S. forces in Europe on a sliding scale-percentage basis in the absence of substantially increased allied contributions. This action was taken in spite of the facts that U.S. troops deployed in Europe had already declined from a high of 427,000 in 1953 to around 316,000 by 1968, and that various cost-offset agreements had already been signed between the United States and West Germany between 1968 and 1971.[13]

The financial burden-sharing debate that surfaced during the Nixon era—the first serious domestic debate on this issue since 1951—also reflected a growing opinion in the United States that Western Europe was an economic success and was, in fact, rapidly becoming a threat to U.S. trade and manufacturing interests. Under these circumstances, a greater European defense contribution was viewed by many Americans as a reasonable request, and one that offered the added benefit of bolstering the relative competitiveness of the U.S. economy.

From the Western Europeans' perspective, any large-scale reduction of U.S. forces in central Europe threatened to compromise the American extended deterrence commitment based upon flexible response. But Nixon sought to turn this argument around in his 1972 Foreign Policy Report to Congress, when he advocated greater European conventional force deployments, precisely because "American forces should not be reduced to the role of a hostage, triggering automatic use of nuclear weapons at the very time when the strategic equation makes such a strategy less plausible."[14] This interpretation of flexible response did little to reassure the European allies.

Congressional pressure for American troop withdrawals from Europe subsided between 1974 and 1976, due largely to an easing of the U.S. balance of payments problem. Many U.S. policy makers were also influenced by military developments during the Yom Kippur War, as well as by improvements in Soviet/Warsaw Pact offensive forces during the 1970s, to back away from earlier demands for U.S. troop cuts in Europe or in other forward positions. Initial Egyptian military successes against Israeli forces during 1973 were generally attributed to Cairo's use of strategic surprise and its maintenance of the offensive. Despite later effective counterattacks waged by the Israelis, the Yom Kippur War had demonstrated that a surprise attack in a modern conventional warfare situation might deprive the defender of the time and space needed to reinforce its lines in preparation for a counterattack. The problem was explicitly linked to NATO in the influential Nunn-Bartlett Report, which was published shortly after President Jimmy Carter came to office. The report warned of the Soviet ability "to initiate a potentially devastating invasion of Europe with as little as a few days' warning."[15]

THE LONG-TERM DEFENSE PROGRAM

The Carter administration came to office convinced of the need for substantial improvements in NATO's conventional defense capability, along the lines proposed in the Nunn-Bartlett Report. Particular emphasis was placed upon improving readiness and enhancing NATO's capacity for rapid resupply. On the occasion of his first North Atlantic Council session in London (May 1977), Carter proposed a comprehensive program for NATO defense modernization, subsequently referred to as the Long-Term Defense Program (LTDP). At a NATO Defense Planning Committee Session, held immediately following the council meeting, U.S. defense secretary Harold Brown outlined specific LTDP objectives: to enhance standardization of weapons and two-way procurement of weapons systems within the alliance, to improve NATO forces' ability to work together, to strengthen capabilities for reinforcement and mobilization of reserves, to modernize air defenses, and to update U.S. and allied maritime postures.[16]

During the London Council discussions, Carter also proposed a broad and symbolic formula for assessing each ally's defense contribution in support of the long-term NATO modernization plan. Each NATO government was asked to commit itself to increasing its annual defense spending in real terms by 3 percent during the period 1979–83. The 3 percent figure was thought roughly to approximate the Soviet Union's defense spending increases between 1970 and 1976, according to estimates by the Central Intelligence Agency.[17] The U.S.

secretary of defense described the "3 percent solution" as a compromise between the need to respond to a rising Soviet military threat and the equally compelling requirement to take into account the strained economies of Western states at a time of still-rising oil prices and attendant recession.[18] Most European governments saw the 3 percent solution proposal as a positive development, since it would reverse a general downward trend in U.S. defense spending increases between 1971 and 1978 (averaging 2.69 percent per annum in real terms). What remained unresolved, however, was whether the 3 percent figure would relate to a nation's total defense spending or only to NATO-related defense costs.[19]

The 3 percent issue and the broader LTDP debate probably deflected a good deal of attention which would otherwise have been focused on the issue of out-of-area policy coordination during this period of growing Soviet (and Soviet proxy) activism in the Third World and extreme Western dependence on oil and raw materials from developing regions. Indeed, a North Atlantic Assembly Economic Committee paper released in October 1979 noted that "there was no debate among experts that the economies of most Allied countries are absolutely dependent on imported oil," and that "tensions or conflicts in a few Third World countries . . . can hurt both the military supply and economic security of the industrialized countries of the Western World."[20]

Tables 3 and 4 provide some information on the state of Western energy and raw material dependence at the time of the 3 percent debate.

The interconnection between Western European energy strategies and out-of-area security politics was also underscored by the strong U.S. resistance to a multibillion-dollar pipeline project involving shipment of natural gas from western Siberia to Western Europe. When negotiations between Moscow and

TABLE 3

Reliance on Oil Imports

(Oil Imports as Percentage of Primary Energy Consumption in 1979)

Denmark	77–83
Japan	73
Italy	64–68
France	61
Belgium	52–57
Federal Republic of Germany	51–52
Netherlands	38–47
United States	22
United Kingdom	18–25

Source: German Tribune, March 25, 1979, and *Commission of the European Community,* Doc. Com. (79) 316, June 14, 1979.

TABLE 4
Industrial Countries' Dependence on Imported Raw Materials (in %)

	USA	EC	Japan	Fed. Rep. of Germany	United Kingdom
Copper	15	82	83	100	82
Lead	15	55	70	87	46
Zinc	59	60	68	68	100
Tin	85	87	93	100	65
Bauxite (aluminum)	87	60	100	100	—
Iron ore	27	79	99	93	89
Nickel	71	100	100	100	100
Tungsten	59	100	100	100	99
Cobalt	94	98	98	100	100
Manganese	98	99	98	99	100
Chromium	90	99	98	100	100

Source: Authors' Compilations from CIA *Handbook of Economic Statistics*, ER 77-10537, September 1977, and *German Tribune*, December 1978.

Western European countries were initiated in 1978, the Soviets planned that the gas would come from the Yamburg fields in the Yamal region of western Siberia; later, the gas extraction site was moved south to the Urengoy fields. The Carter and Reagan administrations were concerned that West Germany, France, Italy, and Belgium were risking Western security by handing Moscow a political instrument for threatening natural gas supplies during future East-West or out-of-area crises. American representatives also complained about Soviet access to European hard currency as a result of the project. David Calleo summarized this last U.S. complaint as follows: "Western Europe's greatest asset, its economic strength, was serving not the common defense, but the common enemy. Yet the Americans were expected to go on defending Western Europe."[21] The Europeans countered that Moscow would supply only about 30 percent of the natural gas they needed, far from enough to force them into making strategic concessions. They also noted that the Soviet Union had proven itself to be an extremely reliable trading partner in the past, based upon its record of delivering on contracts.

CONCLUSION

The question that evolved during the Nixon and Carter administrations had once been framed by Lyndon Johnson in an acerbic response to a group of foreign policy advisers who had provided the president with a broad-ranging survey of problems in the Middle East: "Therefore, what?"[22] What kinds of arrangements could have been made, either within NATO or among selected NATO allies in the mid- or late 1970s, to reduce the risks of an interruption of European and American energy and/or raw material supplies? What more could the United States reasonably ask of its allies at a time when it was pressing them for a renewed commitment to defense modernization and other improvements in the European theater?

With respect to this last question, at least, the European allies had developed a fairly clear position by the end of the 1970s. Undersecretary of Defense Robert Komer and other defense officials within the Carter administration were advised by their European counterparts that any additional European commitments in support of U.S. defense efforts beyond the NATO Treaty area could occur only within the framework of the 3 percent annual defense spending increases that had been agreed upon at the North Atlantic Council meeting in London in May of 1977.[23] The European allies took this position, even though the 3 percent defense spending target was by this time being treated by the Carter administration as an absolutely *minimal* goal. All parties were also aware that the 3 percent figure was not, in fact, being reached by most of the European allies. In 1978, NATO's non-U.S. defense spending average showed a real increase of approximately 2 percent; in 1979, 2.2 percent; and in 1980, 2.7 percent. In 1980, Congress responded to this disappointing trend by requiring the Department of Defense to submit an annual allied contributions report informing it of what efforts were being made by the United States to enforce greater European adherence to the 3 percent standard, and what efforts were being made to increase host nation support for U.S. forces stationed on NATO European soil.[24]

American criticism of allied burden sharing during the 1970s was symptomatic of Washington's frustration at playing the role of *demandeur* after twenty years of being courted by the Europeans for help with their own extraregional security crises. American frustration remained largely unfocused, however, until the confluence of two events at the end of the decade—the Iran hostage situation and the Soviet intervention in Afghanistan.

CHAPTER 7

SOUTHWEST ASIA AND THE PERSIAN GULF: REEVALUATING OUT-OF-REGION SECURITY CHALLENGES IN THE 1980S

ACCORDING to some Western defense analysts, developments in Southwest Asia and the Persian Gulf region during 1979 encouraged all NATO allies to reassess the seriousness of the out-of-area issue. A typical assessment noted that

> the crisis in Iran and the invasion of Afghanistan reduced the different American and European perceptions of security policy in the Middle East to a common denominator; that is, the important relationship between the vulnerability of the West because of its dependency on Persian Gulf oil, and the continued relative decline of its political-military power vis-a-vis that of the Soviet Union.[1]

Such premises, however, are misleading on at least two counts; first, because a number of other considerations influenced the intra-alliance debate as well; second, because key European allies still diverged from Washington on the unavoidable question of "Therefore, what?"

The issue of détente was one complicating element in the post-Afghanistan debate within the alliance. During Carter's last year in office, many European governments continued to argue that détente with the Soviets was still a necessary and achievable policy goal, in accordance with the logic of the 1967 Harmel Report—a document prepared for NATO by Belgian foreign minister Pierre Harmel, which committed the alliance to the pursuit of East-West détente while maintaining NATO's previous goals of deterrence and defense. French president Valéry Giscard d'Estaing and his foreign minister, Jean-François Poncet, accused Carter of overplaying the significance of the Soviet invasion of Afghanistan and speculated that perhaps the American leader was dramatizing the geopolitical danger so as to justify his policy switch in favor of more U.S. military spending. Germany's chancellor, Helmut Schmidt, asserted that U.S. hard-line domestic politics must not be allowed to destroy the East-West ties that had been built up over the previous decade.[2] The Congressional Research Service summarized the points of dispute:

> Europeans [are] more inclined to regard detente as "divisible," to protect the gains of detente in Europe. The United States, carrying the majority of Western global military burdens, has a much greater interest in treating detente as "indivisible" with Soviet actions outside of Europe seen as providing cause for Western response within a European framework.[3]

In his State of the Union message to Congress on January 23, 1980, Carter outlined the basic elements of his administration's response to the Soviet invasion of Afghanistan—a policy statement that later became known as the Carter Doctrine. The president characterized Moscow's December 1979 military intervention as "aggression" that fit into a larger pattern of Soviet global expansionism. Carter argued that the Soviet invasion represented "the most serious threat to peace since the Second World War."[4] The president committed his administration to a campaign to improve significantly America's ability to project force to, and fight a limited war in, the Persian Gulf/Indian Ocean area in the aftermath of Washington's loss of influence in Teheran. The operational aspects of Carter's proposals were developed in Presidential Directive 18 and in the Consolidated Defense Guidance programs, which flowed from that directive.[5] The Middle East and the Persian Gulf were treated in these studies as foci of intensified East-West competition. Recent developments had "created new requirements for the European members of NATO . . . to support the United States within the Southwest Asian region and [to implement] efforts within Europe compensat[ing] for the possible diversion of U.S. forces."[6]

To deter Soviet advances in these areas, it was hoped that the allies would provide "appropriate cooperation . . . without diverting their attention too much from European defense or the defense of Northeast Asia."[7] The Europeans' military ability to contribute to a Persian Gulf deterrent in 1981 and 1982 was limited, particularly in those areas of force projection (airlift and sealift) most critical for responding to any Southwest Asian contingency. If European oil supplies were to be safeguarded, U.S. manpower in Europe would be critically affected and the NATO Europeans would have to make up the difference, a condition that has been labeled "the compensation crisis."[8] Defense Department officials notified Congress that "virtually all" of America's major allies had been consulted on Southwest Asian security problems and that, "under appropriate circumstances," they would be expected to cooperate with U.S. forces on access, overflight, and transit rights pertaining to military operations in the gulf. Moreover, it was expected that "those who have capabilities" would provide more direct military assistance to U.S. efforts.[9] For its part, the Carter administration decided to create a Rapid Deployment Force (RDF) as the most visible and dramatic affirmation of its commitment to the security of this region.

At the time of the RDF's creation, the United States could not hope to match Soviet military power in all of these areas or item-by-item because of geographic and logistical factors. Nevertheless, Carter and his associates had signaled their unambiguous intent to defend peripheral areas with an extended containment formula strikingly reminiscent of that employed by Dulles. The president's announcement was also clearly designed to impress upon the Western Europeans that détente was no longer an option.

At the same time, Carter moved to convince the NATO Europeans of the need to recognize and deal with the possible impact of a deteriorating strategic environment in Southwest Asia. U.S. efforts in this regard culminated in the NATO International Military Staff's *Study on the Implications for NATO of U.S. Strategic Concept for Southwest Asia*. Also known as the Southwest Asia Impact Study (SAIS), the review was prepared over a two-year time span (1983–84). While the exact content of the SAIS remains classified, it appears to have evolved from the Carter administration's request that NATO address the impact of a future American RDF deployment to the Middle East, which would result in a 20–33 percent reduction in U.S. forces stationed in Europe. NATO was also once again asked to consider the growing U.S. congressional sentiments that Europe should assume a greater share of the defense burden in the gulf as well as in Europe.[10]

It has since been revealed that the United States originally requested the NATO Defense Planning Committee in April 1980 to analyze four issues: (1) increased European reserve force levels, either to compensate for U.S. redeployments to the gulf or to deploy some of their own contingents there; (2) strengthened European capabilities to transport U.S. troops to Southwest Asia; (3) European assistance in U.S. reconnaissance operations in both the Mediterranean/Atlantic and northern Indian oceans; and (4) the eventual formation of a NATO quick strike force for out-of-region contingencies. But "the Europeans initially responded to these requests by completely stonewalling the issues."[11]

THE EUROPEAN RESPONSE

Understandably, the Europeans responded cautiously and defensively to the Carter Doctrine; they were aware that some of NATO's worst internal disputes had resulted from differing perceptions of responsibilities in the Third World. While reluctantly acknowledging that it might eventually be necessary for the West to use force in order to secure continued access to raw materials in unstable regions of the developing world, many of Washington's allies clearly felt that President Carter was moving too far, too fast, away from détente and toward a simplistic, unidimensional policy of reliance on military power in response to Third World instabilities.[12] West German defense minister Hans Apel reflected the opinion of many influential Europeans when he argued that selective economic assistance to Third World areas was the most reliable source of Western influence in the Third World, one more in line with the developing world's nonalignment politics.

The European preference for keeping any arrangement for sharing extra-European contingencies as limited and informal as possible was hardly satisfactory to members of the Carter administration. Undersecretary of Defense Robert Komer picked up on arguments about Europe's special relationship with African and Middle Eastern nations and contended that the Europeans should use their political and economic influence with the Third World to elicit greater support for U.S. military objectives in the Middle East and elsewhere. The NATO SACEUR, General Bernard Rogers, noted that European NATO members needed to provide additional military forces and resources in order to meet new out-of-region threats, rather than "simply redistributing existing ones."[13]

Such a fundamental political disagreement made it impossible for Carter to persuade the Western Europeans to enter into a new division of labor concerning extraperipheral disputes. The bland statements adopted at the June 1980 Venice Heads of State summit meeting regarding the impact of Third World conflicts on Western security, and Helmut Schmidt's subsequent comments in the Bundestag debate, which rejected demands by the opposition Christian Democratic party for some type of geographical extension of NATO, were indicative of the gap between Washington and key European allies during this period.[14]

Both European appeals for caution and allied resistance to U.S. solicitations of increased support helped to convince many influential Americans that the European allies were "relatively rich and ungrateful introverts."[15] In January of 1980, Irving Kristol warned that "if American military force intervenes somewhere and our European allies simply stay aloof, there will be overwhelming support in Congress and public opinion for the removal of American troops from Western Europe."[16] The implications of U.S.-European disagreement were highlighted by Carter in notes that he constructed toward the end of his tenure in office "as a benchmark for the next Administration":

> If present trends should continue, the American public will become increasingly dubious about the value of the European alliance, and our primary commitments will be shifted elsewhere in the world. This would not be good for us or them. We have serious doubts among us that some of the European governments will keep their present commitments on defense budgets and other politically sensitive decisions, much less make additional commitments for improved cooperation and defense capability.[17]

THE REAGAN ADMINISTRATION AND
THE RETURN OF SYMMETRICAL CONTAINMENT

During 1981, the newly elected Reagan administration continued to press the allies for greater burden sharing and for a more globalist orientation within the alliance. The new president was swept into power by a U.S. electorate that strongly supported his arguments about America's need to reestablish its standing as a global superpower in the aftermath of the Iran hostage crisis, the Afghanistan intervention, and other setbacks in the Third World during Carter's tenure in office. Reagan's arguments were similar to those used by his predecessor but with even more specific expectations of allied extraregional assistance. For example, President Carter had experienced difficulties in mobilizing sufficient offshore naval and air power to sustain two carrier battle groups with a normal complement of eighteen hundred U.S. Marines in the Persian Gulf without seriously diluting the Sixth Fleet in the Mediterranean or the Seventh Fleet in the Pacific. The incoming Reagan administration therefore pressed the Europeans through NATO's DPC to help the United States prepare for the diversion of U.S. forces from Europe to the Persian Gulf if the need arose (possibly through support by a European civil reserve air fleet). Washington also expressed interest in direct military support for an American contingent in the theater of operations itself. The Reagan administration cited the December 1980 NATO Ministerial Conference communiqué as justification for its requests for more allied help outside of Europe.

The United States pressed its allies to respond actively and positively to Washington's call for a new "consultation-facilitation-compensation" formula.

−*Consultation* between the allies in a future Southwest Asian crisis was to be based upon the recognition that NATO's concept of security had to be "broadened," and that the Carter Administration's earlier proposals for a multilateral strike force specifically earmarked for out-of-region contingencies would be inappropriate.
−*Facilitation* was related to the need for NATO to maintain sufficient military strength within the Treaty area to ensure a credible defense posture even at times when the U.S. and selected NATO powers might have to redirect the deployment of their forces beyond it (a direct legacy of the U.S. JCS geographic/resource constraints outlook).
−*Compensation* was to embody the concept of NATO Europe's making up the manpower and logistical differences if U.S. combat troops originally designated for reinforcement in a NATO defense were required to be redirected to Southwest Asia.[18]

By 1983, NATO was regularly conducting meetings of regional experts to pool national intelligence data relating to out-of-area issues and discussing diplomatic approaches to Third World regions.[19] Throughout 1983, however, the ongoing Southwest Asia Impact Study became mired in the Reagan administration's own reluctance "to specify its highly confidential and repeatedly changing contingency plans for Southwest Asia" and by continued intra-European squabbling about the study's ultimate implications.[20] Accordingly, the study received only "informal" endorsement by the DPC in June 1984.

Concurrent with its campaign to solicit greater allied support for its out-of-area policies, the Reagan administration undertook efforts to enhance America's ability unilaterally to influence events beyond the NATO boundary. In its first defense budget, presented to Congress in early 1982, the Reagan administration requested appropriations to improve air and sea transport capabilities, elevate the RDF to command status as the U.S. Central Command (USCENTCOM), and pursue an ambitious naval building program. This last proposal, incidentally, was in striking contrast to the Carter administration's efforts in 1977 to achieve successful Naval Arms Limitation Talks (NALT) with the Soviets and to reduce overall U.S. naval ship construction.[21] Secretary of Defense Weinberger also upgraded the concept of "horizontal escalation" or "war-widening strategy" to the status of official American policy. As Zbigniew Brzezinski later recalled, the concept had been developed unofficially by previous administrations:

> The point of both the Truman Doctrine and what later came to be called the Carter Doctrine was to make the Soviet Union aware of the fact that the intrusion of Soviet armed forces into an area of vital importance to the United States would precipitate an engagement *with* the United States, and that the United States would then be free to choose the manner in which it would respond. In fact, in our private contingency preparations, I made the point of instructing the Defense Department to develop options involving both "horizontal and vertical escalation" in the event of a Soviet military move . . . by which I meant we would be free to choose either the terrain or tactic or the level of our response.[22]

This was to be a counteroffensive strategy, insofar as it called for the United States to attack the USSR at points of geostrategic and/or psychological vulnerability if U.S. interests were threatened.[23] President Reagan's strategy relied upon manipulating an opponent's insecurity and uncertainty, much as the earlier theory of "massive retaliation" had done. But critics of the president's strategy contended that such an approach was more provocative than stabilizing in an era of superpower nuclear parity.[24]

BURDEN SHARING REVISITED

As the Reagan administration became increasingly frustrated over European stalling tactics concerning the NATO out-of-region agenda, it began implicitly and explicitly to link future European cooperation on this issue with the preservation of U.S. troops in Europe. This approach played to a very supportive congressional audience, once again sensitized to Mansfield Amendment-type arguments about the need for greater allied burden sharing. After all, NATO Europeans were falling far short of their 1977 pledge to achieve the 3 percent spending increase goal, while concurrent U.S. fiscal outlays were substantially above that criterion.

Certain European governments aggravated the situation during the early 1980s by openly rejecting earlier NATO commitments. Belgium informed Washington that it could not afford to follow through on paying its previously agreed-to share of NATO's new Patriot antimissile defense system, thus leaving the alliance's integrated air defense network increasingly vulnerable. Denmark restricted its FY 1983 defense budget to a 0.5 percent increase, far short of the 3 percent annual increase agreed upon in London. Even Margaret Thatcher felt compelled to cut U.S. $360 million from the British military budget in early September 1983 and to spurn U.S. requests to commit the U.K. to an expanded naval role in the Mediterranean (despite its recent large naval maneuvers there) because of Britain's responsibilities in the South Atlantic and its decision to preserve its full British Army on the Rhine (BAOR) contingent.

European governments also resisted Washington's efforts to link their policies on sensitive issues relating to the Middle East and the Persian Gulf to the defense burden-sharing issue. The depth of disagreement between the United States and the European NATO members over Middle Eastern issues was demonstrated at the end of 1981 when the allies rebuffed Secretary of State Alexander Haig's proposal at a NATO foreign ministers' conference that NATO adopt a policy of "firmness" toward Libya.[25] Europeans opposing a NATO-wide challenge to the Libyans cited a September 1981 European Communities (EC) decision to pursue moderate policies vis-à-vis Colonel Qaddafi's regime.[26] Italy was especially concerned about avoiding a direct confrontation with Qaddafi because of the twenty thousand Italian workers still residing in Libya at that time and because of the vulnerability of Sicily, the Lipari Islands, and Malta to military attack from Tripoli (as discussed in Chapter 21).

Led by senators Theodore F. Stevens, William S. Cohen, and Carl Levin, Congress weighed possible legislation for reducing American ground troops abroad, unless the allies demonstrated a willingness to carry their "fair share" of the defense burden. Not all U.S. officials, however, believed that their nation was totally justified in expecting the Europeans to contribute more to Western defense efforts, either within their own continent or on a global basis. Successive Department of Defense *Reports on Allied Contributions to the Common Defense* prepared annually for the Congress actually gave Western Europe and Japan relatively strong performance ratings in their defense efforts. The 1985 report typifies DOD's approach to the debate, citing "encouraging recent developments" in European infrastructure/facilities construction and maintenance, weapons and communication production and procurement and, most significantly in terms of this study's concern, "out-of-area" force goals related to "air and land improvements in areas where [force] capabilities would be significantly reduced by U.S. deployments to Southwest Asia."[27] The report concluded that the NATO allies "appear[ed] to be shouldering their fair share of the NATO and Japan defense burden."[28] The Joint Chiefs of Staff also challenged initiatives by Congress to require cutbacks of U.S. forces in Europe, primarily on the grounds that such actions would communicate a dangerous message of alliance disarray to the Soviet Union:

> Congressionally mandated European troop strength (ETS) manpower ceiling(s) . . . affect adversely European force structure, readiness, modernization and sustainability. The ceiling ignores the increasing capabilities of the Warsaw Pact, discounts improvements made by our allies, creates the impression that the United States is increasing nuclear forces at the expense of conventional forces, and creates a NATO penalty for CONUS defense improvements. . . . There is no ceiling on Soviet forces.[29]

Strong counterarguments to the DOD and JCS positions were nonetheless developed by Congress and independent analysts during the Reagan years. The Congressional Budget Office (CBO), for example, published its own studies directly refuting DOD's selection and computation of burden-sharing data.[30] Senate Foreign Relations Committee staffers, moreover, computed indexes of economic changes in the NATO alliance showing that between 1950 and 1985, the United States slipped from first to seventh in GNP per capita. The U.S. percentage of world exports decreased from 18.3 percent to 12.3 percent, and its total import dependency increased from 15.2 percent to 18.4 percent during that time span.[31] In an era of increased resource constraints and higher government deficits (total U.S. government revenues dropped from 19.4 percent to 18.6 percent of the GNP, while total federal spending rose from 22.2 percent to 24 percent between 1980 and 1985), the United States was nevertheless allocating half of each research and development dollar to defense-related pursuits while West Germany was devoting 90 percent and Japan 95 percent to their respective civilian sectors.[32]

Despite DOD arguments that any effort by Congress to force Europe into higher levels of defense spending would be counterproductive, Congress did enact measures for limiting U.S. troop deployments in Europe to levels attained by the end of September of 1983. Stanley Sloan has noted that this measure marked the first time during the postwar era that Congress imposed a specific limit on U.S. troop levels in NATO.[33] While waiver provisions within this legislation allowed President Reagan some freedom to station additional troops, a clear political signal had been sent to Washington's NATO allies. In the absence of more visible European commitments to support the Americans' globalist strategy, U.S. critics of the alliance were in a strong position to pressure the president to further reduce budget authorizations for the defense of the Continent.

In June 1984, Senator Sam Nunn introduced a follow-up proposal to link

U.S. deployment levels in Europe more directly to the 3 percent standard. According to Nunn's proposal, for each year from 1987 to 1989 that this target was not met, the United States would reduce its troop strength by thirty thousand (a total reduction of ninety thousand) unless the secretary of defense could assure Congress that the Europeans would undertake compensatory measures— for example, improvements in ammunition stockpiles and standard base infrastructures—and/or SACEUR could offer assurances that the NATO European states had carried out "significant measures to improve their defense conventional capacity" needed to lengthen the period of time before nuclear weapons would have to be used in any NATO defense.[34]

The Nunn Amendment failed to pass in Congress owing to the timing of its introduction. Europeans were just beginning to accept newly deployed American intermediate nuclear weapons systems on their soil, and it was feared that too much pressure on the allies at this time would disrupt the momentum of these deployments, given the already widespread resistance to the new INFs by most European publics. But Senator Cohen introduced a compromise measure (worked out with Nunn in advance), which dropped the reference to punitive troop cuts yet retained the originally stated goals "in principle." This proposal passed the Senate by a 94 to 3 vote, reinforcing a congressional signal of the imperative for greater efforts by NATO Europe to provide for its own conventional defense. Nunn himself later justified his effort as a "NATO Conventional Defense Improvements Amendment" rather than a "NATO Troop Withdrawal Amendment" and contended that if the Europeans really wanted to settle merely for an American nuclear tripwire, "the U.S. should recognize this and adjust our own military commitments and defense priorities . . . [providing] an extended [nuclear] tripwire . . . with far fewer conventional forces than the U.S. currently has stationed in NATO."[35] For many analysts, the critical question was no longer whether the allies should be asked to do more, but whether U.S. pressure tactics would actually change European policies before a snowballing process of alliance dissolution set in.

OUT-OF-AREA STRATEGY:
MOVING TOWARD QUALIFIED ALLIED SUPPORT

In view of the tense transatlantic atmosphere during the first term of the Reagan administration, most allies were eager to avoid a highly visible and divisive dispute with the United States over out-of-area issues. Key European governments therefore sought to demonstrate some movement toward upgrading their extraperipheral defense capabilities while simultaneously seeking quietly to restrain Washington's geostrategic ambitions. Thus, the allies supported the U.S.-sponsored North Atlantic Council communiqué in April 1981, which stated that "a number of Allied countries possess or are determined to acquire the capacity to deter aggression and to respond to requests by [Third World] nations for help in resisting threats to their security and independence."[36] Derek Arnould, formerly head of General Political Affairs for NATO, has described the 1981 communiqué as "a departure, in many ways, from the traditional outlook of the Allies" on the out-of-area issue.[37] The communiqué still fell far short of a formal or informal extension of the treaty area. It nonetheless illustrated that at least some European governments shared America's conviction that there was a need for the NATO partners to develop a new "generic frame of reference" (to use Uwe Nerlich's phrase) to cope with extra-European contingencies.[38] By 1983, the State Department's director of Politico-Military Affairs cited the following extraperipheral burden-sharing measures being undertaken by America's allies:

1. British and French development of intervention forces for "contingency use" should national or Western interests be threatened outside of Europe. Specific reference was made to the Thatcher government's announced plans in November 1983 for upgrading the 5th Infantry Brigade to carry out "significant interventions of its own" by 1985 with the purchase of six TriStar strategic tankers and an increase in manpower from nineteen hundred paratrooper/infantry battalion personnel to over five thousand; also mentioned was France's deployment of the "Force d'action rapide," bringing five divisions plus a logistics support group (about forty-seven thousand personnel) under one command either to deal with territorial defense missions within France and Central Europe or to intervene in selected Third World missions.

2. Agreement "in principle" by selected allies to provide in route support to U.S. and other allied force deployments to Southwest Asia in the event of an emergency.

3. Establishment by NATO of procedures to ensure the defense of Europe if U.S. forces should be diverted to Southwest Asia or elsewhere in defense of Western interests.

4. Participation in the multinational forces (MFOs) for Lebanon and for the Sinai.

5. Continued British and French maintenance of military forces in the Indian Ocean, and British deployment of a small naval detachment (about thirty personnel) to Diego Garcia in support of developing U.S. Rapid Deployment Joint Task Force (RDJTF) operations there.

6. Japan's acceptance of responsibility for the defense of its own sea lanes to a distance of one thousand miles offshore, and a significant increase in Tokyo's Third World economic assistance programs. (Japan had already made it clear that it would allow U.S. RDJTF forces to use American military bases in Japan for backup to emergency deployments to the Middle East, Africa, and the Indian Ocean.)[39]

Subsequent developments reinforced this more positive picture. The Department of Defense announced that the NATO allies had committed themselves to meeting the six hundred commercial ship minimum requirement needed to reinforce NATO Europe during wartime, even if European quotas should increase owing to new U.S. out-of-area efforts, while nine NATO members had committed themselves to increasing their contributions of civil long-range cargo aircraft and civil wide-body passenger aircraft under the same circumstances. DOD also announced in June 1983 that eight NATO nations had provided overflight rights and in route access and support to U.S. forces deploying to annual CENTCOM exercises in Southwest Asia during the period 1980–82.

During Reagan's second term, several incidents occurred that reminded all allies that fundamental differences of interest and perception continued to place strict limits on any more ambitious campaigns to stretch NATO's boundaries. But there were also some very positive developments on both sides of the Atlantic.

On the European side, key allied governments began moving away from the policies of the late 1970s, which seemed to be designed to establish Europe as the "good cop" in a classic "good cop/bad cop" arrangement in dealings with the Third World. According to this misguided and divisive strategy, Third World nations were encouraged to view the nations of the European Communities as diplomatic and economic actors, while not forgetting that the EC members were backed up by a United States that was both willing and able to intervene militarily if situations proved threatening or resistant to conciliation. Beginning in the mid-1980s, more realistic, and more assertive, positions were taken by key European governments on such issues as state-sponsored terrorism and Persian Gulf security. These trends will be discussed in detail in other parts of this book.[40]

On the U.S. side, meanwhile, there was a softening in the overall American posture regarding European military contributions to out-of-region crises. It is important to note, however, that this trend was more visible within the Reagan administration itself than within Congress. In mid-1987, Congressman Tom Lantos complained to Assistant Secretary of State for European and Canadian Affairs Rozanne L. Ridgeway that "the [Reagan] Administration is not sufficiently sensitive to the very profound dissatisfaction on the part of the Congress and the American people with the failure of our European friends and Japan to engage in burden-sharing in areas outside Europe." Ridgeway countered that "we must never forget that NATO is a North Atlantic Organization. It is a regional organization. Its heart and soul is found in the division of East and West. . . . It does that alliance no good to forget that is its essential mission."[41] The State Department official concluded by noting that 80 percent of NATO's manpower and 90 percent of its aircraft deployed in the theater are "European." While she was "not prepared to comment on NATO's contingency planning" in the Persian Gulf, she did note that "the obligations imposed" by NATO "apply only in a specified area, which includes the Atlantic Ocean north of the Tropic of Cancer."[42]

Since coming to office in 1989, George Bush has continued to moderate U.S.

criticisms of allied burden sharing and out-of-area support. It was, of course, difficult for the new administration to become too upset over the failure of its allies to meet the established 3 percent goal in a situation in which America's debt and deficit problems had forced Washington to accept a modest one percent defense budget increase for FY 1990.[43] For their part, Washington's allies have publicly accepted the principles of "consultation and concertation" in the event that the United States is confronted with a future out-of-area crisis.[44] A conditional modus vivendi thus seems to be evolving as the 1990s begin. It remains to be seen, however, whether these transatlantic understandings will survive the next out-of-area challenge.

CONCLUSION TO PART I

DEVELOPMENTS during the late 1980s, including the reduction in American criticisms of allied policies regarding out-of-area challenges and a growing, if still very limited, acceptance by key NATO allies of the need for more transatlantic cooperation on out-of-area policies on occasion, are very encouraging. But they must be seen against a backdrop of three much larger trends that have been ongoing since the mid-1960s.

The first, most important trend is the relative decline of U.S. power, particularly in the realm of economics. The contrasts between the U.S. economic situation in the early cold war years and the situation in the 1980s are stunning. To cite just a few of the relevant indicators: in the decade following World War II, the United States accounted for about 45 percent of world economic activity; today it accounts for 20–25 percent. Between 1950 and 1980, the American share of world military expenditures dropped from 50 percent to 23 percent, and during the same period the U.S. share of world monetary reserves dropped from 50 percent to 6 percent.[1] During the second term of the Reagan administration, Congress exerted strong pressure on the executive branch to reduce the federal deficit as a step toward revitalizing the U.S. economy. The defense budget was the principal target of congressional attack; Reagan's budget requests for FY 1988 and 1989 were slashed by $68 billion. Since coming to office in 1989, George Bush has demonstrated a greater willingness than his predecessor to hold down the defense budget, but he has still been forced by Congress to go farther in achieving economies in the military area. Thus, Washington has accepted the need to close eighty-six of its military bases at home and abroad and to reduce funding significantly for such prestigious systems as the B-2 (Stealth) bomber and the Midgetman missile.

American economic problems have contributed to the second trend affecting U.S.-European security relations since the mid-1960s—Washington's quest for ways to induce the allies to carry a greater share of the NATO defense burden. As discussed in Chapter 6, burden-sharing disputes have focused on questions of financial and manpower contributions for the defense of NATO per se, and also on the issue of allied support for U.S. policies beyond the NATO Treaty area. Diplomatic support for American policies in the Third

World has often been treated by Washington as the very least that could reasonably be expected of the NATO allies. More active support—in the form of increased economic backing, logistical assistance, or even direct military contributions—may once again be solicited by U.S. policy makers if out-of-area crises surface during the 1990s.

The European response to demands for a more active out-of-area posture by an overextended American ally will be largely determined by the third trend that shapes the debate today—the "loss" of the European colonial empires. Since the mid-1960s, these European allies have adjusted their foreign policy aspirations and modified their defense forces in accordance with the completion of global retrenchment. Having been forced to abandon their postwar imperial ambitions, however, these allies will be reluctant to support any new demands for out-of-area assistance.

In view of these trends, it is not at all surprising that out-of-area disputes still represent a potentially explosive issue for NATO at the beginning of the alliance's fifth decade. Nor is it surprising that many defense experts looking at the out-of-area problem in the 1990s should assume that the alliance treaty must be renegotiated, in order to make NATO more responsive to problems beyond the existing treaty boundaries. In the conclusion to this book, we respond to some of these arguments. It is sufficient at this juncture to note that the older types of NATO out-of-area disputes (American concerns with "guilt by association" with European colonialism and European resentments over perceived interference in Third World *domaines réservés*) have been replaced by questions of threat definition and burden sharing in the 1980s. If present trends continue into the 1990s, we shall see extraregional events triggering intra-allliance disputes about the nature and degree of the threat posed by the Soviet Union and about NATO's responsibility for dealing with such problems as state-sponsored terrorism and assured access to resources. And in spite of the best efforts of all parties, out-of-area challenges will continue to fuel the debate about the equitable distribution of costs and risks among the NATO allies.

PART II

BRITAIN

Power and influence we should exercise in Asia; consequently in Eastern Europe, consequently in Western Europe; but what is the use of these colonial deadweights?

BENJAMIN DISRAELI
letter to Lord Derby, 1866

It is rather sad that circumstances compel us to support reactionary and really rather outmoded regimes because we know that the new forces, even if they begin with moderate opinions, always seem to drift into violent revolutionary and strongly anti-Western positions. . . . It is a confused position.

HAROLD MACMILLAN
letter to the queen, October 7, 1962

INTRODUCTION TO PART II

B RITAIN'S "long recessional" from empire began well before the creation of NATO. As the alliance moved past its fortieth anniversary, the last notes of the recessional still waited to be played in Hong Kong and still waited to be composed for a few isolated outposts, such as the Falkland Islands. British global retrenchment has already been the subject of several excellent studies.[1] Part 2, by contrast, focuses on one aspect of that complex history: Britain's attempts to use its status as a NATO ally to help preserve portions of its overseas empire. We also consider the issue of British resource constraints in some depth, with special reference to hard budgetary choices between intra-European and extra-European security requirements. As we attempt to demonstrate, however, London's problems of overextension, as well as the frustrating experience of occasionally being treated by Washington like a venerable but somewhat doddering great-aunt rather than an essential ally, are attributable as much to British failures of imagination and foresight as to budgetary limitations.

As one of Western Europe's major powers, and as the nation that could claim with justification to be the initial sponsor of the alliance, Britain was in an excellent position to influence NATO policy during the cold war. But London had one foot in and one foot out of Europe during this period and refused to come to terms with the contradictions inherent in this situation. Instead, it placed too much faith in the Anglo-American "special relationship" that had evolved during World War II. The result was a series of missed British opportunities on the Continent and frustrated initiatives beyond the NATO boundaries.

British defense experts hung their hopes of postwar power and influence on the management of the special relationship with Washington. We attempt to look at that relationship from the point of view of competing intra-European and extra-European defense requirements. We argue that the United States was clear and consistent in communicating its policy preferences to Britain during most of the cold war era. Washington wanted London to help lead the NATO alliance, and the United States was prepared to provide England with the support and the status necessary to perform the role of European "prefect . . . chiding unruly pupils for failing to heed the wishes of the American headmaster."[2] Thus, for example, the United States was willing to make special bilateral arrangements with Britain regarding the development of Britain's "independent nuclear force" while communicating opposition to the acquisition of nuclear weapons by other members of the alliance. But London's ability to parlay this "prefect-headmaster" arrangement into real political influence in Western Europe was confounded by British overseas commitments and Anglo-American disputes beyond the NATO Treaty area.[3]

An internal British security planning memorandum, circulated in mid-1953, was openly skeptical of the likelihood that America and Britain would come to any real understanding over global military strategy following the Korean War armistice.

> As both Lord Ismay and Field Marshall Montgomery have pointed out NATO strategy ought to fit into a global strategic concept. . . . we cannot adequately provide for the defense of NATO without regard to other possible threats of war. We have been anxious for some time to arrive at an agreed global policy with the Americans but there is no hope in being able to do this at present.

In view of these circumstances, the report concluded, it was "better to make some progress on NATO policy on its own."[4]

More than any other event, the Suez Canal crisis of 1956 clearly demonstrated the limits of U.S.-U.K. cooperation beyond the NATO Treaty area. Following Suez, differences between Washington's and London's outlooks toward security problems in the developing world appeared to sharpen. As John Baylis has since argued,

> The growing [military] inequality between Britain and the United States did in many respects loosen the bonds between the two countries. The Skybolt crisis of 1962, the Vietnam War, the [British] withdrawal from east of Suez in the late 1960s and the Arab-Israeli War of 1973 all demonstrated a gradual erosion of the relationship. The lack of reciprocation and Britain's unwillingness to contribute significantly to "the common defense" does seem to have contributed to the decline in the working relationship between London and Washington.[5]

Britain's postwar efforts, first to preserve portions of its empire and then to manage the process of global retrenchment, appear in retrospect to have been detrimental to Britain's national self-image and prejudicial to British influence within Europe. By the late 1970s, Britain's retreat from empire was almost complete, but the U.K. had still not accommodated itself to a new role in Europe. Furthermore, the British economy was in a state of near collapse—the pound had reached record lows by 1976, unemployment was at a postwar high, wage and price restraints were in effect.[6]

During the 1980s, however, Britain demonstrated a new sense of direction in its foreign and security policies and acquired new influence within the Atlantic community as a result. But several hard choices relating to defense must still be made as Britain enters the 1990s. In Chapter 12, we survey the recent defense debate in London and compare various proposals for adjusting British purposes to British power.

CHAPTER 8

POSTWAR BRITISH SECURITY
POLICIES: EUROPE
VERSUS EMPIRE

FOREIGN policy disputes in Washington in the immediate postwar period reflected the multiplicity of options available to the United States at the time, in spite of the fact that much of the debate focused on the rationing of resources. In London, the situation was very different. Internal debates during and after the war tended to focus on problems of British weakness in a postwar world dominated by the United States and the Soviet Union. Lord Halifax, the British ambassador to Washington, reflected the predominant view of most British strategic thinkers in January 1944, when he speculated that, over the long term, Britain, with or without its empire intact, would not be able to claim equal partnership with the Soviet Union, the United States, or even China in terms of global decision making.[1]

Early on, the tension between American "guilt by association" concerns and British *domaine réservé* interests became manifest in Anglo-American relations. Throughout World War II, Winston Churchill attempted to explain to President Roosevelt that an explicit Allied commitment to rapid decolonization would undermine the war effort by its deleterious effect on morale in England. In drafting correspondence to Roosevelt (later modified before being sent to the U.S. leader) concerning the Indian independence issue in early 1942, the prime minister warned that the common Anglo-American wartime cause would be seriously impaired "if it were known that against our own convictions, we were conforming to United States public opinion in a matter which concerns the British Empire and is vital to our successful conduct of the war in the East."[2] Churchill also attempted to convince Roosevelt of the strategic value for overall Western security of preserving at least part of Britain's colonial system during the postwar era. But FDR envisioned Britain and France as junior partners in the international security order that would materialize following the Axis

Powers' defeat. And this point of view significantly impaired the British prime minister's influence over the president's calculations.[3]

Churchill regarded Roosevelt's position as not only incomprehensible but dangerous. Where he differed most fundamentally from Washington was in his estimate of how the Soviet Union would respond to any process of rapid British decolonization. As early as 1943, the prime minister had confided to his political adviser, Harold Macmillan, that he believed the Americans had difficulty seeing that Russia was the real postwar threat to global peace.[4] In a March 1945 letter, Churchill asked Roosevelt to consider the postwar world from the following perspective: "When the war of the giants is over, the wars of the pygmies will begin. There will be a torn, ragged, and hungry world to help to its feet: and what will Uncle Joe [Stalin] or his successor say to the way we should both like to do it?"[5]

One policy available to Britain was to live with the loss of empire, shift its focus to Western Europe, and pursue a "big fish in a smaller pond" strategy. Britain's first postwar foreign secretary, Ernest Bevin, was, in fact, attracted to this approach in principle.[6] But other influential British leaders during the late 1940s, such as Churchill and Anthony Eden, were less enthused about a "Europeanization" of British foreign and defense policy, since they felt that turning toward Europe would be a betrayal of four centuries of British imperial history.

Most British policy makers argued that in order to preserve its global influence London would have to develop a "special relationship" with Washington in which British diplomacy and experience would complement American military power. London therefore endeavored to cultivate an image in Washington of Britain as "the indispensable mediator," willing and able to intercede on America's behalf with the nations of Western Europe and much of the Third World. London also pursued a strategy of encouraging Washington to commit itself to the defense of Europe, both as an end in itself and as a means of permitting London to allocate the bulk of its military assets to the maintenance of residual Commonwealth and imperial interests.[7]

Shortly after V-E Day, however, Washington began to signal to Britain's Attlee government that the wartime "special relationship" would have to be reassessed. British policy makers suffered a particularly strong setback in August 1946, when the McMahon Act was passed by the U.S. Congress, effectively severing British access to American nuclear weapons technology. Significant British and American differences also surfaced regarding the administration of their respective German zones of occupation. Shortly thereafter, Anglo-American disagreements over British policies in the Middle East became a matter of public attention, and the Democratic party's Congressional Conference publicly warned President Truman (in March 1947) against supporting British policies throughout the Mediterranean or even within Europe.[8]

Resisting Continental Defense

Britain's participation in the 1948 Brussels Treaty could not disguise the fact that London had little respect for the will and capability of France and the Benelux countries. Bevin himself related his worries to the U.S. ambassador to Britain in July 1947, indicating that if massive U.S. economic assistance was not forthcoming, "France and most of Europe" would be lost by the following year.[9] Winston Churchill and other British conservative opposition members estimated that at least fifty or sixty divisions would have to be deployed across the European continent opposite the Soviet forces, at a "ruinous" cost to the British economy, in order to deter the developing land threat. Bevin countered that such an arrangement was the best way to create a Europe equal to Russia and America and that the Brussels Treaty would have the strong backing of the "extraregional" (North American and Commonwealth) states sympathetic to British global strategic objectives.

In fact, the foreign secretary's preliminary blueprint for a Western European defense organization called for the affiliation of African and other European colonial territories (but *not* Washington).[10] Events during 1948—notably the Czech coup and the Berlin Blockade—nonetheless convinced most British policy makers, including Bevin, that in the developing situation of tight global bipolarity it was unrealistic to establish a European security system without U.S. participation. The passage of the Vandenberg Resolution by Congress in 1948 seemed to clear the way for such U.S. participation under the auspices of a broad North Atlantic pact.

As the 1948/49 Washington Preparatory Talks progressed, however, it became increasingly evident that the United States was prepared to underwrite British defense interests only on American terms. After the North Atlantic Treaty itself was signed in early 1949, President Truman made it clear in two successive messages to Congress that the United States expected Britain and other NATO nations jointly to "attain a level of *Western European* defenses which would make [an enemy] invasion so costly and so unlikely of success that the danger of it being attempted would become remote."[11] The British had interpreted the new alliance's purpose along precisely opposite lines, viewing it as an opportunity for Britain to focus more of its attention—and most of its air—and seapower—on the defense of its vital extra-European interests. London also continued to hope that Washington's formal commitment to the defense of Europe presaged a new U.S. willingness to help defend European interests in the Third World.

Once the NATO Treaty was established, London's goal was to keep the Americans from feeling satisfied and complacent. This concern was implicit in Bevin's comments to the U.S. Policy Planning Staff, made on April 4, 1949, while the British foreign secretary was in Washington to sign the North Atlantic Treaty. During this top-secret briefing, he admitted that the allies had "done well" in Europe. It remained, however, for Western nations to join forces to protect the "outer crust" extending from "Scandinavia to Turkey and including the Middle East." Bevin also stressed the need for U.S.-British coordination in India and in Southeast as well as Northeast Asia. With regard to the Far East, he advised the group that China seemed to be "lost to us," but that Britain could be relied on to "stand firm" in Hong Kong in the face of the communist threat, "making it, if necessary, a sort of 'Berlin of the East.'" In regard to Bevin's analogy, Dean Acheson mentions in his memoirs that "the thought of another Berlin, if this involved another airlift, filled me with considerable distaste."[12] This last comment by Acheson is worth emphasizing, because it illustrates the extent to which British and American policy makers differed in their views of the contribution that the U.K. could make to the global order. Bevin's choice of the Berlin analogy was certainly a case of bad salesmanship, but the problem went beyond the specific cases of Hong Kong and Berlin. With Hong Kong, Bevin had chosen one of several examples of Britain's residual imperial system, which, from the point of view of London, were important assets in the global Western security framework. But Acheson's remark demonstrates the American sensitivity to the possibility that British global strongpoints could rapidly become unwelcome American strategic responsibilities. Such concerns contributed to Washington's propensity to meddle in Britains's affairs in some regions of the world and, in some cases, to edge Britain out. They also contributed to the difficulty that the U.K. experienced in its efforts to influence American decisions about extending NATO's boundaries or replicating NATO in selected Third World regions.

In spite of these fundamental policy disputes, the United States did attempt to treat Britain as *primus inter pares* within the Western security community during the immediate postwar period. Bevin and other British statesmen also succeeded in sensitizing Washington to the seriousness of the economic crisis in postwar Europe.[13] Finally, Bevin was occasionally successful in his efforts to convince Washington that the Western containment strategy, as it materialized in the late 1940s and early 1950s, depended upon Britain's retaining its far-flung military basing network and its residual political influence in such regions as the Middle East and Southeast Asia. These considerations notwithstanding, most attempts by the British Foreign Office and various British Defense Ministry officials to encourage U.S. policy makers to treat the U.K. as an equal partner in planning and executing the global containment strategy outside of Europe fell on unreceptive ears in Washington.[14]

In spite of problems that British officials experienced in talks with their American counterparts, influential groups within the postwar Labor government (supported by members of the British Chiefs of Staff) argued that the only way to preserve Britain's overseas possessions would be to win American political backing and military support. Otherwise, an overburdened British economy could eventually force the U.K. to make painful geopolitical concessions to the Russians in Southwest Asia or to local anti-British insurgency movements throughout the Third World. Beyond the continent, the Committee of Imperial Defense, in early 1946, "gently solicited" commitments from Canada, Australia, New Zealand, South Africa, and other dominions to provide badly needed funding support for empire and Commonwealth defense missions.[15] London was generally frustrated in its efforts to obtain such assurances from the key Commonwealth nations, however, and growing financial exigencies forced the Attlee government to implement its own program of troop reductions in early 1946 despite the clearly negative effects that such cutbacks would have on British strategic power overseas.

PURSUING AN INDEPENDENT NUCLEAR DETERRENT

When the Conservative government returned to office in 1951, it made much of the potential savings that could be achieved by reliance on nuclear weapons as the cornerstone of Britain's postwar defense policy. A "Global Strategy Paper" was produced by the British Chiefs of Staff in the summer of the following year.[16] Nuclear deterrence against a Soviet attack on NATO was regarded as eminently more rational than any British attempt to match Soviet conventional force deployments in Europe, and Prime Minister Churchill had already asserted in public that without the West's atomic weapons inventory, the Russian army would already have pushed to the English Channel.[17]

The European military balance at the time seemed to corroborate Churchill's dramatic assertion. The Soviet forces numbered around 3.2 million after World War II. Moscow was producing some five thousand armored fighting vehicles annually and over ten thousand aircraft. The Russians deployed over a million men in Eastern Europe alone.[18] By contrast, Britain's army in 1952 comprised only around 450,000, while residual British overseas defense commitments included some 24,000 troops for Malaya (against communist insurgents), 10,000 for Kenya (to quell a separatist movement), 85,000 for the Suez garrison, and some 30,000 for Cyprus. During the early 1950s, many British force planners argued that Britain, with a population of only 50 million, a crippled economy, and residual overseas responsibilities, could not be expected to provide four divisions to NATO when an enormously wealthy United States, with a population four times as large, was then providing only five divisions.[19] Thus, nuclear weapons were seen as the most cost-effective and expeditious means of adjusting British power to the demands of the alliance in Europe. By 1956, Britain was committed to the simultaneous maintenance of a thermonuclear stockpile, extended V-bomber production, and the development of guided missiles, as well as maintaining in Germany four of Britain's ten army divisions.

While both the British Conservative and Labor parties were prone to justify the British nuclear force with arguments similar to those presented in support of the "massive retaliation" nuclear doctrine in the United States during the early 1950s, neither American nor British defense planners appeared able or willing to merge their views on the precise ways in which nuclear capabilities could be employed outside the NATO theater.[20] Early British defense plans, for example, assumed that nuclear weapons could be employed unilaterally as a cost-effective instrument for "active deterrence," not only in Europe, but in the Third World as well. "Active deterrence" as London envisioned the concept at that time has since been defined by Andrew Pierre as "deterrence against aggression aimed at an allied country or an overseas colony."[21]

By the late 1950s and early 1960s, however, improvements in Soviet offensive nuclear forces, along with the Soviet doctrinal emphasis on surprise attack, called into question the continued utility of Britain's nuclear weapons inventory as an "active deterrent" to be used by the U.K. in any contingency apart from that of defending her homeland. Such considerations were not entirely lost on British foreign policy and defense planners at the time. In July 1954, Ivone Kirkpatrick, permanent undersecretary at the British Foreign Office, noted that his country's relinquishing of the Suez Canal Zone military base was directly related to the realities of the nuclear age (the base could be quickly neutralized by Soviet nuclear bombers) and that "the power and numbers of these frightful [thermonuclear] weapons will be so great that the chance of our wanting to conduct a campaign in the Middle East will be less than it is today."[22] Washington, in any case, was justifiably skeptical of any British ability to conduct long-range nuclear deterrence outside the NATO format, given London's already overstretched defense resource base.

CONCLUSION

Britain suffered a more serious postwar identity crisis than other NATO allies because its expectations were greater. It also remained indecisive about whether to participate in or resist the politics of bipolarity. The British leadership's national security aspirations remained imperial, but its financial and strategic capabilities were not sufficient to sustain its ambitions. Subsequent British solicitations of support, however—both to the Americans for understanding and to the Commonwealth nations for material backing—proved unsuccessful. This left the British defense establishment with the incredible option of assigning both European and extra-European defense roles to Britain's nuclear deterrent. In the wake of Suez in 1956 and the Nassau Agreement in 1962, British strategy began to be adjusted to the realities of both the alliance and the international power balance. But the process was neither easy nor steady.

CHAPTER 9

AFTER SUEZ: ADJUSTING
NUCLEAR DETERRENCE AND
INSTITUTING GLOBAL
RETRENCHMENT

B RITAIN'S ROLE in the Suez fiasco is discussed in Chapter 3. At this point, it is sufficient to observe that the problem of cost saving greatly complicated Harold Macmillan's efforts to resuscitate the "special relationship" after the Suez crisis. The prime minister was anxious to salvage, to the extent possible, U.S. defense planners' belief in Britain's indispensability. The big question concerning budgetary allocations was what kinds of defense investments would be most likely to enhance Britain's status in its relations with Washington while at the same time protecting British security interests.

THE "SANDYS DOCTRINE"

The decisions reached by the Macmillan government were summarized in the famous 1957 British Defense White Paper, produced under the direction of Duncan Sandys, secretary of state for defense. The document did not provide much in the way of original thought on how Britain should reorganize its defense priorities to greater advantage. Nor did it demonstrate that the Ministry of Defense had learned very much from the Suez disaster. It did, however, seek to perpetuate the myth that Britain's strategic nuclear striking power could be applied outside as well as inside Europe independent of U.S. and allied backing. It also contended that small, modern, mobile air and ground units could be deployed around the vestiges of the empire to quell local rebellions, even though Suez had demonstrated that the U.K. did not have the requisite logistical infrastructure for such interventions.[1] At the same time, reductions in Britain's active forces, in the Middle East and elsewhere, were to be made as cost-saving measures. In the words of one parliamentary critic of the White Paper, these force reductions overseas would mean that "this country will be incapable of waging any large-scale colonial war again. . . .once we accept the logic of this White Paper we cease to be an imperial power."[2]

Part of the reason why the Sandys Doctrine was laden with contradictions was because British interservice rivalries were still intense, particularly in regard to their differences over the NATO versus out-of-area defense missions. The navy was, by this time, the most ardent supporter of programs designed to enhance Britain's east-of-Suez presence (in particular, development of aircraft carriers). The RAF, on the other hand, saw its greatest responsibilities in the defense of the homeland and in Britain's contribution to NATO. The army was caught in the middle, buffeted from both sides, since troop cuts were seen by most politicians as the most expeditious way of addressing the problem of budgetary limitations. The army was advised that its overall manpower totals were to be reduced—with implications for both the British Army on the Rhine (BAOR) and overseas forces—and that the conscription system (the National Service) was to be abolished. Minister of Defense Anthony Head resigned in the wake of the Defense White Paper's release in order to protest the manpower cuts in British land forces, which he believed would ultimately compromise the U.K.'s ability to project military power below the nuclear level (he disdained the concept of "tactical" nuclear warfare), both in the NATO theater and in future Third World crises.

The Macmillan government, nevertheless, hoped to be able to achieve these manpower cuts—while at the same time increasing Britain's influence in Washington as well as strengthening Britain's security guarantees to developing nations—by improvements in the mobility and quality of equipment and by a greater reliance on nuclear weapons as a substitute for conventional forces. In retrospect, this latter argument seems to have been altogether unrealistic. Washington could not help but be skeptical of Britain's nuclear capabilities at this time. Britain's first hydrogen bomb was not exploded until October 1957, by which time both the United States and the Soviet Union were developing advanced missile delivery systems for their much more powerful nuclear inventories. During the same year, British V-bombers, replacing the old Canberra and Lincoln aircraft, were only coming on line. The Vulcan, Valiant, and Victor aircraft could only be used in a first-strike mode, however, because of the advanced state of Soviet air defenses. Deterrence based on second-strike retaliation was still five years away—in the form of the Polaris missiles provided by Washington. Anthony Verrier has since argued that "all these aircraft and their weapons represented a genuinely independent nuclear force which, so far as a specific role was assigned to it, extended to any part of the world. But such a force could only be used in retaliation against an enemy which lacked nuclear weapons."[3] Verrier might have added, "and which lacked the clear-cut support of a nuclear superpower." If the USSR chose to intervene against

Britain on behalf of a regional ally (in a future Middle Eastern conflict, for example), only America's nuclear deterrent would be capable of actually counterbalancing a Soviet nuclear threat. As Harold Wilson was to argue eight years later, British strategic "independence" had always depended, in the final analysis, on U.S. support.

Subsequent British attempts were made during the early 1960s to maintain its nuclear bombers throughout the world and to present the bomber force as a central component of the West's global containment strategy. The deployment of Canberras on Cyprus was even characterized by London as CENTO's "nuclear strike force"—implying that the U.K. had adapted NATO nuclear weapons stockpiling practices to a Mediterranean/Middle Eastern format.[4] Two Vulcan bomber squadrons, moreover, were regularly assigned to the RAF fields at Episkopi and Akrotirid, under CENTO command, in case they were needed for low-level, deep penetration attacks against the Soviet Union during wartime.[5] NIMROD tracking planes with nuclear capabilities were also eventually introduced to British and allied force contingents tracking Soviet SSBN movements in the Indian and Pacific oceans. This gave successive British governments a rationale for claiming that Britain's nuclear power supplemented American strategic capabilities around the world.

The question remained, however, whether London actually increased its status in its relations with Washington as a result of the changes incorporated in the Sandys Doctrine. From Washington's perspective, a nuclear-equipped ally might contribute marginally to the West's overall nuclear war-fighting capability if the need arose. But this potential contribution had to be judged against the potential risk that such an ally might feel compelled to use its nuclear weapons by default—either in a NATO context or beyond the treaty area—because of insufficient conventional strength. Even the threat of such an action might result in a loss of control by all sides in a conflict. The Kennedy administration was especially concerned about such possibilities, at a time when it was attempting to "get the nuclear genie back in the bottle" through the development of a strong conventional force in NATO and by the short-lived and unsuccessful attempt to place European nuclear forces under American veto control with the proposed NATO multilateral force (MLF).

U.K. Conventional Forces: Deficiencies in Power Projection

Britain's contribution to NATO's upgraded conventional strategy was to be tested by the new U.S. administration during Exercise Spearhead in 1961. This NATO maneuver was designed to assess the West's capabilities for using conventional forces to achieve a "pause" in any Warsaw Pact invasion against NATO Europe, prior to the latter's use of tactical nuclear weapons. The outcome of these maneuvers was considered to be so unsuccessful that it convinced a number of Western strategists that the BAOR couldn't defend itself without nuclear support.

Another disturbing indication of British military projection problems occurred in the summer of 1961, during the British intervention in Kuwait. Prior to this action, British defense planners had expressed concern about Iraq's dictator, Abdul Kerim Kassem, claiming that he entertained designs on Kuwait, which provided the U.K. with 40 percent of its crude oil supplies. In July 1961, over six thousand British troops were dispatched to Kuwait to help deter a suspected Iraqi invasion of the newly independent nation. In operational terms, the intervention was a British military success. Air and naval units sent from Singapore and Hong Kong arrived on the scene within nine days, contributing to a combined task force of over forty-five British ships under the Middle East Command. Even in this case, however, some elements of Anglo-American tension were evident. Because Kuwait was so important to Britain in terms of its oil exports, there was some discussion among British defense planners that London might possibly be compelled to use tactical nuclear weapons as a last resort.[6] Britain actually deployed some of its nuclear assets (Canberra bombers) to the scene of the conflict as insurance against escalation of the brushfire crisis. Such a prospect was obviously alarming to Washington, still intent on disassociating itself from any major action that could alienate Arab nationalists. American policy makers were also concerned that the British forces, with their half-squadron of Centurion tanks and limited carrier-based air cover, would be no match for the Iraqis in a conventional battle.[7]

Equally unattractive to the Americans was the prospect that extensive British air and ground attack operations would inevitably lead to an alliance burden-sharing problem through the withdrawal of significant levels of British contingents from NATO Europe to meet this newest threat in the gulf region. These fears were at least partly borne out by events. The Kuwait intervention, labeled Operation Bellringer, involved British reinforcements from England and Germany, which were transferred to Kuwait via Turkish air corridors. By the time that Ankara subsequently refused overflight permission for the RAF, the Royal Navy had already deployed the commando carrier HMS *Bulwark* off Kuwait's shores, and Britain had assured itself of air superiority in the event that a major confrontation with Iraq erupted. As already mentioned, Britain also deployed its nuclear-capable Canberra bombers to the gulf, with assigned targets in Iraq, while V-bombers dispatched from Germany were readied on Malta for possible duty.[8]

These and other developments appear to have led the Kennedy administration to find Britain's commitment to an independent nuclear force unwelcome, not only because it could complicate East-West and North-South crisis management but because it encouraged British leaders to hang onto the myth of British global influence. Kennedy's undersecretary of state, George Ball, has since aptly summarized the American concern about sustaining a "special relationship" with London at the nuclear level:

> In retrospect, I think that responsible officials of the United States Government—and I include myself—should have quite calmly and dispassionately asked themselves certain pertinent questions: . . . Did we have any obligation to keep Great Britain in the nuclear club? Would it not be better to assist her to phase out her nuclear deterrent?
>   . . . [U.S. support for British nuclear forces] encouraged Britain in the belief that she could, by her own efforts, as long as she maintained a specially favored position with the United States, play an independent great power role and *thus it deflected her from coming to terms with her European destiny.*[9]

The issue came to a head during the 1962 U.S./U.K. Nassau Talks, when Prime Minister Macmillan insisted that the Americans accept the principle that Britain had the right to employ its soon-to-be purchased Polaris missiles for extra-European contingencies if London deemed it necessary. Kennedy was sympathetic to Macmillan's need for at least the appearance of a victory in the Nassau Talks, since the prime minister was facing domestic criticism that he was trading British sovereignty for American missiles. Consequently, the United States agreed to Paragraph 8 of the Nassau Agreement, which provided an escape clause under which Britain could use the Polaris "where supreme national interests are at stake," even *outside* NATO auspices. In subsequent statements, Macmillan and his cabinet argued that Polaris could be diverted from exclusively NATO missions in times of worldwide crisis and could even be employed in the unilateral defense of Singapore or Kuwait under certain circumstances.[10]

In fact, however, by the mid-1960s London harbored no such expectations. From the time of the Nassau Agreement onward, the U.K. was moving away from being an independent nuclear actor in the global power balance to becoming an auxiliary force for U.S. nuclear containment. London's overall foreign policy continued to be guided by the conflicting desires to retain its traditional position as an important player in a combined allied collective defense effort led by Washington while simultaneously achieving reductions in successive defense budgets—a policy which Kenneth Hunt has aptly described as "getting a quart out of a pint bottle."[11] Nuclear weapons did not solve Britain's problems, either inside NATO or beyond the NATO boundary. Britain's desire somehow to use its nuclear weapons to acquire status and influence beyond Europe never completely disappeared, however, even after British retrenchment during the 1960s eliminated those overseas bases that had been a central component of Britain's long-range strategic bomber system.

Coming to Terms with the Limits of Power

The Wilson government, which came to office in October 1964, was at first reluctant to address directly the issue of global retrenchment. But shortly after taking office, Wilson began to cancel those defense procurement programs designed for east-of-Suez missions.

The more controversial issue of British base maintenance overseas was not addressed by the Labor leadership until late 1967. A January 1968 Defense White Paper announced that "Britain's defense effort will in the future be concentrated mainly in Europe and the North Atlantic. . . . No special capability for use outside of Europe will be maintained when withdrawal from Singapore, Malaysia and the Persian Gulf is completed."[12]

The target date for completion of the retrenchment process was 1971; and indeed, some NATO planners saw the decision to retrench as a positive development for NATO. Britain's defense minister, Dennis Healey, had asserted in Parliament that the British pull-out east of Suez would result in "more forces available for the defense of Europe."[13] But, as had been the case after France's retreat from Algeria (see Chapter 16), most of the forces that returned home were deactivated rather than reassigned to Europe. Successive British Defense White Papers that appeared during the early 1970s were more objective in acknowledging the erosion of British military power outside of Europe and explicitly accepting the U.K.'s new status as a Continental security actor.[14]

Wilson's announcement of Britain's strategic withdrawal from extra-European outposts was succeeded over the following three years by force cuts in the Royal Navy which left only five frigates, a detachment of NIMROD long-range maritime and strike aircraft, and a helicopter squadron in the immediate Indian Ocean area. British ships nonetheless still retained basing privileges at Simonstown in South Africa, at Mombasa in Kenya, in Malagasy, in Mauritius, and in the Maldives for the time being.[15] Continuing British access to these and other facilities was cited in support of Wilson's assertion (in December 1971) that "Britain's strategic frontier stretched to the Himalayas." But this claim was a fantasy that generated an appropriate amount of derision abroad and at home.[16] Similarly, Wilson's claim that NATO-designated units could be relied upon for extra-European interventions as needed neither impressed nor reassured anyone beyond the treaty area. It did, however, exacerbate intra-NATO concerns about the reliability of British forces in Europe in the event of simultaneous threats against NATO and challenges to British interests in other regions of the world.

The Wilson government also challenged one basic premise of British defense policy during this period by highlighting the "fictitious assertion of independent nuclear action by Britain," especially as it applied to out-of-area contingencies. In fact, before its election to power in October 1964, the British Labor party campaigned on the position that it, rather than any Conservative government, would be better able to form a more "realistic" special relationship with the Americans by downgrading any vision of an "independent" British nuclear deterrent to the realistic objective of supporting an *eventual* U.S. nuclear monopoly within the Western camp. This triggered a landmark nuclear debate in Parliament during December 1964, which ended, in the words of one commentator, "in a crescendo of fury unparalleled since Suez."[17] Wilson challenged the Tories to offer any reasonable scenario under which Britain would use its Polaris force independent of a U.S. decision. Would Britain really use its Polaris missiles for "some nuclear Suez" in the future? If not a Suez, then what? Only a "go-it-alone war [which] would mean a certain and total annihilation of all human life in Britain" made sense to Wilson as a possible scenario. Under these circumstances, the prime minister held to the position that "there is no independent deterrent because we are dependent on the Americans."[18]

Wilson was, of course, correct when he discounted any prospect that the U.K. would initiate nuclear strikes outside of a situation of global warfare and without coordination with the United States. Furthermore, as Lawrence Freedman has since noted, even the value of Britain's sea-based nuclear force for NATO must be questioned, as these forces may actually complicate alliance defense planning.[19]

CONCLUSION

As events unfolded over the two decades following Suez, NATO defense officials and independent Western defense analysts gradually came to accept overall British military weakness as a permanent aspect of their security calculations and planning. In 1976, for example, the chairman of the U.S. Joint Chiefs of Staff bitterly declared, during an unguarded moment, that Britain could no longer be viewed as a world power because all it had left were generals, admirals, and bands.[20]

As discussed in Chapter 5, the United States began to adjust its thinking regarding the geostrategic value of a British overseas presence during the Kennedy administration, at the same time that Britain began to turn grudgingly toward Europe. Plans for British global retrenchment during the late 1960s and early 1970s were badly received by a U.S. government increasingly mired in Vietnam. By the early 1970s, only about one-fifth of the British defense budget was earmarked for non-NATO functions.[21] The language of the 1977 *Statement on the Defense Estimates* reflected this trend: "Britain's defence can make the most effective contribution to the Common Defence [in] the Eastern Atlantic and Channel areas, the Central Region, the security of the United Kingdom base, and the nuclear deterrent."[22] By this time, however, cumulative reductions in Britain's contribution to NATO had also taken their toll, to the point that NATO Secretary General Joseph Luns felt compelled to send a personal letter to Britain's secretary of state for defense, Fred Mulley, in which he warned that "any further cuts by the United Kingdom would not be understood by its Allies."[23]

When Margaret Thatcher became prime minister in 1979, she attempted to reverse the effects of four successive defense budget cuts since 1975. Her success in this difficult undertaking is assessed in the conclusion to Part 2. Before offering our assessment of current British policy, however, we survey the history of British out-of-area defense policy in the Middle East/Persian Gulf region (Chapter 10), in Asia (Chapter 11), and in the Caribbean and South America (Chapter 12).

CHAPTER 10

BRITISH SECURITY POLICY
IN THE MIDDLE EAST/
GULF REGION

BRITISH strategic presence in the Middle East and Persian Gulf area was tied historically to London's need to control the Suez Canal as the link to India and other distant points of the empire. Postwar British officials regarded British ability to work with the Arabs throughout the Mediterranean, Red Sea, and Persian Gulf area to be critical in building a new commonwealth. Following India's break with the empire, the Middle East/gulf region was accorded an even higher priority as a *domaine réservé* in British global planning, as U.K. defense experts became increasingly concerned about salvaging what they could of the imperial system. Confronted with the Russian threat along the Northern Tier, the British Chiefs of Staff (COS) contended that only British control of Middle Eastern airfields, from which the Royal Air Force (RAF) could strike Russian targets, would make up for the loss of Indian manpower—a strategic reserve formerly constituting over a quarter of a million men which in the past had been moved east or west by the Royal Navy as situations demanded.[1]

The Chiefs of Staff warned in March 1947 that a gradual British departure from important Mediterranean basing and communications centers would mean that the West would have to wage future global warfare from an "outer ring" consisting of North America, Britain, South Africa, Australia, and New Zealand, where air bases were few and remote and where "the U.K. would begin the war by fighting in the last ditch. . . . it is open to serious doubt she would survive so long."[2] Indeed, this scenario had been influential among British defense planners since March 1945, when the Post-Hostilities Planning Subcommittee, composed of representatives from all three services in Britain's military, produced an extensive defense policy paper outlining both the U.K.'s strategic requirements in the Middle East and the measures needed to realize

122

them. Specifically, the paper concluded that Britain had to retain control over the Suez Canal and other Eastern Mediterranean exit-control points for three reasons: first, to secure Middle Eastern oil supply lines; second, to maintain safe use of the Middle East's regional airfields and ports, required for unimpeded air and sea routes to the Far East; and third, to sustain basing systems throughout the Middle East for possible use by imperial strategic reserves.

Because the Soviet Union was viewed as a serious threat to the attainment of these objectives, the subcommittee also recommended that "Western" mobile forces be maintained in the region to delay Soviet force projection through north Persia, Turkey, or the Persian Gulf. It further proposed that a system of alternative bases be established to the west and south of the Middle East, including Libya, Sudan, Eritrea, and other East African locales, in order to provide defense in depth for the British basing network. Above all, the subcommittee's paper advocated that "the U.S.A. should be encouraged to assume a definite defense for the area."[3]

Prime Minister Attlee expressed special concern about such policy recommendations on the grounds that they would divert British attention and resources away from Europe. In January 1947, he complained that Bevin and the chiefs were recommending "a strategy of despair." He argued that Western military preparations beyond Europe would invite greater military pressure against Britain and other Western states in Europe itself; and that, moreover, the countries to be supported (such as Turkey and Egypt) were all relatively weak in defense terms—this at a time when Britain should concentrate its limited resources on a European defense. Bevin countered that if Britain actually withdrew from the Middle East, "it would lead the U.S. to write us off," sorely tempt the Russians to fill the resultant power vacuum, and undermine the morale of the British public regarding the preservation of global influence, at a time when the nation's "economic and military position is now as bad as it will ever be."[4]

The problem of how the U.K. could protect remaining British military interests in the Middle East led Bevin and others to consider ways of expanding the NATO Treaty area. During his Middle Eastern tour in January 1950, Bevin frequently spoke about extending the new North Atlantic Treaty's line of defense to the south and southeast, although Attlee was still arguing that Britain's defense in Europe had to be given priority.[5]

In the end, it was the cost of maintaining its European land and air defense forces, rather than any strategic debate about Britain's global role, that led to the reduction of the Royal Navy's importance in the Eastern Mediterranean and the Middle East. A growing sensitivity to the burden of Middle Eastern responsibilities led British security planners grudgingly to accept some increase in the U.S. defense role for the Middle East/gulf region—either through bilateral arrangements or through a multilateral pact modeled after or explicitly linked to NATO.[6]

COLLECTIVE DEFENSE EXPERIMENTS
IN THE MIDDLE EAST/NORTHERN TIER

Although Britain was anxious to secure U.S. politico-military support and oil production assistance in the region, Whitehall was concerned about the prospect that the United States would attempt to establish strategic leadership from the Middle East to the Northern Tier.[7] As Sir John Troutback, head of the British Middle East Office in Cairo, wrote in May 1951, British security objectives in the Middle East reflected a desire to create a "command organization under *British supreme direction* which we can represent politically as a counter-weight to the American position in the Atlantic."[8] The U.K.'s problem was to convince the Egyptians and other moderate Arab factions in the region to accept an increased U.S. strategic presence in the area, while at the same time continuing to accord political and military preeminence to Britain.[9] At least in retrospect, this appears to have been an impossible demand upon Britain's diplomatic services. British policy makers discovered that, having accepted the need to bring the Americans into the Middle East, it was difficult to control their actions or limit their influence there.

In meetings held during early 1952, U.S. and British Chiefs of Staff discussed the implications of a possible extension of NATO's southern flank. Washington made it clear that any new Mediterranean command would have to be under a U.S. officer. As a compromise, Field Marshal Sir William Slim and other British military officials pressed the "outer ring" argument—that Turkish forces deployed outside of Turkey would constitute the best means for simultaneous Western coverage of both Southern Europe and Middle Eastern defense interests and would prevent Southwest Asian or Arab states from playing the United States and Britain off against each other. General Bradley countered (correctly) that the Turks' interest in Middle Eastern problems was secondary to their concern that Ankara be completely integrated into NATO, in view of Turkey's long northern border with the USSR (see Chapter 22 for further discussion).[10] By May it was clear that this compromise could not be sold to either Washington or Ankara. An internally circulated British COS memo grumbled that American insistence upon broadened and unified command arrangements stretching from the Mediterranean eastward was superfluous in any case, because "a command in the Middle East exists and has existed long before NATO was thought of. In war, the distinction between NATO and non-NATO becomes meaningless. All the forces of the Western Alliance in the Mediterranean Sea and the area around its shores will then be allies facing a common enemy."[11]

U.S. reluctance to defer to Britain regarding any Middle Eastern defense organization was largely attributable to the fact that by the end of 1951 Washington was increasingly doubtful about the wisdom of Britain's Middle Eastern policy. In particular, U.S. policy makers were expressing new concerns about

124

the cost effectiveness, from the point of view of overall Western security, of preserving the residual British military presence in the region. Thus, in October of that year, the United States pressed Britain to withdraw its land and naval forces from Abadan in Iran.[12] As a further example of policy differences, the United States viewed Egyptian leader Gamal Abdel Nasser as a personality requiring delicate U.S. diplomatic and economic cultivation, rather than continued British military pressure.[13] When Nasser rejected British proposals for renewal of the 1936 Suez basing agreement, American suspicion of Britain's inability to translate Middle Eastern military strength into diplomatic leverage seemed to be confirmed.

Washington's suspicions of British diplomacy in, and intentions toward, the Northern Tier undercut the effectiveness of the Baghdad Pact as a Western mechanism for enhancing Middle Eastern security. Britain entered into the pact, along with Iraq, Turkey, Pakistan, and Iran in March 1955 after its efforts to sponsor a MEDO had been foiled. Anthony Eden, then Britain's prime minister, justified the pact as a means of bringing British relations with Iran, Pakistan, and Iraq "into line with those which already exist with Turkey and other partners in NATO"—that is, a tacit linkage of NATO with traditional British strategic interests in the Northern Tier.[14] Meanwhile, his foreign secretary, Harold Macmillan, described the Baghdad Pact as "the most important organization other than NATO," even though he privately regarded the arrangement as "perilous" without full American membership.[15]

By 1955, however, it had become clear to most British defense planners that the United States was pursuing fundamentally different policies concerning the stabilization of the Middle East and the Northern Tier than those pursued by either Britain or France. Nonetheless, London continued to accord the United States military rights to British air bases at Wheelus and Al Adem in Libya, Amman and Mafraq in Jordan, and Habbaniya in Iraq. In return for base concessions, the United States provided Britain with forty-three million pounds of sterling-equivalent military and economic assistance in the form of Defense Support Aid, Agricultural Commodity Aid, Special Aircraft Purchase Programs, and additional programs to strengthen the RAF.[16] Outside of such financial arrangements, however, agreements between the United States and the United Kingdom regarding Middle Eastern security were very tentative. This delicate situation finally exploded in October and November 1956, at the Suez Canal.

SUEZ AND THE CONFIRMATION OF U.S. PREDOMINANCE IN WESTERN STRATEGY TOWARD THE MIDDLE EAST

The disparity of postwar military power between the United States and Britain, coupled with Washington's general skepticism about Britain's ability to manage its Middle Eastern policies, was an even greater source of frustration for

Prime Minister Eden than for his predecessors. Eden is described by Richard Neustadt in *Alliance Politics* as "a sort of tragic hero" in the Suez affair.[17] Eden's urbanity and negotiating skills were interpreted by some American policy makers as an example of what they deemed one of London's worst tendencies—a reliance upon finesse at the expense of realism in postwar international relations. The problem was exacerbated by the personal antipathy between Eden and Dulles, which had come to the public's attention during the 1954 Geneva Conference.[18]

Shortly after Eisenhower took office in January 1953, Eden (then foreign secretary) visited Washington to discuss the prospects for MEDO and for U.S.-British cooperation in the Middle East. Eden subsequently informed Churchill that "the President agreed with me that it was essential to maintain the [British] base in Egypt and that if we were to evacuate the canal zone before making a Middle Eastern defense arrangement we should be exposing ourselves to Egyptian blackmail. In contrast to Dulles, he was firm on this point."[19]

By the time he became prime minister, Eden was prepared to admit that the canal was actually becoming less important to London as a military base:

> The tangled mass of workshops and railways in an area the size of Wales was cumbersome and dependent upon Egyptian labor. It did not seem likely that in this nuclear age we should ever need a base on the past scale. Smaller bases, redeployment, and dispersal would serve our purpose better.

In contrast to the base, however, the canal itself remained "of supreme importance."[20]

> The canal was an international asset and had been recognized as such since the Convention of 1888. In recent years its importance had been greatly increased by the development of the Middle Eastern oilfields and by the dependence of Western Europe on them for a large part of its oil supplies. In 1955, 14,666 ships had passed through the canal. Three-quarters of them belonged to NATO countries and nearly one-third were British.[21]

Broader considerations of prestige and national image also fueled the prime minister's determination to assert British strategic interests during the Suez crisis as strongly as he did. Suez was seen as a test, not unlike Indonesia's test of Dutch control over New Guinea. Eden was most worried that if a revolutionary Third World state such as Egypt was successful in wresting power and strategic access from Britain with impunity, a precedent would be set that would seriously and permanently damage Britain's overall strategic credibility. These concerns encouraged Eden to commit himself to challenge Nasser, even against the advice of his military advisers and without the support of Washington.[22]

In August of 1956, three months prior to the joint British-French-Israeli military expedition against Egypt (Operation Musketeer), opposition leader Hugh Gaitskell pressed Eden to bring the Americans in: "It would be ridiculous to treat ourselves as though we were the only power involved. It is essentially a matter for all the maritime powers of the world, and we must act in concert with other nations."[23] With regard to strategic capabilities, British military leaders such as Field Marshal Sir Gerald Templer (chief of the Imperial General Staff), Lord Mountbatten (First Sea Lord), and Sir Dermot Boyle (chief of the Air Staff) warned Eden that Britain's available forces were not up to the task of taking back Suez. They noted, for example, that the nearest airborne troops (on Cyprus) needed to be retrained and reequipped for Middle Eastern duties and that airborne operations unsupported by a credible ground offensive were bound to fail.[24] By mid-October, however, Eden, the "tragic hero," could see no alternative to intervention, in spite of the risks.

The confrontation between Washington, Paris, and London over Suez is discussed in Chapter 3. It is sufficient to reiterate here that Suez was the low point in British-American postwar strategic relations. Suez also encouraged many British policy makers to reassess NATO's place in Britain's overall national security priorities. In the wake of Suez, many British policy elites, as well as the country's public at large, asked whether London in fact had over-prepared for war in Europe at the expense of its ability to fight a limited war outside of the European continent. The fact that London was unable to use bases in Jordan and Libya during the crisis, because of these countries' opposition to the Suez campaign, only served to throw into greater doubt subsequent claims by British defense analysts that the U.K. could still conduct quick and effective extra-European military operations by relying on its remaining deployments and base facilities (see table 5).[25]

In the wake of the Suez crisis, the Macmillan government agreed with the Chatham House report regarding the need for "collective" solutions to Middle Eastern security problems. Macmillan felt that the best way to repair the "special relationship" was to extend full British support to the postulates of the Eisenhower Doctrine. On a more general level, the new British government saw the crisis as proof of the need for a British recommitment to Anglo-American policy coordination in the Third World. At the same time that Macmillan was pressing the case for a recommitment to "transatlantic interdependence" in the planning and operation of Western military strategy, however, he was arguing for continued "national independence" in defense through a strengthened British nuclear deterrent.[26] As events were to illustrate, however, there were strict limits to how far the United States was prepared to go in encouraging the latter, in view of the limited contribution that Britain could make to the former.

THE INTERVENTIONS IN LEBANON AND JORDAN

Both Macmillan's concept of transatlantic interdependence and NATO's relevance to post-Suez Middle Eastern contingencies were tested in July 1958, with the twin crises of Lebanon and Jordan. In Beirut, radical Sunni Moslems challenged the pro-Western Chamoun government. The radicals were backed by Iraq, where the pro-British monarch, King Faisal, had recently been assassinated and replaced by a leftist, somewhat anti-Western military regime. The Lebanese revolt was put down between July and October 1958 by over fourteen thousand U.S. Army and Marine personnel who relied upon supplies that were built up or prestocked under a NATO infrastructure program at the Adana air base in southern Turkey. Britain played an important support function in Lebanon by permitting the United States to use its Cyprus facilities during the operation.

Britain, for its part, took advantage of the situation to deploy two thousand British troops into Jordan in support of a beleaguered King Hussein, who was fearful that Egypt and Iraq would foster internal disorder to overthrow his regime, or that neighboring Iraq would invade Jordan outright. In Iraq, the Habbaniya air base had already reverted to national control in an enforced modification of the former U.K.-Iraq security treaty. Now it seemed that the last vestiges of British strategic influence in the region were being threatened by the country which, only a short time before, had been regarded by London as the key to Britain's Northern Tier strategy.

The interventions were planned and executed by Washington and London in close collaboration. Joint plans for mutual assistance had been worked out following a visit to Washington by the new British foreign minister, Selwyn Lloyd, and Chief of Staff Sir William Dickson. While London provided access to its Cyprus facilities in support of the U.S. action in Lebanon, Washington airlifted supplies to London's interventionary force deployed to Jordan and provided air cover for British paratroopers with about fifty jet fighters.[27] Macmillan saw the joint operation as a validation of his policy of closer cooperation with Washington. In his elation, he asserted that in the future he would almost prefer to be "wrong together" (with the United States) than "right separately."[28]

This combined Anglo-American intervention did not, however, improve the prospects for policy coordination on out-of-area contingencies within NATO itself. The NATO Council of Ministers was not consulted, and NATO forces were not employed in the intervention. Some allies (Belgium, Greece, Turkey, Italy) provided base access or overflight rights in support of the operations, but others were openly critical. West Germany went so far as to complain that the U.S./U.K. initiatives in Jordan and Lebanon had adversely affected "NATO's global image," and to call publicly for a NATO study of how British and American military activities in the region might incite Warsaw Pact counterpressure in central Europe. Chancellor Adenauer also speculated that, in the future, other European NATO members might have to act as mediators between more belligerent treaty partners and Third World victims of intervention.[29]

Britain's contribution to the 1958 Lebanon/Jordan operations was also interpreted by some critics of the Macmillan government as a public demonstration of London's subservience to Washington and as a further confirmation of the limits of British extra-European interventionary capability. As was the case in 1956, a joint operation in which Britain participated as one of two NATO powers acting in a non-NATO context drew attention to the U.K.'s inability to airlift its own troops and supplies to overseas locales in an emergency. American Globemasters had to be used to reduce the all-too-obvious vulnerability of the British supply line to Jordan—a situation made even more difficult by Britain's failure to obtain overflight rights over Israel and the Sudan, so that planes had to be diverted over the Congo.[30]

The essentiality of U.S. assistance for the British intervention also created important policy leverage for Washington vis-à-vis London in the planning of the joint operation. There is reason to believe, for example, that Britain would have moved against Iraq if President Eisenhower had not strongly resisted such proposals. Eisenhower's actions in this regard reflected his concern about loss of control over the situation in the region, at a time when hawks within his own country, such as Joint Chiefs of Staff Chairman Nathan Twining, were calling for a joint Israeli-U.K.-Turkish counteroffensive against Egypt, Iraq, and Syria, respectively.[31]

Those British policy makers who were pressing for a more forceful military response (along the lines of Twining's proposal) attempted to link instabilities in the Middle East to the issue of NATO security. Sir Charles Mott-Radcliffe depicted the geopolitical situation as follows during parliamentary debate on July 17 concerning the British intervention in Jordan: "Yesterday, Iraq, today Jordan, tomorrow Lebanon, perhaps Libya next week. . . . it would seem to me that the flank of NATO would look a little strange were that process to be completed."[32] With specific reference to Britain, however, William Quandt has recently observed that "the Americans had no intention of helping restore British primacy in Iraq, and this last European effort in the Middle East to keep the remnants of an earlier era intact failed for lack of U.S. encouragement, much as the Suez venture had gone awry two years earlier."[33]

Eisenhower's policies toward Britain during the intervention reflected a sincere desire to bolster Macmillan's public image while at the same time discouraging London from making too much of the new "special relationship" in the Middle East. He was anxious to coordinate this extra-European military venture with the British in order to preclude any replay of the misunderstandings that had arisen during Suez and, if possible, to heal some of the wounds that had been created then. But Washington also sought to discourage London from transforming the Jordan intervention into a more extensive and permanent military presence in the region. Consequently, at a July 31 press conference, Dulles emphasized the prospects of *both* U.S. and British troops withdrawing from Lebanon and Jordan when the political situations in those countries stabilized.[34] As a quid pro quo for British restraint, the United States privately expressed its willingness to protect British oil interests in Kuwait and subsequently moved some U.S. forces from Okinawa to Lebanon and other parts of the Middle East.

THE BAGHDAD PACT, KUWAIT, AND ADEN: ACCELERATING RETRENCHMENT

Following the Lebanon and Jordan interventions, Washington also expressed its willingness to extend a more explicit security guarantee to the members of the Baghdad Pact. In fact, however, the decision had more to do with U.S. doubts about British reliability than with any new American commitment to working with Britain in the Middle East/gulf region as a result of the successes in Lebanon and Jordan. With anti-British sentiments growing in most Arab governments, the original purpose behind the Baghdad Pact's founding—to reinforce pro-Western elements in the Middle East/Northern Tier region—was rapidly becoming unsustainable. Washington nonetheless attempted to resuscitate the pact with new assurances of U.S. support. Meeting with his British counterparts and with other pact members at a ministerial council session in London on July 28–29, Dulles stressed that his country was prepared to act "at great risk" in order to assure the independence of any pact member facing situations similar to those of Lebanon and Jordan.[35] His view was supported by the U.S. Joint Chiefs of Staff and the Department of Defense, who contended that greater U.S. adherence to the Baghdad Pact would "strengthen NATO's southeastern flank and facilitate coordination of planning among NATO, the Baghdad Pact, and SEATO."[36] Other officials within the Department of State, however, privately resisted closer U.S. affiliation with the pact, based largely on their concerns that American policy would be regarded as tacitly supporting the continuation of European imperialism:

> The Baghdad Pact, unfortunately, has been regarded by non-member states of the area as Western-inspired and in large part U.K.-dominated. There is serious doubt, therefore, whether U.S. adherence would alter the prevailing view and muster for the Pact the necessary additional membership and widespread public support necessary to make it a really effective instrument for the furtherance of U.S. objectives in the area.[37]

Prospects for resuscitating the pact declined precipitously when Iraq formally withdrew from membership following the Ba'athist party's takeover of that country in July 1958. As a result the organization's headquarters was moved from Baghdad to Ankara, and in August 1959 the pact's name was changed to the Central Treaty Organization (CENTO).

Britain's general frustration over the situation in the Middle East was demonstrated by the Macmillan government's reluctance to acknowledge Iraq's departure from the pact and by Defense Minister Duncan Sandys's continued public assertions that British Canberra bombers and selected U.K. ground forces designed for pact operations could still use Iraqi ground facilities and overfly Iraqi airspace. Internally, opposition parliamentarians delighted in the government's dilemmas, which stemmed from a Middle Eastern alliance policy in disarray:

> GEORGE BROWN: Did the right honorable gentleman discuss at all [during his recent trip to Iran] the new headquarters for the Baghdad Pact? If so, is he going to put the new headquarters on wheels?
> MR. DUNCAN SANDYS: The new headquarters is already established at Ankara.
> MR. ANEURIN BEVIN: Is it the Ankara Pact now?[38]

By this time, most Egyptians and the majority of other Arab nationalists were irrevocably hostile to what little military power Britain retained in the Middle East. Increasing regional hostility, however, only served to encourage London to accord new importance to its remaining Middle Eastern and gulf outposts, even as the overall process of British military retrenchment continued. During the late 1950s and the early 1960s, Britain therefore attempted to bolster the security of its remaining strategic assets in the region by new deployments and, in the case of Kuwait in 1961, by military intervention.

As previously discussed, the Kuwait intervention involved not only the drawdown of British forces from the NATO central front but also preparation for nuclear attacks against Iraq in the event that British forces were in danger of being overwhelmed. Not wishing to face the difficult decision of supporting or opposing its NATO ally's use of nuclear weapons in the gulf region at a time when the Berlin crisis was heating up, Washington moved to defuse the crisis through negotiations. The United States supported a British resolution in the United Nations urging that Kuwait's independence and integrity be respected, but also moved with all diplomatic haste to facilitate a swift transfer of responsibility for Kuwait's future defense from British to Arab League forces.[39]

British troops departed by October 1962 without firing a shot. As had been the case in 1958 in Jordan, the British military performed efficiently and effectively in spite of the lack of infrastructure support and the logistical problems involved in the intervention. But Macmillan summarized the predicament in a letter to the queen at the time that the troops were leaving Kuwait:

> We have so far been able to sustain our position in the Gulf better than we had dared to hope. Our operation in Kuwait, for instance, was very successful. But so much depends on Aden and if we are driven out of Aden or faced with serious revolutionary troubles in Aden which might make the base useless, our whole authority over the Gulf would disappear. We have spent many anxious hours discussing what can be done and we have put certain actions into operation. Nevertheless, I fear that we shall have great difficulty.[40]

Britain had begun to accord new importance to Aden in 1957, when it was designated the headquarters for the newly created Middle East Command and the site for its new Amphibious Warfare Squadron.[41] Aden's importance was further increased in 1964, when the 24th Infantry Brigade was redeployed there from Kenya. By then, however, insurgencies were raging throughout the South Arabian peninsula, and an official state of emergency was maintained throughout the mid–1960s. It gradually became apparent that yet another British overseas withdrawal, this time from the gulf itself, was imminent. The decision was finally announced in the February 1968 Defense White Paper and completed by 1971.[42]

Retrenchment from Aden represented one more important element in a general process of British adjustment to budgetary and political realities during the 1960s. Collective defense arrangements for Middle Eastern/Persian Gulf security had proven to be unmanageable in part because of America's unwillingness to become formally and fully involved. Prospects for U.S./U.K. coordination had been further undermined by the Suez debacle. Macmillan and his successors during the 1960s continued to express a clear commitment to the goal of increasing U.S./U.K. security cooperation in the Middle East/gulf region. Yet British defense planners tended to classify Baghdad/CENTO-designated units for national service in the region rather than for joint or alliance-wide responsibility.

BRITAIN'S FINAL PULLOUTS "EAST OF SUEZ" AND WASHINGTON'S CHANGE OF HEART

As discussed in Chapter 5, the United States had concluded by the mid-1960s that Britain should be encouraged to preserve whatever it could of its post-imperial basing networks in view of America's own overextension problems. By this time, however, it was difficult for Washington to regard CENTO, or other remaining British security arrangements in the Middle East, as being very valuable instruments for regional defense. The remaining elements of Britain's strategic basing chain in the area were clearly unsustainable by this time, and British military actions throughout the Middle East and Africa—ranging from Aden and Kenya to Uganda, Tanganyika, Zanzibar, and Zambia—had taken their cumulative toll on the British defense budget. In January 1968, Prime Minister Wilson finally announced that all Persian Gulf military positions would be relinquished by the end of December 1971, just two years before the West was forced to undertake a fundamental reevaluation of its security interests in the region in the context of the 1973 Arab oil boycott.[43]

The risk that Britain's departure from the Middle East/Persian Gulf would result in increased regional instabilities or actually encourage Soviet aggression in the Northern Tier area became a subject of considerable speculation among NATO military planners after the boycott. During the 1970s, special emphasis was therefore placed on Britain's continued ability to contribute to NATO flank defenses in the Eastern Mediterranean. By 1974, however, even this "compensatory role" (to use James H. Wyllie's phrase) had been allowed to erode.[44] Successive defense spending reviews significantly cut revenues previously allocated for financing Britain's contribution to Mediterranean security in such places as Cyprus. More significantly, the Defense Ministry announced that same year that Britain would no longer commit forces to CENTO's military command. Further reductions were also scheduled for specialized reinforcement contingents stationed in the U.K. but assigned to the Middle East Command, and for other extra-European contingency forces. These included the elimination of two-air portable brigade groups, one Andover squadron, and a joint airborne task force headquarters, reduction in Royal Marine contingents and army support units, and the rundown of two commando ships.[45] All of these budgetary initiatives made it harder for Western security planners to envision a role for Britain in the event of security challenges in the Middle East/gulf region.

Following the Soviet invasion of Afghanistan, the recently elected (May 1979) government of Margaret Thatcher was among the most active supporters of the American argument that some new initiatives in the Middle East/Persian Gulf region were essential in order to shore up the West's remaining allies in the area and protect Western resource supplies. Britain nevertheless joined other NATO European governments in questioning Washington's contention that the Soviet invasion was a prelude to Russian military interventions in other parts of the Persian Gulf. British diplomats emphasized that the risks of Soviet forces occupying gulf locales were quite limited, when compared to threats of intraregional instability caused by ethnic and religious strife, or to the danger that a new round of Arab-Israeli military conflicts might spill over into the gulf area. Britain's comparatively smaller dependence on gulf oil supplies, due to its North Sea reserves, further tempered whatever inclination the Thatcher government may have had to support the U.S. view that Western security depended on the development of an expensive and potentially destabilizing anti-Soviet military presence in the gulf region.[46]

By the end of 1979, moreover, CENTO was no longer even in existence. NATO—if only by default—was considered by many defense experts as the one security forum within which the Western industrial powers could respond to developments in Southwest Asia in any meaningful way.

When President Carter announced plans for the creation of a Rapid Deployment Force in 1980, Britain expressed support in principle for the administration's idea of developing U.S. long-range interventionary forces, but London adopted its traditional argument that control arrangements for Middle East/gulf forces should be along national (rather than NATO) lines.[47] London thus developed plans for the use of the Spearhead (Parachute) Battalion, the 5th Airborne Brigade, and the 8th Field Battalion in the gulf, but did not envision the incorporation of these forces in America's Readiness Command (REDCOM), European Command (EUCOM), or any other unified U.S./NATO authority.[48]

One reason for the Thatcher government's desire to retain sovereign control over its interventionary forces was to avoid being caught between Washington and the European Communities at a time when EC members were developing their own positions regarding Middle East/gulf security problems—positions that were very different from Washington's. In fact, Britain ended up leaning more toward the EC than toward the United States in its diplomatic response to the Soviet invasion of Afghanistan. Responding to inquiries made during the House of Lords debate in late January 1980, Britain's foreign secretary, Lord Carrington, noted that Soviet motives for invading Afghanistan were "complex" and that the situation did not merit actively considering reestablishing a "substantial, permanent" U.K. military presence in Southwest Asia.[49] One month later, Carrington, while not directly criticizing the American approach to Southwest Asia, nevertheless told the Lords that the West needed to maintain lines of communication with the Soviet Union, continue arms control and other forms of diplomatic negotiations with Moscow, and, over the long term, construct a new system of détente "free from the illusions of the past and provid[ing] a firm framework for the management of [future] difficulties." He also asserted that most Third World nations were quite capable of objectively assessing the abysmal record of Soviet aid programs and the incompatibility of Moscow's policy ends with the Third World nonalignment movement without the insertion of a "crude East-West [strategic] rivalry into their concerns."[50] A NATO RDF was therefore viewed by the British government as an inappropriate response to an admittedly difficult and dangerous situation.[51]

From the time it took office, the Thatcher government demonstrated that its preferred instrument for increasing British influence in the Middle East and (in particular) the gulf region was through the cultivation of its arms trade with key regional actors such as Saudi Arabia and Kuwait—the two countries that supply Britain with 40 percent of its oil imports. By 1980, British arms sales and related military assistance to the region amounted to a half billion British pounds per year. While British levels of arms transfers to this region have been lower than those attributed to the Soviet Union, the United States, and France, British weapons such as the Chieftain and Scorpion tanks and the Nimrod and Rapier missile systems have often been as highly regarded as any comparable systems in Soviet and/or Western inventories. In 1985 and 1988, Britain sold Saudi Arabia the Tornado strike aircraft, as well as trainer aircraft and helicopters, in deals that totaled £15 billion.[52] The British technical support and training firm Airwork Services, moreover, has remained active in the Middle East since its creation in the 1960s. During the 1980s, it provided some three thousand specialists for personnel training at Middle Eastern installations; designed and operated services at Middle Eastern airfields; and provided complete logistical support systems, including radar equipment, computers, vehicle/specialist transport, and light missile systems. The Defense Sales Office

(DSO) and International Military Services (IMS) branches of the Defense Ministry have continued to specialize in the coordination of and liaison with such British defense-related activities in this region and throughout the Third World. Furthermore, as it entered the 1990s, Britain still retained a low-key but effective military advisory presence in Oman and other selected gulf states as a contribution to the continued stability of the region.

Britain has also demonstrated on occasion that it has the will and the capability to deploy naval forces to the region. The Soviet presence in Afghanistan contributed to Britain's decision in 1980 to preserve its force of two warships in the Indian Ocean. Limited British military activities in conjunction with American basing operations at Diego Garcia have continued.[53] Finally, throughout the 1980s and to the present time, the British Indian Ocean Trust (BIOT) bases (along with intermittent Persian Gulf warship deployments to Bahrain, Oman, and Eastern Mediterranean sites) have constituted an important element in the regional security equation.

Britain demonstrated the priority that it still accords to the Mediterranean in its global defense planning in September 1983 when it deployed the Royal Navy's three operational carriers, the *Invincible, Illustrious,* and *Hermes* (since retired), with a supporting task force (including five destroyer escorts) more powerful than that formed at the start of the Falklands crisis, to the Eastern Mediterranean.[54] More recently (1987), Britain was an active participant in the Persian Gulf armada—including British, American, French, Italian, and Dutch warships—designed to protect civilian shipping in the gulf and to encourage Iran and Iraq to accept a cease-fire to their eight-year-long war. After the outbreak of the Iran-Iraq War (1981–82), Britain's Indian Ocean task force was expanded to include a command helicopter cruiser, five frigates, one nuclear-powered attack submarine, four escorts, two oilers, and three replenishment ships. London has also escorted merchant vessels in the region with its Armilla naval patrol.[55]

In addition, Britain has attempted to complement its regional naval presence by improving the mobility of land and air force components earmarked for Middle East/Persian Gulf operations. In 1984, the 5th Infantry Brigade was regrouped into the 5th Airborne Brigade with an improved out-of-region force projection capability designed for future gulf contingencies. Its features include a stronger armored reconnaissance regiment, an artillery regiment, a light helicopter squadron, and increased airborne personnel carried by modified RAF Hercules transport with Viscount and Trident air refueling capacities.[56]

Taken together, these limited and unspectacular initiatives have added up to a relatively successful campaign to "get a quart out of a pint bottle" in the Middle East and Persian Gulf region. The relevance of such activities to the West's overall strategic interests was summarized by a London *Daily Telegraph* article appearing in early 1985:

The buzzword in Whitehall is "horizon-stretching" [even though] the deliberate adoption [by Britain] of a defense policy outside of Europe would complete a 180 degree turnaround over 15 years. . . . It is true we are not wanted as a sovereign power. But from Brunei via the Persian Gulf right round the Indian Ocean, with the conspicuous exception of the Indian Peninsula, British defense assistance has been almost unanimously in demand. . . . East of Suez is precisely where our naval minesweepers have been sent at the urgent request of the Egyptian Government. The Queen's Dragons have been active in Beirut. . . . British warships are patrolling the Persian Gulf at the request of the Gulf Cooperation Council . . . personnel from all three [British] services are active today in over 30 countries outside the NATO area. . . . All this political influence, with its concomitant exclusion of Communist cadres, constitutes a tiny fraction of our defense spending outside Europe, which totals only five percent of the national defense budget.[57]

Not even the most ardent Thatcher government supporter could argue that these activities have compensated for the gradual loss of Britain's basing networks in the Middle East/gulf region over the last four decades. But the Thatcher government has demonstrated a determination to preserve Britain's ability to exercise military options in the Middle East/gulf region as required.

CONCLUSION

It would appear that Britain's assessment of its interests in the Middle East and Persian Gulf region at the beginning of the 1990s is similar to the assessment of early postwar foreign policy and defense planners in several respects. Assured access to gulf oil is still viewed as the preeminent British security concern. Indigenous revolutionary and anti-Western movements are still viewed as the most likely source of regional tensions, but Soviet manipulation of regional instabilities is still considered to be a threat.

In spite of these policy continuities, however, the context within which British defense planners must think about Middle East and gulf contingencies has been irrevocably altered over the last four decades. In particular, the basing infrastructure in the region has essentially disappeared. This has permitted Britain *faute de mieux* to allocate a larger portion of its defense budget elsewhere: toward support of a seaborne, independent nuclear deterrent against the Soviet strategic threat and toward maintenance of land, naval, and air power directed against a Soviet conventional threat in Europe. The Thatcher government attempted to make some improvements in British forces to permit the U.K. to continue to respond to crises in the Middle East/Persian Gulf region in the postimperial era, while at the same time preserving its primary commitment to homeland defense and NATO force planning.

CHAPTER 11

BRITISH SECURITY POLICY
IN THE FAR EAST:
THE UNFINISHED RECESSIONAL

Dᴉsᴘᴜᴛᴇs between Britain and the United States in Asia during World War II gave little reason to expect that the two governments would be anything more than "allies of a kind" in the postwar period.[1] At the close of the war, the issue of Japan's occupation provided the first serious test of this expectation. Following the Allies' victory over Japan, the British desire for an influential role in the administration of that defeated country through the Allied Council for Japan (ACJ) was largely frustrated by General Douglas MacArthur, Supreme Allied Commander of Pacific Forces. The British Foreign Office counseled against an open challenge to MacArthur, however, on the grounds that Britain's interest in Japan (primarily to control Japan's reconstruction in ways that would preclude Tokyo from threatening British commercial activities in the Far East) was less important than its interest in ensuring U.S. political and military cooperation in Europe. In any event, British military manpower shortages forced the U.K. to withdraw its small Commonwealth contingent from southern Japan in October 1946, after a brief and unsuccessful effort to extend U.K. occupation in Kobe and Osaka.[2]

In 1949, a more serious policy dispute surfaced between Washington and London, which would have a much greater impact on each party's assessment of the other's reliability as an Asian ally. As previously mentioned, Ernest Bevin brought up the issue of an imminent Chinese Communist victory during his visit to Washington in April 1949 to sign the NATO Treaty. Bevin attempted to impress members of the U.S. Policy Planning Staff with the strategic value of Hong Kong in the face of an intensified Chinese Communist threat on the mainland. However, American security planners soon became aware that Britain was in fact seeking an accommodation with Mao Zedong in order to ensure the security of Britain's offshore possessions in the region. This pattern of behavior convinced many U.S. policy makers that Britain could not be relied upon to stand firm against Asian communism. Conversely, American opposition to diplomatic relations with a communist regime governing mainland China led many people in London to question America's ability to come to grips with reality.

The limited extent of Anglo-American cooperation during the Korean War did not encourage either side to abandon these suspicions. To be sure, British naval forces operating from the U.S. base at Sasebo, Japan, provided aircraft carriers and other naval units to support U.S. ground forces, and the British Commonwealth Force Korea (BCFK) ground troops fought alongside their American and South Korean counterparts with honor.[3] But the British army's 27th Brigade and selected British naval forces were dispatched to the Korean peninsula as much to influence U.S. combat decision making as to support the UN-sponsored intervention. London's concern about Russian military superiority in Europe, residual British hopes of achieving a *modus vivendi* with the new government in Beijing, and fears that fighting on the Korean peninsula could spill over into Hong Kong all accounted for the Labor government's efforts to restrain the scope of American military operations during the Korean War.

By the end of 1950, British diplomats were pressing for a negotiated solution to the Korean conflict and seeking to discourage Washington from escalating the conflict with the People's Republic of China (P.R.C.). As one internally circulated Foreign Office memo concluded: "Such [U.S. gestures of hostility toward China] can only have the effect of drifting China further into the Soviet camp, which is not in accordance with our common aim. Indeed, the whole policy of the U.S., insofar as a policy exists, can be expected to have this consequence."[4] London also feared that a full-scale confrontation with China could undermine Washington's defense commitments in Europe and contribute to a potentially fatal power vacuum in the North Atlantic.[5] Such reasoning formed the basis for what was to become the longstanding "China differential" dispute between London and Washington regarding economic and diplomatic policies toward the P.R.C.[6]

Although it contributed forces to the Korean War, Britain focused more of its attention and resources on NATO during the early 1950s. The Korean conflict provided Britain with an opportunity to substantially increase its status and influence within the NATO alliance by convincing Washington of the centrality of the British role in the Atlantic defense scheme. This strategy was in fact reasonably successful, since the United States did increase its public support for Britain within the NATO context immediately after the outbreak of the Korean War. Indeed, by the end of the year, Truman was referring to Britain as the "mainspring of Atlantic defense."[7]

In retrospect, Britain's concentration on Europe at a time of U.S. preoccupation with China, Taiwan, and Korea was probably the best course of action, since the general British approach to Asian politics and security during this period was bound to get London into trouble with Washington. Britain could not remain entirely isolated from events in Asia, of course, and Anglo-American policy disputes did erupt from time to time throughout the cold war. Five developments illustrate the limits of Anglo-American defense cooperation in Asia: (1) the American exclusion of Britain from ANZUS, owing to U.S. fears of entanglement with British colonial responsibilities in Southeast Asia; (2) British reluctance to back American military assistance efforts on behalf of France in a deteriorating Indochina situation throughout 1953–54; (3) the failure of the Southeast Asia Treaty Organization (SEATO) to provide a valid counterpart in the Asian-Pacific region to NATO's containment strategy; (4) Britain's difficulties in obtaining American help as Southeast Asian states moved toward independence and nonalignment; and (5) Britain's strategic retrenchment from East Asia at the same time that Washington was becoming trapped in its commitment to defend South Vietnam.

THE ANZUS EXCLUSION

While Britain opposed the United States' uncompromising hostility toward China's new communist government, it also independently undertook to resist Soviet—and/or Communist Chinese-supported insurgencies throughout the Malay Peninsula and adjacent territories. London reasoned that if peninsular Southeast Asia were controlled by forces hostile to the Commonwealth, Australia and New Zealand would be directly threatened and British access to Southeast Asia's natural resources and potentially lucrative markets would also be endangered.

It was generally agreed, however, that the key to any credible British containment effort on behalf of the Antipodes was active American participation. This opinion was certainly supported by Australia and New Zealand, neither of whom had much faith in the staying power of British military forces in the region after the defeat of the Royal Navy at Singapore in 1942. At the Commonwealth Foreign Ministers' conference in Colombo in January 1950, Australian foreign minister Percy Spender and his New Zealand counterpart, Frederick Doidge, nonetheless, for reasons of historical affinity and Commonwealth loyalty, began to explore the possibilities of an Asian containment framework involving both the United States and Britain.[8]

Early in the discussions, however, U.S. representatives communicated their opposition to a security treaty linkage with Britain in the Pacific region at that time, on the grounds that the United States was determined to avoid "the accusation of setting up a white NATO in the Pacific."[9] Borrowing a theme from the universalist/idealist faction in Washington, Dean Rusk, U.S. Assistant Secretary of State for Far Eastern Affairs, advised British ambassador Sir Oliver Franks that if the United States became involved in a Pacific pact with Britain, then France, the Netherlands, and Portugal would also want admittance. As a result, any such treaty would acquire "a colonial nature which would make it an anathema to Asian nations and destroy its realism as a genuine security arrangement among powers with primary Pacific interests."[10]

A more specific U.S. concern was that Britain was attempting to elevate its status and influence in Asia by joining a Pacific defense pact with Washington. This assessment was essentially correct. According to one British planning document, membership in a Pacific pact as an equal with the United States would make "any defense planning in the area . . . unrealistic without us."[11] From Washington's point of view, as well as from the perspective shared by Wellington and Canberra, Britain had done nothing in Asia in the postwar period to justify the kind of special status that it was accorded in NATO as a member of the NATO Standing Group (comprising Britain, France, and the United States).

The United States was also reluctant to permit Britain to join a Pacific pact because of the risk that it would lead to pressures for an Atlantic-Pacific security linkage (perhaps under the auspices of the Standing Group), which could in turn be used by the European colonial allies to draw the United States into risky Third World conflicts. The issue of an Atlantic-Pacific linkage had in fact come up in discussions in 1952 between U.S. secretary of state Dean Acheson and Australian prime minister Robert Menzies. According to a May 1952 State Department dispatch:

> The Secretary . . . stated we are open minded on the desirability of NATO work-ing out some method for dealing with countries outside the NATO area. The Australian belief that NATO engaged in global planning, however, is based on a fundamental misconception. NATO deals solely with the defense of Europe and we and Britain have always resisted developing NATO into a global planning instrumentality. Some smaller countries in NATO even opposed the idea of the same men constituting the NATO Standing Group wearing different hats who could give guidance to the Middle Eastern Command. It is no doubt a defect that there is no place now where international global planning is taking place. The Secretary said we were trying to meet the problem through regional [security] organizations—NATO, MEC, and the establishment of a Pacific Council [ANZUS].[12]

Acheson's inclusion of Britain in this statement, however, was misleading, to say the least; the secretary of state was certainly aware of ongoing efforts by influential British policy makers, including Prime Minister Winston Churchill, to structure precisely this type of arrangement, and he resisted such efforts from their inception. Months, later, at the first ANZUS council meeting, Acheson moved to "dispel any misconception as to the role of the NATO Standing Group [saying] it worked on problems of raising and supporting the forces under [Supreme Allied Commander, Europe] General Ridgway's command and was not [to be] involved in global planning."[13]

To the frustration of London, ANZUS was established in September 1951.

The treaty did not even acknowledge an informal British consultative status. In spite of a feeling of betrayal, London continued to press for membership in the new alliance, arguing the case for the benefits of an explicit NATO-ANZUS linkage—with Britain and the United States as the linchpins of the transregional security arrangement. Lord Ismay, NATO's first secretary general, joined Churchill in arguing that NATO and ANZUS, working independently, were inadequate for responding to Far Eastern security questions that could directly affect Europe in a future global conflict. In a speech before the North Atlantic Council delivered in February 1953, he advocated the need for closer NATO ties with the new Pacific alliance. [14] Churchill subsequently developed Ismay's arguments further, noting that Article 8 of the ANZUS accord allowed for its members to develop special relationships "between the Treaty machinery and other states." Churchill argued that the prospects for coordination between the two bodies (NATO and ANZUS) merited a "strong consideration within Britain and throughout the West." [15]

The Americans, having already expanded their original defense perimeter in the Asian-Pacific region to include the Korean peninsula, and preoccupied with the problem of restraining a difficult ally on Taiwan, were interested in avoiding any more ambitious multilateral security commitments in Asia for the time being. In the case of ANZUS, Washington made it clear that its commitment was limited in both geographic scope and the nature of military responsibilities that the treaty imposed on the signatories. Indeed, certain British policy analysts subsequently tended to argue that ANZUS was effectively meaningless as a collective defense treaty because it did not explicitly commit the United States to military action on behalf of Australia or New Zealand in the event of aggression. [16] The British Commonwealth Office countered, however, that both Canberra and Wellington were actually "quite satisfied" with ANZUS's operational language, and it speculated that critics of the pact might merely be articulating a general British frustration that was due to London's exclusion from the pact. [17]

VIETNAM AND THE ORIGINS OF SEATO

By the end of 1953, the political environment in the Asian-Pacific region reflected tension between a declining British Commonwealth system and a more dynamic U.S.-sponsored system, which included not only ANZUS but a network of bilateral allies and bases stretching across the Pacific. Events leading to SEATO's creation were conditioned by this tension and by the test case of Dien Bien Phu.

The intensity of U.S. feelings soon became apparent to British leaders. In a letter written March 18, 1954, British Embassy personnel in Washington warned Eden that the deepening Indochina crisis had "top priority" with the Americans and that, if the French worked out an accommodation with the Vietnamese communist insurgents independent of U.S. approval, the consequences could be "far reaching" and might even have a serious impact on NATO's continued viability.[18]

During two emergency meetings held on April 25 in London during NATO planning sessions, Dulles asked Eden to provide Royal Air Force contingents for selected air strikes against the Vietminh, in order to help end the siege of Dien Bien Phu. Dulles also speculated on the possible introduction of British ground troops from Malaysia to bail out General Navarre's all-but-defeated French troops. The American secretary of state had introduced this formula for united action in a speech delivered March 29: "any American military intervention taking place in Indochina would need the approval and military backing of Britain and other allies" (i.e., Australia and New Zealand). The "united action" requirement was, in fact, a ploy by Eisenhower and Dulles, designed to head off an attempt by U.S. military officials (such as the chairman of the Joint Chiefs of Staff or Admiral Arthur Radford) and selected Republican senators to create a political atmosphere in which the United States would have no recourse but to intervene on its own. Dulles nevertheless claimed to be "infuriated" with Eden for prompting "total French capitulation" to communist forces and endangering all of Southeast Asia in the process.[19]

As Washington expected, Eden rejected Dulles' requests at the April 25 meetings, proffering instead the same "adjustment to reality" argument that Bevin had presented to the Policy Planning Staff in 1949 in the case of China— that a communist victory was by then all but inevitable. Eden maintained that neither a U.S. airstrike nor the intervention of U.S. and British ground forces would guarantee military success in Indochina and that any such action would turn "world opinion" against the West. Radford, who was also present at the meetings, countered that an Indochina debacle could encourage the P.R.C. to support new communist insurgent movements throughout all of Southeast Asia, and he urged that "vigorous military action" against the Chinese mainland be undertaken without concern about a Soviet response on the P.R.C.'s behalf. Eden replied, however, that Churchill's government wanted to avoid a "major war" over the Indochina issue and that the British rated "very much more highly the risks of such a course of military action."[20]

U.S. policy makers assumed—as they had done in 1949—that Britain's opposition to a vigorous allied response to the communist threat was determined by its concern for the vulnerability of its remaining territories in Asia, especially Malaya and Hong Kong. British leaders, conversely, felt that their U.S. counterparts were setting the stage for a major war in the Far East.[21] London feared that even if the United States could successfully pursue such a war, it would result either in U.S. domination of British allies and bases in the region or, worse, in communist retaliation against Britain's friends and British facilities in the region, as targets of convenience. London consequently maintained its opposition to a joint U.S./U.K. operation to save the French forces at Dien Bien Phu.

Although Eisenhower was willing to let the French position collapse in Indochina, he and his advisers were concerned about the impact that such a development would have on regional stability. Thus, a month before Dien Bien Phu's downfall, the United States sought to encourage British support for a stronger defense position in Asia and "to rouse the French from their defeatism" (Dulles' phrase) by expressing a greater interest in the creation of a new regional defense pact that would include the United States, the United Kingdom, and France. Indeed, "Dulles pursued this line even more vigorously following the Geneva conference with the idea of a permanent regional grouping along NATO lines to compensate for what the Eisenhower Administration's domestic critics labeled yet another humiliating loss to Asian Communism."[22]

Preliminary NATO foreign ministerial discussions held in Paris during late April 1954 provided a natural setting for the British to discuss with their American counterparts the formation of a Southeast Asia Treaty Organization (SEATO). Churchill tried to link British cooperation in SEATO with a U.S. quid pro quo to underwrite British interests in the Middle East and, in particular, Egypt, so as to avoid a loss of British influence in that region. The prime minister also speculated that if the Americans could help Britain to obtain an acceptable settlement of the Suez basing issue, London could transfer more troops to Malaya from the Canal Zone to back up future U.S. military operations in Southeast Asia.[23]

But American military planners involved with organizing SEATO were not interested in offering London very much in return for its membership in the alliance. Although they were attracted in principle to the idea of greater Anglo-American defense cooperation in Asia by this time, they also recognized that London would attempt to manipulate any new multilateral defense arrangement in Asia to advance its own narrow security interests there. British willingness to take military action in defense of what Washington saw as "common security interests" had already been tried, and found wanting, in the cases of China and Vietnam. Furthermore, the U.S. ambassador to Britain reported that the British Chiefs of Staff "did not relate the implications of the situation in Indochina to the future of EDC and the effects on NATO [and] their approach seems to be strictly in terms of local U.K. interest without regard to other areas of the Far East such as Japan."[24] American policy planners were nonetheless in agreement by this time that British exclusion from ANZUS had been counterproductive and that the creation of a more comprehensive Asian defense organization was probably in everyone's interest.[25]

THE CREATION AND TESTING OF SEATO

SEATO was formed in September 1954. The United States, the United Kingdom, France, Thailand, the Philippines, Pakistan, Australia, and New Zealand were formal members, and the noncommunist Indochinese governments were designated as associates. In spite of the fact that Churchill did not obtain the assurances of U.S. support in the Middle East that he sought, he was relatively satisfied with the SEATO arrangement, since (in the words of Dulles) the new Southeast Asian Pact gave him "the enlarged ANZUS that he had always sought."[26] Ironically, SEATO was sold to a skeptical Parliament by Eden (who knew better), not as an enlarged ANZUS, but as an Asian equivalent of NATO.[27] In private discussions with U.S. representatives, however, Eden painted a very different picture.

> Mr. Eden said that the situation in Europe when NATO was formed and the present situation in Southeast Asia were vastly different. In NATO, we had drawn the line around the NATO area before aggression had occurred. In Southeast Asia, the communists were already actively engaged in hostilities in Indochina and to draw a line at the China-Indochina border was not the same since indirect aggression has already taken place.[28]

Eden also made it clear to U.S. policy makers that in view of Britain's situation of depleted global power, it would be difficult for London to contribute ground forces or other scarce military resources to any future SEATO operations. In fact, none of SEATO's Western members—including Washington—were interested in contributing standing armies for the new organization. Consequently, the organization was never constituted as a NATO-style defense pact with its own forces-in-being and its own military command structures. Rather, it was viewed as an institutional framework for ad hoc consultations as crisis situations arose within the Southeast Asian theater of operations.

This very conditional security relationship left all parties free to become involved in, or stay out of, subsequent Asian crises affecting any of the signatories. Thus, when the United States attempted to use SEATO in April 1961 to solicit French and British backing to prevent the Pathet Lao from capturing the key Laotian cities of Vientiane and Luang Prabang, both London and Paris refused to become involved out of concern that the Laos situation could quickly evolve into another Korea.[29]

Britain, much to Washington's consternation, demonstrated its continued willingness to take unilateral actions in Asia which could eventually involve U.S. military action as well in December 1962, when London intervened against a rebellion in Brunei. As had been the case in Kuwait the previous year, British military forces moved in quickly and efficiently, and order was restored in a matter of a few days. But as in Kuwait, London's justifiable satisfaction with the operational aspects of the intervention was overshadowed by the fact that British forces had to be withdrawn from a number of places, including the BAOR assigned to NATO, in order to cope with even this brushfire incident. As Phillip Darby has noted, "In some sections of Parliament and the press, this was taken to demonstrate what many defense commentators had long been saying, namely, that an Army of 175,000 was seriously overstretched supporting existing commitments and that one unexpected crisis could bring down the whole system."[30]

Less than a year later, however, Britain found itself even more severely challenged when the newly independent nation of Malaysia solicited British protection in the face of military threats from Indonesia. Britain recognized that there was little prospect of Washington's actively contributing to Malaysia's security, for four reasons:

1. Washington viewed Malaysian leader Tunku Abdul Rahman's attempts during the early 1960s to consolidate Malaysian control over all of the territories along the peninsula as an unjustified disruption of regional political arrangements.
2. The United States was anxious to stay on good terms with Indonesia's president Sukarno to ensure U.S. oil companies of access to Indochinese reserves—perhaps at the expense of the British company (Shell) that had been doing business in Indonesia.
3. The Kennedy and Johnson administrations were more sensitive to the demands of the Third World nonaligned states that supported Sukarno's claims during the *Konfrontasi* (confrontation, or state of undeclared war).
4. Some territories claimed by the Philippines were contested by Malaysia (most notably, Sabah), and the United States was not about to provide aid to a country that was viewed as a threat by one of Washington's most important regional allies.

In view of these considerations, Washington would not permit London to use SEATO to enlist U.S. support for the government in Malaysia. In any event, the Tunku had demonstrated his own preference for keeping SEATO out of Malaysia by making it a condition of accepting the deployment of Britain's 28th Commonwealth Infantry Brigade at Malacca (in August 1960) that these forces would have to leave Malaysia if they were ever used for SEATO operations.[31]

The *Konfrontasi* operation was, by all unbiased accounts, an extremely impressive British holding operation. It required the coordinated efforts of all three British services, as well as cooperation among the British, Australian, New Zealand, and Malaysian navies. Most of the fighting took place in some of the densest jungle in the world, along the thousand-mile frontier between Malaysia and Indonesia. In spite of problems of terrain, weather, and indigenous support for the insurgents, British forces contained the Indonesian incursion for three years. Indeed, the success achieved by the British troops in Malaysia had a seductive, reassuring effect on U.S. defense experts who were beginning to become involved in the management of their own Asian land war nearby.[32]

The *Konfrontasi* campaign was nonetheless an enormous drain on British resources and (in spite of its success) on British resolve to hang on in Asia. It occupied between sixty thousand and seventy thousand troops—plus artillery and armor units, the aircraft carrier *Victorious,* the strike carrier *Centaur,* and the amphibious carrier *Bulwark,* as well as submarines, destroyers, frigates, four Vulcan bombers, and a variety of other aircraft.[33] Phillip Darby also notes that Britain had to remove "an essential signals component" from the BAOR for service during the *Konfrontasi.*[34] In spite of the extensive commitment of forces, the conflict was ultimately resolved by 1966, not by a British victory, but by Indonesia's growing preoccupation with its own domestic political and insurgency problems.

BRITAIN'S ASIAN RETRENCHMENT AND THE U.S. RESPONSE

The *Konfrontasi* proved to be the last major test of the British government's ability to hold "the whole system" together in the face of a major military commitment abroad. In the aftermath, London seemed to have good reason to reconsider the advantages it had obtained from its continued affiliation with SEATO and its overall military activities in the Far East. The *Konfrontasi's* drain on British military resources, combined with the perpetual financial crisis that plagued the nation, prompted London to declare its formal withdrawal from the area east of the Suez in January 1968. As early as February of the previous year, the Labor government had stated that it was "our aim that Britain should not again have to undertake operations on this scale [the *Konfrontasi*] outside of Europe."[35]

Ironically, however, the United States had by this time reversed its traditional posture, having become more inclined to encourage a continued British security presence in Asia. Washington recognized all too clearly (and all too late) that American military power alone could no longer guarantee the viability of its extra-European containment strategy. As pointed out in Chapter 5, this fact was especially appreciated by Secretary of Defense MacNamara, who was determined to see Britain retain some type of military presence east of the Suez.

By mid-1965, the United States was seeking ways to discourage London from abandoning its Asian and Persian Gulf facilities in view of America's own situation of overextension. In his memoirs, Harold Wilson recounts his first "get acquainted" meeting with President Lyndon Johnson in December 1964. One point that struck Wilson was that Johnson seemed to be unfamiliar with the extent of Britain's Far Eastern commitments.[36] In subsequent discussions with the president, however, the British prime minister underscored his government's determination to cut back the costs of British military commitments in Asia and to reduce the overall British defense budget by over a half million pounds, primarily through east-of-Suez force reductions. Although later denied by Wilson, Johnson is reported to have considered offering to offset the costs of British military activities beyond NATO by employment of a "Hessian concept." According to this plan, the United States would have provided trade and financial incentives to Britain, in order to relieve Britain's persistent sterling crisis, in exchange for a continued British presence east of the Suez.[37] In July of 1965, Johnson also sent Wilson a "very urgent and personal message" regarding Vietnam. According to Wilson, the president stated that "he knew . . . how stretched our [U.K.] forces were, and the heavy commitment we were bearing in NATO. But could we not send even a token force? A platoon of bagpipers would be sufficient; it was the British flag that was wanted."[38]

Wilson had no intention of complying with Johnson's request. He was nonetheless concerned that unless Britain could exercise some restraining influence on Washington, the United States might escalate the conflict in Indochina to the point where it would spill over into Britain's territories in Asia, or even trigger a global war. Such fears had been exacerbated by MacNamara's reported statement at NATO headquarters in late 1965 about the "near certainty of war with China" as an outgrowth of the Vietnam struggle.[39] Not surprisingly, Wilson's attempt to retain some influence over U.S. policy in Asia while refusing to send troops in support of its ally proved to be unsuccessful.[40]

Wilson also discovered that his plans to retreat from Asia were hard to achieve. The ongoing *Konfrontasi* made it impossible for Britain to pull back until mid-1966, and the Labor government was unwilling to abandon other Asian outposts such as Singapore until it was confident of their security. Furthermore, Wilson contended that, as far as Asia was concerned, London had a responsibility to prevent a situation where, by "contracting out" of the region, the U.K. left "the Americans and Chinese eyeball to eyeball. . . . it is the surest prescription for a nuclear holocaust I could think of."[41]

It was nonetheless increasingly obvious to all observers that Britain could not cope with any new crises in Asia without cutting into its NATO commitment. The *Konfrontasi* and the brushfire intervention in Brunei had made this clear. Under these circumstances, some influential politicians, including Labor's defense spokesman, Denis Healey, chose to address the issue directly. Healey argued in January of 1964 that "the immediate need for British forces is obviously greater overseas than in Western Europe" and hinted that he would support a redeployment of portions of the BAOR to Asia.[42] The Wilson government was able to avoid this painful decision, however, in part by redefining the purposes of British power overseas. In the words of Alastair Buchan, Wilson sought to justify Britain's continued presence in Asia during this period as "a sort of an 007—a special agent of the United Nations to mediate between countries."[43]

During the 1970s, the Far East became a less prominent factor in U.S./U.K. discussions and in intra-NATO deliberations, as events in the Middle East and the Persian Gulf (with their threatening implications for Western energy supplies) tended to take priority. Successive British Defense White Papers contended that the United Kingdom Mobile Force was still a reliable interventionary instrument for use on NATO's flanks and beyond. In fact, however, British contingents in the Third World in general, and in the Far East specifically, were increasingly incapable of engaging even in brushfire conflicts. Unfortunately, from the point of view of U.K. security planners, "the likely scale of possible conflicts [had] grown" since the mid-1960s, although "the ability to back up a small force [had] shrunk."[44]

Specific British military reductions in the Far East continued as the 1970s drew to a close. British manpower levels in Hong Kong were reduced from four army battalions and various support units in 1966 to a single battalion and the Gurkha Brigade by 1978—some seven thousand men withdrawn from Britain's three services. Whitehall recognized that such a force "obviously could not stem a Chinese invasion and no one pretends they are there for that purpose." Rather, London tended to envision these forces as an internal police force for the Crown Colony.[45] Another Gurkha Brigade remained on station in Brunei, but its long-term status was at best uncertain, and the British force commitments to the Five Power Defense Arrangements (Australia, Britain, Malaysia, New Zealand, and Singapore) had, for all intents and purposes, been terminated.[46]

In view of the skeletal British force presence in Asia by the end of the 1970s, one could be fairly skeptical of the 1981 Conservative government's Defense White Paper's assertion that it was once more "necessary for the NATO members to look to Western security concerns over a wider field than ever before . . . [and] . . . Britain's own needs, outlook, and interests give her a special role and special duty of this kind."[47]

CURRENT POLICIES

Important questions remain unanswered at the beginning of the 1990s: What precise British security interests remain throughout the Asian-Pacific region? How can they be protected? How do they relate to the U.K.'s role in NATO?

The 1987 Defense White Paper explained London's out-of-area policy in terms of honoring "residual obligations" (defending thirteen dependent territories, including Hong Kong, as well as retaining responsibility for Brunei's security), protecting British citizens abroad, and "helping to maintain stability and ensure the free use of the seas."[48] The U.K. also conducts a fairly extensive arms sales relationship with various Asian countries as a means of preserving its influence in the region.[49] For example, during the late 1980s Britain regained its traditional role as Malaysia's principal arms supplier, with sales of Tornado aircraft, Oberon class submarines, helicopters, air defense missiles, and other items.[50]

Unquestionably, the 1987 White Paper's third stated objective—ensuring Britain's continued economic and strategic access to the Third World by protecting sea lanes—is the most important British goal for the Asian-Pacific theater. For the foreseeable future, this objective can only be achieved if Britain is prepared to sustain a visible (if minimal, by early postwar standards) naval and supporting air presence in the region. To this end, the U.K. conducts a major naval deployment exercise every two or three years to the Far East, North Pacific, Australian, and Indian Ocean areas. The 1986 exercise, Global 86, for example, involved a Royal Navy Task Group headed by the navy's small aircraft carrier, the HMS *Illustrious,* and supported by a Type 42 destroyer, Type 21 and Type 22 frigates, and auxiliary forces. During its eight-month sojourn, the task force participated in the Rim of the Pacific (RIMPAC) maneuvers with the U.S., Canadian, Japanese, and Australian navies (Britain replaced New Zealand, which was excluded in the aftermath of its nuclear-free zone dispute with Washington) and visited South Korea, Brunei, Singapore, various Australian ports, and Pearl Harbor. It even passed through the Suez Canal and the Straits of Gibraltar before returning to its home port. It is interesting that the British Defense Ministry represented the official mission of Global 86 as "demonstrating an effective British presence in the areas to be visited and to achieve operational readiness for the British fleet relative to NATO's out-of-region concerns."[51] London followed this action by participating in September 1988 in the first major maritime air defense exercise conducted by the FPDA (Five Power Defense Arrangements). The U.K. provided the largest contingent and participated more seriously in the FPDA's Integrated Air Defense System (IADS) than it had during the past fifteen years. Four British Tornados were dispatched from the U.K., and a naval task force, headed by the aircraft carrier HMS *Ark Royal* and carrying fifteen hundred British commandos, was incorporated into the IADS. The extensive British participation in these four days of maneuvers was clearly designed to reassure Malaysia, Singapore, and the other ASEAN governments that FPDA remained viable despite New Zealand's decision to withdraw its 740-man defense force from Singapore and Australia's decision to rotate jet aircraft into Malaysia's Butterworth Air Base instead of maintaining its previously permanent deployments there.[52]

CONCLUSION

Showing the flag in the Pacific at regular intervals continues to be within Britain's financial and military means. But as British defense analyst (and former Minister of State for Foreign Affairs) Lord Chalfont has noted, situations could arise in the Far East as well as in other Third World areas where a British government would feel compelled to defend legitimate interests. Lord Chalfont admits that "it would . . . be unwise to overestimate Britain's future capacity in the face of domestic economic and political pressures . . . for engaging in large-scale independent crisis management" outside the context of NATO.[53] If, for example, a future *Konfrontasi* challenges London's paper commitments to FPDA, or if the United States were to call upon British support to safeguard Asian-Pacific sea lanes in the aftermath of a communist takeover in the Philippines, the U.K. would find it extremely difficult to reconcile its

European defense commitment with its residual obligations in Asia.

Throughout the postwar period, the British have found they have had few common interests with their major NATO allies in the Far East. They nonetheless adopted an approach in this theater similar to that developed for the Middle East, which was based upon the assumption that London's experience in dealing with regional elites and projecting a military presence should guarantee the U.K. influence over Western decisions affecting the region's future. America's resistance to such a British role has been determined less by its concern for Asian nationalism (it was Britain, not the United States, that recognized the legitimate nationalist aspirations of Asia's modern communist movements) than by its suspicions about British support for Washington's global containment strategy. Failure to forge a common definition of threat is the primary reason that postwar Anglo-American security coordination in the Far East has been marked by frustration.

CHAPTER 12

BRITISH DEFENSE POLICIES
IN THE CARIBBEAN AND
LATIN AMERICA

IN CONTRAST to the Middle East/Persian Gulf and Asian regions, the Caribbean and South Atlantic area contiguous to Latin America held few major postwar interests for Britain. Consequently, London was generally predisposed to defer to Washington in this area of the world. Britain also considered ways to relinquish the few security responsibilities it did have in the region, in order to focus its energies in other, higher priority locales. A representative policy review was made by the British Secretary of State for Foreign Affairs in a top secret memo dated June 18, 1952:

> A very minor commitment which we could endeavour to dispose of to the United States is the Falkland Island dependencies. I do not, however, advise such action, for public admission of our inability to maintain these territorial possessions would cause a loss of prestige wholly out of proportion to the saving in money obtained. It might precipitate a scramble to various parts of British territory.[1]

PRECEDENTS

The policy of deferring to Washington on security issues in the Western Hemisphere was clearly illustrated by Britain's actions during the 1954 Guatemala intervention. London supported Washington in the United Nations Security Council when the United States backed a so-called liberation army in its action against the Arbenz government in June. Anthony Eden justified his public support for the U.S. intervention on the grounds that "the first priority must be given to the solidity of the Anglo-American alliance," even while he privately complained about America's naval blockade against Guatemala because it threatened British maritime transit rights.[2] London's willingness to support U.S. policy in this case was also due to the fact that Guatemala had made claims

151

upon neighboring British Honduras (which became the independent state of Belize in September 1981). In addition, London decided to support U.S. policy in Guatemala to temper, at least partly, the frustration felt by the Eisenhower administration over Britain's unwillingness to make a more positive contribution to the creation of an EDC in Europe.

The Cuban missile crisis was also a model of Anglo-American policy coordination, in spite of numerous arguments to the contrary. According to some 1960s histories of the missile crisis, London was badly treated by its superpower ally during the crisis itself. For example, Richard Rosecrance describes the British government as "angry at not having been consulted" during the crisis, and John Mander saw the missile crisis as the ultimate proof of the fictional nature of the "special relationship."[3] On the contrary, however, the Kennedy administration clearly treated London as *primus inter pares* in its consultative procedures during the crisis. Macmillan was personally notified by JFK one day before the other NATO heads of state, and the opinions of David Ormsby-Gore, Britain's ambassador to the United States, were accorded special attention by the members of Kennedy's Executive Committee (EX-COMM) and, in particular, by Kennedy himself during the crisis. Macmillan contends in his *Memoirs* that "we were 'in on' and took full part in . . . every American move . . . during the crisis." He also notes—in a statement that is emblematic of Geoffrey Warner's concept of Britain playing "prefect" to America's "headmaster" within NATO—that "our complete calm helped to keep the Europeans calm . . . during the crisis."[4]

On other occasions, however, Britain has demonstrated its willingness to act independently of its principal NATO ally on issues relating to Cuba and the Caribbean basin. For example, London attempted to pursue an independent foreign policy following Castro's takeover in Cuba. This was due at least in part to British concern for protecting financial holdings on the island and for preserving lucrative trading arrangements. Thus, Britain attempted to justify to Washington its plan to sell seventeen Hawker jet fighters to Castro's government on the grounds that these aircraft were merely replacements for the older model Sea Furies, which Britain had supplied to the prerevolutionary regime of Fulgencio Batista. Protestations to the contrary notwithstanding, it is clear that London's subsequent decision to drop the Hawker sale was largely due to U.S. pressure.[5] Macmillan notes in his memoirs, further, that Britain continued to reject Eisenhower's requests for coordinated "economic pressure" against Castro. In a reiteration of the arguments that Britain had used in the early 1950s to justify its rejection of American requests for an embargo against Communist China, Macmillan "expressed doubts as to whether economic hardship would encourage opposition to Castro, especially if it could be blamed on the Americans and mitigated by Russian help."[6] More recently (January 1982), when the Thatcher government's foreign minister, Lord Carrington, was asked how Britain would respond to an American request for NATO support of a hypothetical U.S. blockade against Cuba during some future crisis, he replied that while Europeans recognized U.S. special interests in that region of the world, the Americans should also recognize European special trading interests there and elsewhere.[7]

Britain has also been reluctant to back U.S. anti-Cuban initiatives when such actions have been openly opposed by the "Mini-Commonwealth" actors in the region—the English-speaking Eastern Caribbean islands of St. Kitts, Nevis, Anguilla, Barbados, Dominica, Grenada, Jamaica, Montserrat, St. Lucia, St. Vincent, Trinidad and Tobago, and Belize, most of which constitute the Organization of East Caribbean States's (OECS) membership. Britain's sense of special responsibility for the "mini-Commonwealth" actors in the region has been tested on several occasions. In March 1969, for example, the Wilson government dispatched British troops to Anguilla in response to threats of secession from the newly formed associated territory of St. Kitts by Anguillan separatists. Britain subsequently dispatched 130 paratroopers and 40 London policemen to intervene against separatist leader Ronald Webster and what the British Foreign Office termed as "the disreputable elements" around him, including an American who was suspected of representing Mafia interests planning to establish gambling on the island. But Wilson himself was to admit later that Operation Sheepskin had a "musical-comedy atmosphere."[8]

During the 1970s, Britain undertook more extensive operations to defend what was then British Honduras against periodic attacks by Guatemala. Until the late 1970s, the United States was reluctant to come out strongly in support of British policy in British Honduras, not only because of its traditional concern about becoming too closely identified with British colonialism in Third World areas, but also in the interest of keeping Guatemala's military government in the U.S. ideological camp. In 1979, however, British Honduras obtained independence from London as the new state of Belize. The Reagan administration began to adjust U.S. policy in favor of the newly independent nation in 1984: The United States reportedly extended over $500,000 worth of military equipment to the fledgling Belize Defense Force (BDF) in that year, and by 1986, the total U.S. assistance program had mushroomed to over $5 million.[9]

In return for increased U.S. military assistance to Belize, the British have accepted responsibility for assuring that U.S.-supplied weapons and equipment are not funneled through Belize to Central American insurgency groups. London also continues to maintain its own military presence in Belize with around sixteen hundred British troops, four Harrier jump jets, and Puma and Gazelle helicopter units, along with the artillery and reconnaissance support that has remained in the country since its independence. The annual cost to the British Treasury of this presence is approximately 30 million pounds. For its part, the United States maintains a small military contingent in Belize (about 120 troops) in support of its military aid program. Washington views its own policy, as well as the continued British military presence in Belize, as a deterrent to left-wing

Guatemalan insurgents who operate along the Guatemalan-Belizean border.[10] It has nonetheless been reported that British officers garrisoned in Belize have expressed concern that "the continued presence of U.S. troops could drag Belize into a future Central American conflict."[11]

GRENADA

Anglo-American relations in the Caribbean were severely tested by the U.S. military invasion of Grenada in late October 1983. That island state had been ruled by the pro-Marxist, anti-American New Jewel Movement, headed by Maurice Bishop. Within a year of taking power in March 1979, it had invited Cuban military advisers into Grenada and had begun to develop logistical support facilities for Soviet arms shipments to the region.

Bishop's assassination in 1983 only seemed to make the situation more dangerous from Washington's perspective, since he was replaced by an even more pro-Cuban and anti-American individual, General Hudson Austin. Washington feared for the safety of U.S. citizens on the island at the time of the crisis, and most of the OECS states encouraged the United States to intervene to restore order. While the British High Commissioner in Barbados (Mr. Davis Montgomery) was not invited to take part in crisis deliberations between East Caribbean leaders, he was informed both of initial plans to form a multinational invasion force on October 22 and of later Caribbean Community (CARICOM) decisions to avoid military options and instead to pursue economic sanctions against Grenada.

As mentioned in the introduction to this book, differences between the United States and Britain over Grenada represented a special form of *domaine réservé* situation, since both governments claimed special responsibility for the security of that island-state. From Washington's perspective, Grenada was a test of the continued relevance of the Monroe Doctrine. From London's point of view, Grenada was a Commonwealth affair. The Reagan administration assured British diplomatic personnel in Washington in the days just prior to the invasion that the United States would respond "cautiously" to the Grenada crisis. Consequently, when the American invasion did occur, the British government was shocked by the United States' lack of consultation. The Labor party's shadow foreign minister, Denis Healey, went so far as to denounce the American action as "an unpardonable humiliation of an ally."[12]

The House of Commons Foreign Affairs Committee further concluded in the months following the invasion that Britain's sensitivity to threats against the independence of another Commonwealth nation was well known in Washington. The committee asserted that "the evident lack of consultation" between the United States and its allies in the days preceding the intervention of Grenada "must . . . be a cause of concern to all members of the North Atlantic Alliance and has inevitably worrying implications for United Kingdom-United States and wider NATO-United States relations on other matters in the future."[13] The report also concluded that British policy toward the Caribbean region since 1979 had become too subordinate to American policy in the area.[14]

Most of the British media and public were even more critical of the U.S. intervention. As Malcolm Rutherford observed at the time, "To be overruled by your own best friend, in an area which you are supposed to know most about, must be a pretty stunning experience. . . . Mrs. Thatcher and Sir Geoffrey Howe [U.K. foreign secretary] probably came closer this week than ever before to realizing the limits of British power and influence and the fundamental flaw in the special relationship: it is not a relationship of equals."[15] Labor's Denis Healey reflected the sentiment of many of his countrymen when he argued that "the lack of candor shown by the American President amounted to deceit of a favorite ally."[16]

The tendency to see the U.S. action as a personal slap at Mrs. Thatcher was widespread throughout the U.K. Several factors nonetheless encouraged the prime minister to exercise restraint in response to U.S. actions in Grenada. First, the issues surrounding the intervention were extremely complex, and, as a result, somewhat blurred. This permitted both sides to downplay the conflict between American and British claims of responsibility. Second, the prime minister understood that Grenada was simply too small an issue to justify a major disruption of American-British relations or the close personal relationship that she had developed with Ronald Reagan.[17]

Nor did London wish to derail Washington's growing program of military training of and cooperation with the OECS states—a fiscal burden sustained by Britain alone until the early 1980s. Prior to 1979, the United States had provided no military assistance to the Eastern Caribbean region. By 1980, Washington was providing a small amount ($4 million) to selected governments in the area. After October 1982, however, when OECS-affiliated Antigua, Dominica, and St. Vincent signed a memorandum of understanding with Barbados to work toward the establishment of an East Caribbean Regional Security System (RSS), the Reagan administration began substantially to increase its military assistance to the region. By 1985, the Eastern Caribbean region was receiving $57.3 million under the United States Economic Support Fund.[18] One important determinant of the Reagan administration's decision to increase aid to the Caribbean was its concern about the security of Caribbean sea lanes of communication (SLOC), which would be essential in any American resupply of NATO Europe in the event of an East-West conflict. In this regard, Mrs. Thatcher showed every interest in supporting the American effort.[19]

THE FALKLANDS

The increasingly important U.S. defense assistance factor made it easier for the British government to look the other way when the United States intervened in

Grenada. But the most important consideration that encouraged Mrs. Thatcher to restrain her criticism of the United States over Grenada was the large store of good will that the Reagan administration could still draw upon in London as a result of Washington's invaluable assistance to London during the Falklands crisis. In the Falklands case, a NATO ally successfully solicited the support of the United States despite the specter of European colonialism. It is illustrative of how much things had changed since the 1950s that the United States was no longer preoccupied with the risks of guilt by association with such events. Indeed, since the mid-1960s it had been Washington that had become the target of allied criticism for unilateral extraregional activities. Thus, Americans had become more sympathetic to the kinds of problems that Great Britain faced in the Falklands.

The other European NATO allies (except Spain) extended qualified support for Britain's efforts to protect its *domaine réservé* in the South Atlantic, owing to the general sense that the Argentines had violated international law by seizing the islands. NATO officials, however, viewed the crisis in a burden-sharing context as well, questioning how the diversion of British naval resources to the South Atlantic would affect NATO's overall force readiness.

The crisis was triggered by the Argentine invasion of the Falkland Islands in April of 1982. To the great surprise of the Galtieri regime in Buenos Aires, Britain demonstrated that it was still willing and able to intervene militarily. The Thatcher government consistently emphasized that the Falklands action was a unilateral British initiative, but it could not avoid the fact that the intervention had repercussions for overall NATO preparedness. Under these circumstances, Thatcher treated the Falklands war as a NATO-related issue in a speech to the North Atlantic Assembly in November 1982:

> The attack on *British* territory was outside the area defined by the North Atlantic Treaty. The responsibility to act was ours and ours alone. The fortunes of the Alliance are affected by the developments outside the Treaty area. Although the Alliance *cannot act collectively* outside the area, each of us must discharge his *separate* responsibilities. In doing so, each strengthens all . . . for if the NATO area is bounded by a line, the Atlantic is not. If we had not acted to repel aggression outside the area, the Alliance's resolve *to act within it* might well have been questioned.[20]

When the Royal Navy ventured forth to the Falklands in April 1982, undertaking its most ambitious extra-European military operation since Suez, the resultant naval power vacuum in the Atlantic left primarily U.S. vessels to defend the Eastern Atlantic and English Channel approaches. With Britain having withdrawn two of its Swiftsure nuclear submarines and two-thirds of its total surface fleet from NATO positions, moreover, the alliance's own flanks and Western European sea lane approaches became suddenly more vulnerable. U.S. contingents were not well suited for conducting a NATO maritime defense in the Eastern Atlantic inasmuch as they lacked the experience and defense in depth of their departed British maritime counterparts. With Britain's reallocation of maritime power to the South Atlantic (as the *Economist* observed in retrospect), "the Falklands were not just irrelevant to NATO but a distraction from it."[21] Such was the case even though reports were disseminated from NATO headquarters that Britain's alliance partners welcomed the additional training opportunities that their forces enjoyed in the North Atlantic patrols in the wake of the Royal Navy's departure.

Several studies have pointed out that if Buenos Aires had waited just two months to invade, the British position would have been untenable, because large elements of the Royal Navy, including the carrier *Invincible*, were slated to be dispatched to the Indian Ocean, and any force deployed to fight in the South Atlantic at that time would have done so under extreme winter weather conditions and would have arrived only after long delays. Argentina, by contrast, was only starting to receive new weapons systems—including the Exocet-carrying Super-Etendards from France—and, within a few weeks, might have procured enough of these to have turned the tide of battle. Indeed, even under the military balance as it existed at the outset of the conflict, the prospects for a quick and sweeping British victory in dislodging the Argentinean invaders seemed remote to both the Argentine high command and a number of U.S. and Western military officials as well.[22]

From the point of view of military planning, Britain's ability rapidly to coordinate a successful military response to Argentina's invasion, as well as its mobilization of civilian resources, such as the conversion of passenger liners into troop carriers, was indeed impressive.[23] Yet some questions were inevitably raised about how a long-term Falklands commitment would affect the overall British contribution to NATO defenses in Europe. Dr. Joseph Luns, NATO's secretary general, admitted such a concern in a mid-June 1982 address delivered at Annapolis, Maryland, when he noted that the deployment of much of the British fleet to the Falklands had depreciated alliance defenses across the board. Over the short term, the best that either the Americans or NATO headquarters could do was to "keep a sense of proportion," noting that no real East-West crisis coincided with the Falklands incident and that NATO assets could be temporarily—if inconveniently—shifted by SACLANT Headquarters to perform Greenland-Iceland-U.K. (GIUK) defense duties.[24]

Mr. Luns's expressions of concern notwithstanding, an official British report released a few months after the Falklands incident announced the dispatch of a "substantial naval task group on long detachment for visits and exercises in the South Atlantic, [the] Caribbean, [the] Indian Ocean and further east."[25] The completion of a new airfield at Mount Pleasant in the Falklands, capable of receiving wide-body jets, was designed to allow air reinforcement operations to be conducted there more readily, while allowing reductions of permanently stationed ground forces and supporting naval/air elements (the number of frigates deployed in the Falklands, for example, was reduced from three to two in January 1985).[26] Furthermore, as of 1985, over four thousand army personnel were still stationed in this South Atlantic outpost.[27] That these deployments detracted from Britain's ability to contribute to NATO was admitted by the House of Commons Foreign Affairs Committee in October 1984. The relevant passage states that "until there is agreement with Argentina as to the future of the Falklands, [the British commitment there] will continue to require the substantial army, air force, and naval resources in and around the Falklands . . . and the consequential diversion of these resources from the United Kingdom's regular commitments, particularly to NATO." [28]

Washington officially supported the British claim that the 1982 Argentinean seizure of the islands was an act of aggression under international law. Nonetheless, facilitating British-Argentinean negotiations over the administration of the islands was important to the United States, given its geopolitical perspective. But Secretary of State Alexander Haig's "shuttle diplomacy" between Buenos Aires and London probably served to confuse the situation more than it helped.[29] The failure of his shuttle diplomacy convinced the secretary of state of the necessity for America to "come off the fence" and publicly support the British government. He was opposed within the administration by Jeane Kirkpatrick, ambassador to the UN, who had been carrying on her own discussions with Latin American leaders, and who favored a "publicly neutral" U.S. posture. Haig reportedly accused the U.S. ambassador of being "mentally and emotionally incapable of clear thinking on this issue." Kirkpatrick is reported to have retorted that Haig and his staff at the Department of State were "amateurs . . . Brits in American clothes" with a "boys' club vision of gang loyalty." She is also reported to have asked, "Why not just disband the State Department and have the British Foreign Office make our policy?"[30]

Eventually, however, U.S. officials moved toward the obvious, if painful, choice of providing military assistance to Britain at the expense of incurring the criticism of its Latin American neighbors, most of whom were supporting Argentina. Washington calculated that Britain's defeat at the hands of a second-rank military power in the Third World would result in serious damage to overall Western credibility in future contingencies as well as seriously undermine British morale—a result to be avoided even at the risk of temporarily alienating most of the Organization of American States (OAS).[31] Washington also accepted "guilt by association" with residual British imperialism in the opinion of NATO's newest member, Spain. Madrid had made it clear on the day after it joined the NATO alliance that membership in the pact "in no way" implied Spanish approval of Britain's policies in the Falklands.

Actual U.S. military-related assistance to Britain included almost all of the intelligence information used by British forces in the campaign. Most of this material was transmitted to British defense planners by U.S. communication satellites. American satellites were also used for optical and electronic surveillance in the theater of operations.[32] Significantly, the United States also agreed to supply 100 replacement Sidewinder air-to-air missiles so that Britain could draw upon its own NATO stock of Sidewinders without running afoul of NATO commitments not to touch these stocks except in response to a European crisis.[33]

Some of Britain's other NATO allies also were active in rendering critical and timely support. Belgian Mirage aircraft fought mock battles with British Harrier pilots at the height of the Falklands crisis to enable U.K. pilots to learn more about how to combat Argentinean Mirages, while the French did the same with their Super-Etendard to allow the Royal Air Force to practice combat against that aircraft as well.[34] There were limits, however, as to how much logistical support the United States and other NATO powers were able to extend to the U.K. For example, the Royal Navy's task force was operating in the South Atlantic without airborne early warning and reconnaissance systems because the U.S. aircraft carrier-based forces assigned to NATO's SACLANT were too preoccupied with making up the difference for naval and naval air shortages in its operations area caused by RN and RAF diversions from NATO to the South Atlantic theater. As one U.S. admiral subsequently observed, "Satellites don't substitute for tactical airborne reconnaissance."[35]

The Falklands war demonstrated that the United States and Britain are still capable of coordinating their policies and merging their intelligence and defense assets on an ad hoc basis in order to protect each other's security interests in times of crisis. Furthermore, the crisis illustrated that NATO is still strong enough and flexible enough to adjust to temporary emergency drop-downs in forces designated for defense missions beyond the European continent.

But a December 1982 British Defense White Paper, released just after the conflict ended, recommended caution "in deciding which lessons of the [Falklands] Campaign are relevant to the United Kingdom's main defense priority—[the] role within NATO against the threat from the Soviet Union and its allies."[36] The White Paper left the geographic nature of such a Soviet threat specifically undefined, while strongly implying in its conclusion that threats beyond the NATO Treaty area would need to be addressed in terms of improved flexibility, mobility, and readiness.[37]

CONCLUSION

As of this writing, an ambiguity still exists in Britain's military policy concerning how its limited military assets should be apportioned to its residual strategic interests in the Western Hemisphere. The Falklands episode did little to clarify in doctrinal or operational terms the interrelationship between British Atlantic/NATO seaborne operations and those applicable to future out-of-area contingencies. Furthermore, there remains a concern on the part of at least some Western defense analysts that "a certain unreality may be entering the debate as to what Britain can achieve alone in the military sphere" as a result of post-Falklands euphoria.[38] Reports that British air defense forces in the Falklands could be quickly recalled to NATO Europe and could perform at a high state of combat readiness from the outset seemed, at best, somewhat hyperbolic.[39] Some observers also worried about the detrimental effects of the Falklands commitment on Britain's ability to respond to other out-of-area challenges. As the *Financial Times* reported in late 1982 in an editorial, "The point of the so-called 'out-of-area' forces is to achieve flexibility; they can be moved wherever necessary. But it is hard to see how flexibility is gained from a force specifically designed for the defense of the Falklands; nor, incidentally, what other engagements it might be called upon to undertake in the South Atlantic."[40]

On the whole, however, the Thatcher government resisted the temptation to treat the successful intervention as any kind of precedent. This is entirely understandable in view of the fact that the Falklands campaign alone was estimated to have cost over 2.5 billion pounds ($4.2 billion) for the recapture, subsequent garrisoning, and equipment replacement, at a time when Thatcher was already coming under heavy fire for her decision to procure the Trident II nuclear submarine while simultaneously keeping British Army on the Rhine (BAOR) detachments at current NATO treaty levels.[41] Britain's ability to keep this many balls in the air is the subject of the Conclusion to Part 2.

CONCLUSION TO PART II

Bʀɪᴛɪsʜ efforts since World War II to manage simultaneously the demands of the "special relationship," the NATO commitment, and the residual responsibilities of empire appear in retrospect as an audit of frustration. It is tempting to explain Britain's inability to square the circle in terms of unavoidable budgetary constraints. But as we have attempted to illustrate in Part 2, the British failure to develop an effective global defense strategy since 1945 has been attributable as much to problems of conceptualization as to those of economics. This situation, in turn, has affected Britain's ability to manage, or to derive benefits from, its role as "prefect" to Washington's "headmaster" within the NATO community.[1]

Britain's decision to develop a nuclear force, moreover, did little to clarify the debate, since it was never clear how independent the British nuclear force really was. It was equally uncertain whether nuclear weapons could ever really be used as a substitute for conventional forces in or out of the NATO Treaty area—in spite of the fact that successive defense estimates used this argument to justify troop reductions. As early as 1952, when the government had argued that primary reliance on nuclear weapons meant that Britain could reduce its overall manpower contributions to NATO, the British Chiefs of Staff Committee opposed such reductions on both political and military grounds.[2] This same concern was still being voiced by the British Chiefs of Staff three decades later despite the advances of technology and the changes in the global power balance which had occurred.[3] Nuclear weapons have been seen by British defense planners primarily as a quick fix for manpower and budget problems within the NATO Treaty area. Our study demonstrates, however, that on occasion British defense planners have also dabbled with the idea of using nuclear weapons as a military quick fix, or at least as a fallback option, in the face of out-of-area disturbances in such places as Kuwait (1961). The very fact that London had gotten to the point where it was willing to consider a nuclear "solution" to a minor disturbance such as Kuwait speaks volumes about the frustration of British power in the postwar era.

The centerpiece of British postwar defense planning, and the primary source of British frustration, was the famous "special relationship" with Washington.

During the first two decades of the postwar era, U.S. policy makers tended to be positively disposed to Britain in principle—as a traditional ally that shared America's fundamental values. The problem was at the operational level, where British military weakness and doctrinal incoherence led U.S. planners increasingly to question the U.K.'s reliability.

On occasion, London's efforts to bolster its image (and self-image) by "standing tough" against Third World challenges got the U.K. in trouble, not only with Washington, but with other NATO allies as well (such as West Germany and the Scandinavian states in the case of Suez). Instances of British assertiveness were often interpreted by these allies, and by the alliance leader in particular, as confirming Dulles' suspicion that Britain was a country that, "realizing it was weak, felt it had to act strong." British out-of-area activism was also seen by critics within the alliance as defense of narrow national interests at the expense of wider Western security concerns.

In other extra-European situations, however, Britain opted for adjustive diplomacy, owing to a sense of its own geostrategic vulnerability, even though Washington was more inclined toward a tougher stance. British policy toward the P.R.C. between 1949 and 1955 is a good illustration of this type of situation. By its actions, the U.K. encouraged Washington to doubt British strategic reliability as a participant in the Third World containment scheme.

The United States came increasingly to resent British recommendations for caution and moderation during the 1970s when British east-of-Suez retrenchment and defense budget cuts made London appear as an even less valuable participant in the overall Western defense system. Table 5 contrasts British retrenchment during (and since) the 1970s with overall British global strategic commitments during the 1950s and 1960s.

Since the accession of Margaret Thatcher in 1979, the process of British defense budget cutting has been reversed, but the problem of doctrinal contradiction has persisted. For example, Britain's former secretary of state for defense, John Nott, argued in 1981 that Britain had to be prepared to respond, in cooperation with its allies, to challenges at any point on the globe because of the increasingly expansionist nature of the Soviet military threat.[4] Yet when the government was pressed during parliamentary debate to offer specifics regarding Britain's ability to contribute to Western initiatives outside of the NATO Treaty area, "the Thatcher government admitted that the actual British contribution . . . 'in terms of size and scale would be very small and it would tend to be more political than military.'"[5] In fact, the British defense agenda in 1981 involved plans to cut the Royal Navy's surface ship inventory and to relegate that service to the basic missions of an almost exclusively Atlantic defense. This was not what the newly elected American president, Ronald Reagan, wanted to hear at a time when he was committing his own nation to substantial defense budget increases in response to what he viewed as an intensifying Soviet challenge to free world interests.

TABLE 5
Selected Deployments of British Extraregional
Military Presence: 1950–1989

NAVY

Mediterranean Command

1950

Largest and most important overseas command; included Malta, Middle East, and
Gibraltar subcommands; liaisons with the French naval command at Algiers, the Italian
naval command at Naples, and the Turkish naval command at Ankara. After 1954, the
Libyan and Egyptian coasts as well as the Levant were placed under the purview of the
Commander in Chief, Mediterranean Fleet.

1960

Cyprus patrol reduced, owing to internal political resistance against British presence,
and U.K. minesweeping efforts redeployed to east-of-Suez sites. Mediterranean Fleet
retained a proximate configuration of a cruiser, 10 frigate/destroyers, and a submarine
squadron.

1970–1983

Port facilities at Cyprus maintained. Naval frigate and special boat detachment also
maintained at Gibraltar. British naval presence in Malta relinquished in 1979. After
1976, British maritime forces were committed to the NATO On-Call Force, Mediterranean, in support of NATO, but only one guard ship permanently stationed at Gibraltar.

1984 Onward (residual deployments)

No permanent presence, but joint military exercises frequently conducted at Cyprus.

South Atlantic Squadron

1950

Headquartered at Freetown/Simonstown, South Africa, and covering that part of the
Mediterranean not under the Gibraltar subcommand; to the eastern limit of the Americas
and West Indies station in a westward direction; and around South Africa into the south
Indian Ocean in an eastward direction. Bermuda military installations reverted to U.S.
control in 1950.

1960

British presence largely depleted but sustained by greater aircraft carrier power (4 full-
sized carriers compared to 2–3 in the earlier 1950s). Also greater emphasis on guided
missile frigates vs. older cruiser deployment. Fifty-four destroyers and frigates deployed in the British fleet worldwide, Simonstown transferred to S. African navy in
1957. Small British naval presence left Simonstown permanently in 1975.

Continued on next page

TABLE 5—Continued

1970–1983

Permanent deployment of 2 frigates to the Caribbean until 1976.

1984–1989

One frigate and 1 auxiliary ship intermittently patrolling Belize and the West Indies. Immediately following the 1982 Falklands War, 1 hunter-killer submarine, 1 ASW carrier, 4 escort units (destroyers/frigates), a survey vessel, and an offshore patrol vessel. Carrier force removed following hostilities, but escort and auxiliary units remained deployed.

East Indies/Persian Gulf/Indian Ocean

1950

East Indies squadron headquartered at Trincomalee, Ceylon (Sri Lanka); weakened by emergence of India as an independent republic (1948); active in bombing insurgent concentrations in Malaya; dissolved in 1958.

1960

Remnants of East Indies command incorporated into Far Eastern, South Atlantic, and Persian Gulf command missions or under CENTO command direction; small permanent detachment (usually 4 frigates) deployed in Persian Gulf at Aden or other ports along with the Amphibious Warfare Marine Squadron.

1970–1983

Build-up of Diego Garcia's refueling station/communication center; patrols gradually decline in the Indian Ocean as 2 escort/frigates and 1 tanker with limited maritime reconnaissance support constitute the Beira Patrol. Communications base maintained at Mauritius throughout most of this period, but British forces leave in 1976. CENTO military commitment dropped in 1976 along with presence at Gan.

1984–1989 (residual deployments)

A small Royal Marine detachment at Diego Garcia and "Armilla Patrol" (2–3 escort ships) in Persian Gulf. Temporarily supplanted by 3 additional surface units and 3 minesweepers during 1988 Persian Gulf patrolling operations.

Far Eastern Command

1950

Headquartered at Hong Kong and at Kure, Japan, during Korean hostilities; also active in Malayan Peninsula—the 5th Cruiser Squadron and the China Squadron consolidated during Korean War owing to lack of sufficient units to sustain separate subcommands.

1960

Formed in 1959 to replace Far Eastern Fleet gradually; headquartered in Singapore. Included an autonomous submarine arm, constantly added destroyers and frigates (by

TABLE 5—Continued

1961, more operational naval units were deployed east than west of Suez [1–2 fleet carriers and 12–15 escorts] mostly under command of all-purpose fleet based at Singapore). Far East Squadron built up to 50 total units at height of Indonesian/Malaysian confrontation (1964–65), including 2 carriers, a commando ship, 2 missile destroyers, 17 destroyers and frigates, 11 minesweepers, and various auxiliaries.

1970–1983

Singapore naval dockyard transferred to Singapore control in 1968; throughout most of 1970s, 5–6 frigates/destroyers, 1–2 submarines, along with selected support ships, maintained in Far East Squadron. In Hong Kong, 1 frigate with accompanying patrol vessels and minesweepers deployed. Also 1 Royal Marine detachment in the Falklands; 1 Royal Marine detachment in Gibraltar.

1984–1989 (residual deployments)

Periodic deployments of home-based Hong Kong naval task forces with a VSTOL carrier and 5–6 escorts; retention of patrol craft and a Marine raiding squadron in Hong Kong until its 1997 reversion to China; a Marine company at Brunei.

ARMY

Total Active Duty Manpower in Extra-European Locales

1950

100,000 plus assigned to extra-European defense roles. Middle East: $1^2/_3$ divisions = 55,000 plus 20,000 East African military personnel. Malaya, Korea, Hong Kong: 2 divisions = Malaya, 20,000; Hong Kong, 12,000; Korea, 15,000.

1960

Approx. 90,000 (note: from 1955 to 1962 the U.K. total manpower base for active duty army personnel decreased from 422,000 to 201,000). In 1964, U.K. deployed 58,000 east of Suez (mostly in Malaya), 23,000 in Mediterranean areas, and 9,000 elsewhere (mostly in Hong Kong).

1973–1974

Singapore: 1 infantry battalion group (approx. 3,000)
Brunei: 1 Gurkha battalion (approx. 3,000)
Hong Kong: 2 brigades with 2 British, 3 Gurkha battalions (approx. 9,000–10,000)

1979–1983

Belize: 1–2 infantry battalions, 1 artillery battery, reconnaissance and engineering personnel (approx. 1,600)
Brunei: 1 infantry battalion (approx. 3,000)

Continued on next page

TABLE 5—Continued

1984 Onward

Out-of-area force capability projected at approx. 17,000 in extra-European locales, including residual extra-European deployments in Belize (1,600); the Falklands (2,000 and declining); Gibraltar (1 infantry battalion, or 1,950); Cyprus (4,650); Hong Kong (8, 950); and minor deployments in other locales.

Selected Global Deployments/Home-based Deployments for Global Missions

1950

Dispersed, limited land force commitments in the Caribbean, Cyprus, Gibraltar, Libya, Malta, Aden, East Africa, Bahamas and Jamaica, and the Persian Gulf.

1960

Creation of U.K. Mobile Force, including a Land Element of 3 air-portable brigades plus divisional troops plus logistical support forces (primarily earmarked for NATO support roles but usable in extra-European contingencies).

1970–1983

After 1975, U.K. Mobile Force reduced to one air-portable brigade group plus support and logistic forces. After 1975, U.K. Joint Airborne Task Force abandoned.

1984

5th Airborne Brigade stationed in the U.K. under command of Joint Force Headquarters, which could also command the 3 Commando Brigade, Royal Marines.

Withdrawal Patterns of British Ground Units: The Middle East and Africa

1950

Two divisions in Palestine withdrawn in 1948; Suez Canal base signed in October 1954 pledging U.K. to withdraw troops from the canal by June 1956 as a result of indigenous resistance to British presence, poor logistical conditions, vulnerability to nuclear attack, and draining of British Strategic Reserve manpower.

1960

Most of the 30,000 British troops deployed in Cyprus were removed in 1956–60. 7,000 British military personnel stationed at Aden until 1968 withdrawal announcement (24th Infantry Brigade group, Amphibious Warfare Marine elements, etc.). 6,000 British troops withdrawn from Kenya to Aden and Britain during mid-1960s.

1970–1983

Withdrawal of all British land forces from Bahrain, Qatar, and the United Arab Emirates by end of 1971.

TABLE 5—Continued

1984–1989

Sovereign Base Areas (SBAs) in Cyprus for Eastern Mediterranean Middle Eastern operations (3,500 personnel, later increased to 4,500). Gibraltar garrisons with 1,800 personnel can also support Mediterranean missions. 700 military advisers in some 30 Third World countries; mostly posted to Middle Eastern locales.

Withdrawal Patterns of British Ground Units:
The Far East

1950 Onward

1950–53: 2 brigades—intermittently the 27th Commonwealth, 28th, and 29th—10,000 infantry personnel withdrawn from Northeast Asia by 1954. 1950–60: 17,000 British and 10,000 Gurkha troops constituted 28th Commonwealth Brigade/17th Gurkha Division. In 1964–65, this total swelled to 59,000 British military personnel deployed in Malaysia at height of Indonesian/Malaysian confrontation. Following 1965 cease-fire, however, a decline took place and only 3,000 British military personnel were left in Malaysia and Singapore under ANZUK auspices, 1970–75. The 28th Commonwealth Brigade itself was withdrawn in 1975; Five Power Defense Arrangements (FPDA) formed with Malaya, Singapore, Australia, and New Zealand with all British army personnel removed, save a Gurkha battalion in Brunei. The Hong Kong garrison has declined from 10,000 through much of the postwar time frame to about 7,480 army personnel, including 1,897 British, 4,703 Gurkha, and 1,240 indigenous personnel. Manpower strength of Brunei garrison has been declining since 1983 (from approx. 1,500 to 900 personnel), with a Gurkha battalion and a company of British Marines still deployed.

South Atlantic/Caribbean Force Deployments, 1984–1988

Falkland Islands garrison with Infantry Battalion Group plus supporting arms and services has been declining from 4,000 personnel in 1984 to less than 1,000 by end of 1988. The strength of the Belize garrison with 1,500 army/infantry, artillery, engineering, and reconnaissance personnel has remained steady.

OUT-OF AREA COMMAND AND DEPLOYMENT PATTERNS
FOR THE ROYAL AIR FORCE

Middle East Air Force

1950

Headquarters in Ismalia, Egypt, with Lower Formation commands in Fayid, Egypt (no. 205 Group); Malta; East Africa Habbaniya air base in Iraq; and Headquarters, British Forces, Aden. Largest geographic command of the Royal Air Force (RAF), with Aden and Iraq RAF commanders exercising jurisdiction over any British army elements

Continued on next page

TABLE 5—Continued

deployed there; the command was regarded as the critical staging post for East-West air routes (replacing India and the Canal Zone) and the first line of defense against a Soviet attack commencing from Iran and moving southward/westward against NATO positions.

1960

Operations increasingly conducted under CENTO authority; Canberra bombers and Hunter & Javelin fighter squadrons were the mainstays of the air force, but Iraqi air base access lost. Headquarters, British Forces, Aden now redesignated as British Forces, Arabian Peninsula, with an upgraded role in Persian Gulf insurgency warfare from airfields at Khornaksar, Masirah, Sharjah (by 1966, however, only 1-plus squadrons remain in this command).

1970–1983

Aden base access relinquished by 1971; by 1976 RAF has essentially stopped operations as a Mediterranean/Middle Eastern air power except for Oman and Cyprus, where 2 RAF fighter/light bomber squadrons are still deployed; Gibraltar, where air surveillance missions are conducted; and Malta, where British components partly make up 2 NATO fighter squadrons. RAF technicians help man FPDA Integrated Air Defense Systems (IADS) at Butterworth Air Base, Malaysia—no other significant operations. Five Hercules Air Transport Squadrons abandoned as part of U.K. Joint Airborne Task Force phase-out.

1984–1989 (residual deployments)

Cyprus: 1 squadron of Wessex helicopters and 1 RAF Regiment squadron.

Far East Air Force

1950

Headquarters in Changi, Singapore, with Lower Formation commands in Ceylon, Malaya, and Hong Kong. Primarily used in a tactical role against Malayan communist insurgency and for rapid reinforcement in other Far Eastern contingencies. Long-range strategic bomber exercises/maneuvers—e.g., Operation Red Lion, Sunray—also conducted.

1960

1 V-bomber detachment, jet fighter ground attack detachments, and reconnaissance elements constituted a command of "greatly reduced scale" for RAF operations following the Malayan emergency and, again, following the Indonesian/Malaysian confrontation (primary emphasis is moved toward transport support for remaining ground troops in the region). After Cyprus reductions in 1959–60, British air presence reduced to 1 fighter squadron and 1 strike wing by 1966. By 1966, only 1 reconnaissance group remains on Gibraltar. Upgraded RAF staging posts at Gan for better linkage of Middle East/Far East Command operatons. Transport Command post on the Seychelles.

TABLE 5—Continued

1970–1983

Gan retains RAF satellite communications base Skynet for use in Indian Ocean/Far Eastern Operations—British Nimrod tracking aircraft and Whirlwind helicopters conduct intermittent ASW tracking operations with the Royal Navy in the Indian Ocean. Air Support Command conducts occasional reconnaissance operations in the Caribbean. Small jet fighter detachment (2 squadrons) retained in British Honduras (Belize).

1984 Onward (residual deployments)

Hong Kong: 1 squadron of Wessex helicopters. Departure from Gan in 1979; no permanent deployment pattern in the Indian Ocean but selected task force deployments are carried out intermittently; selected airfield access to Diego Garcia. Falklands: 1 Phantom squadron and 1 Harrier fighter flight, assorted Buccaneer aircraft, Sea King and Chinook helicopters, plus Hercules transports. Belize: 1 Harrier flight and Puma helicopters. Brunei: British personnel man Rapier Aid Defense Battery, but strength of this contingent has declined since 1983.

Sources (Note: All the following sources incorporate data from the annual British MOD Cmnd. Papers plus additional data bases.)

"Air Estimates, 1960–61," in *Brassey's Annual, 1960* (New York: Macmillan, 1960), pp. 342–43; "Ajax," "Operational Training in the RAF, 1950," in *Brassey's Annual, 1951* (New York: Macmillan, 1951), pp. 347–51; "Army Estimates, 1960–1961," in *Brassey's Annual, 1960,* pp. 330–31; C. N. Barclay, "The Imperial Army," in *Brassey's Annual, 1951,* pp. 228–29; *Brassey's Annual, 1971* (New York: Praeger, 1971), pp. 281–83; Neville Brown, *Strategic Mobility* (London: Macmillan, 1963); Phillip Darby, *British Defense Policy East of Suez, 1947–1968* (London: Oxford University Press, 1973); "Extracts from Navy Estimates by the First Lord of the Admiralty" (Cmnd. 949), in *Brassey's Annual, 1960,* pp. 308–12; International Institute for Strategic Studies, *The Military Balance, 1971* (London: IISS, 1970), pp. 23–24; ibid., *The Military Balance, 1984–1985* (London: IISS, 1985), pp. 33–35; Catherine McArdle Kelleher, "The Conflict Without: European Powers and Non-nuclear Conflict outside of Europe," in *Non-nuclear Conflicts in the Nuclear Age,* ed. Sam C. Sarkesian (New York: Praeger, 1980), pp. 277–78; Lt. Cmdr. P. K. Kemp, RN, "Royal Navy—Organization and Administration," in *Brassey's Annual, 1951,* pp. 145–46; A. R. W. Low, "The Army Seen from Parliament," in ibid., p. 224; William P. Snyder, *The Politics of British Defense Policy, 1947–1962* (London: Macmillan, 1963); Stockholm International Peace Research Institute, *World Armaments and Disarmaments: SIPRI Yearbook, 1972* (New York: Humanities Press, 1972), pp. 262–64; ibid., *SIPRI Yearbook, 1975* (Cambridge: MIT Press, 1975), pp. 78–81, 86–87; United Kingdom, Ministry of Defense, *Statement on the Defense Estimates, 1984,* Cmnd. 9227-I (London: HMSO, 1984); Anthony Verrier, *An Army for the Sixties* (London: Macmillan, 1966); James Wyllie, *The Influence of British Arms: An Analysis of British Military Intervention since 1956* (London: Allen and Unwin, 1984).

The only truly global element in Mrs. Thatcher's 1981 defense program was the plan to improve Britain's ability to participate in a global nuclear war by the 1990s, by the development of the Trident II ballistic nuclear missile submarine complemented by British attack submarines and other anti-submarine warfare (ASW) forces. As Thatcher was moving Britain even closer to its original 1952 strategy of according priority to the nuclear deterrent, many NATO allies worried about the long-term implications for Britain's conventional defense contributions to the alliance. The Reagan administration nonetheless encouraged Britain's purchase of the Trident II, based upon the Pentagon's argument that a supplementary nuclear force under NATO command would enhance the United States' own Single Integrated Operations Plan (SIOP) for nuclear targeting.

The Falklands crisis interrupted the trend toward an even greater reliance on nuclear weapons in Britain, although the commitment to Trident II was preserved. In the wake of the fighting in the South Atlantic, various British defense spokesmen (most notably Defense Undersecretary Geoffrey Pattie) expressed increased support for improving Britain's conventional forces. They also expressed a renewed interest in U.S. proposals for greater NATO out-of-area cooperation.[6]

In the aftermath of the post-Falklands euphoria, however, British defense spokesmen attempted to downplay London's interest in developing a stronger out-of-area intervention force, or in substantially resuscitating Britain's out-of-area basing system. In a May 1985 interview in *NATO's Sixteen Nations,* then-British secretary of state for defense Michael Heseltine contended that "more than 95% [of the U.K. defense budget] is spent within NATO." He went on to assert, "I believe the British commitment to central Europe is absolute and I have recently slightly increased the number of troops we keep in Germany."[7]

Proponents of continued BAOR deployment have correctly focused on the credibility problem of Britain's continued commitment to European defense at a time when West Germany, with its declining population, is unable to compensate for British manpower cuts on the Continent. They warn of a domino effect upon current NATO ground force commitments. ("If the British go, the Belgians and Dutch can't be far behind.") In late 1982, Supreme Allied Commander General Bernard Rogers observed that the continued deployment of British troops in the North German Plain represented a critical element in the West's ability to sustain the central European power balance.[8] The status of the British forces in Central Europe may nonetheless be affected in the near future, as NATO and the Warsaw Pact enter into conventional arms reduction talks.[9]

Some British defense experts have nonetheless viewed the BAOR as the best target for cuts. Peter Foot represents this revisionist school of thought:

> Does it make sense, for example, for the British to continue to keep 55,000 troops in West Germany? Would it not better serve the common good if some—perhaps all—of the United Kingdom's small but highly professional land (and tactical air) forces were assigned to other roles, their positions on the Central Front being taken up by troops drawn from the larger, conscript-based forces of the continental countries? . . . Is the envisaged degradation of a general purpose navy capability sensible, from the Alliance's standpoint, at a time when demands for precautionary or reactive deployments outside the NATO area are likely to grow?[10]

It seems very likely that the fifty-thousand-strong BAOR—which is presently maintained at an annual estimated cost of more than three billion pounds—will eventually be reduced.[11] London continues to resist pressures for deep cuts in its armed forces, however, and defense budget projections for the period 1989–92 assume a real growth of 2.9 percent in defense spending. According to the 1989 *Statement on the Defense Estimates,* this level of spending "brings valuable certainty and confidence to our forward planning. And it disposes of talk of the need for a defense review."[12] Such reassurances notwithstanding, it will be extremely difficult for Britain to maintain this level of defense spending into the early 1990s, and BAOR is the most vulnerable big-ticket item in the British defense inventory. Under these circumstances, improvements in British mobile reserve elements designed for either quick reinforcement in a European conflict or rapid deployment in extraperipheral operations may represent the most practical conventional emphasis for Britain in the future. Mobility is usually more conducive to the kinds of defense-in-depth strategies currently being developed within NATO. Indeed, recent reports filtering out of both NATO's Defense Planning Committee and the Defense Ministry in London indicate that British military planners are now implementing plans designed to improve the in-theater force mobility of the U.K.'s European forces (as opposed to the traditional emphasis on battlefield attrition). Thus, for example, the British army is now introducing greater members of armored personnel carriers and other infantry combat vehicles in its quest to achieve higher levels of mechanization in the Central European region.[13] Such efforts fit into recommendations advanced by the NATO Defense Ministers' December 1988 report, *Enhancing Alliance Collective Security,* with its "Conceptual Military Framework" stressing Follow-on Forces Attack (FOFA), electronic warfare, and tactical reconnaissance.[14]

In regard to Britain's future military role beyond the NATO boundary, the Falklands episode demonstrated that Britain could still mobilize a substantial emergency force for an out-of-area crisis in spite of severe resource constraints. But the Falklands effort would be extremely difficult and costly to replicate. Furthermore, barring unforeseen changes in the British defense posture, even a limited out-of-area initiative would probably require London to cut into its contribution to the NATO central front and/or its naval contribution to Atlantic defense. But NATO demonstrated an impressive ability to make the necessary adjustments to accommodate temporary drawdowns in the Falklands case. Depending on the circumstances, the alliance could do so again.

PART III

FRANCE

It was the Atlantic Alliance that in years past enabled France to commit the bulk of her forces abroad, and that, in years to come, may make it possible for her to reduce conventional forces in favor of the atomic program.

RAYMOND ARON
The Great Debate

During his brief tenure as leader of France's Provisional Government at the end of World War II, Charles de Gaulle set the direction of French foreign policy for the next fifteen years. In particular, the general locked his successors into a commitment to colonial reassertion, which would prove disastrous for France—first in Indochina and then in Algeria. Ironically, it was de Gaulle, who more than anyone else was responsible for involving France in the postwar colonial morass, who was called back to office by the French people in 1958 for the express purpose of resolving the colonial crisis in Algeria.

By 1958, de Gaulle had convinced himself that many of France's problems in the Third World were due to the conditional nature of the support that France was receiving from its two leading NATO allies, the United States and Britain. De Gaulle communicated his resentment, first by removing French vessels from the NATO Mediterranean fleet, then by taking France out of the NATO military command altogether.

Much of the history of French defense policy since that time has involved the gradual, de facto return of France to the NATO military command. But the limits of that process of reconciliation continue to be set by the themes of national independence and self-reliance established during the de Gaulle era. Part 3 will focus on the role played by out-of-area events in shaping that commitment to national independence and self-reliance.

CHAPTER 13

EMERGING FROM
OCCUPATION

AT ONE POINT in his war memoirs, de Gaulle observes that "war resembles certain plays in which, as the denouement approaches, all the actors appear on the stage at once."[1] It may be more accurate to state that the principal actors had all been on the stage for some time, but that the general had been unable to see them from his disadvantaged position in the back of the chorus. De Gaulle spent much of his time during the war years in political isolation, developing his vision of France's proper role in the postwar international order and reflecting on the barriers that would have to be overcome in order for France to play such a role. An essential prerequisite, according to the general, was the restoration of French sovereignty in the wake of the betrayals of national honor and identity by Marshal Pétain and the *gouvernants de rencontre*. To achieve this goal, and to protect French interests in the new international system, the nation would have to secure a position of influence over postwar developments in Europe and reestablish France's control over its prewar empire.

Shortly after the Provisional Government was established in Paris (September 1944), de Gaulle began negotiations with the Soviet Union aimed at advancing the first of these two goals. His experiences with the Anglo-Saxons during World War II had convinced him of the need to obtain Moscow's support for an influential French role in Europe. De Gaulle's efforts were rewarded with the December 1944 Franco-Soviet Treaty of Mutual Aid and Assistance, an explicitly anti-German pact that also committed both signatories "not to enter into an alliance or to join any coalition directed against one of the partners of the treaty."[2] The treaty was viewed by de Gaulle as a logical continuation of prewar French security policy. He expressed some interest in permitting Britain to join France and Russia "to form a European bloc," but his enduring suspicions of British motives and goals in Europe and the Third World encouraged the general to bide his time. By the fall of 1945, however, de

Gaulle's hopes for Soviet cooperation had dimmed considerably, and the general was forced to accept a Westward reorientation in his European strategy. With the end of the Provisional Government in January 1946, it was left to de Gaulle's successors to dismantle the last vestiges of the Franco-Soviet strategy and to adjust French foreign policy to the benefits and the constraints of Atlanticism.

The notion of empire was the second element in de Gaulle's plan for reconstruction of French sovereignty and influence in the postwar world. His speeches and statements prior to and during World War II illustrate that he shared the basic premises of classical French imperialism, built upon the concepts of sovereign right, economic self-interest, the *mission civilisatrice,* and the essentiality of colonies as a source of strength during periods of national vulnerability.[3] In his first "Free France" radio broadcast (June 18, 1940), de Gaulle developed the theme that "France was not alone" because it could draw upon the resources of its empire in a crisis. Throughout the war, the victories of Free French forces in Francophone Africa were frequently cited by the general to justify his demands for status in his dealings with the Anglo-Saxons. These victories also served as a major source of inspiration to the anti-Vichy forces within France and abroad. It is not surprising, then, that the general was committed to the preservation of the empire at the end of the war, both as a reward to Free French forces, which had helped to liberate the colonies, and as a source of power and influence for a physically weakened and psychologically insecure state.

Throughout the war, de Gaulle had pressed the Allies for statements acknowledging French sovereignty over all prewar colonial territories as a means of stopping any attempts by London and Washington to redraw the world map at French expense when hostilities ended. Churchill's reluctance to provide the kinds of formal and public guarantees that the general sought was a special source of concern and insecurity. These fears were confirmed for de Gaulle when Britain signed the Saint Jean d'Acre agreement with the Vichy forces in Syria and Lebanon during the summer of 1941. De Gaulle interpreted the agreement as a pure and simple transfer of Syria and Lebanon to British authority: "By signing this capitulation, Vichy showed itself faithful to its wretched vocation. But the English were apparently lending themselves to it with all their ulterior motives."[4] The general refused to accept the assurances of Oliver Lyttelton (British minister of state) that "Great Britain is pursuing no aim in Syria and Lebanon other than to win the war."[5] De Gaulle's options were limited, however, and he chose to control his reaction to the British initiative ("casing myself in ice") while increasing his vigilance. On a few occasions during the war, the general exhibited less self-control in response to what he perceived as Allied infringements on French sovereignty. On being advised *ex post facto* of the start of Operation Torch (the U.S.-U.K. invasion of French North Africa), the general expressed his frustration at having been left out of the planning for the attack. "Well, I hope the people of Vichy throw them into the sea. You can't break into France and get away with it."[6]

Once the Provisional Government was installed in Paris, de Gaulle undertook to make the French position regarding its imperial possessions clear to the major powers. Roosevelt provided the general with one opportunity to deliver this message when he invited de Gaulle to meet with him in Algiers immediately following the Yalta Conference. The general rejected the proposal, not only because he had not been invited to the Big Three conference in Yalta, but also because he could not accept "a summons from the head of a foreign state to go to a place that is part of our national territory."[7]

De Gaulle's formula for postwar metropole-colony relations was introduced at the Brazzaville Conference of February 1944 and served as the outline for the subsequent policies of the Provisional Government. The conference served notice to the Third World and to the Anglo-Saxons that France intended to reassert its control over its empire, and that Paris would resist both nationalist pressures within the colonies and decolonization demands from the international community. No native leaders representing indigenous peoples actively participated in the conference. Its philosophy is captured in a concluding statement: "The idea of a possible, even ultimate establishment of self-government in the colonies must be discarded."[8]

De Gaulle illustrated the scope of his imperial ambitions on March 24, 1945, when he announced that France would retain its sovereign control over Indochina. He underscored this announcement five months later by sending a forty-eight-thousand-man expeditionary force to the region, under the command of General Philippe Leclerc, who had led the first French armored division into Paris in 1944.[9] De Gaulle's purpose during these months was to reestablish a French presence in the region, both legally and physically, in the face of a rapidly changing situation.

In the words of Brian Crozier, "It was a confusing time."[10] At the Cairo and Potsdam conferences, arrangements had been made for British forces to replace the Japanese in Southern Indochina, while the Chinese Nationalist forces under Chiang Kai-shek took over these responsibilities in the north. De Gaulle was opposed to these arrangements as an infringement on French sovereignty in the region. In particular, he feared the establishment of a permanent Chinese presence in the northern region at French expense. This concern was reinforced by reports from General Leclerc during the fall of 1945 which stressed the military potential of any alliance between Nationalist China and the Vietminh forces of General Vo Nguyen Giap.[11] According to Leclerc, Indochina was "first of all a Chinese problem," and France could not hope to retain control of the region in the face of a coordinated Sino-Vietnamese opposition. Leclerc therefore encouraged Paris to pursue a policy of negotiating with Chiang Kai-shek in order to achieve Chinese support for French sovereignty claims in

Indochina. This was achieved in February of 1946 by the Sino-French Treaty of Chungking, according to which Chiang accepted French sovereignty in Indochina in return for a French commitment to provide specific trade concessions to China and to abandon its "capitulation" claims against the Chinese government. [12] Once he had reached an understanding with Chiang, it was easier for de Gaulle to obtain U.S. and U.K. acceptance in principle for the reassertion of a French *domaine réservé* in Indochina.

De Gaulle attempted to employ the same strategy of establishing French legal claims backed by a military presence in the Levant, but by the time that the Provisional Government took over it was impossible for the general to impose the Brazzaville formula in this area. Events subsequent to the signing of the St. Jean d'Acre Treaty had permitted the growth of pressures for Syrian and Lebanese independence, and de Gaulle found himself faced with a situation of negotiating the terms and timing of such an outcome. The question was what kind of quid pro quo France could extract from Damascus and Beirut in return. As negotiations progressed, de Gaulle became increasingly convinced that Britain was encouraging the representatives of Syria and Lebanon behind the scenes to resist French demands for a "special position" in the region following independence, in the hopes of replacing French influence in the Levant.

The situation reached the crisis stage in the spring of 1945 when de Gaulle sought to strengthen the French negotiating position relative to Syria and Lebanon by reinforcing the remaining French garrisons in the region under question. Anticolonial demonstrations began on May 8, one day after French reinforcements arrived in Beirut. By the end of May, Syrian armed forces were actually engaged in support of the public uprising against the French. As the risk of a major military confrontation grew, British forces, which substantially outnumbered the French military contingent in the region, were ordered to enforce a cease-fire. As had been the case at the time of the St. Jean d'Acre accords, de Gaulle once again found himself with few options in the face of a British *fait accompli* in the Levant; but on this occasion, the general at least was able to articulate the anger that he had been forced to repress four years earlier. "We are not, I acknowledge, in a position to make war on you at present," de Gaulle advised the British ambassador. "But you have outraged France, and betrayed the Occident. This cannot be forgiven." [13] De Gaulle nonetheless was forced to accept the less than optimal bargains that were offered to France in the region, since Britain enjoyed the general support of Washington in the negotiations that were subsequently carried on for the establishment of Syrian and Lebanese independence. All of this would reinforce for de Gaulle, and for many other French policy makers who were to take office following the collapse of the Provisional Government in 1946, the conviction that France could only hope to retain its influence and achieve its foreign policy goals in the Third World if it was able to convince the Anglo-Saxons that it was in their interest to treat France as an equal. Alternatively, Paris could attempt to neutralize the restraining influence that London and Washington had over French policy in the immediate postwar order.

De Gaulle's campaign to establish "a place for France" among the great postwar powers was carried on with less direction and less success by the twenty-one governments of the Fourth Republic. The demand for some form of global directorate in which Paris would share responsibility with London and Washington for the management of overall Western security was a recurrent theme during this period, and each successive Fourth Republic government came to share de Gaulle's frustration at not being able to entice or compel the Anglo-Saxons into accepting such a plan.

As previously mentioned, the French came into the Western alliance hesitantly, after dabbling with an opening to the East in the later stages of World War II. Several factors during the period 1945–48 contributed to this reevaluation of French foreign policy. These included Stalin's opposition to French participation at key summit conferences (Potsdam, Moscow), the creation of the Cominform and Soviet support for the Parti Communiste Française's (PCF) campaign of national strikes and demonstrations, the Prague coup, and the Berlin blockade. The danger of Soviet-sponsored subversion, leading perhaps to a replay of the Prague coup in Paris, was in fact the most immediate concern of the Fourth Republic leadership by 1948. The significance of this concern is perhaps best illustrated by the fact that the first substantial increase in the size of the postwar French army (eighty thousand men in November of 1948) was specifically designated for peacekeeping functions within metropolitan France.[14]

A decision to bolster French military forces at home was controversial in 1948, not only because of the missions that the forces were expected to perform, but also because of the budgetary demands that such a decision made at a time of serious economic difficulty. U.S. reconstruction aid was still earmarked exclusively for nonmilitary uses at this time, and what few funds were available for defense were being consumed by what Guy de Carmoy has described as France's "war without war aims" in Indochina.[15]

During the fall of 1945, French forces under General Leclerc occupied all of Cochin China in an attempt to establish the military context for French negotiations with the various regional and extraregional actors. Leclerc was nonetheless painfully aware of the vulnerability of the forces under his command, and of the limited prospects for reimposing effective French control over Indochina in the face of concerted nationalist opposition. His concerns were shared by Jean Sainteny, the French commissioner for Tonkin, who communicated to the Viet Minh on March 6, 1946, that he would support a negotiated settlement that would recognize the Republic of Vietnam and would commit France to abide by the results of any popular referendum for the unification of Tonkin, Annam, and Cochin China. These preliminary understandings encouraged Ho Chi Minh to travel to Paris in the late spring of 1946 to seek formal recognition of his government. He found a newly elected regime in Paris that was without foreign policy direction and unwilling as well as unable to undertake any new foreign policy commitments at that time. After three and a half months in Paris, Ho returned to Indochina with nothing to show for his efforts; by the end of the year, the French expeditionary forces were engaged in the war that Leclerc had sought to avoid, with limited manpower and equipment and even less purpose.

During the ensuing eight years of warfare, French policy toward Indochina became, if anything, even less clear. Much rhetoric was generated regarding the preservation of the French Union, resistance to world communism, and commitments to the French-sponsored regime of Bao Dai, but no administration during this period really succeeded in resolving the contradictions between these policy goals, or in clearly establishing guidelines for what constituted an acceptable price to pay for the achievement of these ends. Fourth Republic governments were anxious to avoid the domestic political costs associated with any unambiguous commitment to military victory in Indochina during the late 1940s. They therefore resisted the entreaties of Leclerc, who, as early as January 1947, had estimated that 500,000 troops would be required to achieve such a victory in the region.[16] The size of the expeditionary force did grow incrementally during the latter half of the 1940s—from 48,000 in 1945 to 221,000 by 1950, but this was much less than was needed for the job.

It was also far more than the French economy could sustain. Primarily because of the special logistical problems of managing a war across a distance of twelve thousand kilometers, the Indochina campaign cost France an estimated 805 billion francs from 1945 to 1951,[17] representing about 25 percent of the overall French defense budget during the first five years of the conflict and 37 percent of the overall defense budget by the end of 1950.[18] French casualties during the first five years of the war exceeded fifty thousand.

The drain on French manpower and materiel was a source of concern not only to Paris but also to Washington. During the latter half of the 1940s, France represented the greatest potential source of ground forces in the critical region of Western Europe. That this potential contribution was being diverted to support French neo-imperialist pretensions in Asia angered many U.S. policy makers, particularly those members of the universalist/idealist school who were still in positions of influence.

During the first two years of the Truman administration, the United States maintained a policy of rhetorical support for French sovereign claims in Indochina while consciously avoiding becoming entangled in the complex issues involved. France succeeded in drawing the United States farther into the Vietnam conflict during 1947, however, as the fear of a worldwide communist conspiracy under Soviet control began to take hold in Washington. Neither Washington nor Paris succeeded in establishing a direct link between Ho Chi Minh and Moscow during this period, but by the end of the year the United

States was becoming sensitive to circumstantial evidence of Soviet-Vietnamese cooperation. In April of 1947, Acheson expressed suspicion of Ho's links to Moscow on the basis of the fact that the French communist newspaper *L'humanité* did not criticize the Vietminh leader.[19]

U.S. fears of a Vietminh takeover in Indochina were at least partly mitigated, however, by enduring American doubts about the wisdom and propriety of French policies in the region. A general U.S. suspicion of French motives, compounded by a feeling among many American policy makers that France had neither the right nor the capability to pursue a globalist foreign policy in the postwar era, contributed to U.S. reluctance to provide material or political support for the French campaign in Indochina during the late 1940s. But the inevitable tendency to err in favor of caution was already apparent. In a cable sent to the U.S. ambassador in Paris, the State Department demonstrated a classic ambivalence in expressing its own position on the Indochina conflict:

> In spite of any misunderstanding which might have arisen in [French] minds in regard to our position concerning Indochina they must appreciate that we have fully recognized France's sovereign position in that area and we do not wish to have it appear that we are in any way endeavoring undermine that position . . . and French should know it is our desire to be helpful and we stand ready assist any appropriate way we can to find solution for Indochinese problem. At same time we cannot shut our eyes to fact that there are two sides to this problem and that our reports indicate both a lack of French understanding of other side (more in Saigon than in Paris) and the continued existence dangerously outmoded colonial outlook and methods in area. Furthermore, there is no escape from the fact that trend of times is to effect that colonial empires in XIX Century sense are rapidly becoming thing of past. . . . On other hand we do not lose sight fact that Ho Chi Minh has direct Communist connections and it should be obvious that we are not interested in seeing colonial empire administrations supplanted by philosophy and political organizations emanating from and controlled by Kremlin. . . . Frankly we have no solution of problem to suggest.[20]

Washington was searching for ways to resolve the contradiction between Roosevelt's universalist prescriptions regarding anticolonialism and Truman's more recent worries pertaining to the implementation of containment against a global Soviet threat. As the 1940s drew to a close, the latter instinct began to prevail, especially in the aftermath of the victory of the forces of Mao Zedong in China and the invasion of South Korea.

CHAPTER 14

THE WASHINGTON
PREPARATORY TALKS OF
1948-1949

OVEREXTENSION in Indochina placed strict limits on France's ability to contribute ground forces for the defense of Western Europe. This, in turn, undermined French efforts to induce the Anglo-Saxons to grant France equal status in the evolving Western alliance. A special French concern during the latter half of the 1940s was that Paris would be left out of the planning for any collective security system that committed Washington to the defense of Europe; indeed, this anxiety proved to be justified. As noted in Chapter 1, negotiations for the creation of the North Atlantic Treaty Organization were carried on in Washington during the period March 22–April 1, 1948, between the United States, Canada, and the United Kingdom. At U.S. insistence, Paris was deliberately excluded from the first round of talks. Washington preferred to establish a basic understanding with Britain, in particular, on questions relating to the U.S. role in Europe and the potential contribution of Germany to the future defense of the West before confronting the French. The continued influence of the PCF in French politics at the time provided a convenient pretext for keeping Paris out of the preliminary negotiations on the grounds that France represented a security risk.

Under these circumstances, it was not surprising that when France was invited to the second round of talks (June–September 1948), it approached the negotiations with its guard up. As preparations for the second round of the Washington Preparatory Talks progressed, French foreign minister Georges Bidault pressed the case for French inclusion in the Washington-based U.S./U.K. Combined Chiefs of Staff so that Paris could participate in global strategic planning with the Anglo-Saxons. Bidault implied that this was a precondition for French support of any North Atlantic Treaty Organization.

But these preliminary French solicitations met with strong resistance within the U.S. government, with the U.S. Joint Chiefs presenting the main arguments against any French participation in a "Tripartite Chiefs of Staff" arrangement. The position of the Joint Chiefs regarding French participation in the formulation of Western global strategy reflected the logic of the resource/geographic constraints school of U.S. postwar alliance planning (see Chapter 1). It was summarized in a memo from the director of the State Department's Office of European Affairs to Secretary of State Acheson in February 1949: "[According to the Joint Chiefs], the French have basically only European and North African responsibilities, and inadequate strength to play any role in other theaters and therefore are not entitled to participate in consideration of global strategy."[1] The Joint Chiefs even opposed official visits to the United States by French military delegations during this period, on the grounds that French military representatives might attempt to raise the issue of a Combined Chiefs of Staff. Bidault's efforts to establish a special status for France before entering into the negotiations were consequently rebuffed by Washington, although the United States did agree to consider the creation of a three-party "Standing Group" within the context of the treaty negotiations.

During the ensuing nine months of negotiations, the United States sought to skirt the issue of a Combined Chiefs of Staff by recourse to two arguments. First, the U.S. delegates to the Washington Preparatory Talks stressed the need for organizational efficiency in global strategic planning. Theodore Achilles, chief of the West European Desk of the State Department during the talks, attempted to turn away the arguments of the French ambassador by citing General Marshall's injunction against the creation of a "military parliament" to coordinate defense plans. The ambassador assured Achilles that France did not favor the creation of a parliament for global strategic planning, merely a triumvirate. The second American argument was that the U.S.-U.K. Combined Chiefs was a holdover from the war which had no policy significance and, in fact, had not met officially in two years. The French discounted this argument as evasive; they attempted to focus the discussions upon the well-known fact that British and U.S. defense policy makers were in constant touch regarding issues of global security, and that this habit of consultation and cooperation had been developed to the disadvantage of France.[2]

In the face of French persistence, U.S. policy makers sought a compromise solution that would satisfy French sensitivities without granting France an unjustified position in the formulation of Western global strategy. Charles Bohlen proposed such an idea to representatives of the Joint Chiefs in the closing days of the Washington negotiations. He favored an arrangement that would

> give France full membership in whatever was the real controlling body from the military point of view in the Pact, but at the same time confine the functions of any of the organizations under the Pact to the immediate question of the implementation of the Treaty. Under such an arrangement France would be on a full equal

184

footing within the framework of the Pact with any other member, but on matters lying outside of the immediate purposes of the Pact which might involve global strategy—Far East, Middle East, etc.—no mechanism of the Pact would be called upon to deal with such subjects.[3]

This approach to the problem of French status within the new North Atlantic Treaty Organization ultimately served as the basis for the ensuing U.S. position. Washington publicly deferred to France by accepting in principle the creation of a Standing Committee (later called the Standing Group) within the alliance—comprising only France, Great Britain, and the United States. But it was a Pyrrhic victory for Paris, in that the Standing Committee was understood to have no purview beyond the officially designated treaty area—and in any event, all parties understood that the formal creation of the Standing Committee in no way assured its utilization by the Anglo-Saxons.[4] To Washington and London, France still appeared too vulnerable to domestic political turmoil and too reactionary on the question of a viable German state to be trusted with the responsibilities of cooperating on global defense.

CONCESSIONS TO PARIS REGARDING NATO'S BOUNDARIES

Although the French delegation to the Washington talks could claim only limited success in its quest for status, it did achieve two specific concessions—both relating to the territorial scope of the treaty. First, Paris obtained the unanimous support of the conference participants for the inclusion of Algeria in the alliance treaty area. Second, the French succeeded in convincing the signatories to accept the application of Italy for membership in the defense organization.

At the start of the Washington talks, France had taken a position in favor of extending the alliance treaty guarantees to all of its North African possessions. This argument was opposed by all of the other participants as an unnecessary and perhaps ruinous diversion from the central issue of Atlantic defense. Robert Lovett was particularly concerned that "to get into Africa would open up a limitless field" and jeopardize treaty ratification.[5] Paris subsequently settled for a fall-back agreement to incorporate only Algeria in the treaty area. Having offered this accommodation, however, the French representatives dug in their heels. Henri Bonnet, chief of the French delegation to the talks, presented the inclusion of Algeria as a nonnegotiable precondition for French membership: "Algeria was a part of France and in the same relation to France as Alaska or Florida to the United States."[6]

In view of the interest that France had expressed in the creation of an Atlantic Alliance, and the dependent status of Paris within the Western community in 1949, the tough French position with regard to Algeria was probably seen as a bluff by most of the participants in the Washington talks. In fact, however, the unstable domestic political situation in France lent some weight to the French warnings. While Paris could not reasonably threaten to reject Atlantic Alliance membership over the issue of Algeria, it could realistically warn that the government would not succeed in obtaining public or parliamentary support for such an alliance if Algeria was not included. The government was being criticized by some domestic factions for not pressing its case for the inclusion of the protectorates of Morocco and Tunisia in the treaty area, but all parties in France agreed that priority had to be given to the protection of Algeria, both because of its status as a department of France and because of the historical, economic, and social ties between France and the one million European residents of Algeria.

American policy makers appreciated the vulnerability of the French government and were willing to help Paris accommodate domestic pressures on the Algerian issue as long as France's problem did not disrupt the entire treaty process. The sticking point was the wording of the treaty. The State Department encouraged France to accept verbal assurances of support for the French position in Algeria. Acheson argued that "the United States did not see how there could be an attack on Algeria without there being also an attack on European France, unless it was a local scrimmage which would not be within the scope of the treaty. The U.S. would much prefer merely referring to an attack 'in Europe or North America.' "[7]

But Paris held out for a specific statement in the treaty as a matter of principle. If the treaty was to designate a specific area of responsibility, Algeria, as a part of French national territory, had to be included.[8] There was also an unstated concern on the part of the French delegation that Paris and Washington might disagree about the definition of a "local scrimmage" in North Africa at some time in the future, in which case the more binding the contractual commitment on the part of the United States, the better.

At the same time that Paris was pressing for the inclusion of Algeria in the proposed Atlantic treaty area, it was also encouraging the participants in the Pentagon talks to permit Italy to become a founding member of the alliance. Paris was alone in its active sponsorship of Italy, although several participants in the negotiations expressed an appreciation of the value of bringing Rome into some Western defense arrangement—either in an affiliate position in the Atlantic treaty or in a separate Mediterranean defense arrangement. French foreign minister Bidault had originally preferred the inclusion of Italy in a separate collective defense treaty, but by the fall of 1948 he had shifted his position, partly in response to Rome's submission of a request for membership and partly to balance the decidedly North Atlantic orientation of the treaty participants.[9]

U.S. and British accounts of the Washington talks frequently resorted to the term *ad nauseam* to describe French persistence on the issues of Algeria and Italy. In the end, this perseverance was rewarded. France discovered that it had some leverage over the Anglo-Saxons during the first part of 1949 for six reasons: First, as previously mentioned, the United States and Britain were resigned to keeping France in the Atlantic Alliance and were sensitive to the

French government's domestic political problems; second, London and Washington were anxious to reassure France about its security before beginning to revitalize the German economy; third, French agreement was required for the admission of Norway into the alliance—favored by both the United States and the United Kingdom—and Henri Bonnet had made it clear that "French public opinion" would demand a quid pro quo; fourth, Acheson notes in his memoirs that by February of 1949 Truman and the two key congressional participants in the ratification process, Senators Tom Connolly and Arthur Vandenberg, had "lost patience with this haggling" and were willing to agree to French demands so that ratification could be managed expeditiously.[10] The fifth factor working in France's favor was Dutch support, which had been obtained as a result of a secret deal betwen Paris and The Hague. In exchange for Holland's backing on the issues of Italian and Algerian membership, France reversed its voting pattern within the UN Security Council and opposed America's efforts to use the United Nations as a forum for pressuring the Netherlands to modify its colonial policies in Indonesia.[11] Sixth, and perhaps most importantly, although many U.S. and British policy makers were concerned about the risk of jeopardizing the treaty by geographic overextension, the Anglo-Saxons were not insensitive to French arguments regarding the geostrategic importance of the Mediterranean and North Africa for European and Atlantic security.

THE MEDITERRANEAN "TURNTABLE"

During the late 1940s and the 1950s, French military and political elites developed an elaborate geostrategic thesis to press the case for greater allied attention to the Mediterranean and North African region. According to this popularly held French argument, any Western collective security arrangement that did not extend to the southern and eastern shores of the Mediterranean was fundamentally flawed from the outset. From this viewpoint, European history taught, and the experience of World War II had recently confirmed, that North Africa and Western Europe constituted a single organic theater of operations. North Africa represented either the "soft underbelly" of Western European defense or a source of geostrategic depth, manpower, and material, depending upon the foresight of the European leaders of the time. Under these circumstances, the Mediterranean was not the natural southern boundary of a U.S.-European alliance against Russia, but rather the strategic core of a Eurafrican defense.[12] The role of North Africa in World War II was frequently emphasized in support of this argument, and Operation Torch—the combined British-American landing in North Africa and the subsequent utilization of North Africa as a logistical springboard for the Allied Southern European campaign—was held up as the best example of the geostrategic continuity of the northern and southern shores of the Mediterranean. Western Europe and North Africa were consequently to be viewed as constituting a unified theater of operations for the next war, much as they had been in the last—with the Eastern Mediterranean serving as the "turntable of the Atlantic system."

Both London and Washington accepted the basic elements of the geostrategic argument put forward by Paris during the formative period of the alliance. Britain and the United States had shared in the victorious outcome of Operation Torch during World War II, and both had been developing a network of bases in the North African region since the war. The United States in particular recognized that recent technological developments in fact enhanced the geostrategic significance of French North Africa in postwar strategic planning. According to a memorandum from the U.S. Policy Planning Staff dated March 22, 1948,

> With the rapid development of air power, the geographical position of North Africa assumes added importance. In hostile hands, the air and naval bases of this area, especially those in French Morocco, could exercise control over the Atlantic approaches to the Mediterranean and the sea lanes down the West African coast. Such hostile bases could neutralize potential U.S. Atlantic bases in the Azores or other neighboring islands and cut the most direct line of access to the petroleum of the Middle East. Conversely, a North Africa in friendly hands could afford corresponding advantages to the U.S. It would be a valuable base for the launching of air attacks, naval operations or amphibious landings against an enemy-occupied Europe. Its utilization by the U.S. or a friendly power would complement and strengthen any U.S. bases in the Atlantic islands.[13]

Having accepted the geostrategic value of French North Africa, many U.S. planners were prepared to support the recommendation of the Policy Planning Staff: "We should at every opportunity point out to the French that we are not seeking to disrupt their empire or to place in jeopardy their position in North Africa."[14] There was nonetheless a general suspicion in Washington that a policy of reassuring Paris might encourage French insensitivity to nationalist sentiments and demands for reform which had been growing in the region since World War II. The aforementioned report of March 22 noted that "US wartime propaganda was in part responsible for the recent spur to North African nationalism, and for the present unrest in the region."[15] Unless Paris was prepared to deal with these issues constructively and to accommodate the understandable desire for independence over the long term, the West was in danger of losing the region to communist subversion. Many American policy makers agreed with Dean Acheson that "the real difficulty with the French position was that France had no policy in North Africa except repression and hanging on."[16]

In spite of such suspicions, U.S. and British policy makers were sensitive to the fundamental premises of the French geostrategic argument. This fact, plus the aforementioned American and British desires to incorporate France in the alliance and to achieve treaty ratification in the United States as quickly as possible contributed to the decision by the Anglo-Saxons to defer to Paris. In March, Acheson advised the participants in the Washington talks that the

United States was "open minded" on the issue of Italian membership and was prepared to include Algeria in the treaty area as well.[17] French success in obtaining the grudging approval of the treaty signatories for at least a partial orientation of the alliance toward the south and southeast represented one of the most important foreign policy successes in the generally abysmal record of the Fourth Republic.

CHAPTER 15

THE INTERNATIONALIZATION OF THE WAR IN INDOCHINA AND THE FAILURE OF THE EDC, 1950–1954

As PREVIOUSLY noted, U.S. doubts about France's reliability as a guarantor of long-term Western security interests in the Third World had prompted Washington to distance itself from the French in Indochina during the second half of the 1940s. Following the overthrow of Chiang Kai-shek, however, American doubts began to be overshadowed by concern about the spread of communist influence in Asia. No event was more influential in forcing Washington to reassess the fundamental premise of its containment doctrine in Asia. With the "loss of China," America's vision of two-front containment of Russia was placed in jeopardy, and Washington began to reevaluate the contributions that the European colonial powers might make to a rimland containment network in Asia.[1]

From the French point of view in 1949, increased American support was a minor consolation when weighed against the prospect of concerted Chinese Communist support for the Vietminh. The question of how France might buffer itself against such a development had occupied much attention in the quai d'Orsay during the latter half of the 1940s. General Leclerc's warning in 1945 that France could not reestablish control over Indochina in the face of active opposition from China was accepted by many influential policy makers in France at the time. Many of these leaders transformed this thesis into an argument for a policy of accommodation toward Mao Zedong as it became increasingly more apparent that Chinese Communist Party (CCP) forces would eventually be victorious. However, France had chosen the wrong side to negotiate with in 1946 when it had signed the Chunking Treaty with Chiang Kai-shek, and by the fall of 1949 France was scrambling for an opening to the advancing communist forces and investigating the possibility of recognizing the government headed by Mao Zedong. Specifically, four problems made it difficult for Paris to strike a bargain with the CCP during the closing months of 1949:

1. The strategic Sino-Vietnamese border region remained in the hands of the Chinese Nationalists throughout 1949. Accordingly, Paris had to consider the possibility that French cooperation with Mao's forces or an offer of recognition for the incoming Chinese Communist government might precipitate anti-French retaliation by the residual forces of Chiang Kai-shek still deployed in Tonkin.

2. Formal negotiations with Mao or outright French recognition of his government might further undermine the legal status of the government of Bao Dai, which the French had sponsored as a sop to Vietnamese nationalism, and might weaken the morale of the anticommunist Vietnamese forces that were fighting against the Vietminh.

3. State-to-state relations between Paris and the regime of Mao Zedong would not necessarily preclude Chinese support for the Vietminh. Indeed, it would have been naive to expect such a development, in view of the network of cooperation that had already been developed between China and the Vietminh.

4. France could not move too far or too fast in a policy of accommodation toward Mao without running afoul of Washington, which was pressing the allies to stand firm against the incoming Chinese Communist regime.[2]

Paris continued to struggle with the question of recognizing the CCP government throughout 1949, always alert to the risk that the Anglo-Saxons might strike a deal with Mao ahead of France, thereby eliminating whatever negotiating leverage Paris still had. The issue was finally resolved for France in January of 1950, when Mao became the first communist leader to extend diplomatic recognition to the regime headed by Ho Chi Minh. For the next six months, Foreign Minister Bidault hinted that France would consider recognizing the People's Republic of China if the Chinese limited their military support of Ho.[3] But the strategic moment for an accommodation had passed—if it had ever existed. With the start of the Korean War, France was forced to conclude that it had no choice but to follow Washington's lead in regard to China, and to accept the consequences in Southeast Asia.

During 1949 and 1950, the People's Liberation Army (PLA) cooperated with the Vietminh in establishing a vast system of supply routes by land (across the Sino-Vietnamese border along five routes converging on Hanoi) and by sea (mostly through Hainan Island off the North Vietnamese coast). Once the infrastructure of support for Sino-Vietnamese military cooperation had been established, Peking and Moscow were able to provide an uninterrupted supply of materiel to the forces of General Giap. During this period, the PLA also established training schools for Vietminh troops in the Gaungxi region north of the Sino-Vietnamese border and on Hainan Island. By the spring of 1951, between fifty thousand and seventy-five thousand Vietminh had been trained and equipped by PLA cadres. East German, Russian, and Chinese instructors were also engaged in training Vietminh pilots at the PLA air force school on Hainan.[4]

French expeditionary forces along the border sought to preserve their positions but were dangerously overextended. France finally lost the region in September of 1950, when Chinese and Vietminh forces overran the French strongholds of Cao Bong and Lang Son, resulting in the death or capture of six thousand French troops.[5] The collapse of French positions along the Sino-Vietnamese border encouraged Washington to reconsider plans to provide Mutual Defense Assistance Program (MDAP) funds in support of the French war effort. The United States had, in fact, initiated a program of aid to France in the early spring of 1950. An appropriation of $10 million had been approved by Congress on March 8; on June 28 (three days after the North Korean invasion of South Korea), Truman had directed the secretary of state to increase the size of the U.S. contribution to the French campaign against Ho Chi Minh.[6]

In the wake of the catastrophic French defeats in the border region, however, some U.S. policy advisers began to question why Washington should support France in Indochina at the expense of other U.S. security commitments. John Ohly, deputy director of MDAP, presented Acheson with a particularly forceful argument in favor of backing away from an Indochina commitment. It was a position that would surface time and again during subsequent burden-sharing discussions about the level of support that the United States should provide to the French in Indochina.[7] By way of introduction, Ohly cited reports by recent U.S. military missions to Indochina which were highly critical of French management of the war effort. He charged France with obduracy and a failure of political leadership in the region. He then turned his attention to the costs that the United States and the Western alliance could reasonably expect to incur in the near term in support of the French campaign in Indochina. French military equipment costs, most of which would be borne by the United States, were expected to be about $500 million during 1951, and "we have already indicated our belief . . . that these requirements will substantially increase."

Along with these direct costs, Ohly recommended that Washington consider the indirect cost of diverting French troops from continental Europe to the Indochina theater. Ohly cited a CIA memorandum completed at the end of 1950, which noted that 147,000 French army regulars were tied down in Indochina in support of 200,000 "native forces." The regular army forces deployed in Indochina represented 49 percent of all French career enlisted personnel at the time, as well as 20 percent of all regular army officers and 28 percent of all career NCOs. French officers were being killed at a faster rate than the French military academy at St. Cyr was producing graduates.[8]

France was expected to contribute ten fully equipped divisions to the new

NATO alliance by the end of 1951 and twenty-seven divisions by the beginning of 1954. Ohly warned of "bottlenecks" in the staffing, training, and equipping of French forces earmarked for NATO in 1950, which would make it difficult for France to achieve its force goals for 1951 or 1954. (In fact, by the end of 1951, only three fully equipped French metropolitan divisions were available for NATO services.)[9] He noted that U.S. efforts to compensate for shortfalls in French contributions to NATO would have a ripple effect in other components of the "Medium Term Plan" for Atlantic defense, including the training and equipping of units from other European countries. Ohly also warned that a decision to provide the necessary support for the French war effort could result in a six-month delay in plans for forming and equipping German, Greek, and Turkish units and a "six month delay in the date when North Atlantic Treaty forces will be adequate to resist Soviet aggression." Ohly closed his analysis with an "additional caveat":

We are . . . slowly (and not too slowly) getting ourselves into a position where our responsibilities tend to supplant rather than supplement those of the French. . . . We may be on the road to being a scapegoat, and we are certainly dangerously close to the point of being so deeply committed that we may find ourselves completely committed even to direct intervention. These situations, unfortunately, have a way of snowballing.[10]

In his memoirs, Acheson credits Ohly with "presciently" assessing the situation and implies that he took special note of Ohly's "perceptive warning."[11] Acheson nonetheless weighed Ohly's report against the assessments of the Indochina situation made by the CIA, the Joint Chiefs of Staff, and the Joint Strategic Survey Committee in the late 1940s and 1950. These studies tended to share—and in some cases exceed—Ohly's skepticism regarding French reliability, but they tended to place greater emphasis upon the danger that "a Vietminh victory would lead to the transformation of Indochina into a communist satellite" and upon the domino effect throughout Southeast Asia in the event of a victory for the forces of Ho Chi Minh in Indochina.[12] Under these circumstances, Acheson says somewhat wistfully, "I decided . . . that having put our hand to the plow, we would not look back."[13]

By 1950, the United States was therefore resigned to a policy of support—but not blind support—for France in Indochina. All of the above-mentioned policy studies emphasized the need to press France for a sincere commitment to reform the political system in Indochina as a condition of U.S. assistance. According to a memorandum from the JCS, "Popular support of the Government by the Indochinese people is essential to a favorable settlement of the security problem." To achieve such popular support, the French would have to abandon their colonialist pretensions and pursue a program leading to the "eventual self-government of Indochina either within or outside of the French Union."[14] The French sponsorship of Bao Dai was generally viewed as a cynical and (more importantly) an untenable deception. According to one State Department assessment, the emperor was "a figure deserving of the ridicule and contempt with which he is generally regarded by the Vietnamese."[15]

The Joint Chiefs further recommended that Washington institute a system of checks to ensure that its conditions for U.S. aid were met by the French. No such specific set of policy conditions was established between the United States and France during the period 1950–54, but American field representatives in Paris and Saigon were routinely encouraged by Washington to press the French for assurances of support for Indochinese nationalist demands. These requests, whether in Paris or Saigon, were consistently rebuffed as interference in French domestic politics. French representatives were also alert to any hint of U.S. meddling in the relations between Paris and the governments of the three "associated states" of Vietnam, Cambodia, and Laos. During the Franco-American Washington Conference (September 17, 1951), General de Lattre complained that in 1950, "a number of young men with a 'missionary zeal'" had managed the distribution of U.S. economic aid to the associated states, "with the result that there was a feeling on the part of some that they were using this aid to extend American influence." He warned that "the results could only be bad "if somebody was attempting to 'put rocks' into the machinery . . . particularly when the French Commonwealth was involved."[16]

From the perspective of French military planners, France was doing more than its fair share to protect Western security interests by means of its anticommunist campaign in the Third World. The NATO alliance was threatened by a *guerre révolutionnaire* of global proportions, coordinated by Moscow and exploiting the nationalist sentiments of Third World peoples. Only the *grande position française* was sufficiently global in scope and sufficiently well established at strategic points in the Mediterranean, North Africa, and Southeast Asia to provide a viable basis for resisting a communist encirclement strategy targeted against out-of-area footholds held by Atlantic Alliance members. Paris was not opposed to a situation in which the United States would provide the weapons and the financial support so that France could do most of the fighting against a common enemy, but Paris would not permit Washington to assume direction or even to establish oversight regarding a war fought under these terms. French leaders also claimed that because French troops were being killed in pursuit of common Western security interests, French demands for equal status with the Anglo-Saxons in the formulation of global strategy were justified. Failure on the part of Washington and London to accord equal status to Paris during the period of the Indochina war convinced many members of the Fourth Republic of the eventual necessity of greater independence in security affairs.

In the interim, however, there was no alternative to American sponsorship of French defense policy. Following the collapse of the French positions along the Sino-Vietnamese border, Paris solicited a firm commitment from its Anglo-

Saxon allies that they would provide immediate military assistance in the event of a People's Liberation Army offensive in North Vietnam. A succession of French military delegations sought to alert British and American defense planners to the imminent threat posed by the presence of 250,000 PLA troops in the Sino-Vietnamese border region, and to the mutual interest of all Western governments in the preservation of the French military presence in North Vietnam. Tonkin was the "keystone to the entire defense system for Southeast Asia," according to Marshal Juin, commander in chief of the Allied Land Forces in Central Europe. If the Chinese invaded and were not confronted with a coordinated Western military response, the allies would see the collapse of the Western security framework in Asia and "horrible disaster for the 80,000 men of the Expeditionary Force" in Tonkin.[17]

According to French military sources, the prospect of such an invasion had greatly increased by the end of 1951.[18] Washington and London responded to such warnings by reassuring Paris that they appreciated the strategic importance of Tonkin, but they continued to resist French requests for a specific prior commitment. The Anglo-Saxons did agree to coordinate their defense activities in Asia and to transmit a joint deterrent threat to Beijing to discourage intervention. But, in spite of these reassurances, the fear was to persist among French military leaders that if the PLA moved south, the allies would temporize and fiddle with the UN machinery until the fate of Tonkin was already sealed.

Factions within the U.S. government (in particular, the U.S. delegation in Saigon) were in favor of a prior commitment to France as early as January 1951.[19] But the general inclination of U.S. planners (in particular, the Joint Chiefs of Staff) was to coordinate plans internally for a U.S. response in support of France while avoiding bilateral or multilateral commitments that might limit U.S. foreign policy flexibility in a crisis and force Washington to misallocate scarce military assets in the global struggle against communism. Indeed, during this period the Joint Chiefs even tended to oppose discussions between U.S./U.K. and French defense ministers on issues relating to Asian security, on the grounds that such discussions might unnecessarily constrain American military planning for the region.[20]

Influential factions in Washington also encouraged Truman and Eisenhower to block French efforts to obtain the official sanction of the Atlantic Alliance for its efforts in Indochina. These critics warned that France would use any official NATO statement as a lever in negotiations with Washington to obtain more military aid. Concern was also expressed that such a statement, while consistent with the consultation clause of the NATO Treaty (Article 4), might undermine the specific boundary designations of the treaty incorporated in Article 6 and set a precedent for requests for similar statements relating to Malaya or other out-of-area disputes.[21]

Washington nonetheless acquiesced in French arguments that a formal blessing of the Indochina defense effort was necessary to overall Western containment efforts. In December 1952, the NATO Council, under the chairmanship of Lord Ismay, issued its first official statement regarding a conflict beyond the established treaty area. The council asserted its "wholehearted admiration" for the French war effort in Indochina, which was "in fullest harmony with the aims and ideals of the Atlantic Community" and deserved "continuing support from the NATO governments."[22] The statement remains one of the most ambitious NATO positions regarding an out-of-area question. It also represented a victory for French foreign policy makers and a step toward the fulfillment of French premier Edgar Faure's "Grand Plan" for the Western alliance.

The "Grand Plan" had been introduced at the Lisbon Conference in February 1952. It called for the *OTANization* of the French war effort in Indochina (i.e., associating NATO with the French campaign in Vietnam) as one component of a coordinated global strategy of Western resistance to the forces of worldwide communism.[23] Faure's success at the Lisbon Conference was nonetheless overshadowed by the fall of his government four days after the close of the conference. Its demise came as a direct result of France's proposal to increase the defense budget by 15 percent in order to meet European troop commitments agreed upon in Lisbon while simultaneously maintaining the war effort in Asia.

When the NATO Council memorandum was published, it also represented a personal victory for Lord Ismay in his campaign to encourage the members of the alliance to accept a globalist orientation and to develop institutional mechanisms for global security consultation within NATO. Dean Acheson could nonetheless reassure Truman on the day that the resolution was drafted that "it does not point the finger at us for more help or involve NATO out there."[24] Indeed, Washington encouraged other alliance members to "carry the burden" of argument against any more ambitious resolution that would formally bind NATO to the French military cause in Indochina. This permitted the United States "to remain in [the] background" and avoid "the appearance of overt U.S. minimizing of French contributions to Western security interests in Southeast Asia."[25] The American tactic did not fool Paris, however, and it became a major long-term irritant in French-American relations.

U.S. support for the French in Indochina increased after the Eisenhower administration came to office in January 1953. The new president was anxious to make good on his campaign commitment to achieve a quick end to the war in Korea, and he was eager to obtain the cooperation of France and Britain in the pursuit of this goal. Eisenhower was therefore more sensitive than his predecessor had been to French arguments regarding the need for a coordinated "hemispheric" view of the threat posed by international communism in Asia and to French requests for increased economic and political support for the war effort in Indochina. The French government was alerted to the change in the U.S. position when Eisenhower announced in his first State of the Union Message (February 2) that the U.S. Seventh Fleet would no longer be employed to "shield communist China" from attacks from Taiwan. This message was reinforced two weeks later when French military officials in Taiwan obtained confidential information that the United States was coordinating plans with the Nationalist government of Chiang Kai-shek for a three-front anticommunist offensive—in Korea and Indochina and on the eastern coast of the Chinese mainland, with plans for the occupation of strategic points in eastern China modeled after earlier Japanese war plans.[26] As a result of these encouraging signs, French political and military representatives redoubled their efforts to solicit direct and indirect American backing for the Indochina war effort.

Edgar Faure's "Grand Plan" for Indochina defense cooperation was officially approved by the U.S. government in September of 1953—in part to encourage France to persevere in its floundering war effort, and in part to attract votes within the National Assembly for the creation of the European Defense Community, which, by this time, had been entirely co-opted by Washington.[27] The United States agreed during the latter half of 1953 to lend France two aircraft carriers and to equip fifty-four additional French battalions stationed or earmarked for duty in Indochina.[28] Washington nonetheless held to its policy of resisting pressures for direct military intervention by American forces and continued to demand some oversight of the flow of aid to the Indochina war effort. It also tied further U.S. military assistance to signs of progress in the French military campaign and to commitments by Paris that the Indochinese states would soon gain their independence.[29]

DEFEAT IN INDOCHINA: RAMIFICATIONS FOR NATO

In spite of the increased U.S. military contribution, Bidault warned Eisenhower and Churchill at the end of 1953 that the French public was becoming increasingly critical of the war effort and that a series of decisive victories was required in order for the French to persevere in Indochina. General Henri Navarre, commander in chief of the French forces in Indochina, favored Dien Bien Phu, in a remote northwestern Vietnamese valley, as a "mooring point" for a major confrontation with the forces of General Giap. Some military leaders in the United States questioned the selection of Dien Bien Phu. In particular, Dwight Eisenhower asked the French why they were inclined to gamble everything at an "isolated fortress . . . whose only means of resupply was by air."[30] Washington nonetheless deferred to Paris while reserving the right to criticize in the event of a catastrophe.

The valley had been a Vietminh stronghold that Navarre's forces had recaptured during November and December of 1953. The French quickly reinforced the garrison in expectation of a counteroffensive in the spring. When it came, however, Navarre's commanders were totally unprepared for the size of the enemy attack. After the first day of battle (March 13), the Vietminh had routed the French from two of the three key artillery positions defending the valley. Following the first attack, fifty thousand Vietminh encircled the French contingent of twelve thousand and then settled in to prepare for a final offensive. The consensus among French military experts was that only a military intervention by U.S. forces, or at least U.S. air power, could raise the siege.

On March 20, General Ely, the French chief of staff, met with Admiral Radford, chairman of the U.S. Joint Chiefs, to solicit U.S. aid. As noted in Chapter 11, Radford strongly backed a more aggressive U.S. military posture in Asia. He entered into discussions with Ely about providing several hundred U.S. bombers and fighter aircraft to support the garrison at Dien Bien Phu. When he presented his plan to the Washington defense community, however, Radford discovered that his offer of support was not unanimously approved by the Joint Chiefs. The plan, known as Operation Vulture, was viewed by Army Chief of Staff Matthew B. Ridgway and other U.S. military leaders as a "serious diversion of limited US capabilities" which could precipitate a military response by China.[31] More importantly, Dulles and Eisenhower were skeptical of the plan's military feasibility and of the potential political costs. Fearing a new Korea, Eisenhower, as we have related previously, made any U.S. military commitment contingent on congressional support. Key congressional leaders in turn advised the administration that they would withhold support unless Washington's NATO allies were actively and publicly behind any U.S. action. Special reference was made to the need to elicit British backing for any military initiative.

The issue came to a head on April 23, following a NATO Ministerial Meeting in Paris at which a communiqué was issued that officially "paid tribute to the gallantry of the French Union forces fighting in Indochina."[32] On that day, Navarre communicated to Paris that the situation could only be saved by a U.S. air strike within seventy-two hours. John Foster Dulles' presence in Paris on this occasion provided Bidault with an opportunity to communicate the Navarre message directly and to solicit a response. The U.S. secretary of state, fresh from discussions in London on a united front for collective action in Indochina, advised Bidault that the British remained firmly opposed to military intervention and that the provision of U.S. bombers "seemed to me out of the question under existing circumstances."[33]

At the same time, Prime Minister Laniel was meeting with Douglas MacArthur II (Counselor of the U.S. State Department in Paris) to advise him that in the event that Dien Bien Phu was overrun, his government would have great difficulty in maintaining any public support for a presence in Indochina, and the US-sponsored EDC proposal would probably fail as well. MacArthur reported that he told Laniel that "the picture he had painted seemed to me catastrophic in terms of France's future. . . . I could not conceive how any Frenchman could reason that the fall of an outpost in Indochina must result in the abandonment of that area and the destruction of the collective defense system which we had together developed for the defense of Western Europe." Laniel agreed with MacArthur's argument that it was not "logical," but lectured the American diplomat that "Dien Bien Phu had become a symbol in the minds of the French people and Parliament . . . a tremendously emotional thing and Frenchmen were no longer capable of reasoning about it." MacArthur warned the French prime minister that such developments "would seem to leave the US no choice but to rethink, not only its strategic policy, but its entire political relationship with respect to France." Laniel could only express his desire that a rift be avoided, but doubted that he would be in office to help "control the ground swell."[34] Laniel's political prediction was confirmed seven weeks later when his government fell by a vote of 306 to 293, to be replaced by a cabinet headed by Pierre Mendès-France.

When it came, the groundswell of criticism in France was largely aimed at the United States, which was viewed by many Frenchmen as having given just enough support and encouragement to successive Fourth Republic govern-ments to maintain the illusion of ultimate victory. During the period 1950–54, U.S. financial and political support for the Indochina campaign had accelerated until Washington had effectively supplanted Paris—precisely as John Ohly had warned in 1950—as the financial sponsor of the war. According to U.S. con-gressional sources, American military aid to the French in Indochina totaled $2.6 billion during the first four years of the 1950s, representing 80 percent of the funding for the war effort.[35] The aforementioned U.S. efforts to monitor the French military campaign nonetheless contributed to a growing resentment of U.S. Vietnam policy on the part of both mass and elite French publics during the period of rapidly escalating American support. Moreover, French press reports at the end of the war stressed French contributions to the war effort almost exclusively, downplaying U.S. aid as too little, too late, and with too many strings attached.

Georgette Elgey's analysis of the U.S. role in Indochina reflects the general orientation of many French historians of the period. In her interpretation of why France was eventually defeated in her Asian colony, she contrasts U.S. backing during the early 1950s with U.S. indifference or opposition during the for-mative period of the Indochina war. Elgey notes, for example, that the United States and China provided $100,000 per month in equipment and supplies to the forces of Ho Chi Minh during World War II, much of which was subsequently used against the forces of the French Union.[36] Many French political figures were completely able to discount the contribution that Washington had made. Jacques Soustelle articulated this mood with a retrospective assessment in *Foreign Affairs* in 1956: "In the Far East, France has derived no help from the fact that she is an ally of Britain and the United States. . . . she has found herself ousted from the south of Indochina under conditions that lead an impor-tant part of French public opinion to suspect that the United States actively contributed to this result."[37]

On the other side of the Atlantic, the fall of Dien Bien Phu and the subsequent French retreat from Indochina confirmed for many U.S. policy makers the 1949

assessment by the Joint Chiefs—that the French were "not entitled to participate in considerations of global strategy." In spite of his sympathy for the
French plight, Eisenhower could not resist judging the French harshly for their
overall management of the war and, more specifically, for their mismanagement of the Dien Bien Phu campaign. The fiasco of Dien Bien Phu appeared to
many U.S. policy makers as the logical culmination of a long history of
failures—for four years Washington had given France the tools with which to
win in Indochina, but the French had proven themselves unable to do the job.

The French "loss" of Indochina had both direct and indirect repercussions
within the Atlantic Alliance. The direct impact was the failure of the EDC and
the subsequent remilitarization of Germany under NATO auspices. The issue
had been kept in the background of Western debates during the late 1940s, but it
had become a much more visible and tendentious topic after the establishment
of the Medium Term Defense Plan in 1950 and the subsequent establishment of
the Lisbon Conference force goals in 1952. As discussed in Chapter 2, increasing NATO's ground forces was a central component of both of these programs.
The question was, where would the troops come from? A study by the Royal
Institute of International Affairs summarized the problem.

> Of the French army . . . eight divisions were in Indochina, two in North Africa
> and two in other parts of the French Union. Nevertheless in the event of (a
> European) war the burden of the first months must fall on France which was
> expected to raise and put into the field five divisions in three days after the
> declaration of a state of emergency and another fifteen divisions by the end of the
> month. . . .
>   . . . In effect, therefore, General Eisenhower [NATO's SACEUR] was ex-
> pected to fight a holding campaign for two or three months . . . reinforced by the
> mobilized French army. This prospect was not particularly attractive to the French,
> nor was it reassuring to those in other countries who still measured French capacity
> by the events of the 1940s.[38]

French foreign minister M. Robert Schumann, in discussions with his counterparts at Lisbon, noted that his nation's forces could not indefinitely maintain
their strategic position in Southeast Asia on behalf of the West if Paris was
required to meet the necessary force level criteria set out by the Wise Men at
Lisbon. British foreign minister Anthony Eden alluded to similar problems that
the U.K. would face in continuing to subdue Malayan communist insurgents.
The projected German manpower contribution to the EDC was clearly perceived as the only realistic short-term option for upgrading Western European
conventional defenses while the British and the French still felt compelled to
pursue their national security interests abroad.[39] Shortly after the Lisbon Conference, the French government signed the Treaty of Paris (May 27, 1952),
which committed France, West Germany, Italy, and the Benelux states to the
creation of the European Defense Community. All parties recognized it for

what it was—the best deal that Paris could get in a situation of extremely limited French influence.

More than two years were to pass, however, before France made a final decision on ratifying the treaty. Mendès-France decided to face the issue in 1954, while French mass and elite opinion was still in an uproar over Dien Bien Phu. The result was that "the national assembly refused by 319 to 264 votes to even take up proper discussion of the Treaty," which was shelved as a consequence.[40]

West Germany's contribution to European defense had to be renegotiated after the EDC was rejected by the French Assembly in August 1954. The United States announced that it would have to "reappraise its foreign policies" in response to the French rejection, and Secretary of State Dulles went so far as to condemn publicly France's "one country nationalism." But a paper prepared by the U.S. Policy Planning Staff was somewhat more balanced in its assessment of the reasons for French rejection of the EDC.

> EDC failed, in the last analysis, because in the early showdown it represented to many Europeans, particularly the French, a *U.S.* project to force *premature* [European] federation along *military* lines involving a high risk of ultimate *German* predominance in a European union, and with a too apparent concern for the realization of EDC as a device for mobilizing German armed forces.[41]

Washington nonetheless subsequently slowed military assistance deliveries to France, although it continued to provide arms and materiel for the final stages of the war effort in Indochina.[42]

The "loss" of Indochina also had a more significant, if indirect, impact on France's role in NATO. Having found a way to blame unreliable allies, many influential French policy makers came away from Dien Bien Phu impressed with the rightness of de Gaulle's arguments for a defense policy oriented around the themes of national self-reliance and independence. Interestingly, no one seems to have questioned the logic of empire, which de Gaulle had reintroduced in 1944 and which had ultimately led France to the catastrophe of Dien Bien Phu. Finally, the fact that NATO's first official statement of support for an ally's out-of-area activities was subsequently tested by France and found to be a meaningless diplomatic nicety was not lost on the other members of the Atlantic Alliance who still maintained colonial outposts throughout the world.

CHAPTER 16

"LACHONS L'ASIE,
PRENONS L'AFRIQUE"

IN HIS DRAMATIC account of the Algerian War, Alistair Horne has described the way in which the problems faced by France in Vietnam were transferred directly to North Africa after the collapse of the Indochina war effort. On May 7, 1954, the day that the fall of Dien Bien Phu was announced to the world, the Comité révolutionnaire d'unité et d'action (CRUA) held its first plenary meeting in Algiers. The purpose of the meeting was to establish at least a temporary and conditional truce between factions that had been competing for leadership of the Algerian independence movement, in preparation for a general revolt. Ho Chi Minh's victory was a key factor in encouraging these groups to cooperate at a time of French political, psychological, and military vulnerability. In subsequent meetings, a collective leadership was established, a new name was created—the Front de libération nationale (FLN)—and a date was chosen for a major uprising against French rule.[1]

The FLN struck in thirty locations in eastern Algeria on the morning of November 1, 1954. François Mitterrand, the minister of the interior, epitomized the French government's position in his response to the news of the revolt: "There can be only one form of negotiation: war."[2] The 25th Airborne Division was immediately deployed from the metropole to Algeria—to be followed during the next several months by troops drawn from other units in Indochina, Germany, and metropolitan France. The size of the French force grew from 50,000 to 117,000 within days, and by the end of 1956 the figure was 500,000.[3] Jacques Soustelle was appointed governor general of Algeria in early 1955, with a mandate to pursue a policy of "pacification" in the rebellious

---

The title of this chapter is the title of an article by Onesime Réclus, written during the late nineteenth century, which favored giving priority to Africa in French imperial policies. Cited in Christopher Andrew and A. S. Kanya-Forstner, *The Climax of French Imperial Expansion, 1914–1924* (Stanford: Stanford University Press, 1981), p. 35.

colony. In April, the French government approved the suspension of civil liberties in Algeria. Throughout the summer, both sides established their positions and engaged in periodic offensives, culminating with a confrontation between French and FLN forces in August at Philippeville. From that point on, Soustelle recounts, "there had been well and truly dug an abyss through which flowed a river of blood."[4] France was once again inextricably at war with her empire.

Along with the prospects of another long and bloody war, Paris faced the possibility of once again having to solicit U.S. and NATO support for its war efforts. Many French policy makers, however, felt that the Western allies could be relied upon to provide greater support for French efforts in Algeria than they had in Indochina. After all, Algeria had been officially recognized as part of the NATO Treaty area since 1949. Others, chastened by the Indochina experience, sought assurances.

As had been the case in Indochina, however, French policy makers were reluctant to bring NATO into the Algerian situation in some direct way, for fear that the United States would meddle in France's *domaine réservé*. In fact, successive Fourth Republic governments had been seeking assurances from Washington since 1951—in the form of a public statement of noninterference in North African affairs—as a means of enhancing French foreign policy flexibility in the region. The U.S. State Department stalled on this request through the spring of 1953, at which time the French intensified their campaign. Washington's position was established in an aerogram from Acting Secretary of State Walter Bedell Smith to the U.S. embassy in Paris. The United States regretted that "as a matter of principle" it could not offer a noninterference statement for North Africa. While Washington was prepared to reiterate its "unequivocal support" for a continued French presence in North Africa, France should appreciate that the United States had interests and ties in the region as well. Finally, Smith reminded the embassy that "French policy has heretofore contributed little to [the] solution [of] nationalist problems" in the region, and that the situation was too important to be disregarded by Washington.[5] But balanced against the dangers of French mismanagement was the persistent U.S. concern that "effervescent nationalism" would ultimately undermine the Western security system throughout North Africa if the French loosened their grip.

In the face of such contradictory concerns, Washington once again opted for a "middle-of-the-road approach," involving constant monitoring of French actions at the same time that the United States provided public and private assurances of its support in principle for a continued French presence in the region. To the extent possible, the Americans sought to avoid any actions that could be interpreted by Paris as meddling in Franco-Algerian relations during this period. But Washington was somewhat more willing to involve itself in the cases of Morocco and Tunisia if French policies threatened to jeopardize the network of U.S. bases in the two French protectorates (which at this time consisted of four major air bases in Morocco and the huge facility at Bizerta in Tunisia).[6] The United States also believed that the situation in Algeria was more stable than in the two French protectorates during the first half of the 1950s and, consequently, was more inclined to keep out of Franco-Algerian affairs.

By the end of 1955, however, the situation had changed. Paris had succeeded in managing its relations with Morocco and Tunisia to the general satisfaction of the NATO allies during 1954 and 1955. Both protectorates had been able to work out compromise arrangements with Paris which allowed them to acquire national independence (officially established in the spring of 1956) while permitting the French to maintain sizable forces on their territories for an unspecified period of transition. In Algeria, however, things had completely unraveled following the imposition of Soustelle's pacification campaign.

French policy makers were concerned that Washington could not long resist the temptation to meddle in Algeria as the situation became more dangerous. On the day Prime Minister Mendès-France addressed the National Assembly (November 12, 1954) on the gravity of the Algerian situation, the French secretary of the army, Jacques Chevallier, acknowledged that French utilization of military equipment obtained from Washington was "a politically important problem in the United States." He assured U.S. ambassador Douglas Dillon, however, that the crisis in Algeria was under control and that MDAP materiel represented less than 1 percent of the equipment in use in Algeria and Tunisia.[7]

Throughout 1955, the issue received increased public attention in the United States. Washington, nonetheless, maintained its policy of noninterference in French policies in Algeria, and the United States backed France in its decision to withdraw three of its five ground divisions from NATO for service in Algeria. The North Atlantic Council officially approved this French initiative on March 27, 1956, stating that "the Council recognizes the importance to NATO of security in this area. Expressing the hope of an early and lasting settlement, the Council noted the determination of the French Government to restore, as soon as possible, its full contribution toward the common defense of Europe."[8] Washington and London also offered to provide Paris with helicopters that had been earmarked for NATO, for combat support in Algeria in 1956, based upon French reassurances that the insurrection was under control and reforms were being instituted.

As had been the case in Indochina, American initiatives in support of the French war effort in Algeria satisfied neither public nor elite opinion in France. The consensus was that Washington still did not appreciate the contribution that France was making to overall Western security by its efforts in North Africa. Soustelle reflected the feeling of the majority within the French electorate in the aforementioned October 1956 *Foreign Affairs* article. He complained that the Anglo-Saxons had "taken our troubles rather lightly and have accepted without excessive regret the prospect of seeing French Africa—that is to say, French power—collapse."[9] Robert Murphy, U.S. undersecretary for political affairs, cabled Washington on March 3 to warn of a "psychological phenomenon . . . a curious, and from our point of view very unhappy, French attitude developing which seeks to place the onus for the French predicament in Algeria . . . on the United States."[10]

Soustelle, like many other Frenchmen, was particularly critical of the "apparently inexhaustible complacency" of most NATO allies regarding the behavior of Egyptian president Gamel Abdul Nasser. French opinion was virtually unanimous that Nasser was one of the driving forces behind the Algerian revolution. According to Soustelle, "Egyptian Pan-Arabism and Algerian terrorism" were the "two inert chemicals" that had combined to create the revolution.[11] Premier Guy Mollet claimed that 25 percent of all the arms captured from the rebels had been funneled through Cairo.[12]

Mollet was pleased to discover, however, that, at least on questions relating to Egypt, the Anglo-Saxons were not unified in opposition to French policy. He found a sympathetic listener in British foreign secretary Anthony Eden as long as the discussion focused on the threat posed by Nasser or on the difficulty of working with John Foster Dulles. The two leaders met on March 11 and 12, 1956, to discuss general problems relating to the Middle East. Both men appear to have come away from these initial meetings convinced that something should—and, more to the point, could—be done to restrain "an upstart like Nasser." During the next seven months, French public and elite opinion generally worked to reinforce Mollet's resolve on this point. Eden, on the other hand, was subjected to a barrage of conflicting arguments relating to Egypt, Nasser, and the evolving Suez crisis.

As the confrontation approached, Eden in particular was anxious to obtain the imprimatur, if not the active support, of NATO for a strong Franco-British position against Nasser. The allies were consulted on September 5, and the British delegation to NATO was pleased to find a "vigorous ally" in the person of Joseph Luns, then Dutch foreign minister. Support in principle was also offered by Lester Pearson of Canada and P.-H. Spaak of Belgium. Efforts to develop a common position among the NATO allies nonetheless foundered on U.S. opposition, as discussed in Chapters 3 and 9.

In France, the "psychological phenomenon" that Murphy had warned about—composed of anti-Americanism, national frustration, and humiliation—took on increased clarity and focus during the summer of 1956 as Paris and London made plans to "chase Nasser out of Egypt." The press, the politicians, and the general public stressed Nasser's ties to Moscow, his threats against Western security interests, and, most importantly, his support for the FLN. Thus, when

Mollet called for "an energetic and severe counter-stroke" against Nasser in the wake of the nationalization of the canal, he knew that he could rely upon the French mass and elite publics to support him.

British support came as something of a happy surprise to the French government during the summer of 1956. But American taciturnity on the Suez issue confirmed the expectations of Mollet, the French press, and the general public. There was widespread suspicion that Washington was maneuvering to supplant French influence in North Africa in general, and in the oil-producing states in particular. U.S. opposition to coordinated NATO action on the issue of Suez was interpreted in France as one component of that strategy. But even the hypercritical French press was unprepared for the rebuke that Paris suffered from Washington in response to the launching of Operation Musketeer on October 31. As events during the next few days were to demonstrate, Eisenhower and Dulles were in essential agreement that Washington was relieved of all responsibility to support its NATO allies by the fact that Britain and France had developed their war plans in complete secrecy, with an eye toward presenting the United States with a *fait accompli*. Eisenhower felt a special sense of betrayal at having been presented with a choice between "following in the foot-steps of Anglo-French colonialism in Asia and Africa or splitting our course away from their course."[13]

Faced with an unexpectedly strong American reaction to the intervention and direct Soviet threats against Paris and London, the British were the first to agree to a cease-fire. Mollet and French foreign minister Christian Pineau implored Britain to hold out for two more days. But Eden admitted that he had already agreed to American demands for a cease-fire even before consulting his French ally. Eden's unilateral action permitted the French public, and the French military in particular, to foster the myth of an imminent military victory betrayed by the perpetually perfidious British.

For Britain, the psychological fallout from the Suez fiasco was at least partly reduced by the fact that the nation had not been completely behind the intervention. Donald Neff mentions the alacrity with which major newspapers and magazines in Britain took to calling the intervention "Eden's war."[14] In France, on the other hand, there was no way to mute the shock. In a phrase that was curiously similar to Eisenhower's remark, an article in the generally pro-Atlanticist newspaper *Le Figaro* warned the United States not to force France "to choose between its African vocation and its friendship for America."[15]

In the wake of the Suez crisis, FLN forces redoubled their efforts to force the French to agree to independence as the precondition for negotiations. The Algerian rebels also sought to take advantage of the animosities between Washington and Paris by soliciting American support for their cause. Throughout 1957 and 1958, the FLN achieved a number of victories in its efforts to internationalize the Algerian conflict. The most important success in terms of U.S. opinion was achieved when John F. Kennedy chose the issue of Algeria for his first major speech as a member of the Senate Foreign Relations Committee in July 1957.

Kennedy considered himself something of an expert on the general problem of French colonialism. As early as 1951, he had traveled to Indochina with his brother on a congressional fact-finding mission. On his return, he criticized the evolving U.S. policy of support for the forces of General de Lattre in Indochina. "In Indochina we have allied ourselves to the desperate effort of a French regime to hang on to the remnants of Empire . . . through reliance on the force of arms. . . . To do this apart from and in defiance of innately nationalistic aims spells foredoomed failure."[16] Three years later, when the U.S. government found itself caught up in a debate over the possible use of U.S. military power to raise the siege of Dien Bien Phu, Kennedy spoke out in the Senate against any U.S. military action with a statement that would haunt American policy makers for the next two decades: "I am frankly of the belief that no amount of American military assistance in Indochina can conquer . . . 'an enemy of the people' which has the sympathy and covert support of the people."[17]

Based upon prior experience, Paris had every reason to be concerned when the FLN's representative in New York, Abdelkader Chanderli, began to cultivate an acquaintance with Kennedy in 1957. The Senate speech on July 2 demonstrated that Kennedy had listened attentively and sympathetically to Chanderli's arguments. Kennedy did not challenge the French contention that security and order in North Africa were of immediate concern to all of the Western allies. In fact, he turned this argument against Paris, as a justification for the application of U.S. power and influence on the issue of Algeria. He criticized the Republican administration for its inaction and its insensitivity to the legitimate nationalist demands of the Algerian people and recommended that Washington begin immediately to collaborate with France and the other nations of the NATO alliance to resolve a situation that was "no longer a French problem alone."[18]

With one speech, an issue that had by common agreement been out of bounds was thrown open for international debate. Schlesinger mentions that "it is hard now to recall the furor that his remarks caused. . . . It produced great irritation not just in official circles in Paris and Washington but throughout the foreign policy establishment in the United States. . . . Kennedy had criticized an ally; he had imperiled the unity of NATO. Even Democrats drew back."[19]

The French press and public were still attacking Kennedy for his statements on Algeria when reports of the Anglo-American decision to sell arms to Tunisia were published in November of 1957. In the face of a threat from the government of Habib Bourguiba that Tunisia might turn to Moscow for arms, the United States and the United Kingdom had agreed to provide a small quantity of weapons. Washington and London had initially sought French support and participation in the sale of arms to Tunisia. But, for France, which was constructing a two-hundred-mile electrified fence (the Morice Line) along the

Tunisian-Algerian border to stop FLN forces from retreating to safety in Tunisia and to stop the flow of weapons from Tunisia to the FLN, the allied provision of arms to Bourguiba represented an indirect subvention of the Algerian rebellion and a serious encroachment onto Paris' *domaine réservé*. The recently formed government of Felix Gaillard refused to participate in arms sales to Tunisia unless Bourguiba was prepared to assure the allies that the equipment would not be transferred to any third parties. Bourguiba refused to offer such a guarantee, and on November 12, the Anglo-Saxons decided to approve the Tunisian arms sales without France.[20] Alfred Grosser notes that on the day that the news of the arms sales decision was published, the French delegation to a NATO conference walked out of the proceedings, stating that "every effort to achieve an Atlantic solidarity as desired by all of the participants in this conference has become pointless."[21] Prime Minister Gaillard warned at the time that "if the Atlantic Pact should fall to dust one day we will know the artisans of its failure."[22]

French public and elite accusations notwithstanding, the Eisenhower administration was acutely sensitive to the problems that Paris faced in North Africa, and the White House continued to resist demands for U.S. interference in Algeria throughout this period. On the day that Kennedy addressed the Senate, Dulles told a press conference that Washington backed the January 1958 French request to the NATO allies for emergency financial assistance in the face of a budgetary and balance of payments crisis that was largely attributable to the cost of the Algerian campaign. But Washington found it far more difficult to keep the United States or NATO out of the developments in North Africa after French bombers and fighter aircraft attacked the Tunisian village of Sakiet-Sidi-Youssef on February 8, 1958.

The raid was an attempt to strike at Algerian rebels in hiding across the border, but to the international community it appeared more like an act of French desperation in response to an increasingly unmanageable colonial war. Rather than disrupt rebel activity in the frontier region, it served to force the Algerian issue into the open and to place France's allies in a position where they could no longer abstain from taking a stand. "We do have a NATO ally," Eisenhower stated, "and we also are great friends of the North African area, so it is a very hard problem."[23]

The problem was particularly difficult because Washington had developed much of its North African policy around the friendship and support of Tunisia. Under these circumstances, Eisenhower felt compelled to act in response to the formal complaint that Tunisian president Bourguiba filed against France in the United Nations following the bombing of Sakiet-Sidi-Youssef. Eisenhower's solution was to offer U.S. and British mediation between Paris and Tunis. For many in France, the offer was seen as a wedge for further Anglo-Saxon meddling in French North African affairs. Strong public and political pressure was exerted on the Fourth Republic government of Felix Gaillard to resist the U.S.

proposal. Gaillard's decision to defer to American pressure and accept Anglo-American involvement in the settlement of the Franco-Tunisian dispute resulted in the collapse of the Gaillard government and a renewed commitment by the more conservative elements in France to strike back—against the forces of terrorism in Algeria, against the untrustworthy allies across the Atlantic and across the channel, and against the forces of capitulation in France itself.

The Fourth Republic effectively ended as a result of the backlash against Washington's involvement in the Sakiet-Sidi-Youssef incident. For Charles de Gaulle, these developments represented a further confirmation of the arguments against overreliance on the NATO allies, as well as a mandate for a new direction in French foreign and defense policy. To pursue a new policy, however, France needed to break out of its situation of excessive dependence upon NATO. To the extent that this dependence was in large part attributable to France's need for allied support in order to prosecute the Algerian War, de Gaulle appreciated that his Fifth Republic government would have to reassess the importance of Algeria for France. The great irony of de Gaulle's return to power was that he was more responsible than any other postwar political figure for reestablishing the philosophy of empire in postwar France. His diplomatic and military initiatives during the brief period of the Provisional Government were designed to dispel any doubts about the necessity of retaining France's prewar colonial territories. As previously mentioned, de Gaulle saw the empire as a confirmation of French sovereignty and a source of French power in a period of national weakness and vulnerability. He had in fact welcomed combat in Indochina: "However painful the immediate results of such issue, I must admit that, from the point of view of national interest, I was not distressed by the prospect of taking up arms in Indochina. . . . French blood shed on the soil of Indochina would constitute an impressive claim."[24]

But in spite of his rhetoric of national honor, national right, and the *mission civilisatrice,* de Gaulle had an essentially pragmatic vision of what the colonies could do for the parent country. Although during the late 1940s he frequently asserted in public that France's position vis-à-vis its former colonies was permanent and nonnegotiable, the general personally understood that the colonies were an adjunct to the nation, rather than its core. Several passages in de Gaulle's memoirs illustrate that he viewed the colonies as an important potential source of French power and prestige that could be translated into influence on the European continent—but only if the relationship between France and the colonies was positive and collaborative. De Gaulle also recognized that a continuing colonial struggle, requiring the allocation of a large portion of France's military and economic power for the preservation of order, would only serve further to disadvantage France in its dealings with other European governments and with the superpowers.[25]

During the latter period of the Fourth Republic, de Gaulle had maintained a studied reserve in his comments on the prospects for Algeria, presumably to avoid foreclosing his options in the event of his return to power. He nonetheless made it clear to his inner circle of confidants that France could not afford to be hung up indefinitely on the Algerian issue if it hoped to preserve its interests within the Western Alliance. As a military leader, de Gaulle was especially concerned about the precipitous decline in the quality of French military equipment from 1954 to 1958, as successive French governments allocated the bulk of the French defense budget to manpower for the war in Algeria.[26] Once in power, de Gaulle was anxious to get on with the business of modernizing the French army—permitting France to "wed her times."[27]

But the Algerian War showed no signs of ending during the first two-and-one-half years of the Fifth Republic. All of de Gaulle's early efforts at revitalizing French military forces and establishing an influential position for France on the continent foundered on the problem of Algeria. De Gaulle had been convinced prior to taking office that the NATO allies could not be relied upon to provide real support for France in its North African campaign. In particular, he was sensitive to the growing impatience of the U.S. government over French handling of the Algerian problem.[28]

De Gaulle thus came to the conclusion—haltingly and reactively—that only a policy of triage, of cutting Algeria loose, would save France. The subject of de Gaulle's movements to end the Algerian War is beyond the scope of this book and has already been described with great clarity and force by Alistaire Horne. For our purposes, however, it needs to be mentioned that de Gaulle's earliest Fifth Republic initiatives toward NATO—his opposition to the basing of U.S. nuclear-equipped fighters in France, his decision to remove the French fleet from the NATO Mediterranean Command, and, in particular, his demand for the creation of a tripartite directorate within NATO—were all inextricably linked to his campaign to manage the process of French retrenchment from Algeria.

Conclusion

From the standpoint of the French national interest, the cases of Suez and Algeria tended to confirm de Gaulle's earlier suspicion that the United States and Britain could not be relied upon to support French efforts made on behalf of the Occident. Paris discovered that its particular interests were increasingly incompatible with Washington's, and the American extended deterrent guarantee in Europe had little meaning relative to the Fourth Republic's quest to reestablish a national strategic identity on its own terms. By the time that the Fourth Republic collapsed, many French policy makers were convinced that the greatest barrier to the achievement of French independence was within NATO itself, rather than to the east. And de Gaulle had little trouble in translating this mood into a foreign policy mandate.

CHAPTER 17

POSTCOLONIAL FRANCE: GLOBAL SECURITY ASPIRATIONS STYMIED, ALLIANCE COLLABORATION MODIFIED

T HE DESIRE to reestablish France as an equal partner with the Anglo-Saxons in the formulation and management of global strategy represented one of the most consistent themes in post-World War II French foreign policy. De Gaulle had articulated this goal as early as 1949 when he criticized the exclusively Atlantic orientation of the proposed NATO alliance, which "could eventually present serious problems in terms of strategic preparation for a common effort."[1] During the ensuing nine years of the Fourth Republic, he came more and more to share Soustelle's opinion that NATO's principal defect was that it was "merely Atlantic" in an era of globalized *guerre révolutionnaire*. Events during the 1950s confirmed de Gaulle's suspicion that the NATO allies did not—could not—appreciate the contribution that France was making to Western security in Southeast Asia and North Africa.

THE DIRECTORATE: PRETEXT AND PORTENT

Shortly after his return to power in June 1958, de Gaulle met with John Foster Dulles in Paris. During the meeting, the general developed the argument that, in the modern age, France could no longer be certain of its security if the Mediterranean—in particular, its southern coast—was excluded from the NATO defense zone. De Gaulle argued that the existing NATO Treaty did not reflect the fact that France was "torn" between Africa and Europe. He proposed that the "field of action" of NATO be enlarged to include the Middle East and North Africa, and that Washington, Paris, and London undertake to improve the decisional efficiency of the alliance by establishing a system of three-power collaboration to direct NATO activities within and beyond the treaty area.

The general elaborated on these comments on September 17, in letters and official memorandums to Eisenhower and Macmillan.[2] First, he expanded on the demand for out-of-area consultation beyond the Mediterranean region, calling for a "new body" consisting of the United States, Great Britain, and France, "[with] responsibility for taking joint decisions on all political matters affecting world security, and of drawing up, and if necessary, putting into action, strategic plans."[3] Second, de Gaulle specifically recommended that the new body should have authority in global decisions regarding the use of nuclear weapons by the Western powers (i.e., the United States). Finally, de Gaulle asserted that France would make its continued participation in NATO contingent upon the response of the Anglo-Saxon governments to the September memorandum.

In the wake of the Suez fiasco and the Three Wise Men's report, there was ample reason to believe that the United States would look favorably on proposals for improving NATO consultation procedures. The problem, as de Gaulle realized, was in convincing Washington to accord a special status to France within some resuscitated version of the old NATO Standing Committee. Still burdened with the confetti of empire and unable to fulfill its troop commitments for the defense of the central front, France had few cards to play. The U.S. Joint Chiefs were especially critical of any new arrangement that would increase French influence over American security planning beyond the treaty area:

> This [the Tripartite Proposal] represents a de Gaulle attempt to increase French power, prestige, and voice in world affairs and an equal partnership in the formulation of global political and strategic policy. While it is recognized that the risks incurred are equally shared and that consultation and cooperation among the Free World allies are essential, the responsibilities for the maintenance of the Free World posture rest primarily on the United States. . . . For the Western world to adopt a committee type system would hopelessly confuse and complicate the decisionmaking process and place us at a great disadvantage vis-a-vis the Communist bloc.[4]

As soon as de Gaulle's proposal was made public, it triggered widespread resistance from virtually all of the other Western allies. NATO Secretary General P.-H. Spaak warned other Western leaders that a formally established directorate "would mean the end of the Atlantic Alliance."[5] Adenauer railed against what he viewed as de Gaulle's duplicity, since the two leaders had met only three days prior to de Gaulle's transmission of the proposal for a directorate, and the general had not even advised the chancellor of his plans.

On the other side of the Atlantic, Eisenhower initially expressed suspicions of the general's motives for proposing the directorate. The president did not reject the idea on the spot, but he was not prepared to accept de Gaulle's most extreme demand—for French influence over nuclear decisions. Nor was he willing to associate himself officially with the establishment of a politically disruptive system of first and second class membership within NATO. Finally, Eisenhower resisted efforts by the Fifth Republic leader to tie the directorate issue to the problem of Algerian independence, or to the issue of U.S. and British sales of small weapons to Tunisia.[6]

Dulles appears to have been more firm than Eisenhower in his opposition to the directorate scheme. Dulles advised the president just before the latter was to meet with Spaak in late September that "with regard to harmonization of Western policies vis-a-vis Asia, the Middle East and Africa, we [should] be willing to discuss fully our policies in these areas with our NATO partners, but [should] see dangers in having any country press for adoption of an agreed NATO 'common policy' with respect to them." Dulles also argued, however, that as long as de Gaulle understood the U.S. position in this regard, the United States should be willing to meet with British and French representatives at least to discuss the directorate proposal, making clear in advance to the Germans, Italians, and other NATO partners that the purpose of any such meeting would be to discuss the plan, not implement it.[7] Washington subsequently advised de Gaulle that it would consider creation of an institutionalized directorate to deal with issues beyond the NATO boundary and a less conspicuous, informal system of tripartite consultation within NATO.

But the general would not be mollified. Throughout 1959, he attempted to increase the pressure on Washington by attacking the military foundations of NATO. During a meeting with Dulles' successor, Christian Herter, on February 6, de Gaulle and Prime Minister Michel Debré communicated their concern "because the Allies are not united in their support for France in Algeria" and linked this complaint to the need for independent French control over its Mediterranean fleet. Herter, in a secret report to Eisenhower, nonetheless observed that the tone of the discussions was positive ("We had a happy surprise . . .") and that de Gaulle viewed as a "very important" development a U.S. offer to negotiate a new status within NATO for the French Mediterranean fleet—equal to the American Sixth Fleet and the Royal Navy, both of which could be dispersed, under national command, to defend "overseas territories."[8]

Herter's optimism proved to be unfounded. On March 14, de Gaulle announced that, in the "absence of a common policy" on African security among the NATO allies, the French government had decided to place the one-third of its Mediterranean fleet which was earmarked for NATO under national control. De Gaulle justified this action with the claim that France was compelled to preserve its "national mission" of protecting the link between North Africa and the parent state. Herter interpreted the French attempt to link the Algerian issue to the question of French naval participation in the Mediterranean as "blackmail." He informed French ambassador Hervé Alphand that de Gaulle's unilateral action contradicted the principle of tripartism to which the French had recently expressed a strong commitment. De Gaulle, of course, turned the argument around, noting in a press conference on September 9, 1959, that the decision to remove French forces from NATO Mediterranean command was forced on France. "How could we leave our fleet in the hands of an organization having nothing to do with Africa, where we are so constantly involved?"[9]

In the midst of the directorate debate, de Gaulle concluded that the time was right to revive French complaints against Washington and London. Six months after its decision to remove French naval vessels from NATO's Mediterranean fleet, the French leadership dropped the other shoe. In a meeting with Debré on April 29, Herter was advised that France had decided that two conditions would have to be fulfilled if the United States wanted to retain bases for nine nuclear-armed fighter squadrons in France: first, the establishment of a global directorate in accordance with de Gaulle's September memorandum (to include nuclear cooperation); second, U.S. sponsorship of allied support for French policies in the Mediterranean, the Maghreb, and Africa.[10] Herter protested that the issue of deploying nuclear forward-basing systems in Europe was entirely separate from the other issues, which France had chosen to present as a quid pro quo, but his argument does not appear to have had any impact on the Fifth Republic leadership. On July 9, in compliance with French demands, NATO's Supreme Allied Commander, General Lauris Norstad, announced plans to move two hundred U.S. aircraft and six thousand support personnel from France to Great Britain and West Germany. By the second half of 1959, France was well down the road toward a complete break with the alliance.

De Gaulle's exact reasons for pressing the directorate issue during the first two years of the Fifth Republic remain unclear. The Fifth Republic leadership was certainly attracted to the possibility that France could derive some specific political benefits by challenging the alliance structure and purview. In particular, de Gaulle, Premier Debré, and Foreign Minister Maurice Couve de Murville sought to use the directorate issue as a means of pressing Washington and NATO for more support in Algeria. In a broader context, however, the French leadership probably regarded its proposal as a low-risk gamble that would significantly enhance French influence in the alliance and throughout the world if it worked.

John Newhouse asserts that "in return for very little—an occasional bow to NATO, a commitment to remain an active partner—de Gaulle at various moments could have had anything he wanted from the Americans and British."[11] This is certainly an exaggeration. First, Washington at no time appears to have considered de Gaulle's vague request for tripartite global planning on nuclear issues, although Dulles did apparently allude to the possibility of granting Paris the right of "advance authorization" in any decision to use nuclear weapons based in continental Europe.[12] Second, Washington consistently opposed a formal division of NATO into senior and junior members.

If Newhouse's interpretation is somewhat extreme, it is nonetheless much closer to the truth than many earlier accounts of the directorate episode which depict the Eisenhower administration as totally unresponsive and unsympathetic to de Gaulle's proposals. Indeed, in view of the fact that many U.S. policy makers still harbored resentments over Suez, Eisenhower and Dulles appear to have been extraordinarily open-minded and moderate in their responses to De Gaulle's demands.

Part of the reason why the United States was at least mildly sympathetic to de Gaulle's requests for coordinated action beyond the NATO Treaty area was because the French president was not alone in arguing for a globalized perspective on Western security during this period. For example, at about the same time that de Gaulle's September Memorandum was made public, Field Marshal Montgomery published his memoirs, in which he recommended a series of improvements in NATO based upon his experience as NATO Deputy SACEUR during the period 1951–58. In particular he argued that the geographical limits of NATO had to be enlarged to "a world-wide scale" in view of the fact that the primary threats to Western security were located in the Third World. Montgomery's precise words deserve quotation, if only for their eccentricity: "A major war can now be considered unlikely—in fact, the 'test match' (in American the 'World Series') is postponed indefinitely because of the internal strength of the Western alliance. But . . . what might be called 'village cricket' (In American 'Sand-lot Baseball') . . . on overseas fields must be handled firmly so that they do not become the forerunners of a test match."[13] In response to the de Gaulle memorandums, NATO Secretary General Paul-Henri Spaak also recommended procedures for improved out-of-area policy coordination, including the establishment of regional committees within NATO and the formation of subcommittees under the NATO Council of Ministers for global oversight.[14] As previously mentioned, Lord Ismay, Spaak's predecessor as Secretary General, had been even more insistent and ambitious in his demands for a wider purview for the alliance.

In an interview after leaving the White House, Eisenhower complained that he had made several offers of unofficial consultation on global issues in his dealing with de Gaulle: "I'll consult you as you request, I'll promise to make no move and neither will the British unless we've all agreed that we'll do this thing by study, but let's don't proclaim it publicly as a three power Directorate."[15] On certain occasions (as in his meeting with Herter on February 9, 1959), de Gaulle expressed some tentative interest in these offers and admitted that progress was being made on the directorate issue.

At times, the general attempted to advance the directorate debate by what he apparently viewed as inducements, as in his offer to participate with Britain and the United States in the formulation of Western positions on the Jordanian (1958) and Congo (1960) crises and in his offers of French troops to back up a tripartite foreign policy. But when Eisenhower pressed de Gaulle to enter into three-power talks for the establishment of a common policy in Africa, de Gaulle failed to nominate a French representative. When, subsequently, Washington backed a plan for UN peacekeeping in the Congo, in the absence of any coherent three-power policy for responding to the crisis, de Gaulle attacked this effort to bring "global incoherence . . . to the local scene" and refused over-flight rights to UN planes.

It appears that by the fall of 1960, de Gaulle himself had lost all interest in his directorate campaign. This may have been because he was unable to envisage a practical directorate scheme that would not provide the Anglo-Saxons with new opportunities for meddling in French foreign and defense policies in the Third World. In particular, a commitment to tripartite policy coordination in North Africa might have enhanced French prestige in the region, but at the risk of giving Washington and London increased influence over Paris in its manage-ment of the Algerian issue. Under these circumstances, only a sphere of influ-ence arrangement, in which the United States and the United Kingdom ex-plicitly deferred to France in the Mediterranean, North Africa, and continental Europe, would have reassured de Gaulle, and there was no doubt that this was unacceptable to both Washington and London.

In the absence of a satisfactory solution, de Gaulle let the directorate issue devolve into a vague discussion topic in meetings between midlevel defense and foreign ministry representatives of the Big Three powers. By the time that Kennedy took office, the scheme was effectively dead, if not officially buried. Kennedy and de Gaulle did touch on the issue of tripartite policy coordination outside of NATO during the U.S. president's state visit to Paris in May 1961, and Kennedy's National Security Adviser (McGeorge Bundy) did attempt to engage the general in discussions "about improving the need for our machinery for worldwide consultation" in a diplomatic—but not military—context.[16] Kennedy also directly solicited de Gaulle's advice on a number of issues, including Laos, the Congo, and the utility of the United Nations as a peacekeep-ing mechanism. In general, however, the young president was too caught up in his own sense of power and mission to accord de Gaulle more than polite attention and interest. De Gaulle could not miss the implication of the fact that Kennedy's visit to Paris was meant as a pleasant interlude—a bonanza for the White House photographers and a chance for Jackie to practice her French—on the way to the more important business of meeting Khrushchev in Vienna.

Atmospherics aside, the two leaders were too far apart in a political and, indeed, an epistemological sense. Even if de Gaulle and Eisenhower had suc-ceeded in establishing some system of tripartite consultation, it probably would have collapsed under the guidance of two so disparate personalities as Kennedy and de Gaulle.

BREAKING WITH NATO, PRESERVING THE ALLIANCE

Seven and a half years elapsed between the time that de Gaulle issued his first directorate proposal and his announcement of plans to remove France from the military structure of NATO. During this time, the general consolidated his control over domestic French politics, extricated France from Algeria, and set the direction of French defense policy based on nuclear weapons as the ultimate guarantee of French security. From de Gaulle's point of view, there were innumerable instances of bullying, disdain, and manipulation by Washington during this period which confirmed his opinion that NATO was essentially an instrument for the institutionalization of U.S. hegemony. From Washington's perspective, the general became more and more obsessive, vindictive, and unreasonable during this period.

John F. Kennedy had come to office with a deep respect for de Gaulle as a leader and as a "historic personage." He also believed that the French leader was moving in the right direction in his policies toward Algeria. But it became much more difficult for Kennedy to support de Gaulle's policies in North Africa after the French invasion of Tunisia in July 1962—only two months after Kennedy had hosted the Tunisian leader, Habib Bourguiba, in Washington and had arranged a ticker-tape parade for him in New York. According to most accounts, the incidents that led up to the French intervention were precipitated by Bourguiba. On July 6, he surprised de Gaulle with a letter demanding the immediate removal of French troops from the naval facility at Bizerta and challenging the French interpretation of Tunisia's southern boundary with Algeria. Two weeks later, Bourgiba punctuated his demand by encouraging demonstrations around the Bizerta base and by deploying Tunisian forces into the disputed southern territory. When the Tunisian government subsequently intensified its pressure on Paris by open military attacks against the Bizerta facility, de Gaulle responded with what Brian Crozier referred to as "ruthless dispatch."[17] In a move that was clearly designed as a lesson to FLN representatives who were then engaged in negotiations with Paris, de Gaulle sent French aircraft and seven thousand paratroopers to the trouble spots in northern and southern Tunisia. The Casbah district in Bizerta was subjected to mortar barrages, and demonstrators were confronted with brutal counterattacks. Seven hundred Tunisians and twenty-one French troops died in the confrontation, which lasted three days. Thirteen hundred Tunisians were wounded and over six hundred taken prisoner. To much of the West, as well as most of the Third World, de Gaulle's actions looked reactionary and unjustified.

France subsequently contributed to its own isolation within the United Nations by a public policy of disdain toward international criticism or inquiries. In an effort to avoid guilt by association, two NATO allies (Norway and Denmark) voted with the Afro-Asian block to condemn France in the General Assembly. The Anglo-Saxons abstained, but Washington did place pressure on Paris to enter into bilateral negotiations with Tunis to short-circuit the developing crisis. Kennedy felt frustrated that he could not take a stronger stand against the French action, and he sent a personal letter to Bourguiba apologizing for the abstention in the UN. JFK explained his decision to Arthur Schlesinger: "Ev-

FRANCE

eryone forgets how shaky de Gaulle's position is. . . . If the Tunisian affair goes really sour, it might just start a new military revolt. We don't want the ultras to take over in France. With all his faults, the General is the only hope for a solution in Algeria."[18]

Kennedy's desire to assist France as much as possible in its efforts to end the Algerian conflict was motivated by his longstanding opposition to colonialism, but also by a desire to see French forces return to continental Europe as soon as possible. As Eisenhower had pointedly observed during his conversation with de Gaulle in 1959, Algeria and NATO had necessarily been linked in U.S. security thinking in a burden-sharing context since the mid-1950s. The United States assumed that the six divisions that it had assigned to NATO at the start of the 1950s represented a *temporary* measure in support of Atlantic solidarity and in light of the French involvement in Algeria.[19] JFK was particularly anxious to see France cut its losses in North Africa, so that its forces in Algeria—tested and trained over seven grueling years—could be incorporated into the NATO land forces. Kennedy's vision of a flexible response strategy for NATO was anchored in the improvement of the alliance's conventional forces. Only France, unencumbered by Algeria, was in a position to make the kind of dramatic new contributions to a Continental defense force implied by NATO's new strategic posture. In this regard, as in others, de Gaulle's program for asserting French grandeur after Algeria did not dovetail with Kennedy's Grand Design.

As early as 1958, de Gaulle had advised a confidant that "as soon as the Algerian War is over, I shall form five atomic divisions."[20] He began to make good on his plans for a French nuclear force during the spring of 1962, at the same time that the French troops began returning from Algeria in large numbers.[21]

De Gaulle announced that French Algerian forces would not be integrated into the NATO command upon return to the Continent. The forces were to be maintained under exclusively national control: "It is absolutely necessary, morally as well as politically, for us to associate the army more closely to the nation."[22] This strategy was designed to permit the general to contain any residual antigovernment tendencies within the army and to allow him to make whatever changes might be required in the size or composition of French continental forces to support the priority goal of acquiring a *force de frappe*.

France officially recognized the independence of Algeria on July 3, 1962. The implications of this event for Article 6 of the NATO Treaty were discussed within the North Atlantic Council on January 6, 1963. According to the French delegation to the council meeting, the establishment of Algeria as a sovereign nation implied that the NATO Treaty reference to "Algerian Departments of France" no longer held any meaning. No effort was made formally to revise the treaty to reflect this development, and the 1949 reference to the "Algerian Departments" remains in the body of the text to this day.

218

De Gaulle's Postimperial Policy in the Third World

De Gaulle attempted to compensate for a radical reduction in the French military presence abroad by an active foreign policy based on the related themes of North-South cooperation and opposition to the traditional cold war politics of blocs. In Asia, this strategy was reflected in de Gaulle's opening to the People's Republic of China in 1964 and his progressively more strident criticism of U.S. policy in Vietnam from 1963 until his departure in 1969. In Africa and the Middle East, de Gaulle's strategy was characterized by the twelve bilateral defense accords that established the guidelines for a continued French security role among the Francophone African states. The General also moved— although with only moderate success—to establish a role for Paris in resolving Arab-Israeli disputes during the 1960s.

De Gaulle's decision to extend diplomatic recognition to the P.R.C. in 1964 was justified by Paris as an adjustment to one of the overwhelming realities of the postwar international system. France had, in fact, been seeking ways to make this adjustment since 1949. Paris was nonetheless consistently rebuffed by Mao Zedong, who preferred to align his government with Ho Chi Minh in the early 1950s and with the FLN during the second half of that decade. With the end of the Algerian War, the most difficult barriers to Sino-French mutual recognition had disappeared.

De Gaulle was quick to communicate his interest in reconciliation as soon as practicable. The general's writings and actions indicate that he accepted the Leclerc thesis that a successful Asian policy for any Western nation required some accommodation to mainland Chinese power. He also believed that Washington would share the French fate in its efforts to extricate itself from Vietnam. As long as the United States was trapped in Vietnam, opportunities would arise for France to establish itself as an important and perhaps indispensable mediator between Washington and the regimes in Moscow, Beijing, and Hanoi. Furthermore, Washington's involvement in Vietnam seriously constrained U.S. foreign policy options with respect to other states in both Northeast and Southeast Asia—providing potentially rich opportunities for *gestes* by de Gaulle. But these opportunities could only be pursued by France after formal diplomatic ties were established between Beijing and Paris.

From the point of view of Beijing, de Gaulle's offer of bilateral recognition must have looked like a gift, and, beyond that, like confirmation of the inevitability of recognition by all of the Western powers on Beijing's terms. From the point of view of Washington, seen through the filter of the Vietnam entanglements, de Gaulle's actions looked like "pure and simple 'treason.'"[23]

De Gaulle had warned Kennedy against military involvement in Vietnam during their meeting in May 1961. The general had observed that French experience proved that Southeast Asia was not a "propitious battle field" for the West. De Gaulle went on to say that in Cambodia, Laos, and Vietnam, "it appeared that the exercise of influence and the exercise of a military role were incompatible. In the eyes of the inhabitants, all military action reflected a desire to govern."[24] By 1963, de Gaulle was expressing those doubts in public; and by 1965, he had become a frequent and strident critic of U.S. intervention in Vietnam and had begun to treat this issue as one more reason for France to distance itself from NATO.

Several members of de Gaulle's government defended the general's policy direction relative to the alliance on the grounds that the United States could otherwise use the treaty as a means of dragging the Europeans into a war in Asia, "even if we did not wish it."[25] Indeed, British prime minister Harold Wilson later recalled June 1967 discussions with de Gaulle in which the French leader observed that the U.S. involvement in Vietnam "dominated everything" in the wider world situation and that the French government left NATO's command structure, in part, because it did not propose "to be drawn into somebody else's war." The longer American forces stayed in Vietnam, de Gaulle contended, the greater was the prospect of a general war breaking out.[26]

René Pleven challenged the Gaullist line of argument in the National Assembly.

> Assuming the outbreak of a conflict between China and America in Asia, why should NATO become involved since the area covered by the treaty is limited to Europe and the North Atlantic? Did NATO become involved in the Korean War? And when we engaged ourselves in Indochina, NATO was certainly not dragged into the conflict.[27]

Pleven's comments highlight the fact that the Fifth Republic's use of the issue of Vietnam to justify getting out of NATO represented a reversal of de Gaulle's directorate argument and the earlier *guerre révolutionnaire* arguments of the Fourth Republic. These earlier positions—developed in an era of French military involvement outside of NATO—emphasized global containment, the domino theory, and the mutuality of Western security interests in the Third World. De Gaulle's criticisms of Vietnam, on the other hand, downplayed the need for coordinated Western action in the face of a globalized communist threat and warned that, because of the common membership in NATO, repercussions from U.S. adventurism in Southeast Area would be felt in Europe. De Gaulle subsequently went a step further with the argument. When the general was pushed by NATO Secretary General Manlio Brosio during the spring of 1966 to provide the allies with recommendations for reforming NATO to accommodate French concerns, de Gaulle refused, arguing that any proposals would be lost on the Americans, who were too preoccupied with Vietnam to take such initiatives seriously.[28]

Thus, Washington and Paris had reversed positions. By 1966 it was the United States that was beginning to use NATO as best it could to shore up its effort to achieve a military victory in Southeast Asia, while France attempted to play the role of tutor within the alliance. There were, nonetheless, important differences. For all of its meddling in Fourth Republic foreign policy, the United States had in fact provided economic assistance, materiel, and, for the most part, political support (or at least benign neglect) for the French war effort in Indochina. It was within Washington's power to use its economic and political influence within NATO to pressure France to cut its losses and get out of Indochina long before Dien Bien Phu. For reasons that have already been discussed, the United States chose not to do so. By the mid-1960s, Washington's ability to determine policy for its Atlantic allies had declined radically, but France was still unable to do more than harass and inconvenience the United States over its participation in Vietnam. The danger, then, was that in his effort to link the issue of NATO and Vietnam, de Gaulle risked doing irreparable damage to the former (never his intent) without having an appreciable impact on Washington's handling of the latter.

De Gaulle's criticism of U.S. policy in Vietnam was one component of a broader strategy for bolstering French status and influence in the Third World. Another important element in that strategy was the preservation of a French military presence in Africa following the end of colonialism. De Gaulle had begun to develop a formula for cooperation with French-speaking Africa shortly after returning to power. In the first months of 1959, de Gaulle argued in favor of an imperial military structure linking France to the "Republics born in Africa under the Tricolor."[29] During the next four years, however, he modified his vision of a single unified defense system in accordance with African desires for greater sovereign control over defense.

In March 1964, at Dakar, the twelve Francophone African states renounced their support for a cohesive "union d'afrique militaire" in favor of separate bilateral treaties of security with France. Nonetheless, France retained considerable influence according to the terms of these separate arrangements. The treaties permitted the retention of small but effective French forces in a few African bases (most notably Dakar, Pointe Noire, and Fort Lamy) and included arrangements for the French provision of military aid and arms to the dependent African nations. Paris also sought to preserve the link between France and the military elites in Francophone Africa by means of an ambitious program of military training at French military academies. During the 1960s, approximately ten thousand representatives of the military services of Francophone Africa took advantage of this opportunity.[30]

In retrospect, France was extremely successful in managing the transition from a colonial to a postcolonial military posture in Francophone Africa. French troops were reduced from 58,500 in 1962 to 6,420 by 1965. In spite of this major cutback, Paris preserved much of its influence in the region and could even claim with some justification to be a model for North-South cooperation and Third World conflict management during the 1960s.

De Gaulle was somewhat less successful, however, in his attempts to articulate a coherent policy for the Middle East and North Africa. With the signing of the Evian accords on March 18, 1962, de Gaulle ended eight years of warfare against the FLN and released his country from the foreign policy constraints associated with the Algerian conflict. Unfortunately, France did not pursue an innovative policy in the Middle East once it was freed from this lingering colonial imbroglio. It continued to tie its Third World policies in general, and its North African policies in particular, to Algerian support. Paris held to this policy in spite of the fact that Algeria began to break key elements of the Evian accords almost as soon as the agreements were completed. There were, of course, residual economic and cultural links that encouraged de Gaulle to maintain close ties with the governments of Ben Bella and then (in 1965) Boumedienne. But a more important factor in pushing the French to preserve relations with Algeria was a desire for an exoneration from its colonial past that only the FLN could grant.

The desire to preserve good relations with Algeria ran afoul of the second key element of French Middle Eastern policy—a commitment to the security of Israel which had been galvanized by the Suez action of 1956 and reinforced by a bilateral arms trade in excess of $400 million between 1950 and 1969 (over 50 percent of the total French arms trade during this period).[31] Paris was able to finesse these contradictory commitments until the Six Day War in June 1967. On June 2, three days before Israeli forces attacked Arab-occupied territories in Gaza, the Sinai, and the Golan Heights, de Gaulle took the position that "any state that is the first to resort to arms anywhere will not have approval or . . . support of France."[32]

France subsequently voted with the Arab states on a resolution calling for the immediate withdrawal of Israeli forces from all occupied territories and introduced a partial embargo of arms to Israel. In one of his more baroque performances, de Gaulle succeeded in linking the events in the Middle East to U.S. policy in Southeast Asia. In a speech to the Council of Ministers (June 21, 1967) on the Middle East situation, he observed that "France sees no chance for a peaceful resolution in the present world situation unless a new element appears in world politics. This element could and should be the end of the Vietnam war in that this would be the end of foreign intervention."[33]

CONCLUSION

In his June 1967 speech, the general called for a four-power solution to the problems of the Middle East—adding the Soviet Union to the former tripartite vision. This four-power approach to global conflict management illustrates how de Gaulle's foreign policy had evolved during the first nine years of the Fifth Republic: from preoccupation with Algeria to national independence in the security realm, from a position of national independence to the break with NATO, from the rejection of U.S. hegemony on the Continent to open opposition to U.S. policies in the Third World, from the rhetoric of the directorate to four-power management of international tensions. In view of the constraints on French action, it was an impressive record of progress for French foreign and security policy. French global influence and freedom of movement in the international system were increased during the period, along with de Gaulle's personal stature in the Third World and the Eastern bloc.

Nevertheless, much of the progress was purchased at NATO's and, more particularly, Washington's expense. In the end, the general was unable to achieve his major goal of establishing France as a leading power in world affairs. Nor was he able to convince Washington that his idea of allied burden sharing, as set out in the directorate proposal, was consistent with overall Western security interests.

CHAPTER 18

THE OUT-OF-AREA QUESTION
SINCE 1966

DE GAULLE had always been careful to distinguish between the Atlantic Alliance and the NATO military structure. His argument, dating back to the early 1950s, was that the alliance was a necessary but not sufficient element in the preservation of Western security, while the NATO High Command was an unacceptable American invention designed to perpetuate hegemony over Western Europe. In retaining his commitment to the Atlantic Alliance, de Gaulle, by implication, reaffirmed the French commitment to consult with the other members of NATO regarding issues outside its geographic purview as implied in Article 4 of the 1949 treaty. It is nonetheless important for the purpose of this study to reiterate that an essential component of de Gaulle's challenge to NATO was his argument that an institutionalized system of U.S. military hegemony permitted Washington to influence the foreign and security policies of the Western European allies *beyond* the established treaty area as well as within it. By pulling France out of NATO planning and command functions in 1966, de Gaulle was asserting French independence not only within the Atlantic region but on a global scale as well.

Under these circumstances, all Fifth Republic governments since 1966 have interpreted the consultation clause of the Atlantic treaty very loosely, according to French national interests and as determined by the circumstances of each separate out-of-area crisis. Thus, for example, when the NATO Council passed a resolution in June 1968 which expressed concern about the USSR's maritime expansion in the Mediterranean and proposed discussions on NATO measures to counteract Moscow's naval projection capabilities, de Gaulle felt no compulsion to sign the document. But five months later de Gaulle approved a second NATO Council statement, which went even farther in describing the Soviet naval presence in the region as a threat and warned of "an international crisis with serious consequences" if Moscow attempted to use its Mediterranean fleet "directly or indirectly." Edward Kolodziej has attributed this reversal of the general's position to a heightened French concern regarding the risk of Soviet intervention following the Warsaw Pact invasion of Czechoslovakia in August 1968.[1]

FRENCH SECURITY POLICY IN THE POMPIDOU ERA

Although Georges Pompidou concentrated his foreign policy interests on the Mediterranean and the Middle East, he was no more successful than the general had been in reestablishing French influence over events in these regions. Pompidou continued the Gaullist policy of condemning superpower involvement in the Middle East and criticizing the superpower naval build-up in the Mediterranean basin. In view of the fact that the Soviet Union's average naval presence in the region had grown from twelve ships in 1966 to over seventy vessels by 1970, however, Paris had become increasingly reluctant to press the United States to take the first step by pulling back the Sixth Fleet. He justified such actions as the sale of 108 Mirage fighter jets to Libya as a French "duty" to "combat" other (i.e., Soviet) "influences" that could enter the Mediterranean, but he nevertheless felt compelled to seek the participation of both Washington and Moscow in a four-power arrangement to solve outstanding Arab-Israeli differences.

In the face of constant rebuffs to his diplomacy by both the United States and the Soviet Union, Pompidou solicited the support of the European Community (EC) members for the development of a unified position regarding UN Declaration 242 as a basis for a coordinated European policy in the Middle East. This effort also met with limited success during the first three years of Pompidou's administration. Following the Yom Kippur War of 1973, however, a renewed French call for EC political involvement in the Middle East gained new support.

Four developments relating to the Yom Kippur War added weight to Pompidou's arguments for a unified European position. First, the superpowers had attempted to manage the Middle Eastern situation from the top, without the participation of their respective allies. Second, Washington attempted to pressure the NATO allies to provide logistical support for its efforts to supply Israel during the 1973 war. Third, on October 25, in the later stages of the war, the United States unilaterally placed its military forces on alert as a means of deterring further Soviet involvement in the Arab-Israeli conflict on behalf of Egypt. Fourth, in the aftermath of the war, the Arab states retaliated against members of the Atlantic Alliance by recourse to the oil weapon. These four developments were interrelated, and they had a cumulative negative impact on alliance cohesion. They also enhanced the credibility of Pompidou's, and French foreign minister Michel Jobert's, warnings that the West Europeans must act in unison to assert their interests if they wished to avoid similar problems in the future. And the Pompidou government was well placed and well disposed to present the European position to—or, more accurately, against—Washington.

Of the four developments listed above, Washington's attempt to induce the NATO allies to provide logistical support for its efforts to supply Israel triggered the most vindictive and intense arguments within the alliance. From Henry Kissinger's perspective, the American efforts were entirely consistent with the principles of cooperation and mutual assistance articulated in his "Year of Europe" speech of April 23, 1973. From the perspective of most Europeans, however, the U.S. campaign effectively vindicated the Gaullist critique of NATO as an instrument for the perpetuation of U.S. hegemony. Among the NATO allies, only Portugal and Holland provided consistent support for the U.S. supply effort. Kissinger castigated the U.S. allies for their "stampede of dissociation" and for their attempt to "opt out of any possible crisis with the Soviet Union."[2]

Michel Jobert developed the Western European counterargument in statements before the French National Assembly and the press during October and November. He attacked both superpowers for perpetuating and intensifying the conflict by their sponsorship of their respective clients, viewing it as further proof that "under the cover of détente and disarmament, the superpowers were prepared to sacrifice Europe's autonomy and mortgage its future."[3] Jobert leveled particular criticism against Washington for its insensitivity to special European concerns for peace and security in the Middle East, despite the political and economic ties between Europe and that region and despite Europe's dependence on uninterrupted access to Arab oil. Jobert also argued that America's failure to consult with its allies was contrary to the principles of alliance solidarity and could only have negative consequences for NATO. He concluded that the only solution was a united Europe, capable of identifying and protecting European interests in the Middle East.

Kissinger complained that Jobert was "turning the Year of Europe into a wrestling match."[4] He directly challenged Jobert's efforts to establish a "Euro-Arab dialogue" to ensure against future oil boycotts, and he left Paris isolated and frustrated outside of the U.S.-sponsored International Energy Agency (IEA). The events of the second half of 1973 nonetheless served as a strong impetus for the EC members to support the Pompidou government's efforts to establish unified European foreign policy positions, particularly on issues relating to the Middle East. Attempts to establish a Euro-Arab dialogue continued, and European Political Cooperation (EPC) initiatives which materialized within the EC during the early 1970s emphasized the Middle East as the area of primary concern.

The successful completion of the Washington Conference represented the most serious rebuff of the Pompidou government. By Kissinger's account, the alliance had been preserved in spite of France. But in this case, as in others,

France was articulating concerns and criticisms that other alliance members shared but had chosen to suppress. The Middle East had become a high-priority issue for NATO and a permanent threat to alliance solidarity. It would not go away during the next eleven years.

POLICY ADJUSTMENTS UNDER GISCARD

Pompidou's death and the subsequent election of Valéry Giscard d'Estaing defused the conflict within the alliance. As the first non-Gaullist Fifth Republic president, Giscard was in a position to make some cautious adjustments in French defense policy which could accommodate France to its political and geostrategic location in the center of the alliance. Yet there was still no chance of a formal reconciliation, since French public opinion remained overwhelmingly supportive of the basic premises of Gaullism on European and global security. These premises centered on the necessity of preserving the *force de dissuasion* and keeping France out of the NATO military command. Giscard was also sensitive to the broad-based French public support for a foreign policy of independence from both superpowers and the public's vision of France as the spokesman for Europe in the East-West balancing process.

Giscard nonetheless diverged from his predecessors in two important respects. First, he did not share the Gaullist fear of a superpower condominium; "the Russians and the Americans aren't getting together to rule the world," he asserted. "They are getting together to avoid being drawn into a war."[5] Second, although pursuing his own détente initiatives with the Soviet Union, he expressed appreciation of the need for a strong and coordinated Western bloc as a precondition for East-West cooperation, and he was prepared to recognize the centrality of the United States within that bloc.[6] He approached foreign policy from the point of view of a technocrat: solution-oriented and instinctively suspicious of the kinds of dramatic initiatives that had characterized the politics of de Gaulle and Jobert. Not surprisingly, Kissinger publicly applauded the "new spirit" that Giscard and his foreign minister, Jean Sauvarnargues, brought to Paris in May 1974. The new spirit was reinforced by the replacement of Willy Brandt by Helmut Schmidt as chancellor of West Germany, and by the close personal ties that Schmidt and Giscard began to develop. "Suddenly," Kissinger subsequently recalled, "key issues were handled easily; consultations were regular and intimate. Mid-1974 ushered in one of the best periods of Atlantic cooperation in decades."[7]

The major tests of Giscard's predisposition to cooperate with NATO in response to crises occurring outside of the treaty area were the two Shaba interventions of 1977 and 1978. Shortly after coming to office, Giscard communicated his government's interest in a more active foreign policy toward Africa. Zaire was singled out for special attention because of its potential as a resource supplier to France (it produces 60 percent of the world's cobalt) and because it was the largest Francophone state on the continent. In May 1974, Paris confirmed its commitment to the security of the regime of President Mobutu Sese Seko by a bilateral defense cooperation agreement. One year later, Giscard paid a state visit to Kinshasa, during which he assured Mobutu of Zaire's status as *primus inter pares* among France's African allies.[8] Giscard's efforts to reassure Mobutu increased after the Soviet Union and Cuba established a powerful military presence in Angola in 1976.[9] Indeed, next to Cuba, France maintained the largest external military force presence on the African continent and used them in a number of interventions during the 1970s—in Mauritania in 1977, in Morocco (through transfers of military aircraft from Dakar, Senegal) in 1978, and in both Chad and the Central African Republic the same year.

From Giscard's point of view, Africa was the last realm of French responsibility, and the network of Francophone African states represented an essential national interest in terms of geostrategy, politics, and resource dependence. He argued that any "local disequilibrium of forces" in Africa would have a direct impact not only on French power but on European security in general. Soviet or Soviet-proxy victories in any Third World region were also viewed by Giscard as a threat to East-West détente in the long term, since an essential precondition for détente was a stable international order. The French president considered U.S. post-Vietnam retrenchment as an invitation to the Soviet Union to upset the balance in key Third World regions. Under these circumstances, Giscard claimed that Washington's European allies had to accept new responsibilities for guaranteeing Third World security. For France, this implied a special responsibility for the safety of the Francophone African states.[10]

The first Shaba crisis began on March 10, 1977, when approximately fifteen hundred members of the Front de libération national congolaise (FLNC) attacked the rich Zairian mining region of Shaba, bordering Angola. Only France among the members of the Atlantic Alliance felt compelled to draw public attention to the 1977 Shaba crisis as a potential threat to regional stability and, by implication, to overall Western security. During the first month of the FLNC incursion, Giscard expressed his desire "to tell the French that Africa is quite close. So that a change in the political situation in Africa, a general situation of insecurity, subversion in Africa, would have consequences for France and Europe."[11] Without informing or consulting members of the Foreign Affairs Commission of the National Assembly, he approved the provision of eleven French military aircraft to transport fifteen hundred Moroccan troops to the combat area.

Morocco's offer to provide troops relieved Giscard of the decision to engage French forces in the first conflict since World War II outside of the community of former French colonies, but Paris did provide sixty-five military advisers to assist the Moroccan forces, as well as spare parts and other forms of military-related equipment. Giscard was criticized by members of the National Assem-

TABLE 6
Selected French Forces Abroad

Far East/Pacific (Indochina)

1945–1950

NAVY
Five destroyer/cruisers, six corvettes, and nine transport vessels.

AIR FORCE
One transport group of 12 Dakotas. Two groups of fighter/bombers. One transport group of JU-52s.

LAND FORCES
Initial deployment of 35,000 in 1946. Approximately 150,000 by end of 1949, supported by 300,000 Vietnamese.

1950–1954

NAVY
1 aircraft carrier and a destroyer escort.

AIR FORCE
70 FWX 63s, 20 Spitfires, various JU-52s. About 75 air transport aircraft. Fifteen B-26s transferred from South Korea in 1953.

LAND FORCES
150,000 French Expeditionary Corps personnel backed by 300,000 Vietnamese. French forces reduced to 45,000 by end of 1954; 5,000 by end of 1955; 200 by end of 1957.

Middle East/North Africa

1954–1969

NAVY
14,000 naval personnel manning bases in Algeria and Tunisia until Algerian independence.

AIR FORCE
Early 1950s, 24 bomber/fighter squadrons deployed throughout the region; later these squadrons were retired or redeployed to French Somaliland, Chad, and Senegal.

LAND FORCES
In 1954, 141,000; in 1955–56, increased to over 400,000 concentrated in Algeria, Tunisia, and the Sahara. By 1961, French forces totaled 500,000, plus 160,000 Muslim Algerians. In that year, France began withdrawing their last 12,000 troops from Morocco and removing forces from Algeria. By 1966, 7,000 French troops remained deployed in the French Community states of Africa, about 4,000 in Algeria. By 1968, these had been shifted to French Somaliland, Chad, the Ivory Coast, Senegal, and Madgascar, or had been reassigned to France.

Continued on next page

TABLE 6—Continued

1970–1989

West African Command included around 4,000 land forces and a few (usually 3–4) naval frigates, 2–3 landing craft, some minesweepers and coastal escorts. 1–2 fighter squadrons and 1 transport squadron constituted regional air support. UNIFIL force in Lebanon (1978–79) totaled 1,250 but later reduced to 650.

Indian Ocean

1968–1971

NAVY
One frigate, two minesweepers, and one landing craft in the Malagasy Republic.

AIR FORCE
One fighter squadron of A-1D Skyrider ground support aircraft. One medium-range (N-2501 Noratlas) air transport.

LAND FORCES
Three battalions (later reorganized to two regiments) in Malagasy; approx. 1,250 personnel.

1973–1980

Malagasy (Reunion/Diego Suarez after September 1973).

NAVY
1 destroyer, 3 minesweepers, and assorted landing craft.

AIR FORCE
Same as 1968–71.

LAND FORCES
Reduced to one battalion in 1978.

Djibouti
Built up to a 4,000-plus strong garrison by 1980, including two infantry regiments, an artillery regiment, and 2 squadrons of light tanks.

1981–1989

Djibouti/Reunion/Diego Suarez now constitutes South Indian Ocean Command.

NAVY
Approx. 5 frigates, 3 minor combatants, 2 amphibious, and 4 support ships.

Continued on next page

bly for his unilateral action, and some political parties—most notably the communists—accused the government of neocolonialist behavior to protect French cobalt, uranium, and copper interests. In general, however, the public approved of the initiative, accepting Giscard's arguments that quick French

TABLE 6—Continued

LAND FORCES

2,700–3,250 army and marine infantry/airborne personnel deployed at varying intervals.

Caribbean/South Pacific

Combined deployment strength in 2 theaters reached 65,000 in 1955 after Indochina drawdown but had been reduced to two regiments in the Caribbean (Guyana and the French Antilles) and 2 battalions in the South Pacific (Polynesia and New Caledonia) by 1969. By late 1982, deployments had been increased in the Caribbean to 3 infantry regiments and a marine regiment and in the Pacific to 2 marine infantry regiments and one army regiment. 3 frigates/corvettes are usually attached to the Antilles-Guyana Command with supporting maritime reconnaissance; 3 frigates, 8 landing craft, and 12–15 support ships are deployed in the Pacific.

French Capabilities For Overseas Intervention:
1983–1989

In 1983, the French government formed a Rapid Action Force from existing French army units to defend its overseas interests. This included 1 parachute division (12,800) comprising 6 parachute infantry battalions, 1 light armed battalion, 1 artillery battalion, 1 engineer regiment, 1 support battalion; 1 air portable marine division (8,100); 1 light armored division (6,400–7,400); 1 air mobile division, including helicopter regiments, logistical support brigades, and additional infantry. The French Foreign Legion is also available for overseas duties and numbers around 8,000.

Sources: Henry Alleg et al., *La guerre d' Algérie*, vol. 2 (Paris: Temps actuels, 1981), p. 51; *Défense nationale* (various journal articles); Paul Marie de la Gorce, *The French Army: A Military-Political History* (New York: Braziller, 1963), p. 405; Institut Charles de Gaulle, *De Gaulle et la nation face aux problèmes de défense (1945–1946)* (Paris: Plon, 1983), p. 227 and annex 1; International Institute for Strategic Studies, *The Military Balance* (London: IISS, 1961–present); Michel Martin, *Warriors to Managers: The French Military Establishment since 1945* (Chapel Hill: University of North Carolina Press, 1981), app. A, pp. 350–51; Lothar Ruehl, *La politique militaire de la 5' république* (Paris: Fondation national des sciences politiques, 1976); Stockholm International Peace Research Institute, *World Armaments and Disarmament Survey* (Stockholm: SIPRI, all); David Yost, *France's Deterrent Posture and Security in Europe*, pts. 1 and 2, Adelphi Papers, nos. 194, 195 (London: IISS, Winter 1984–85).

action was required to ensure the safety of the European community in the region. The French president downplayed the East-West aspect of the 1977 crisis, however, in light of inconclusive evidence of Soviet or Cuban involvement in the FLNC incursion.

The rapid victory of the Moroccan forces in 1977 provided Giscard with a foreign policy success and enhanced his domestic political image. This in turn may have contributed to the disruption of the Socialist-Communist union of the left and the electoral victory of the center-right coalition, which Giscard led at the time of the March 1978 National Assembly elections.[12] Giscard's moderate but forceful actions also improved France's image within the Western alliance. All parties were in agreement, however, that this was a relatively minor event, one that could not be used as an indicator of future French security policy in Africa.

To the surprise of many—not least the FLNC—Giscard illustrated fourteen months later that he was prepared to repeat his performance as the guarantor of Zaire's sovereignty in the face of a new round of internal tensions.[13] The second Zairian invasion force, comprising approximately four thousand French troops, began action on May 11, 1978, eleven days before the opening of the fifth Franco-African summit in Paris. On this occasion, he opted for a more active military role in view of the greater threat posed by the FLNC; but precisely because of this threat, the French president also sought the backing of the United States and other key Western allies in developing a military response.

Under the circumstances, Paris was not at all reluctant to emphasize the Soviet and Cuban presence in Zaire as a basis for soliciting American military assistance in the second Shaba crisis. As events were to illustrate, the Carter administration was somewhat more willing to listen to such arguments in the spring of 1978 than it had been during 1977, in particular because it was more convinced than it had been the year before that the USSR and/or Cuba was actively backing the FLNC, either directly or through the government of Agostinho Neto in Angola.[14] A steady shift to the right had also been under way within the general U.S. public, as well as within the administration itself, by the time Shaba II occurred. The influence of Secretary of State Cyrus Vance and UN Ambassador Andrew Young had declined and had been supplanted by that of Harold Brown, James Schlesinger, and Zbigniew Brzezinski, who tended to be much more willing to consider U.S. activism in the Third World in response to perceived challenges from Moscow. The 1978 incursion also represented a more serious threat to the safety of the Europeans living in Kinshasa—thus providing an additional, humanitarian justification for U.S. support of French military action.[15] The Carter administration consequently applauded the initiatives by Paris and, subsequently, Brussels to shore up the Mobutu regime with arms and troops.

Once Giscard had concluded that the situation required direct intervention by French military forces, U.S. support became essential because of the deficiencies in French air transport capability. Giscard and the chief of the General Staff, Guy Méry, had been committed to a program designed to enhance the mobility of French conventional forces since 1975.[16] However, French air transport at the time of the second Shaba intervention continued to be based primarily on its fleet of Transall C-160 cargo planes, which were designed for intra-European transport and have a maximum range of between 1,350 and 1,600 miles (depending on payload). The limited range of the Transalls and their comparatively small air transport capability (fifty-four tons maximum) were considered to be insufficient for the medium-scale intervention required by the 1978 Shaba crisis. The initial rapid deployment of French troops to Kinshasa was accomplished with French aircraft (four chartered McDonnell-Douglas DC-8s and one Boeing 707), but the subsequent supply of arms and equipment to support the French intervention required the assistance of Washington.[17]

In spite of its official support for the French and, subsequently, Belgian decision to send troops to Zaire, the United States was reluctant to do more than provide logistical support—a "carefully limited, one-time deployment of US transport aircraft."[18] This decision was based to a large extent upon the Carter administration's concern about running afoul of Congress in this first test of the president's war powers since taking office.[19] The United States consequently agreed to provide C-141 transports to lift arms, materiel, and "logistical personnel" to Zaire, but no U.S. combat troops actually participated in the conflict. No U.S. military aircraft, moreover, came closer than a hundred miles to the combat area. To skirt restrictions of the 1973 War Powers Resolution, U.S. pilots were removed and U.S. air support was terminated once the immediate crisis was resolved.[20] When Washington subsequently received a request from Brussels for a U.S. military contribution to help maintain order in Kinshasa, Vance notes that "the President's response was an emphatic no."[21]

Washington nevertheless emphasized the collaborative elements of the Zairian mission in its public statements. President Carter used the occasion of the NATO Ministerial Meeting of May 30 to applaud the "efforts of individual NATO Allies for the help they gave to nations and peoples who need it—recently in Zaire" and to observe that "our Alliance is centered on Europe, but our vigilance cannot be limited to that continent."[22] During and after the crisis, Giscard echoed these themes of common action in support of common interests in his discussions of the second Shaba intervention.

French and U.S. statements notwithstanding, Shaba II was not a model of ad hoc NATO out-of-region policy coordination. Most Western allies offered muted and conditional approval of the intervention on humanitarian grounds, but attempts by Giscard, Brzezinski, and others to underscore the East-West aspects of the Zairian crisis in stronger terms were rebuffed by several NATO governments. When questioned about prospects for the development of a NATO-backed European peacekeeping force for use in future African conflicts, NATO Secretary General Joseph Luns felt compelled to emphasize that "any European force in Africa will not be realized. All the Allies agree that NATO as such should not get involved in Africa." Furthermore, attempts by defense experts to treat Zaire as a first step toward a de jure or de facto extension of the NATO Treaty's purview to Africa were summarily rejected by the other NATO allies during the Washington Conference, which occurred shortly after the Shaba intervention.[23]

There was also very little agreement between the two principal European actors. Paris had opted for a quick military response to the Zaire crisis with a great deal of fanfare. But while placing his major emphasis on the rescue aspects of the intervention, Giscard also stressed the long-term Soviet/Cuban threat and French responsibilities as a guarantor of Western security. Brussels, by contrast, was much more cautious. The mission was presented by Belgian leaders almost exclusively as a humanitarian act. To reinforce this image, Brussels expressed its interest in a quick operation, lasting only seventy-two hours, and Belgian foreign minister Henri Simonet distinguished between the French and Belgian philosophies guiding the intervention during a television broadcast on May 20: "The French government has an African policy which is not the same as ours. France seeks to maintain *points d'appui* in the dark continent while Belgium seeks cooperation with a country rather than a regime."[24] Brussels also saw an economic motive in the French propensity to intervene and feared that Paris was seeking through military means to undermine the preponderant economic position that Belgium had maintained in Zaire since colonial times.

As noted above, the Shaba intervention represented only one of three French military engagements in Africa during May 1978. Two weeks before the French intervention in support of Mobutu in Zaire, French Jaguar bombers destroyed a column of Algerian-supported Polisario rebels, in defense of Mauritanian and Moroccan claims to the former Spanish Sahara.[25] To the extent that this initiative pitted France against Algeria in Northern Africa, it represented an important break from the Gaullist foreign policy tradition of cooperation with post-independence Algiers. During this same period, France continued to wage a war against rebel forces challenging the regime of Félix Malloum in Chad. Unlike the Mauritanian case, Giscard's military involvement in Chad represented a continuation of ten years of French foreign policy, with no end in sight.

From the French perspective, a militarily active policy in Africa was a logical concomitant of both North-South and East-West relations, perhaps best summarized by Foreign Minister Luis de Giringaud's formula, "No development without peace, no peace without security."[26] For some other NATO allies, however, France's concurrent military involvement in three African conflicts represented a dangerous exercise in imperial nostalgia, which threatened to disrupt developing European ties in the Third World and perhaps undermine détente. The governments of Denmark and the Netherlands were particularly outspoken in condemning French military activism under Giscard and opposing any attempt to place the NATO imprimatur on French initiatives in Africa.[27]

There are four reasons why the events of May 1978 did not precipitate greater dispute within the alliance. First, the French actions in Mauritania and Chad were overshadowed by the more dramatic developments in Zaire; and by virtually any standard of measure, the Franco/Belgian intervention in Shaba was a success. Even the most ardent Western critics of neoimperialism could not challenge the fact that the European community in Kinshasa was in danger of being massacred by the FLNC in 1978. Under these circumstances, the rescue mission—involving the evacuation of two thousand Europeans in three days—was an impressive feat that all the allies applauded. Second, Giscard had already established his *bona fides* as an active proponent of détente politics to the satisfaction of the other Western European governments, so his assurances that he was not seeking a return to the cold war by his initiatives in Africa were accepted. Third, several NATO governments accepted (at least unofficially) Giscard's argument that some French military activism in Africa was needed during a period of post-Vietnam retrenchment in the United States. Finally, even if the United States had been more willing or able to use force in Africa in the late 1970s, many European allies recognized the advantages inherent in using French forces instead. As James Goldsborough observed at the time: "French paratroopers jumping into Shaba are not the same as US paratroopers jumping into Shaba—even if the French are wearing US parachutes. French diplomacy enjoys a latitude that other nations do not have, and the recent French actions in Africa are proof that Giscard is not afraid to take advantage of it."[28]

Events during May 1978 illustrated, however, that the latitude of French military action in Africa was really more limited than Goldsborough implies. In fact, concurrent challenges in Mauritania, Chad, and Zaire stretched French military capabilities beyond their limits. As a consequence, Giscard had to make a virtue out of the necessity of Western support for French initiatives in Africa. Both the right and the left in France reacted predictably. Gaullists, socialists, and communists were united in interpreting U.S. support for the Franco/Belgian intervention in Shaba as confirmation of Giscard's interest in returning France to NATO. Giscard was accused by Jacques Chirac of seeking the *OTANization* of Africa. Chirac also saw France slipping from a great power role in Africa to a "second rank" position by its deference to Washington during Shaba. François Mitterrand also warned against a French return to a new and enlarged NATO alliance that would include not only Europe but Africa as well.[29] He also criticized French interventions in Africa as a destabilizing factor in world politics because such actions contributed to the inclination of others—the superpowers, Algeria, Libya—to employ military force beyond their borders.[30]

In the weeks following the successful rescue mission, however, Giscard's critics fell silent. As in 1977, public opinion polls showed overwhelming support for an action that had enhanced French prestige and had probably averted the slaughter of French civilians at very small cost (five French soldiers killed, twenty wounded). Criticism from left and right shifted to Giscard's proposals for the establishment of a Pan-African force to preserve order in the aftermath of the Shaba crisis.

During the summit meeting arranged in Paris on June 5 (attended by Belgian, U.K., U.S., and West German representatives), Giscard called for the creation of such a force as a follow-up to the ad hoc grouping of Francophone states which had assisted in the 1977 Zaire intervention. He envisioned a standing security force of four thousand to five thousand African troops, to be trained, equipped, and logistically supported by the Western allies. In response to Giscard's initiatives, *Tass* complained of Franco/American attempts at "coordination of NATO politics with an eye toward extending the influence of the [Western] bloc to Africa."[31] This provided fresh ammunition for Giscard's critics, who described the plan as a *"petit OTAN"* for Africa. It was also much too ambitious for the assembled governments, who preferred to maintain their diplomatic flexibility in Africa and did not wish to become tied to an arrangement that would be primarily or exclusively oriented to the Francophone states of the region. As Christopher Coker has observed, "It was precisely because NATO was a pragmatic alliance that it wanted nothing to do with the training and equipping of a Pan-African force."[32]

Peter Mangold has described the second Shaba intervention as a "minor incident" that nonetheless "forced Western countries to answer some basic questions about their policies toward Africa."[33] The incident was of special significance for France because, contrary to what Giscard's critics claimed, it bolstered France's reputation as a reliable protector in Africa while enhancing Paris' image as a supportive Western ally.[34] Because it was a "minor incident," Shaba did not become a seriously divisive issue within the alliance. Historical Franco-Belgian suspicions were aroused, but the two nations nonetheless acted to defend a common interest in the context of crisis. Efforts by Giscard to solicit the support of NATO, or coalitions within NATO, were rejected, but NATO allies were publicly supportive of the humanitarian aspects of the French and Belgian actions. As the principal test of Giscard's inclination to cooperate with other Western nations in response to an out-of-area crisis, Shaba showed that the more defensive, insecure, and xenophobic elements of Gaullist foreign and security policy had been abandoned by the third president of the Fifth Republic. After two decades of dealing with an obstructionist French approach to alliance relations, it is not surprising that Western analysts gave an exaggerated amount of attention to Giscard's handling of the "minor incident" in Shaba as an important symbolic breakthrough.

MITTERRAND'S "NEW ATLANTICISM"

During his presidential election campaign (April–May 1981), François Mitterrand attacked Giscard for subservience to both superpowers. He played up the familiar theme of *OTANization,* arguing that the defense strategy of "enlarged sanctuarization," which had been introduced by Giscard and General Méry in 1976, represented a step backward into the alliance military organization. At the same time, he criticized Giscard for seeking to accommodate the Soviet Union in spite of events in Afghanistan and Poland.

Mitterrand maintained a studied ambivalence on the issue of Third World interventions during the campaign. He was critical, in principle, of Giscard's efforts to make France "Africa's policeman" in the late 1970s, but he did not press this issue during the campaign. This may have been due to Mitterrand's sense that he would be giving Giscard an opportunity to play up the successful and popular Zairian operation.[35] Mitterrand's reticence also reflected a general lack of consensus within the Socialist party on the issue of whether and when France should use force to protect its interests in the Third World.

Following Mitterrand's election victory, some analysts focused on the Socialist government's rhetorical commitment to improving relations with the Third World as the cornerstone of Mitterrand's plans for foreign policy. Much attention was given to the appointment of Jean Pierre Cot as minister for overseas cooperation as indicating Mitterrand's interest in a more active policy of support for "progressive" forces in the Third World, and a more accommodating approach to North-South relations in general. This initial interpretation was reinforced by the French decision actively to challenge the United States in Central America, by publicly supporting Nicaragua and recognizing the Revolutionary Democratic Front, which spearheaded the guerrilla war in El Salvador.[36] According to one African editorial, which was published two months after Mitterrand's election, "Seldom do we have cause to comment favorably on the pronouncements of a non-African leader. . . . We are indulging ourselves on this occasion because we see in the public stance of France's new President . . . a significant departure in France's policy vis-à-vis Africa."[37] Within a few months of his election, however, Mitterrand began to act in ways that were entirely consistent with the Gaullist tradition of military activism in the Third World.[38]

The first major test was Chad, which had been an enduring source of difficulty for France for fifteen years. French troops had been involved in an ongoing civil war raging throughout Chad on and off since 1968. Giscard had removed French forces in May of 1980 in compliance with a request by the Organization of African Unity (OAU), which was attempting to construct its own peacekeeping force.[39] Four months after the departure of the French forces, Muammar el-Qaddafi announced plans to provide military support for the revolutionary forces of the Gouvernement d'union nationale de transition (GUNT), under the leadership of Goukouni Oueddi, in their offensive against the government of Hissen Habré. Backed by Libyan tanks, GUNT succeeded in expelling Habré from N'Djamena by the end of 1980. On January 6, 1981, Qaddafi announced his plans to merge Libya and Chad.

Libya's bold moves were universally condemned in the West. Even the normally indecisive and reticent OAU felt sufficiently alarmed to condemn Qaddafi's initiatives and call for the departure of Libyan troops from Chad. French troops were nonetheless held in check as the government of Habré collapsed, and Giscard came under attack from several African states for his failure to react forcefully to the Libyan intervention. A number of North African political leaders viewed Qaddafi's actions as contributing to the establishment of a "red belt, extending from Afghanistan to Aden, from Angola to Ethiopia, from Syria to Libya and to Chad," and were perplexed as to "why Giscard has permitted this to happen."[40] Others, both inside and outside of France, asked the same question in the wake of Qaddafi's annexation announcement. For many African leaders, the credit that Giscard had acquired by his initiatives in 1977 and 1978 was being squandered by French inaction in the Chadian crisis. Julian Hollick described French African policy as "at best vacillating, at worst unreliable and hypocritical."[41] For many critics, the explanation was to be found in the lucrative arms and oil trade between Paris and Tripoli.

The situation remained essentially unchanged until the month following the French presidential election, at which time it became clear that the OAU's efforts to create its own peacekeeping force in Chad were floundering. This placed increased pressure on François Mitterrand's new government to take some action, either unilaterally or in conjunction with other Western and African leaders, to challenge Qaddafi.

Mitterrand's initial reaction was to attempt to resuscitate the OAU peacekeeping scheme as a means of expelling Libya from Chad. Significantly, he was not at all reluctant to solicit U.S. cooperation in this effort. During the Cancun Conference (October 1981), Mitterrand obtained a U.S. commitment to join forces in guaranteeing economic and logistical support for a new OAU effort in Chad. Such Western assurances did give a temporary boost to the floundering efforts of the organizers of the OAU peacekeeping force. In the face of increased OAU pressure and the prospect of the deployment of a forty-eight-hundred-man inter-African force (IAF) composed of Zairian (two thousand), Nigerian (two thousand), and Senegalese (eight hundred) troops, Qaddafi withdrew his forces.[42] As Herbert Boyd has correctly noted, "no one was more relieved than Mitterrand."[43]

But the situation in Chad deteriorated throughout 1982. The IAF attempted to maintain a neutral position with regard to the struggle for power between Habré and Goukouni which erupted shortly after the departure of the Libyan forces. The French, meanwhile, were highly ambivalent regarding a preferred outcome in the power struggle. Mitterrand continued to pursue a policy of support for the IAF without actively committing French forces. He was anxious to avoid a major shift in the power equation within Chad which might force both Libya and France to reenter the conflict. Paris was also critical of what it viewed

238

as an increased propensity by Washington to become involved in Chad during this period, independently of Paris, and in particular of the U.S. provision of arms to Habré's forces. Having initially brought the Reagan administration into the crisis in 1981, Mitterrand found it difficult to get the Americans out a year later.

Over time, the troops under Habré gained the upper hand over Goukouni's GUNT forces. N'Djamena fell to the U.S.-supported forces of Habré on June 7, 1982. Washington subsequently recognized Habré's regime, provided $25 million in arms to N'Djamena, and began to pressure the French for similar commitments.[44] As Mitterrand had feared, Goukouni's expulsion was followed in early 1983 by a new GUNT counteroffensive against Habré, with logistical and material support provided by Qaddafi. Mitterrand, however, continued to resist demands from Washington to deploy troops to Chad. As Monsour El-Kiklia has noted, the French president "disliked being pressured by Washington, . . . which he considered to be quite ignorant about the politics of the area," but by the late summer it had become increasingly apparent to Mitterrand that "France was faced with the choice of either intervening or being replaced by the United States in Central and West Africa."[45]

Ronald Reagan had publicly identified Qaddafi as "the most dangerous man in the world," bent on destabilizing Central and North Africa.[46] Washington's preference was to present Chad as a replay of 1978, a case of French fulfillment of its responsibility for the stability and security of a large portion of Africa, with economic, logistical, and political support provided by other Western governments as requested by France. All of this was to be proclaimed, moreover, in the name of alliance solidarity and common security interests. If properly orchestrated by Paris, this approach might have been politically advantageous to Mitterrand as well.

Unfortunately, the process was mismanaged by both sides. As Qaddafi's forces scored one victory after another, Mitterrand came under increasing domestic and international pressure to do something. The Libyan leader added to Mitterrand's difficulties by trumpeting his disdain of French warnings. A representative article in the French weekly *L'Express* quoted Qaddafi's assertion that "the French people cannot stand another Algerian war or a repetition of Dien Bien Phu."[47] The article was accompanied by a drawing of Mitterrand kneeling before a sneering Qaddafi in jackboots. Mitterrand nonetheless continued to resist taking an action that communist coalition members and the left wing of his own party would attack as Giscardian neocolonialism.

Mitterrand was finally forced to act on August 9, in response to a major offensive by Libyan and GUNT forces against the strategic city of Faya Largeau in northern Chad. In response, French defense minister Charles Hernu announced that France was "now ready to do everything the Libyans are doing except for bombing civilians."[48] France launched Operation Sting-Ray, the largest French military intervention in Africa since the Algerian War. By the end of August, two thousand paratroopers and French Legionnaires were in Chad, supported by four Jaguar and four Mirage aircraft as well as a squadron of combat helicopters.[49] To counter any accusations of subservience to Washington, Mitterrand made it clear that he would brook no American meddling in Chad and that he was "annoyed" by the fact that he had learned "through the newspapers" of the U.S. decision to deploy two AWACS electronic intelligence-gathering planes to Sudan for the explicit purpose of providing support for French air force units in Chad, if requested.

The subsequent U.S.-French squabble over the AWACS deployment was a classic example of the right military decision being undermined by the demands of politics. In view of the impressive air forces and mobile antiaircraft systems (including SAM-7 missiles and ZSU-23-4 guns) that Qaddafi had at his disposal, Mitterrand had every reason to welcome the American offer of the AWACS. And in view of the public opinion support that Mitterrand enjoyed as a result of his decision to intervene in Chad, the French president was in a strong position to defend Franco-American military cooperation on grounds of concern for the safety of French air force units in Chad. Instead, Mitterrand took the easier, if militarily less defensible, approach of publicly attacking Washington and foreclosing, at least for the time being, the option of relying on U.S. intelligence data collected by the AWACS. In the wake of the destruction of a French Jaguar fighter by Libyan forces, one French article cited disgruntled French military officers criticizing the "purely political decision of the Socialist government to refuse US help."[50]

The record of U.S.-French relations over the issue of Chad illustrates approximately equal quantities of insensitivity on the part of Washington and defensiveness on the part of Paris. The circumstances that had contributed to efficient collaboration between Paris and Washington at the time of the Cancun meeting in 1981 were no longer in place two years later. After an initial period of indecision, Paris aligned itself with Washington's policy of support for Habré against the Libyan-GUNT alliance. Mitterrand nonetheless resented what *U.S. News and World Report* later described as Reagan's "strategy of psychological warfare directed at France . . . to pressure a reluctant Socialist government in Paris to assume responsibility for the defense of its former colony."[51] From Mitterrand's point of view, the United States was guilty of attempting to internationalize a local conflict in Francophone Africa.[52] He also opposed the U.S. interpretation of the threat posed by Qaddafi. He continued throughout the crisis to accept the possibility that Libyan goals were limited to defensive reinforcement of its own southern border and used this argument as the basis for bilateral discussions aimed at resolving the French-Libyan confrontation.[53]

It would be misleading, however, to make too much of the disputes between Paris and Washington over Chad. In fact, Mitterrand proved to be more willing than any of his Fifth Republic predecessors (including Giscard) to analyze security issues and to articulate French defense interests in an Atlantic Alliance context. The three most significant illustrations of Mitterrand's "Atlanticism" are (1) his support for the NATO dual track decision of 1979, (2) the French contribution to the Multilateral Peacekeeping Force in Lebanon and subsequent French participation in Western naval operations in the Persian Gulf, and (3) his efforts to develop a Force d'action rapide (FAR).

During the intense and disruptive debates over the issue of U.S. deployments of Long Range Theater Nuclear Weapons (LRTNF) in Europe, Mitterrand never wavered in his support for the NATO LRTNF modernization campaign. He was among the most outspoken critics of the Soviet Union's attempt to "decouple" Europe from the United States by its SS-20 and Backfire bomber deployments. Like all other Western European leaders, Mitterrand expressed the hope that the problem of the Soviet LRTNF advantage could be resolved through superpower disarmament talks in Geneva; but unlike some Western European leaders, Mitterrand held to the position that the deployment of American Pershing II and ground-launched cruise missiles (GLCMs) in Europe should proceed on schedule after the collapse of the Geneva talks in November 1983.

The French decision to contribute two thousand troops to the Multilateral Peacekeeping Force (MLF) in Lebanon is a second important illustration of Mitterrand's "Atlanticism," in spite of the fact that Mitterrand took pains to distinguish French motives and interests in Beirut from those of the United States. The French president stressed that the United States could not bring to the crisis in Lebanon the sense of history, based upon "nuanced relations spanning several centuries," upon which France relied.[54] The French took pride in the fact that their troops were the first to arrive in Beirut, on August 21, 1982, and the last to leave, on March 31, 1984. Paris also pursued its own diplomatic initiatives in the Middle East during the time that the MLF was in Beirut. In the wake of the massacres at two Palestinian refugee camps during September 16–18, 1982, for example, France sided with the Soviet Union in support of a UN Security Council vote calling for a worldwide arms embargo against Israel. Washington vetoed the Security Council initiative.

The record of the MLF nonetheless reflects Mitterrand's recognition of the need for unobtrusive allied policy coordination in certain out-of-area cases. The French decisions to contribute to the first and second Lebanese peacekeeping experiments during the period of 1982–1984 were worked out in consultation with Washington, London, and Rome, as were subsequent decisions to increase the size of the French forces in Beirut and to wind down the operation in the spring of 1984. Paris also demonstrated concern for policy coordination in the wake of the late October bombing attack against French and U.S. troops in Beirut. Four days after the attack, a special meeting of representatives of the peacekeeping states (France, Italy, the United States, and, by fall 1983, Britain) was convened in Paris to establish a consensus on the issue of retaliation.[55] When three weeks later French fighter-bombers attacked an Iranian stronghold in Baallbek, Paris described the retaliatory strike as a unilateral French initiative. U.S. government spokesmen subsequently admitted, however, that the French government had developed the plan in cooperation with Washington, and up until the last minute American bombers were to be included in the air strike.[56]

In 1987, the Mitterrand government (in "cohabitation" with centrist-Gaullist premier Jacques Chirac) again demonstrated its willingness to collaborate—quietly and conditionally—with key NATO governments in order to enhance stability in the Middle East/gulf region. The French fleet participated in loosely coordinated naval manuevers in the Persian Gulf to protect merchant vessels caught in the middle of the Iran/Iraq War. In fact, France contributed the largest European contingent in the region—fifteen ships, including the attack carrier *Clemenceau*. France actively discouraged any attempts to interpret this initiative as a move closer to NATO or as an accommodation to U.S. wishes, but according to one American defense expert at the time, "The British and French both are cooperating much more closely with the U.S. Navy than anyone is saying publicly."[57]

The third indication of Mitterrand's "new Atlanticism" was his support for the creation of the FAR and his willingness to justify this force as a direct contribution to allied security.[58] The FAR was developed for the express purpose of providing French conventional forces with greater operational mobility. Plans for new weapons and equipment acquisitions in support of the FAR are nonetheless quite limited, and the FAR has not escaped the defense budget cuts that followed the arrival of Michel Rocard as prime minister in May 1988.[59]

Most students of French defense policy who have commented on FAR have focused attention not on the actual improvements in French mobility and interventionary capability but on the doctrinal and political adjustments that it reflects. Some specialists, such as General François Valentin, have argued that FAR only makes sense from a military point of view if it is interpreted as an integral part of an allied forward defense strategy.[60] Gaullist critics have stressed this point as proof that the Mitterrand government is moving in the direction of de facto reintegration of France into NATO. David Yost has cited four "implications" of the FAR plan which collectively indicate a fundamental "attitudinal shift" on the part of the Mitterrand government on the issue of defense.

(A) A stronger public commitment than has ever been made since 1966 regarding participation in the forward battle; (B) Closer coordination and possible combined operations with allies in West Germany; (C) A potentially larger commitment of forces to the conventional forward battle; and (D) New seriousness about possible Soviet non-nuclear options.[61]

242

Although most discussion of the FAR stresses its potential contribution to NATO's flexible response and forward defense strategies for Central Europe, the French government has repeatedly stressed that it is also being developed to respond to contingencies that could arise beyond continental Europe as well.[62] Some logistical problems remain to be solved, however. France continues to rely upon its fleet of forty-six Transall C-160 aircraft for long-range troop and equipment transportation. As previously mentioned, the limited range and lift capability of this aircraft was a constraining element in French interventionary decisions in Africa in both the Giscard and Mitterrand eras. The French government has announced plans to purchase twenty-four newer models of the Transall—ten of which will be designed as tankers capable of aerial refueling. Until Paris acquires a more effective airlift capability, France will probably be compelled to rely once again upon air transport assistance from the United States in the event that a crisis in Central Africa or in one of the French overseas dependencies requires a rapid response by more than a token French military force. Developments in the French overseas territories, including new terrorist actions in Guadalupe or riots among the Kanak population of New Caledonia, could present the Mitterrand government with this type of interventionary decision in the near future.

CONCLUSION

Statements and policies made by the Mitterrand government illustrate that a fundamental change is under way in French thinking about defense. The change is best understood as the culmination of a steady, incremental move away from the more extreme elements of the Gaullist military doctrine. Two earlier stages in the incremental trend are easily recognizable:

1. Pompidou's reorientation of French defense policy away from the extreme Gaullist logic reflected in the *tous azimuts* (all targets) doctrine, and his concentration instead upon developing French capabilities around the assumption of an identifiable threat from the East.
2. Giscard's continuous, if faltering, attempts to introduce the concept of "enlarged sanctuarization" and his willingness to coordinate out-of-area military actions with other Western allies—in particular the United States—when circumstances made unilateral action too difficult or too risky.

When viewed from this perspective, French defense policy since de Gaulle appears as a gradual, perhaps inevitable, readjustment to international realities; to France's geostrategic placement in the center of Western Europe; and to France's political, economic, and strategic affiliation with the nations of the Western alliance. The development of the FAR and the progressive reorientation of French defense thinking do not, however, imply abandonment of the principles of independence articulated by de Gaulle. In the words of former defense minister Charles Hernu, "The space of freedom [in French defense planning] is an irreversible phenomenon."[63] But the Mitterrand government has come to accept the fact of a great potential for enhanced intra-alliance cooperation that will not jeopardize France's "space of freedom," including increased cooperation in training, logistical support, and coordinated air defense.

This is all to the good, from the point of view of Western security. The danger is that Paris' allies will focus too much public attention on these limited initiatives and will publicly encourage Mitterrand's "new Atlanticism." This would tend to create the kinds of opposition within France which forced Giscard to back away from his "enlarged sanctuarization" campaign in the late 1970s. The West, and in particular the United States, therefore, must recognize the limits that French domestic politics place on Mitterrand's ability to publicly coordinate out-of-area initiatives with members of the alliance.

CONCLUSION TO PART III

THE HISTORY of France's relations with the Atlantic Alliance cannot be understood in isolation from French security policies outside of the NATO Treaty area. In particular, de Gaulle's decision to remove the French Mediterranean fleet from the NATO High Command, and the subsequent French decision to leave that command altogether, must be seen against the backdrop of a series of events in the Levant, Indochina, Suez, Tunisia, and Algeria. De Gaulle's earliest postwar foreign policy initiatives were based upon a belief in the need to preserve the bulk of the French empire as it had existed before World War II. The general was fearful that Washington and London either would not assist France in the pursuit of this goal or would actively oppose French efforts. By the time that de Gaulle returned to power in 1958, the French Union was in the final stages of collapse, and the general's worst fears regarding the Anglo-Saxons had been confirmed. De Gaulle's antipathy toward the NATO Alliance and his decision to pursue a security policy based on the theme of national independence were largely determined by this experience.

In the case of the two most important French postwar campaigns—Indochina and Algeria—the historical record illustrates that influential factions within the United States were prepared to offer conditional economic and political support for French military efforts abroad where these efforts were viewed as contributing to the global containment struggle. Furthermore, this group of policy makers was not at all hesitant on occasion to recommend the use of NATO's institutional framework to funnel such support. But this faction consistently ran afoul of a second influential group in Washington—strongly represented within the U.S. Joint Chiefs of Staff—who believed that successive Fourth Republic governments had neither the conceptual nor the military tools required to achieve the goals that they were pursuing outside of the NATO Treaty area. According to this assessment, U.S. political, economic, and, in particular, military support for France in the Third World was at best a maldeployment of scarce resources, and at worst a morally indefensible sponsorship of the politics of another age. The compromises that were inevitably achieved between these two factions contributed to a posture of hesitant, grudging, and condescending support for French extra-European campaigns. U.S. skepticism, in turn, fueled

245

French mass and elite public resentment against Washington, even as it drained American political and economic capital. French public reaction to the nation's cumulative geopolitical setbacks overseas set the stage for the return of de Gaulle, and the subsequent French policies toward NATO and the alliance leaders which have come to be associated with his name.

Other NATO allies were understandably reluctant to involve themselves too deeply in the out-of-area debates between Washington and Paris prior to 1966, but their general inclination was to exercise a restraining influence on the United States in those cases where France sought extraregional assistance. Those allies who had freed themselves of their colonial possessions saw little to be gained from supporting France and a very real risk that, if they supported Paris too overtly, they would be called upon to provide direct or indirect subventions for any French out-of-area actions that NATO officially approved. In fact, only Britain, with its extensive postwar Commonwealth network, was in a position to collaborate with France to move NATO toward a more ambitious commitment to out-of-area security coöperation in the 1950s and 1960s, but London generally preferred to play its own game with Washington.

Since the departure of de Gaulle in 1969, France has moved incrementally back toward the direction of military cooperation with NATO. The process of tentative reconciliation with NATO will continue, we believe, if only because French defense planners have come to accept the doctrinal implications of France's location in the center of Western Europe. But no one inside or outside of France argues that this process of adjusting French defense plans to geostrategic realities will end in the formal reintegration of France into NATO, since the theme of military independence has become one of the most pervasively influential sources of consensus and legitimation in French politics. Under these circumstances, French defense experts can be expected to continue to develop technical cooperation with NATO military planners up to the point at which such cooperation confronts the themes of autonomy and sovereign control, which the French mass and elite publics alike have come to associate with the myth of national independence. As Philip Gordon puts it, "Gaullist boundaries have bent, but they have not broken."[1] NATO planners will have to content themselves with the limitations that this situation implies.

Similar conclusions appear warranted as regards policy coordination beyond the NATO Treaty area. Successive Fifth Republic governments since de Gaulle have accepted the need to coordinate certain Third World policies with other Western European governments and, on occasion, with Washington. But the limits of this policy coordination are, and will remain, determined by the enduring potency of the symbol of national independence for the French people. France continues to refine and develop its capabilities for rapid military intervention outside of Europe. But these improvements will in fact increase the ability of the French government to act alone in Africa, the Middle East, or Asia if Paris chooses to do so. Western security planners can nonetheless applaud improvements in France's capability to project force abroad, even though such improvements do not necessarily imply a change in French defense thinking in favor of increased cooperation beyond the NATO Treaty area. This conclusion is justified by the fact—too often overlooked in intra-alliance debates—that France's global security interests continue to be fundamentally in accordance with the security interests of the Atlantic community as a whole.

PART IV

THE OTHER NATO MEMBERS

INTRODUCTION TO PART IV

As DISCUSSED in our Introduction to this book, Washington initially favored a small NATO, comprising perhaps the United States, Canada, and the five signatories of the Brussels Treaty. Even Dean Acheson and the members of the "Europe first" faction were reluctant to accept the idea of an alliance extending beyond the immediate North Atlantic community. The Joint Chiefs of Staff and other representatives of the "resource/geographic constraints" faction were even more concerned about an overcommitment to Europe. As the Washington Preparatory Talks progressed, however, all factions in Washington came to accept the need for a much larger, and consequently less manageable, NATO.[1]

The fundamental rationales for including both the northern and southern regions in the overall alliance was to gain access to mid-Atlantic "stepping stones" such as Greenland and the Azores, and to provide the alliance with additional space for a Western European defense-in-depth in preparation for an allied counterattack against Moscow. As Roger Hilsman argued a decade after NATO's formation, "Try as they might, the Allies only had a slim chance of holding the Rhine if war came. . . . each of the participants, in consequence, wanted a sector that would permit retreat. This was not cowardice, but merely prudence. In a sector permitting maneuver, one could hope to live to fight another day."[2]

THE NORTHERN REGION

In Chapter 19, we discuss the ambivalent and conditional nature of Scandinavian membership in the alliance. We trace this situation back to the formative period of the alliance when Norway, Denmark, and Iceland saw an Atlantic Alliance as *one of three* options available for ensuring their security. Those Scandinavian policy makers who favored membership in NATO competed with factions within their countries which favored either an exclusively Nordic defense pact or a return to traditional policies of neutrality. Domestic political compromises were necessary to bring these competing factions around. These domestic compromises translated into qualified and restrictive membership in the new alliance.

The postwar Scandinavian perspective on security in general, and NATO in particular, was informed by a sense of the region's marginality to the evolving East-West conflict. It was assumed by many Scandinavians that in the event of an East-West confrontation, the bulk of the fighting would occur in Central Europe. This theory encouraged supporters of the two alternatives to NATO membership to believe that the Scandinavians could and should stay out of any future East-West war, either through a policy of deterrence (by means of an exclusively Nordic defense pact) or by a policy of scrupulously preserved neutrality.

Scandinavian acceptance of NATO membership would have been impossible if more opinion leaders in the Nordic region had been certain about the theory of marginality. The idea nonetheless endured as a recurrent theme in Scandinavian foreign policy debates after the decision to join NATO had been made. This suspicion that the Nordic region was marginal to the evolving East-West struggle encouraged Scandinavian governments and publics to be especially skeptical of any out-of-area initiatives by other NATO members which were justified as a contribution to global anti-Soviet containment. The Nordic states often proved to be more anticolonial than their NATO colleagues, more inclined to favor UN involvement in North-South disputes, and more publicly critical of military interventions by NATO members in the Third World. Their sentiments on such issues have been so strong that neither Washington nor the other NATO allies have seen any value in soliciting Scandinavian support during most out-of-area crises.

In Chapter 19, we focus on those situations in which the Scandinavian allies have become involved in NATO out-of-area disputes since 1949 and comment on the enduring influence of the theory of marginality in shaping Scandinavian positions on out-of-area issues. We attempt to demonstrate that the theory of marginality has been an exercise in nostalgia since 1945 and is even more unrealistic today than it was four decades ago. We discuss changes during the last ten years in the military capabilities and strategies of the two superpowers which have shifted the center of gravity of any future East-West conflict northward. We also discuss the impact of these technological and doctrinal changes on the ability of both NATO and the Warsaw Pact accurately to judge the boundaries of the NATO alliance in the north. Finally, we consider the special case of Canada, the only ally that shares a land border with the alliance leader.

THE CENTRAL REGION

The special characteristics and concerns of the nations composing the central region of the alliance (Belgium, Holland, and West Germany) are the subject of Chapter 20. Since the mid-1960s, these governments have tended to take a strict constructionist position regarding most out-of-area issues. This is not surprising, since their principal security concern during the last two decades has been the preservation of NATO's central front, and they have generally viewed out-of-area involvements by NATO allies as immediate or potential problems of resource diversion.

The three Central European allies nonetheless differed in their approaches to the general issue of out-of-area cooperation during the first two decades of the alliance, when Belgium and Holland were still involved in the difficult process of decolonization. We will accord special attention to the case of Belgium during this period, because of its status as a nation strongly committed to the principles of European unification and Atlanticism, but still burdened with its own national commitments abroad.

THE SOUTHERN RIM

Any survey of the alliance's southern flank must necessarily take a country-by-country approach because of the political and geostrategic heterogeneity of the region. Indeed, the lack of a geostrategically coherent southern flank was recognized by NATO defense planners as one of the defects of the alliance at the time it was established. As originally designated, the southern region hopscotched from Portugal to France to Italy and went no farther eastward. Over time, the southern flank was strengthened by the accession of Turkey and Greece, by the establishment of U.S. bases in Spain, and by the steady build-up of the U.S. Sixth Fleet in the Mediterranean. These positive developments were at least partly offset during the 1950s, however, by the removal of the French Mediterranean fleet from the NATO command in 1959 and by the growth of animosity between Greece and Turkey over the issue of Cyprus.[3]

Since the 1950s, the picture has continued to be characterized by a combination of positive and negative developments. On the plus side of the ledger, Portugal has extracted itself from a crippling colonial involvement in Africa and is gradually rebuilding its economy. Italy has begun to take greater responsibility for its own security. Greece returned to the NATO alliance in 1980 after a six-year absence. Spain has transcended the Franco era to become NATO's sixteenth member. Among the minuses, however, are the continuing Greek-Turkish dispute; the conditional status of both Greece and Spain, along with their bases, in the alliance; the steady, if unspectacular, growth of the Soviet naval presence in the Mediterranean; and new threats arising (outside the venue of East-West competition) along the southern and eastern littorals of the Mediterranean. Chapters 20–23 briefly survey the patchwork of security interests and concerns that constitutes NATO's southern region and relate these interests and concerns to the issue of out-of-area cooperation.

CHAPTER 19

NATO'S NORTH:

CAP, FLANK, OR RIM?

As previously mentioned, the question of what constituted an Atlantic—as opposed to a more geographically comprehensive Western—defense system was the subject of considerable debate and compromise during the 1948–49 Washington Preparatory Talks. Early in these discussions, Washington and London agreed that the inclusion of Iceland and Greenland was necessary, because they represented essential stepping stones between America and Europe.[1] Likewise, it was clear that both Iceland and Denmark (which controlled Greenland) would be unwilling to join a Western defense arrangement if Norway was not included.

The three Scandinavian governments were reluctant to join an Atlantic alliance, since joining would represent a fundamental break from the two traditional security policies favored by the Scandinavian states: neutrality and an exclusively Nordic defense arrangement. Both of these approaches to security were based upon the aforementioned idea of *marginality*—the belief (more accurately, the hope) of many Scandinavians that the Nordic region could be kept out of any future conflict originating in Central Europe. By 1948, many policy makers in Oslo, Copenhagen, and Reykjavik had become convinced that the bipolarization of the post-World War II system made both of these traditional options impracticable. But some key political figures remained suspicious of a policy of trusting Nordic security to the United States. For example, during the Washington Preparatory Talks, Danish foreign minister Gustav Rasmussen sought specific promises of support from the U.S. government prior to Denmark's decision to sign the treaty.[2] The U.S. government, in the person of Dean Acheson, assured both the Danes and the Norwegians that the NATO Treaty guarantee was unconditional.

Such guarantees helped pro-NATO politicians such as Norway's foreign minister Halvard Lange to convince majorities in Norway, Denmark, and

Iceland (grudgingly) to accept membership in the alliance. In the face of strong domestic opposition, however, all three governments attempted to reduce the potential costs and risks of NATO membership by establishing conditions for their participation. The two most well-known conditions were (and remain) no allied bases or troops except under special arrangements (such as the U.S. bases in Iceland) and no nuclear weapons on Scandinavian soil.

NATO's acceptance of these stipulations did not eliminate the Nordic countries' concerns about the dangers of membership in the alliance. And in retrospect, it seems clear that some of their doubts about the reliability of their new allies were at least partly justified. Thus, at the same time that Washington and London were offering Copenhagen and Oslo unconditional assurances of protection against the Russians, U.S. and British defense planners were formulating contingency plans that allowed for the at least temporary loss of NATO's northern flank in the event of an East-West conflict. According to a July 1950 report by the U.K. Joint Planning Staff, London and Washington agreed to contribute only limited manpower to the northern region, on the grounds that the West could "fight a major war even if [the Nordic region] fell into enemy hands and [the region] is not therefore as essential."[3] This position was affirmed by the NSC and the Joint Chiefs of Staff, both of which took a relatively soft line on the question of Scandinavian defense. The NSC also equivocated on the issue of Soviet claims to the Svalbard Archipelago throughout the early cold war, insisting only that Norwegian economic rights spelled out by the 1920 Svalbard Treaty be respected by Moscow.[4]

During the 1950s, Scandinavian defense experts periodically tried to convince American and NATO defense planners to strengthen and clarify alliance defense guarantees in the northern region, but without overwhelming success. In early 1953, for example, a Danish request that non-Danish military personnel replace departing Norwegian troops in the Kiel Canal area was summarily rejected by U.S. and NATO officials as "an internal Danish military problem."[5] American limitations on strategic commitments in the north encouraged the suspicion in both Denmark and Norway that U.S. forces might not respond automatically if Norwegian or Danish security interests were challenged. Nils Orvik put the matter this way in 1963:

The Norwegian Storting can decide that NATO troops and weapons should be kept *out*. But it requires more than a unilateral resolution to bring them *into* the country. A formal request for troops or nuclear [weapons] is unlikely to have an automatic response. It would no doubt be given immediate and serious consideration, but the Russians would know that the outcome could not be taken for granted.[6]

Doubtful about allied guarantees, and still holding onto a residual hope that the northern region could be kept out of any East-West conflict, the Scandinavian allies have continued to view NATO with suspicion and ambivalence.

Under these circumstances, it is not surprising that the Scandinavian allies have generally opposed any attempts to increase NATO's membership or expand its area of responsibility. The Nordic members have been guided by three considerations in their tendency to take a strict constructionist view of the NATO Treaty:

1. Scandinavian governments realize that any expansion of alliance membership can only dilute the already qualified Western commitment to the defense of NATO's northern flank.
2. Scandinavian governments have sought to establish themselves as brokers in the North-South dialogue, as well as in the struggle for decolonization and Third World independence. Extension of the NATO Treaty area into the Third World has been viewed as undermining these foreign policy priorities.
3. Scandinavian governments have been anxious to avoid entanglement in actual or potential East-West confrontations in the Third World, in accordance with their strategy of simultaneously deterring and reassuring the Soviet Union.[7]

During 1950, Norway and Denmark actively opposed enlarging the southern region of NATO when Washington began to press for the inclusion of Greece and Turkey. Norway and Denmark, with the support of the Benelux states, opposed Greek and Turkish membership in the alliance primarily on the grounds that it would shift NATO's operational center of gravity away from the North Atlantic. Norwegian foreign minister Halvard Lange lectured Dean Acheson on preserving the "original concept" of an *Atlantic* Alliance as an integrated security community, while his Danish counterpart, Ole Bjørn Kraft, noted that Denmark and "other small countries" in NATO resented the method by which the proposal for consideration of Greek and Turkish admission was introduced in the form of a Standing Group (U.S.-British-French) paper.[8] In analyzing the Danish resistance to an expanded NATO southern flank (five years after Greece and Turkey entered into the alliance), Joe Wilkinson named the five Danish concerns that led to Denmark's threat to veto the expansion:

1. The lack of mutual cultural ties between the two Mediterranean states and the rest of the Atlantic community;
2. The increased risk of war by the extension of alliance commitments and activities, particularly into such a traditionally sensitive area as the Balkans and the Dardanelles;
3. The precedent that such an action would establish for admitting other nations into the alliance, nations perhaps even farther away, or nations with undemocratic and totalitarian institutions;
4. The possibility of aggravating Soviet anxieties by appearing to form an *indkredsningspolitik,* an encirclement policy; and

5. Preference for having Greece and Turkey included in a Middle Eastern defense pact, outside the automatic collective security purview of NATO.[9]

During the first half of 1951, the Americans and the British pressed the northern allies and the Benelux states to drop their opposition to Greek and Turkish membership. By the summer of that year, this campaign had succeeded in convincing Norway, as well as the Benelux states, to reverse their policies. The Danish government held out for a bit longer and then (in September 1951) abandoned its opposition to extending NATO into the Mediterranean, to avoid being singled out as the one nation still resisting Athens' and Ankara's membership. It is curious, however, that when Danish foreign minister Kraft explained his government's decision to his nation's parliament, one of the reasons he offered for the policy reversal was that his government had concluded that in the event of aggression in the Middle East, NATO would inevitably be drawn into the conflict; and that to prepare for such a contingency, it was in the interest of the alliance to establish a geostrategic bridge between the Middle East and Europe.[10]

Kraft's argument is interesting precisely because it is so inconsistent with the standard Scandinavian position of concern about "guilt by association" with the Third World initiatives of NATO allies. In retrospect, however, Scandinavian acquiescence on the issue of Greek and Turkish membership did not really signal a fundamental change in the foreign and security policies of Norway and Denmark.

The Nordic allies have frequently been the most vociferous critics of specific out-of-area initiatives by other NATO members since 1949. To a large extent, this has evolved from what one Swedish analyst has characterized as "an old neutralist position, a UN ideology and a special egalitarian ambiance with idealist overtures. The small Scandinavian states have [assigned themselves] a special responsibility in world affairs as the conscience of the world."[11] For example, Norway and Denmark were highly critical of Portuguese colonialism during the 1960s and early 1970s. The Scandinavians opposed the Salazar regime's attempt to justify its colonial wars as a contribution to Western security. Instead, they challenged Portuguese policy as dangerous, debilitating, and morally reprehensible. The Scandinavians continued to criticize Portugal's military campaigns in Africa, even though Washington, London, Paris, and Bonn supplied Salazar with bombers, jet fighter trainers, and helicopters—some of which found their way to Africa in spite of prohibitions against such uses.[12] In 1971, at a NATO Council meeting in Lisbon, the Norwegians went so far as to recommend forwarding "humanitarian assistance" to African liberation movements; and in 1973, Oslo hosted a combined UN-OAU conference that concluded by decrying the principle of white supremacy in Africa.[13]

Denmark and Norway have also attempted to distinguish their Third World policies from those of other NATO allies by their contributions to UN peace-keeping operations. UN Secretary General Dag Hammerskjöld's report on the basic principles of peacekeeping (submitted to the Thirteenth General Assembly in the wake of the 1956 Suez crisis) constituted the basis for Swedish, Norwegian, and Danish establishment of UN stand-by forces in 1964.

Participation in UN peacekeeping initiatives was primarily a manifestation of the priority accorded to the UN in Oslo and Copenhagen. But the Scandinavian allies also saw the value of developing an effective UN alternative to NATO peacekeeping in the Third World. In fact, Denmark's Seidenfaden Committee, which convened in 1970 to measure the impact of such UN activities, concluded that great-power intervention in Third World conflicts could escalate to draw Denmark and NATO's other northern flank members into far-off conflicts if other means of conflict control and resolution were not available.[14]

In view of the Scandinavian record regarding out-of-area issues, it is interesting to note that during the Vietnam era, Oslo and Copenhagen were reluctant to criticize Washington publicly, due in large part to the fact that the United States remained the only Western power able to counterbalance what was seen by many Scandinavians as a dangerous growth of Soviet naval and air power along the Kola Peninsula. By the late 1960s, the USSR was maintaining 40 percent of its cruisers and destroyers, 55 percent of its escort ships, and 63 percent of its submarines in its Northern Sea and Baltic Sea fleets. Most of the Soviet submarines patrolling in the area (an estimated 70 percent) carried nuclear weapons—prompting one prominent Norwegian admiral to conclude by late 1971 that "the threat to the U.S. is not coming from Vietnam and not from Central Europe, either. It is sailing from Murmansk."[15]

NATO'S NORTHERN PERIPHERIES: "FLANK" OR "FRONT"?

Beginning in the mid-1970s, strategic developments in NATO's northern region altered the geographic identity of NATO and changed the way the Western allies think about security and war fighting. Such developments made it increasingly harder for the Nordic governments to maintain faith in the theory of marginality.

Upgraded Soviet military deployments in the Kola Peninsula region, the discovery of oil and other natural resources in the "gray area" north of the sixty-second parallel—which is claimed by both Norway and the Soviet Union—and the dramatic increase in both U.S. and Soviet submarine activity in the Arctic region all contributed to a shift to the north in both NATO and Warsaw Pact security planning.[16] As Soviet SLBMs were improved in both range and accuracy, the need for Soviet ballistic submarines to breach the Greenland-Iceland-U.K. (GIUK) gap declined. Soviet Delta-class SSBNs, for example, are routinely deployed in the Arctic and in the Barents Sea as part of an overall "sanctuary" strategy. Western strategists responded by focusing their attention on these locales rather than on the North Sea.

NATO and Warsaw Pact exercises now routinely prepare for massive engagements in the Northern Cap region. U.S. maritime strategy has emphasized the absolute requirement for forward deployment of American carrier battle groups at the first sign of war.[17] Spitzbergen and the polar regions, which were considered to be the outer reaches of NATO defense in the late 1940s and early 1950s, are now daily command responsibilities of SACLANT (Supreme Allied Commander, Atlantic Forces) operating out of Norfolk, Virginia.[18] Spitzbergen itself has become increasingly more important to NATO planners as a control area for NATO maritime forces in the Barents Sea operating against the Kola Peninsula.[19] In short, the previously quiescent and, arguably, "marginal" Northern Cap area is becoming "Mediterraneanized."[20]

Perhaps the most dramatic illustration of the increasing priority accorded to the northern region by the Soviet Union is the frequent sightings of Soviet submarines off the coasts of Norway and Sweden. Between 1969 and 1982, Norway and Sweden reported the same number of certain, probable, or possible sightings—122.[21] Moscow appeared to be relatively sanguine about the risks involved in its own naval build-up proximate to NATO's northern flank during the 1970s, since combined NATO forward projection capabilities in the region were, in fact, deteriorating. For example, the UK mothballed its large-deck aircraft carriers while the USSR introduced its Kirov-class cruisers, V/STOL carriers, and Backfire naval aviation support capability in the region. Unlike the late 1940s (when the Royal Navy was the preeminent maritime force in Northern European waters), Norway now "finds itself in a precarious geopolitical position since, for all practical purposes, it is behind Soviet strategic lines" with "only airlift-prepositioning . . . countervailing what Soviet sea power has wrought."[22] Moreover, as U.S. defense analyst Dov S. Zakheim noted in 1982, an additional factor had to be considered in the overall power balance in the north: "what has shifted over the past two decades has been the degree of ground force capability disparity between Soviet, East German, and Polish forces, far out-numbering active Danish, Norwegian, and West Germans committed to NATO's Allied Forces North."[23]

The Carter administration took steps to improve (at least partly) NATO's ground force capability in the north by prepositioning some weapons and equipment in Norway.[24] But the prospects for a successful local defense of northern Norway continue to look so bleak to some Scandinavian security planners that even the effort required to create permanent advanced stockpiles of supplies in northern Norway has been debated in Oslo. As the Norwegian general who commanded the North Norway military region observed in early 1986:

> I do not believe that the [NATO] alliance has the resources for a permanent presence in the Norwegian Sea. . . . Norwegian defense forces are only partly capable of moving American advance supplies from Trondelag to North Norway.

Air defense is the weakest point. . . . Static positions are generally difficult to defend in our time with the threat of [Soviet] aircraft and helicopters that we confront.[25]

Many other experts have questioned NATO's ability to coordinate a northern flank defense in any future contingency. The British-Dutch Marine Commando Force (UK/NL MCF) is designated for immediate deployment to northern Norway if Norwegian positions are threatened there.[26] Likewise, NATO's Allied Command Europe (ACE) Mobile Force (AMF), formed in 1960 in conjunction with NATO's move toward the doctrine of flexible response and made up of Belgian, Canadian, Italian, Luxembourgian, West German, British, and U.S. forces, is expected to play a key role in the early stages of a northern flank campaign if the Warsaw Pact were to attempt a future attack against northern Norway with the intent of carving out an enclave in the northern region.[27] Yet the effectiveness of the AMF as NATO's only available version of an intra-alliance rapid deployment force remains very doubtful. For example, reports during 1984 by the Canadian Senate's Subcommittee for Defense and by the Canadian Defense Ministry have sharply criticized Canada's inability to protect North American reinforcement convoys to Europe. Denmark, in the meantime, remains worried that Canada is more concerned about the remote Northern Cap area than the Jutland Straits along Denmark's Baltic shores.[28]

The 1987 Canadian Defense White Paper did, in fact, assess Canada's commitment to the ground and air arms of AMF as a "dilution of valuable combat resources" that "cannot be reasonably supported or sustained from an ocean away in the brunt of hostilities." As such, "difficulties with reinforcement and resupply" led to the redeployment of the two small Canadian VF-18 jet fighter squadrons deployed in northern Norway, as well as the Canadian Air-Sea Transportable (CAST) Brigade Group, to other locations outside of Norway. In June 1987, the Canadian defense minister concluded that

if these [Canadian] commitments in northern Norway were to be met fully and effectively, the deficiencies cited above would have to be rectified. This could only be done at great cost. If they were not corrected, it would be as obvious to our opponents as it is to us and, consequently, these commitments would contribute little to deterrence.[29]

The Canadian forces in the Nordic area have consequently been pulled back from positions in Norway to new deployment areas in West Germany (the air component) or to Canada itself (the mobile brigade element).

While British officials continue to assure Oslo that U.K. forces will reinforce Norway in a future conflict, Norwegian defense planners are still less than reassured. As John Ausland has noted, "There is a widespread feeling among Norwegians that the U.K. is simply using Norway to give their Commandos winter training . . . [and] . . . without at least [more] stocks of ammunition in

Norway, the Commandos will not find it easy to make their intention to reinforce Norway credible." To date, London has been reluctant to allocate the expenditures necessary to stockpile enough ammunition and supplies in northern Norway to give the Commando preposition plan sufficient credibility.[30]

Lingering doubts about NATO's ability or willingness directly to defend its northern members have thus combined with new demands on finite resources, traditional ambivalence toward NATO, and a general sympathy for Third World nationalist movements to make the Scandinavian allies especially critical of U.S. efforts to encourage the NATO allies to cooperate in out-of-area contingency planning. Furthermore, U.S. support for nondemocratic regimes in Latin and Central America has been a point of special concern for the Nordic states, as illustrated by the resolution passed by a Norwegian Labor party majority in 1982. The resolution refused to welcome U.S. troops to Norwegian territory for NATO exercises until the United States began to accord the same degree of attention to human rights abuses in other countries that it was demonstrating in the case of Poland.[31]

DIVERGING STRATEGIC PERCEPTIONS OF HOW TO DEFEND THE NORTH

Underlying tensions between the United States and the Scandinavian allies were exacerbated during the 1980s by the Reagan administration's application of the aforementioned maritime strategy doctrine to northern flank defense. American strategists defending this approach emphasized that it was the most cost-effective and potent means of coping with NATO's relative vulnerabilities in the north. The maritime strategy's advocates contended that NATO's "Standing Naval Force, Atlantic" (STANAVFORLANT) could deal with the increasingly formidable Soviet naval surface units with relative ease by putting a "full court NATO press" on Soviet submarines, bottling them up inside the Kola Peninsula. Admiral Wesley McDonald, Supreme Allied Commander of the Atlantic at the time, justified the strategy in early 1985: "I just cannot build a barrier at the Greenland-Iceland-UK gap and not go into the Norwegian Sea. That allows the Soviets too much freedom in the Norwegian Sea. . . . If we have forces in the Norwegian Sea and the Soviets are not at sea in great force, I think it is to our advantage."[32]

The U.S. Navy continues to be committed to the themes of forward defense and "initial containment" of the Soviet Northern Fleet "as far forward as possible."[33] In the face of severe budget constraints during the latter part of the Reagan era and the first year of the Bush administration, however, navy spokesmen have expressed doubts about America's ability to accomplish these tasks. In testimony before the Senate Armed Services Committee, Admiral Lee Baggett, Jr., Commander in Chief of the U.S. Atlantic Command, noted that the FY 1989 budget was 8.8 percent less than the 1988 budget in real terms, and he warned that deficiencies in naval forces (in particular, carrier battle groups and combat ships) in the Atlantic Command would make it difficult and dangerous for U.S. forces to undertake the missions associated with the maritime strategy.[34]

The tendency to plan and train for a Soviet-American naval confrontation in the Norwegian Sea ran counter to the traditional Scandinavian preference for reassuring the Soviet Union. Norway's approach, in an era of an increasingly offensive U.S. naval doctrine, has been to restrict NATO military exercises in the northern region—allied maneuvers must be at least eight hundred kilometers from the Soviet-Norwegian border. Oslo also requires allied military aircraft and naval vessels to stay west of the 24° East Meridian, while Copenhagen restricts allied air and naval exercises east of the 17° East Meridian line.[35] Norway maintains its own major defense line in Troms Province, five hundred kilometers from the Soviet border. Finally, Norwegian opposition forced the United States to preposition heavy equipment for its amphibious brigade six hundred kilometers south of Troms, rather than in the far north as the Pentagon had preferred.[36]

ALLIANCE SCOPE AND PURVIEW: AN ELUSIVE CONCEPT REVISITED

If an East-West crisis should develop in the northern region in the foreseeable future, it could well take on the trappings of an out-of-area dispute, precisely because the northern and northeastern borders of NATO have never been that clearly established. This is a particular problem in the Arctic region, where there has been a dramatic increase in U.S. and Soviet submarine activity since 1983. The problem is not restricted to the Arctic, however. Norway may find it difficult to solicit allied assistance—with the exception of the United States—if a conflict were to erupt with the Soviet Union in the disputed gray area in the Barents Sea.

In the event of a Norwegian-Soviet confrontation along the Svalbard Archipelago, the Southern and Central European NATO allies might seek to disassociate themselves from a crisis that risks a major U.S.-Soviet confrontation in an area of growing geostrategic significance for both superpowers.[37] A related concern is the possibility of what Johan Holst has called a "Pearl Harbor Problem" and Barry Posen has referred to as "inadvertent nuclear war," if U.S. naval forces in the Norwegian Sea threaten, or appear to threaten, Soviet maritime assets in the Kola Peninsula region, thereby precipitating a Soviet overreaction.[38]

Scandinavian concern about loss of NATO control over the northern region in a future East-West confrontation correlates with the aforementioned concern about "guilt by association" with allied interventions in the Third World. Miroslav Nincic has speculated on how a crisis in the Third World could spill over to the northern region of NATO:

The Danish Straits would be sealed in order to block Soviet vessels in the Baltic Sea. As a result of this, Denmark would be caught up in the confrontation and Soviet action against this member of NATO could be expected. In addition, every attempt would be made to impose as high a rate of attrition as possible on enemy submarines as they passed through the GIUK and Bear Island Groups. . . . the USA might launch offensive operations against the Kola Peninsula and this would mean that Norwegian troops . . . would be drawn into direct combat with Soviet forces. At this point war would have spread to much of Europe.[39]

Under these circumstances, it is not surprising that the Nordic allies remain especially sensitive to U.S. statements that implicitly or explicitly link possible Soviet aggression in the region to Western retaliation in other combat theaters according to the logic of "horizontal escalation." Former secretary of defense Harold Brown's reported assertion that the Soviet Union might face retaliation "as far north as Norway" in the event of aggression in the Middle East, for example, did not enhance U.S.-Scandinavian defense relations.[40]

Various American efforts to encourage greater out-of-area cooperation under the auspices of NATO have thus struck sensitive nerves in the alliance's northern flank affiliates. Oslo and Copenhagen have maintained their traditional reservations about projecting their very limited military power capabilities beyond their own geographic parameters in any significant way. A March 1981 statement offered by then-Norwegian foreign minister Knut Fryden remains operative for both the Scandinavian allies: "Norway has always been consistent in its opposition to any possible expansion of the NATO area, and we will continue to do so. If the British and the Americans want to set up a force in the Persian Gulf, that is a matter between the two countries."[41]

If the alliance is to preserve its northern flank, the Norwegians and the Danes will need to remain confident that NATO military resources earmarked for out-of-area-operations or even for NATO southern flank defense do not undermine Scandinavian security. In the future, this will require a greater appreciation of Scandinavian security concerns in NATO councils, even though this is not likely to lead to a new enthusiasm for out-of-area cooperation by the Nordic members.

NATO allies will also need to continually reassess the geostrategic characteristics of the northern region in the light of technological, military, political, and economic developments. In 1987, the North Atlantic Assembly designated the northern part of the alliance as stretching far beyond the formal Northern European Command (NEC) to encompass Norway, Denmark, Schleswig-Holstein, and the land between the Elbe-Trave Canal to the east and the Norwegian north cape to the west. The assembly report contends that NATO's purview now spans a much larger area, which the assembly study designates "the Northern Waters." This vast area of security responsibility includes the land and sea masses "found within the latitudes of 80 degrees N and 60 degrees N and the longitudes 90 degrees W to 30 degrees E . . . [including] the islands of Arctic Canada, Greenland Iceland, the Faroes, the Shetlands, Jan Mayen and Svalbard."[42] This broad definition of NATO's northernmost area covers most Soviet intercontinental ballistic missile flight paths, key sea lanes of communication through which U.S. reinforcements of NATO must pass, and the area in which most of NATO's surface fleet would operate and ASW operations would be conducted in the event of an East-West war.

The key point for purposes of this discussion is that the North Atlantic Assembly's interpretation of what constitutes the northern region is only one conception. It competes with, among others, NATO's official definition of a northern flank, the Nordic Council's concept of a Northern Cap, and Canadian references to a "Northern Rim." All of these interpretations will have to be routinely compared for points of overlap and, in particular, for points of disagreement.

At present, the biggest change in the region involves the increasing attention that both Washington and Moscow have accorded to the Arctic Circle in their respective defense programs.[43] The Canadian government has been concerned about *both* superpowers' accelerating interest and involvement in the Arctic region, especially since 1970, when Ottawa extended its territorial waters from three to twelve miles. Canada has complained that this territory is routinely traversed by both U.S. and Soviet forces without Canadian permission. Canadian political support for asserting territorial sovereignty over the Arctic archipelago has grown rapidly at a time when Canadians are becoming more sensitive about preserving a distinct identity vis-à-vis the United States. In particular, Canadians are increasingly resentful of U.S. and British submarines traversing ocean channels between islands in the Arctic territory without informing Ottawa of their movements, and are showing a new interest in the concept of "Canadianizing the North."

To date, Soviet strategic nuclear ballistic missile (SSBN) and hunter-killer (SSN) submarines have avoided venturing beyond the NATO surveillance systems placed in the GIUK and into Canadian Arctic waters on a regular or systematic basis. But both Ottawa and Oslo remain concerned about the recent completion of a new air base at Schagui in the Kola Peninsula that will enhance Moscow's ability to hit Canadian and U.S. targets with Blackjack strategic nuclear bombers. The new base may be a hedge against either a future U.S. strategic defense initiative (SDI) or a NATO European antitactical ballistic missile (ATBM) component.[44] Soviet TU-95 Bear-H bombers patrolling the North Pole and testing the U.S.-Canadian Defense Early Warning Identification Zone likewise underscore the threat to "the major ocean going trade route between North America and northeast Asia and the polar route for airplanes between Europe and Asia."[45]

At least as worrisome to many Canadians has been U.S. submarine presence in Canada's northern waters to pressure their Soviet counterparts deployed in the Barents and White seas and to deprive Soviet SSBNs of any future prospects for using the Arctic as a nuclear sanctuary. In May 1986, the U.S. Navy did, in fact, disclose that three of its SSNs linked up and surfaced at the North Pole for the first time in history, "signal[ing] a boosted U.S. submarine presence under the Arctic ice pack."[46] This forward projection of U.S. SSNs is consistent with the maritime strategy's doctrine of cutting off Soviet naval projection capabilities at the outset of war and as close to the Soviet homeland as possible.

In its 1987 Defense White Paper, the Canadian government announced that it would take independent action in response to such trends by building between ten and twelve nuclear-powered submarines to patrol its northern seas. The program was canceled in 1989, but not before triggering significant disagreements within NATO.[47] The first repercussions for NATO were in fact felt in the 1980s, because the decision by Canada to purchase the nuclear-powered submarines limited the ability of the Canadian government to respond to the recommendations of the 1983 Report on Maritime Defense of the Sub-committee on National Defense of the Canadian Senate. The major conclusions of the report were:

–That Canada's navy cannot fulfil its NATO commitment at present, as indicated by the fact that on paper Canada contributes 20 escorts to NATO's Canadian-American region, while in fact 3 of these escorts are stationed on Canada's west coast.

–Canadian defense requirements call for a fleet of between 69 to 82 "major weapons platforms" (including destroyers, submarines, and long range naval patrol aircraft). Canada at present has about half this amount. As a result of the de-emphasizing of defense by successive Canadian governments . . . the country is now confronted with two problems: the necessity of replacing virtually the whole fleet at once, and the need for a short term solution to the lack of numbers.[48]

The Conservative government presented the 1987 White Paper as a major step toward Canadian defense modernization. In reality, however, it only committed the government to a 2.2 percent per annum increase in overall defense spending over the next fifteen years—which meant that Canada would continue to spend about half of the alliance's per capita average for defense and would continue to rank thirteenth out of sixteen NATO members in terms of overall defense spending.[49] By 1989, however, even the modest defense modernization goals of the 1987 Defense White Paper had come under intense attack at home, and the government was forced to scale back even farther its planned contributions to NATO defense. As a result of the new round of budget debates, fourteen Canadian military bases will be closed or downgraded during the early 1990s, orders for main battle tanks have been halved, and no new fighter aircraft are to be added to the Canadian inventory as older aircraft are phased out. According to one source, budgetary constraints have made Canada's military role in Europe increasingly untenable.[50] Thus, the evolving East-West discussions on troop reductions came none too soon.

CHAPTER 20

THE CENTRAL EUROPEAN
NATO POWERS AND THE
OUT-OF-REGION ISSUE

It is not surprising that during the last two decades the Central European NATO allies—the nations that are most directly dependent upon the maintenance of a strong NATO presence on the central front—generally have been suspicious of out-of-area developments that threaten to divert alliance attention away from continental Europe. These countries nonetheless came to this common position by very different routes. In the case of West Germany, which entered the alliance in 1955, the problem of managing residual colonial possessions had perforce been resolved with the German defeat in World War II. Belgium and the Netherlands, on the other hand, were middle-sized European powers that struggled unsuccessfully for the first twenty years of the postwar era to retain at least some influence over their extra-European colonial outposts. Only after events had relieved them of the "burdens of Empire" were they in a position to concentrate their interests and energies on Central Europe. Since the 1970s, the policies of Bonn, Brussels, and the Hague have been more in harmony on questions of out-of-area cooperation. The characteristics of that shared perspective are discussed in this chapter.

West Germany

Since joining NATO in 1955, the Federal Republic of Germany (FRG) has traditionally assumed the unmistakable posture of "NATO for Europe and Europe alone." Even Konrad Adenauer—whose foreign and security policies were anchored in the "good ally" role—was unwilling to support the principal NATO governments in out-of-area interventions after the FRG became a member of the alliance. This is ironic, since prior to joining NATO, Adenauer had derived considerable advantage from out-of-area situations. The fact that sig-

266

nificant portions of the French and British armies were tied down in extraregional contingencies during the early 1950s greatly enhanced the German leader's leverage during the negotiations that led up to the FRG's entry into the alliance. Likewise, the Korean War also worked to Adenauer's advantage by contributing to the growth of anti-Sovietism in the United States. After the outbreak of that Asian conflict, few influential U.S. policy makers questioned the indispensability of a remilitarized Germany at the heart of NATO.

Once Germany was firmly established within the alliance, however, Adenauer's perspective on out-of-area crises shifted. From that point on, the German chancellor became preoccupied with the risks of "guilt by association" with the Third World adventures of NATO allies and with the possibility that an out-of-area crisis might lead to the diversion of allied troops or materiel for service abroad. Thus, Adenauer argued that West German security was directly threatened by the French decision of March 1956 to pull 200,000 troops out of the NATO central front for service in Algeria.[1] And when France and Britain intervened in Suez just a few months later, Adenauer joined his other NATO partners in issuing "criticism [that] was . . . unanimous and exceptionally blunt" against Paris and London.[2] Similarly, when American and British troops used West German military bases for transit during the July 1958 Lebanon/ Jordan campaigns, the chancellor's office expressed "regret for the gaps in the treaties with the West that permit forces to fly into and over the country at their pleasure . . . [and] . . . the lack of a common constructive political policy for the future, not only in the Middle East but also in Africa and Asia."[3] Finally, when Lyndon Johnson made cautious inquiries in the mid-1960s about the willingness of Germany to contribute troops to the Vietnam campaign, German chancellor Ludwig Erhard reportedly refused, on the grounds that Bundeswehr deployments beyond "the zone of German defense" would contravene the "spirit" of the West German constitution.[4]

Subsequent governments in Bonn maintained this posture of concern and suspicion regarding out-of-area initiatives by key NATO allies, and supplemented it with an expressed interest in preserving and advancing East-West détente.[5] In accordance with his commitment to a "steadfast peace policy," Brandt was willing during the 1970s to participate in conflict avoidance and mediation efforts beyond the NATO Treaty area over such issues as the Cyprus conflict in 1974 and the status and future of Southwest Africa in 1978. The only instance of German military (to be precise, paramilitary) activity beyond the NATO parameters during the 1970s was the attack by twenty-six members of the West German antiterrorist squad GSG-9 (aided by two members of the British Special Air Services) against hijackers occupying a Lufthansa airliner at Mogadishu Airport, Somalia, in October 1977.[6]

The key test of West Germany's policy regarding out-of-area cooperation was the 1973 Arab-Israeli War. Occurring as it did at the height of the détente era, Bonn was unwilling to jeopardize the progress that was being made in its

Ostpolitik campaign by acquiescing to U.S. requests for basing access during the Yom Kippur War. On October 23, Bonn informed Washington that no shipments of American equipment slated for Israeli use could issue from German airfields or ports. West German public opinion backed this decision (an Allensbach Institute poll conducted two months later showed that 57 percent of respondents approved of the government's decision and only 19 percent were opposed). Bonn subsequently argued in defense of its decision to reject the U.S. request that the Israeli army had already won the decisive battle in the October 1973 conflict *before* the U.S. airlift operations which would have involved German airfields had commenced.[7] This rationalization had no effect on Secretary of State Henry Kissinger, who railed against the West German betrayal of American trust and alliance responsibility (see Chapter 6).

By 1982, however, West Germany had begun to demonstrate a greater willingness to collaborate with the United States in planning for future contingencies in the Persian Gulf, while continuing to resist U.S. pressure to cooperate in other Middle Eastern locales. Bonn agreed to implement new airspace access arrangements and related defense burden-sharing measures to help Washington prepare a military response to future Persian Gulf crises should the occasion arise. Bonn and Washington also signed the U.S.-FRG Wartime Host Nation Support Agreement (WHNS) in early 1982. The agreement represented West German compliance with a November 1980 request by the United States that FRG reserve units stand ready to provide logistical support and augment rear-area security if U.S. combat troops stationed in Europe were redeployed in the Middle East/Persian Gulf.[8] In return, the United States committed itself to assign an additional six divisions and "appurtenant air elements" to the FRG within ten days following the outbreak of a NATO/Warsaw Pact conflict.[9]

The CDU/CSU-controlled coalition government under Helmut Kohl also distinguished itself from its predecessors by its restrained response to the April 1983 American attack against Libya. Kohl responded to intense criticisms by the SPD and other German opposition parties in a frank speech to the Bundestag, carried on West German National Television. The chancellor noted that "[it] is easy to criticize the United States for eventually applying means we would not have taken. If we Europeans do not want to follow the Americans for our reasons, we must ourselves develop meaningful political action. Mere compliance will not be able to handle international terrorism."[10]

Two factors appear to have contributed to this policy adjustment. First, and most important, was the election of the conservative Kohl government in 1982, which was clearly more sensitive than its predecessor to the risk that a public dispute with Washington regarding an out-of-area issue (a replay of 1973) would prompt a resurgence of Mansfield Amendment politics in the U.S. Congress.[11] Second, by the early 1980s West Germany was more inclined to accept Washington's argument that protecting oil supplies was an alliance-wide problem—not just, or even primarily, an American task.

The West German government nonetheless continues to support the general Western European approach to Middle Eastern security politics, which emphasizes that no country in this region—even Libya—should be permanently ostracized, and that deliberately heightening tension in the Middle East through military action should be avoided whenever possible. Former West German chancellor Helmut Schmidt stressed these points in a speech to an American audience in 1985:

> The idealistic American perception that an American Grand Strategy for the Middle East can solve its complex problems and bring about a just and stable peace seems unrealistic and outdated. . . . In spite of all its intercontinental strategic power to destroy. . . . [the United States] could not even rescue American hostages from Teheran. . . . The best one can hope for is to defuse explosive situations on a case-by-case basis, stop wars, and otherwise carry on . . . diligent psychological diplomacy.[12]

Bonn also realizes, however, that hand wringing is no substitute for a positive foreign policy, as Schmidt said in another section of his speech:

> But of course diligent diplomacy does need a certain amount of cooperation between the Americans and those European powers that have traditionally had influence in the Middle East, namely Britain, France, and to a surprising extent, Spain and some other European countries.[13]

The FRG will continue to consult with its NATO allies on specific out-of-area problems. It is also likely that West Germany will offer at least diplomatic support for Western positions on such issues as state-sponsored terrorism. Certainly, the highly visible dispatch of three FRG naval vessels (a destroyer, a frigate and a support ship) to the eastern Mediterranean during October-December 1987, in what the Defense Ministry called "a clear sign of solidarity" with the United States and other NATO allies "who are maintaining the freedom of movement of shipping in the Gulf region," was welcomed in Washington and London.[14] Bonn will nonetheless oppose any attempt to transform NATO into an instrument for out-of-area interventionism. According to Catherine Kelleher, "However more self-confident and assertive they may be on NATO affairs, most of the German political elite believe the cost of extra-NATO involvement will still be too high." Kelleher goes on to list four "alternatives" offered by various German experts and government spokesmen faced with U.S. solicitations of support for RDF activities in the Persian Gulf region:

> –Substantial economic assistance to two Western anchors in the [Gulf] region, Turkey and Pakistan.
> –The assumption of certain unspecified functions in Europe to allow greater American flexibility.
> –Increased diversification of energy imports.
> –Increased diplomatic links with the Gulf states.[15]

All of these efforts are, in fact, being pursued by the Kohl government, but in the words of former FRG defense minister Hans Apel, "the thought of extending NATO's contractual sphere could not be entertained."[16]

THE NETHERLANDS

Holland, like Germany, is a heavily industrialized country but is even more dependent upon international trade to sustain its economy. Some Dutch policy makers cite this dependence on international trade in support of a globalist foreign and defense policy for Holland. In 1986, the commander in chief of the Royal Netherlands Navy reflected this global perspective when he summarized Holland's "special maritime role" as a NATO ally:

> In principle, the Royal Netherlands Navy has the high seas all over the world as its action ground, as well as its territorial and home waters. . . . the emphasis of the Dutch [NATO] contribution is on the defense of the eastern part of the Atlantic. . . . [and] the Dutch Fleet will be mainly deployed in these areas. [Yet]. . . . the Royal Netherlands Navy has a world-wide mission to protect its merchant fleet and maritime commerce, as part of its national interests.[17]

The majority of the Netherlands' leadership and electorate-at-large, however, has accepted a much more restrictive and geographically limited Dutch defense posture. The Dutch government recognized shortly after World War II that it would have considerable difficulty in preserving its colonial holdings in a hostile international environment. The war had disrupted Holland's network of colonial control and weakened the economy of the country. The Hague understood that, at a minimum, it would need the diplomatic backing of the United States in order to preserve some elements of its earlier global influence. But the Dutch government had little leverage in its dealings with Washington, other than a claim on Western solidarity. This proved to be a very weak reed. At about the same time that Washington began to consider the establishment of a North Atlantic Alliance, U.S. policy makers turned their attention to the issue of Dutch control over Indonesia. Exceedingly strong U.S. pressure led to the Renville Agreement (January 1948), the Critchley-Dubois Plan, and the Hague Agreements, which, in turn, led to Indonesia's independence and the final pullout of Dutch military forces from Jakarta in 1953.[18]

Few Western governments appreciated the priority that Dutch policy makers accorded to preserving the last vestiges of the colonial empire during the late 1940s. Indeed, Dutch foreign minister Dirk Stikker warned during the Washington negotiations that if his country were forced to choose between continued "responsibilities towards the peoples of Indonesia" and alliance membership, it would reject NATO and continue its rule over the East Indies. Stikker continued to communicate this threat in confidential communications to Washington until two days before the formal signing of the NATO Treaty, in the vain hope that he could influence Washington's Indonesia policy. But when he was advised (again, in strictest confidence) that the United States would not be overly concerned if the Netherlands were unable to join NATO, the Dutch foreign minister had no choice but to back down. Stikker signed the treaty, and the Dutch Parliament ratified the agreement four months later, by overwhelming majorities in both houses. Washington subsequently attempted to smooth things over with The Hague within the NATO alliance, and the United States extended close to a billion dollars in military aid to the Netherlands over the next eight years. The United States nonetheless continued to meddle in Dutch-Indonesian affairs, to the persistent frustration of The Hague. Holland's resentment of America's encroachment on its *domaine réservé* in Southeast Asia continued to influence official Dutch policy well into the 1950s, as reflected by the Netherlands' support for Britain and France during the intra-NATO disputes over Suez. There is no way to judge how long Dutch resentment continued at the unofficial level.[19] In a brilliant history of his country's foreign policy, written during the late 1950s, Dutch historian S.I.P. van Campen summarized the Dutch perspective on the issue of Indonesian independence as follows:

> Did such friendly relations exist between the Netherlands on one hand and Great Britain, the United States and Canada on the other? Were embargoes on arms deliveries [to Holland] not a sign of unfriendly intentions and did they not show an unfriendly tendency to interfere in what was according to the official Netherlands point of view, a purely internal affair? . . .
> . . . These were obviously grave questions and it was impressed upon the Government that they could not be disposed of by saying that the [NATO] Treaty was so important to Holland's security; this was true but it was equally true that Holland was no less important to the other powers, for what would be the Treaty's value if Holland, the delta of Europe's great rivers, that point of intersection of [European] strategic lines, did not participate [in NATO]?[20]

In August 1962, the United States once again involved itself in a Dutch-Indonesian dispute over sovereignty, this time concerning Irian Jaya. The Hague argued that Western collective defense interests were tied to this crisis, and it sought the backing of SEATO for its policy of holding onto this territory. But SEATO's other members refused to play any role—much less support Holland's position. The Hague also had to contend with domestic pressure; within Holland's own borders, members of the Dutch business and religious communities called for an end to Holland's control over Irian Jaya. In the face of both domestic political opposition and allied nonsupport, The Hague succumbed to U.S. pressure and accepted the New York Agreement. This arrangement brought contested areas under UN trusteeship and made Jakarta responsible for managing a subsequent election campaign leading to Irian Jaya's self-determination.[21] This effectively guaranteed eventual Indonesian control of the territory. It also isolated two hundred thousand settlers of Dutch extraction who had already moved from an independent Indonesia to Irian Jaya. The lesson was driven home once more to the Dutch government that Washington could not be trusted to throw its weight behind the European colonial allies when issues of decolonization or self-determination were involved.

The transition from a colonial power to an Atlantic security actor was more abrupt for The Hague than for other NATO allies. Furthermore, the Dutch had been in the business of colonialism far longer than the Belgians, and unlike the French and English, they retained no special arrangements or ties with their former colonies after their liberation. In view of these facts, Henri Baudet is justified in crediting The Hague with "an astounding pragmatism" in its acceptance of Atlantic power status after being "cast back on her small territory between the Dollart and the Scheldt."[22] By the end of the 1960s, however, the Dutch experience with decolonization had contributed to a general mood in Holland of frustration and cynicism on issues relating to out-of-area cooperation. It also contributed to a widespread inclination to question the need for defense modernization in general. As a result, defense improvements have become more difficult for The Hague to carry out in recent times.[23]

Even the traditionally revered Dutch maritime heritage has become less important to the Dutch electorate as The Hague has come to concentrate its foreign policy aspirations in Europe. Holland remains one of the world's shipbuilding centers (the thirteenth largest in the world), but the total number of ships in the Netherlands' own fleet available for deployment outside of the Atlantic approaches is quite limited. At present, the Dutch navy includes sixteen frigates and five submarines. The 1984 defense program committed Holland to acquiring eight new frigates and possibly six new submarines by 1994. The vast bulk of Dutch naval assets are assigned to two NATO commands: the Eastern Atlantic Command (ACLANT) and the Channel Command (ACCHEN). The Royal Netherlands Marine Corps still has a peacetime strength of twenty-eight hundred personnel, however, and is available for limited long-range amphibious operations under a single battle group command (the First Amphibious Combat Group). Ordinarily earmarked for northern flank defense missions, the Combat Group could be used to reinforce, for example, the small Dutch marine contingent (some four hundred twenty personnel) based in the Dutch Antilles (Aruba and Curaçao, in the eastern Caribbean). As part of its residual defense commitments to the Antilles, the Netherlands maintained one destroyer, one amphibious detachment, and one marine reconnaissance detachment in the immediate vicinty during the 1980s.[24]

With specific reference to NATO out-of-area cooperation, Dutch policy makers and defense experts tend to be automatically suspicious of U.S. solicitations of support, particularly concerning contingencies in the Persian Gulf region. This is due primarily to Dutch concerns about keeping the lid on defense spending and preserving a strong allied presence along NATO's central front. It is exacerbated, moreover, by residual Dutch resentment over what the Netherlands perceives as the legacy of U.S. interference in its foreign policy and—to a lesser extent—by the continued priority that the Dutch public accords to East-West détente. After interviewing Dutch officials at NATO headquarters in Brussels in March 1984, Charles Kupchan observed that they "were opposed to an out-of-area strategy for NATO on the grounds that it would diminish the autonomy of their foreign policy; it would widen the scope of activities falling under the auspices of the Alliance while potentially reducing the input of smaller countries into the nature of those activities."[25] In interviews conducted with NATO planners during the two immediately preceding years, the authors of this book derived precisely the same impression.

All of this makes Holland's October 1987 deployment of two minehunter/ sweepers—the *Hellevoetslius* and the *Maassluis*—to the Persian Gulf highly significant.[26] The joint Dutch-Belgian contingent, totaling five units (Belgium deployed two minesweepers and one supply vessel under Dutch command), was sent to the gulf as much to symbolize an independent European interest in retaining economic and political access to Gulf Cooperation Council (GCC) nations as to back American policies or UN initiatives in the region. The small Lowlands fleet nonetheless operated under the protection of the Royal Navy in the less dangerous lower area of the gulf, leaving the more dangerous upper and middle portions in the hands of the American navy. Furthermore, the British *Sunday Telegraph* reported London's criticism of what it saw as an essentially cosmetic, and potentially disruptive, allied participation in the gulf: "the European operation ran the risk of ending in fiasco as a result of the attitude of the Belgian, Netherlands and Italian Navies. They have not as yet found a single mine and were said to be doing everything possible to remain in the background."[27]

In the final analysis, the Dutch have attempted to make the best of being "cast back" on Europe over the past three decades. But finding a foreign policy direction has been especially difficult. The Hague has come to recognize since the mid-1960s that the alternative to an imperial foreign policy is membership in, rather than leadership of, the European or Atlantic community. Furthermore, Holland recognizes that being a more integral component of Continental defense does not automatically make it safe from the repercussions of extra-European crises. Indeed, Dutch policy makers harbor a special sense of vulnerability to out-of-area developments, owing to the fact that during the 1973 Arab oil embargo Holland was singled out for special punishment because of what Arab governments claimed was a pro-Israeli policy during the 1973 Yom Kippur War. These considerations will continue to establish the limits of Holland's willingness to invest—financially, militarily, or politically—in NATO out-of-area initiatives for the foreseeable future.

BELGIUM

Whereas the Netherlands' out-of-area military history is largely maritime or amphibious in nature, Belgium's postwar experiences in central Africa demanded a much more ambitious colonial administration and a fairly extensive land mobile paratrooper force. The Belgian Congo independence movements in the late 1950s provided the initial impetus for Belgian military planners to develop the requisite military capabilities for intervention beyond Central Europe. The Congo was granted independence in June 1960—a much earlier date than originally anticipated by politicians in Brussels. The accelerated pace of decolonization was at least partly in response to pressures exerted on Brussels—diplomatically and quietly, for the most part—by Washington.

As the colonial bureaucracy began to be dismantled in the Congo, former Belgian colonial administrators and the greater Belgian community still residing in the new Republic of the Congo (some one hundred thousand strong) found themselves the targets of rioting and violence soon after independence day. These outbreaks precipitated the dispatch of Belgian troops to bases at Kitona and Kamina, still retained by Brussels under the old *Force Publique* infrastructure in a Treaty of Friendship signed the day before the Congo gained independence. (The bases were recognized as an unpopular economic necessity by the Congolese nationalists because they employed more than fifteen thousand people.)[28] To protect its citizens and its financial interests, Belgian paratroop companies then fanned out throughout areas of hostility, even though, by doing so, they were in violation of the Treaty of Friendship's stipulations that Belgian troops would remain in base areas. The subsequent secession of Katanga Province precipitated further Belgian military deployments, which eventually totaled over ten thousand troops.[29]

In a NATO context, the Congo episode was yet another example of alliance strains materializing over a Third World problem of *domaine réservé*. As discussed in Chapter 4, the crisis eventually was referred to the UN, and a United Nations Force (UNF) of over twenty thousand personnel was deployed to the Congo for what proved to be an extremely difficult peacekeeping operation. Military transport aircraft provided by the United States and Britain played an important role in support of the UNF throughout 1960.[30] France, however, was opposed to the UNF largely because Charles de Gaulle saw it as an American-led effort to sponsor a system of global collective security at European expense. Yet any possibility of close collaboration between Paris and Brussels in opposition to the UNF operation never materialized, owing to the Belgian government's suspicion of de Gaulle's motives against a backdrop of traditional Franco-Belgian competition over Africa. As noted in Chapter 17, Brussels was particularly sensitive to and worried about de Gaulle's efforts to create a directorate within NATO, which the Belgians viewed as tantamount to making the smaller member countries satellites of a Western security condominium managed by the United States, the UK, and France.

The Congo situation was a personal crisis for NATO Secretary General P.-H. Spaak. He saw the actions of the Kennedy administration in Africa as a betrayal of the principles that had held NATO together since 1949; indeed, the Belgian diplomat felt sufficiently compromised by what he viewed as President Kennedy's interference in the Congo issue that he resigned from his position as NATO Secretary General in February 1962. In a now famous recriminatory letter to Kennedy, Spaak argued that,

> regarding problems which occur outside of the geographic limits of the Alliance, the practice of consultation is generally accepted, but the results are not always very satisfactory. What occurs is that states act without consulting their partners. . . . The last unfortunate example of this occurred quite recently in the case of the politics relating to the Congo. The American ideas, as made public, could be approved neither by France, nor by Belgium, nor by the Portuguese nor, I believe, by the English; that is to say by none of those states most directly interested in African problems. What has come to be called the American plan was never made the object of discussion within NATO. The allies of the United States were apprised of it at the same time as their enemies. . . . I remain convinced that a basic choice has to be made. . . . Does the United States accord more importance to the U.N. than to NATO? In other words, in order to assure itself of the support or friendship of the non-aligned states is it willing to sacrifice the interests or bruise the feelings of its allies in NATO?[31]

For its part, Washington became increasingly frustrated at what it viewed as Belgian hypersensitivity on the Congo issue. But U.S. representatives still tended to be fairly optimistic about the long-term prospects. In a cable forwarded by the U.S. State Department to its embassies in Paris and Brussels, it was reported that in recent discussions about the crisis with American officials, Spaak was

> deeply moved emotionally and . . . the Belgian problem for the time being wholly occupies [the] forefront [of] his mind. . . . given time [however, he] will realize that the Belgian problem and its outcome, [and] also U.S. positions taken with respect to that problem do not affect [the] basic importance and continuing need for [the] NATO alliance.[32]

The Congo and Katanga—subsequently known as Zaire and Shaba, respectively—continued to test the will and the military capability of key NATO governments long after the independence issue had been resolved. The 1978 French intervention in Shaba has already been covered in Chapter 3, but it should be briefly mentioned here from the point of view of Belgian perceptions and interests.

The Shaba crisis was similar to the earlier Congo crisis in that it provided an opportunity for cooperation between Paris and Brussels. In both the Shaba and Congo crises, however, the cooperation that actually occurred was limited by

Belgian and French doubts about each other's long-term strategic intentions in central Africa.

Belgium eyed the French military intervention in this episode with considerable suspicion, because it still had $6 billion worth of investments in Zaire as compared to France's comparatively small ($20 million) holdings. Similarly, 85 percent of Zaire's copper was still being shipped to Belgium for processing. As the *Economist* subsequently reported, talks between Zaire's president Mobutu and French president Valéry Giscard d'Estaing during the crisis raised concerns in Brussels that "the French were out to enhance their political and economic influence over mineral-rich Zaire at *Belgium*'s expense."[33] Brussels also claimed to be motivated by different foreign policy goals than Paris (see Chapter 18).

Both governments sent military forces—six hundred French legionnaires and seventeen hundred fifty Belgian paratroopers—to rescue three thousand European (mostly French and Belgian) citizens held hostage by rebels contesting the legitimacy of Zaire's ruling government.[34] One significant difference between the Belgian and French interventions was that French forces were deployed first, from Corsica on May 17, and landed in Kolwezi in about 12 hours. Belgian forces took off at midday on May 18. The flight time was about twice as long, not only because the troops were stationed much farther to the north, but also because Algeria refused Brussels' request for overflight rights. Belgium did obtain assistance from two NATO allies, however. The United States provided the transport aircraft, and Portugal permitted the Belgian forces to refuel at the Lajes facility in the Azores.

As a result of the greater difficulties that Belgium had in making a decision and then carrying it out, French forces did most of the fighting. Indeed, when an informal military staffing group of French and Belgian, as well as American and British, officers met on May 18, the French had already made the key decisions for wrapping up military operations related to the intervention.[35]

The Shaba intervention is a good example of how two allies can carry out parallel out-of-area operations with a minimum of coordination in a situation of competing interests. The Belgians acted at the national, rather than the alliance level, and only after the Socialist government in Brussels became sufficiently repulsed by rebel atrocities committed against European hostages did they put aside their earlier concerns about helping the authoritarian, right-wing Mobutu regime. They relied upon the assistance of other allies to the extent that it was required, but restricted efforts by various Western officials such as General Alexander Haig to elevate the operation to the status of a model for future out-of-area coordination. The French government, meanwhile, really only "informed" Brussels of its pending military operation in Zaire rather than consulting with the Belgian government about the management of the Shaba intervention. For its own reasons, Paris was more willing to treat the crisis as if it were a coordinated Western response to a situation of "local disequilibrium" and to emphasize its broader implications for Western security and East-West relations.

The Shaba experience did nothing to encourage Belgium to become more active beyond the NATO Treaty area. Brussels, like The Hague, was generally suspicious of American efforts during the 1970s and 1980s to solicit allied support for its activities in the Middle East and Persian Gulf region. Belgium did participate in the aforementioned Persian Gulf task force in 1987, but Brussels joined most of the other European members of the task force in distancing itself from Washington during and after the operation and in emphasizing that the task force did not represent a precedent.

Prospects for a greater Belgian role beyond the treaty area are limited not only by the lack of Belgian interest but by Brussels' limited military capabilities. Like Holland, Belgium faced considerable difficulties during the 1980s in its effort to satisfy American requests for increased financial burden sharing. In a mid-1987 interview, Belgian defense minister Xavier-François de Donnea admitted that "for some time and to some extent we will not achieve our force goals. . . . what I am doing is to try to make an optional allocation of the scarce resources I have, so as to do much more with less than we had before." De Donnea specifically cited projected Belgian efforts to strengthen the country's already "excellent" paracommando regiment for use by NATO's Allied Mobile Force in defense of the alliance's northern flank.[36] Foreign Minister Leo Tindemans echoed de Donnea's philosophy of "increased cost-efficiency ratios" in a November 1987 interview with *Le Soir,* noting that Belgium and other small European powers must realize their responsibility for bearing an equitable proportion of the West's overall defense burden but also insisting that Brussels was doing far better in this regard than was thought by "badly informed U.S. public opinion and U.S. Congressmen."[37]

Brussels will continue to attempt to fullfil its commitments to NATO, in spite of the very real economic problems. Furthermore, the participation of Belgian warships in the Persian Gulf armada demonstrates that Brussels is willing to make temporary and conditional contributions to particular out-of-area operations on an ad hoc basis. But no long-range, extra-European deployments of Belgian paracommando units such as those conducted in 1960 could be justified to the Belgian electorate today. Only an emergency humanitarian operation along the lines of the 1978 Shaba crisis, or a short-term contribution to a peacekeeping initiative such as the Persian Gulf task force, could obtain the necessary support from the nation's elite and its mass publics. And such operations would probably be presented as either a unilateral or a "European" initiative, rather than a NATO undertaking. Indeed, the upcoming economic integration of the European Communities in 1992 should reinforce the tendency on the part of Brussels and other European allies to analyze and deal with out-of-area crises in a European, as distinct from a NATO, context.

*good background to the
Patijn report.*

CONCLUSION

The change that has occurred in Belgium and Holland regarding out-of-area security cooperation can perhaps best be understood by recalling the arguments of Belgian diplomat Paul-Henri Spaak. Initially, Spaak contended that NATO should act as a global alliance, but that this should always be consistent with the "Europe first" school of thought: that alliance-wide interests should be given priority over national interests on Third World issues. The Congo crisis convinced Spaak that the United States did not share his vision, and over time he became disillusioned with what he regarded as Washington's insistence on pulling Europe into the American camp on North-South issues, without giving credence to Europe's own considerable politico-diplomatic experience with Third World regimes.

NATO may have missed opportunities to redefine itself along the lines of Spaak's globalist view during the 1950s. But neither Spaak, nor Lord Ismay, nor Churchill, nor Kennan—nor any of the individuals who periodically expressed interest in a more globalist NATO during the cold war era—ever offered a clearly developed plan for how and when this global security arrangement would be called into operation in the Third World. This was certainly not because of lack of thought or effort. The problem was more fundamental. All parties understood that any attempt to encourage debate on such a plan would only have highlighted the fact that key NATO allies' alliance-wide interests were at odds. Under these circumstances, such a debate could only have undermined the commitment to common security interests in the Atlantic Community itself.

CHAPTER 21

ITALY

IN SPITE of its location on the Mediterranean, Italy was viewed—and viewed itself—primarily as a component of the NATO central front during the first three decades of its membership in the alliance. It is only since the late 1970s that Italy has seriously begun to consider the security implications of its geostrategic vulnerability to threats from "the South."[1] This recent Italian reassessment of defense requirements is one element of Rome's more general reassessment of its proper role in world affairs as a founding member of NATO and of the European Community and as a Mediterranean country.

THE ORIGINS OF ITALY'S ALLIANCE POSTURE

Italy suffered from an identity problem and a serious sense of inferiority in the period immediately following World War II. It had been an ally of Germany during the first half of the war, and its subsequent transformation into a "cobelligerent"—but under armistice conditions—was not viewed by the United Kingdom or the United States as sufficient justification for treating Rome as an equal when the war ended.[2] Italy's wartime record was one of the arguments used by American and British policy makers during the Washington Preparatory Talks to oppose Italian membership in the NATO alliance. But a more fundamental concern on the part of Washington and London (and the Scandinavian allies, as argued in Chapter 19) was that Italian membership might shift the base of gravity of the alliance to the Mediterranean and undermine its identity as primarily a North Atlantic defense arrangement.

It was precisely this latter consideration that attracted France to the idea of Italian membership in NATO. Paris saw Rome as the necessary second anchor for the alliance in the Mediterranean. In the absence of such a Mediterranean ally, France feared that its own security interests and concerns in the Middle East and North Africa would be disregarded by the other signatories to the North Atlantic Treaty.

As negotiations continued, France held firm in its demand for Italian membership and discovered—somewhat to its surprise—that its influence was strong enough to carry the issue. But Italian membership did not result in a fundamental reorientation of the alliance toward the South. On the contrary, defense plans for Italian participation in NATO tended to stress the contribution that the Italians could make to the defense of the central theater. Emphasis—in terms of budget, hardware, and planning—was on the northeastern region of Italy. The northeastern Italian theater is geographically situated in such a way that its occupation by Warsaw Pact forces would leave southern Germany and eastern France highly vulnerable to Soviet air strikes.[3] Italy's location, bordering two nonaligned states (Yugoslavia and Austria) in the northeast, led NATO planners to envision Italian forces performing two principal functions: first, shoring up the resolve of Italy's northeastern neighbors so that they would be more willing to preserve their nonaligned status in the face of Warsaw Pact political and/or military pressure; second, preparing to resist a Warsaw Pact push through one or both of these countries into the area known as the "Gorizia Gap" in the event that deterrence failed.

Three factors contributed to the decision by NATO planners to orient Italian forces toward the northeast. First, it was consistent with the desire of the alliance leaders (Washington and London) to downplay the "Mediterranean element" of the alliance. Second, an Italian northeast posture appeared to be justified by the actual military situation as it unfolded during the late 1940s and the 1950s—when Western governments believed that the overriding military threat was located in Central Europe, while the Mediterranean theater looked comparatively secure. Finally, a European defense orientation for Italian forces corresponded with Rome's own general foreign policy approach during the early cold war era, which was designed to integrate Italy into the Atlantic and Western European communities as quickly and completely as possible in order to enhance its standing among other NATO governments.

This arrangement did, in fact, help Italy to secure its position within the second rank of the Atlantic community, and ensured that Rome obtained its slice of each year's allocation of U.S. Military Assistance Program (MAP) funds. But the Italian decision to develop its military program around assisting in the defense of NATO's central front was not without long-term costs. It led to an Italian *overconcentration* on land power at the expense of critical air and naval components within the Italian military establishment. Furthermore, since Italian defense planning was effectively an adjunct of NATO training and planning for central and southeastern defense, decisions about Italian security were usually made in NATO and SHAPE Headquarters. This contributed to the tendency among Italian politicians to pay little real attention to security questions. Rome's acquired habit of letting NATO rather than sovereign decision makers identify Italian defense priorities also encouraged the separate Italian services to regard themselves primarily as part of the alliance military infrastructures, with whom they trained and coordinated their activities, at the expense of Italian interservice cooperation and to the detriment of internal debate regarding alternative missions and threats.[4]

ITALY'S STRATEGIC REORIENTATION

Italy's northeastern security orientation began to be questioned by domestic politicians and defense experts in the late 1970s in response to a number of international developments, including the growth of East-West détente, the 1973 Arab-Israeli wars, the Arab oil boycott, and the growth of the Soviet Mediterranean fleet. But these developments would not have precipitated a national debate on Italian security if they had not coincided with an important change in the domestic political environment as well. The change occurred in the mid-1970s, as the Christian Democrats (DC) lost their monopoly control over postwar Italian politics and were forced to work harder to defend publicly their positions on foreign and defense affairs. Concurrently, the Communists (PCI) began to compete for the support of center-left voters by moderating the more extreme ideological elements of their earlier platforms. A major event in this process of Communist adjustment was then-PCI general secretary Enrico Berlinguer's assertion during the Fourteenth Party Congress in March 1975 that the PCI is "not raising the question of Italy's departure from the Atlantic Pact" after twenty-six years of staunch opposition to NATO membership.[5]

Once the external and internal environments permitted a national debate on general issues of security, Italy's Defense Ministry began to develop its own capability for strategic planning and public information. The results of this effort can be seen in the Defense Ministry's articulation of a "new defense model" for Italy since the late 1970s. The campaign to develop this model began in 1977 with the publication of the Defense Ministry's first White Book—a very general and preliminary effort. This was followed by a series of more interesting public documents in 1980 (*Indirizzi di politica militare*), 1981 (*Modello di difesa secondo la proposta del governo*), and 1984 (*Nota aggiuntiva allo stato di previsione per la difesa*), culminating in 1985 in the publication of Italy's second Defense White Book. These publications trace a striking progression in Italian defense thinking:

–toward a more independent defense posture which recognizes that Italy has national interests and concerns that may not be covered by the NATO guarantee;
–toward a new sense of responsibility for the security of portions of the Mediterranean;
–toward an explicit commitment to interservice coordination, particularly in situations requiring quick response and/or rapid intervention.

Italian defense minister Lelio Lagorio summarized the thinking behind the "new defense model" in 1982: "Italy's role is primarily in the Mediterranean . . . its interests are not fully met in the Alliance. There is a vast area outside NATO in which our country has many reasons and opportunities to make its own independent and autonomous voice heard."[6] A year later, however, Lagorio's successor, Giovanni Spadolini, appeared to be more cautious when he warned that

> no political-military role may be realistically conceived for Italy except in the context . . . of NATO and the EEC. . . . We must, therefore, resist temptations to theorize a "Mediterranean vocation" or East-West mediation roles outside the Western sphere. In the tense competition between East and West, which is becoming even more polarized and is moving into areas of the Third World also, there is no room for spontaneous actions by medium powers, such as our country, which have their own serious internal economic problems. Any illusion of this nature would be tragically crushed by political-military requests beyond our capability.[7]

The disparity between the Lagorio and Spadolini statements illustrates a fundamental tension inherent in Italy's quest for a more ambitious and balanced international role. On the one hand, Rome seeks to assert its independent identity in the Mediterranean region and to take greater responsibility for its own security in the face of what it recognizes as new foreign policy opportunities and new threats beyond the NATO Treaty area.[8] On the other hand, the Italian government is sensitive to the dangers of overextension and concerned about the risks of being caught between the demands of recently cultivated Arab governments and the expectations of old (and essential) Atlantic allies. It should also be noted that a shrinking military manpower base and related defense spending questions have complicated the choice between greater strategic independence and NATO obligations: since 1971, Italy has experienced close to an 8 percent decline in active duty personnel even while it remains fifth among the NATO states in this category. Rome commits 2.7 percent of its gross national product to defense, but is outspent by ten of its NATO allies.[9]

ITALIAN OUT-OF-AREA ACTIVITY IN THE 1980s

Between 1981 and 1983, Rome made a fundamental break with its postwar tradition of military noninvolvement outside of the NATO Treaty area by its decision to contribute to four different peacekeeping contingents: two UNIFIL operations, the Sinai force, and, most notably, the 1983 Multilateral Force (MLF) in Lebanon. The last-named commitment involved a two-thousand-man Italian force whose activities were closely coordinated with those of Britain, France, and the United States—the other three member nations in the MLF.

In spite of its willingness to coordinate such out-of-area operations with other NATO members, Italy was also anxious to distinguish its MLF activities from those of the other participants, in terms of both its political rationale and its operational style. Thus, for example, the Italian government headed by Spadolini was quick to express concern when U.S. aircraft attacked Syrian

ITALY

army units while the MLF was still in Lebanon during late 1983. The United States claimed that the strikes were in retaliation for Syrian ground fire against U.S. warplanes. But Prime Minister Spadolini noted that such military actions by the United States, coming soon after Israeli strikes against Syrian gun emplacements, threatened to blur the peacekeeping identity of the MLF force and undermine the efforts of all of the participants.[10] Likewise, the Italian contingent sought to distinguish its day-to-day activities from those of the other NATO allies involved in the MLF by establishing less of a garrison presence in Beirut, by encouraging its troops to interact with the local populace, and by attempting to communicate a nonthreatening image.[11] The result was an enormously successful peacekeeping operation, which was applauded at home and abroad.

Italy's policy of balancing its Atlantic and Mediterranean commitments underwent an even more severe test in October 1985, when Arab terrorists hijacked the Italian cruise liner *Achille Lauro* off the Egyptian coast. The initial response by the Italian government was prompt and efficient, in spite of the fact that Italy lacked (and continues to lack) appropriate decision-making mechanisms for unilateral resolution of such crises.[12] The government of Bettino Craxi then began negotiations with the hijackers at the same time that Italian air and naval forces were being quickly deployed to the vicinity of the ship, and an Italian special operations team was readied for intervention if the situation required. But Rome was spared the decision to intervene militarily when the terrorists agreed to release the passengers and crew of the vessel and surrender to Egyptian authorities in Port Said. Cairo subsequently provided the terrorists with an Egyptian Boeing 737 and crew, with instructions to fly to Tunis. The immediate terrorist crisis had ended for the Italian government, but a serious Italian/American diplomatic crisis was only beginning.

The confrontation began when Washington sent four U.S. F-14 Tomcat fighters from the aircraft carrier USS *Saratoga* to intercept the Egyptian airliner over the Mediterranean. The U.S. fighters forced the Egyptian crew to land at the NATO facility at Sigonella, in Sicily, without obtaining the prior approval of the Italian government. In a situation unprecedented in the history of NATO, U.S. Delta Force troops actually confronted Italian forces with guns drawn across the tarmac at the Sigonella base over the issue of which side had authority over the plane and its occupants. Direct orders from Washington were required before the U.S. troops agreed to stand down and permit Italian authorities to take the terrorists into custody. But U.S. aircraft subsequently followed the airliner as the Italian military moved it from Sigonella to Rome. During the flight, the crews of the U.S. aircraft refused to respond to the demands of the Italian air traffic controllers to identify themselves and to state their purpose and destination over Italian airspace.

The extent to which the U.S. use of the Sigonella base was justified by its status as a NATO facility has been debated by international legal experts since the *Achille Lauro* incident.[13] But there was no doubt about the illegality of the U.S. intervention into Italian airspace. In any event, the Italian government and public were united in their interpretation of the U.S. moves as a direct affront to Italian sovereignty. President Reagan exacerbated tensions even more by demonstrating a casual disregard for the issue of Italian sovereignty, bragging to reporters at the time that "we did this all by our little selves."

The diplomatic crisis intensified when Rome released one occupant of the Egyptian airliner—Mahmoud Abul Abbas, leader of the Palestinian Liberation Front—who had been found aboard the plane. Abbas had been one of the architects of the plan to "seajack" the *Achille Lauro,* but he had also been instrumental in subsequently convincing the terrorists on board the vessel to surrender to Egyptian authorities. Prime Minister Craxi's decision to release Abbas was motivated primarily by a desire to maintain good relations with the PLF and the PLO. But Rome was also looking for a means of communicating its resentment, and reasserting its sovereignty, in response to the unilateral American actions.[14]

Craxi's decision to release Abbas led to the resignation of Defense Minister Spadolini and the withdrawal of his party from the Socialist-led coalition. Spadolini also used the occasion to force a debate on Italian foreign and defense priorities, accusing Craxi and his foreign minister, Giulio Andreotti, of excessive deference to Arab and, in particular, PLO demands at the expense of traditional Atlantic allies.[15] Spadolini was subsequently brought back into a cabinet post as part of a reconstructed government coalition, however, and Craxi succeeded in weathering the political crisis.

The longer-term impact of the *Achille Lauro* affair was felt in the relations between Rome and Washington. Many Italians shared Spadolini's dissatisfaction regarding Craxi's handling of the affair; but a much larger and more vocal portion of the population was outraged by America's insensitivity to Italian sovereignty.[16] After five years of especially close cooperation, Italian/American relations fell to perhaps the lowest point in postwar history.

Only five months later, Rome was once again caught up in an out-of-area dispute when Washington challenged Libyan claims of sovereign control over the Gulf of Sidra. The U.S. action was clearly motivated by Tripoli's support for international terrorist activity (including the attack on the *Achille Lauro*), but a fundamental issue of freedom of navigation and exploration was also involved. Italy had its own reasons for challenging Qaddafi's claims over Sidra—including Italian offshore oil exploration and drilling activity in the region—but Rome's highest priority was to avoid an escalating confrontation between Tripoli and Washington in which Italy might become a Libyan target of convenience.[17] Italian concern intensified when Qaddafi specifically cited the NATO facilities at Sigonella, Comiso, Taranto, Naples, and Bagnoli as possible targets of retaliation.[18]

Qaddafi subsequently attempted to make good on his threats to punish Italy for the sins of Washington, after U.S. F-111s based in Great Britain attacked Tripoli and Bengasi on April 14–15, 1986 (following yet another terrorist incident in Western Europe). Qaddafi struck back by firing two Soviet-made SCUD medium range missiles at the Italian island of Lampedusa—in spite of the fact that Rome had refused base access and overflight rights to the U.S. F-111s at the time of the Tripoli/Bengasi bombing.

The fact that both missiles missed their target permitted Rome to make a restrained, diplomatic response to the Libyan attack. It also allowed NATO governments to skirt the difficult problem of deciding whether the attack against Italian territory constituted an attack against the alliance as a whole.[19] But Italian faith in the security provided by the "transatlantic bargain" was badly shaken by the event. As one Italian editorial put it, "Since the time of the 'Achille Lauro' and Sigonella incidents something has evidently changed in our relations with the United States." The article concluded, "For us . . . the issue is not participation in the Alliance, but the mode of participation; the margin of autonomy and reciprocal respect; and the possibility of contributing in a concrete way to common decisions . . . for which we will suffer the consequences."[20]

FUTURE OUT-OF-AREA OBJECTIVES AND CAPABILITIES

The 1985 Italian Defense White Book argued that traditional "conceptual and operational certainties" have been "undermined" by changes in the relative strengths of NATO and anti-Western forces. Closer to home, the White Book noted that the "Mediterranean 'complex' (Middle East, NATO countries, North Africa, Balkans) has been subject more often than in the past to . . . politico-diplomatic instability [which] has entailed a notable shift of European crises toward the south."[21] In view of this new situation, the document stressed the need to improve Italian capabilities for rapid force projection into the Mediterranean region and deterrence of threats against the southern islands.

During the early 1980s, the central element in the Defense Ministry's program to achieve these goals was the proposed development of a Forza Operativa di Pronto Intervento (FOPI). The FOPI was expected to protect "sensitive [Italian or Allied] positions and installations to a maximum radius of 2500 kms, for airguard operations and 1000 miles for air naval operations." It would function as a "rapidly deployable strategic reserve" for NATO's southern region and fight in NATO's central region as well to establish "a symbolic but effective means for NATO to avoid the political-military isolation of its Southern Region." It would also carry out operations supplementary to NATO's Ace Mobile Force (AMF) in the event the latter was confronted with simultaneous threats and/or defense missions on both the northern and southern alliance flanks (AMF cannot handle combat emergencies on both NATO fronts at the same time).[22]

By the time that the 1985 White Book was published, however, the FOPI concept had become a casualty of Italian domestic political debate. In fact, the force has been transmogrified into a civil protection and emergency assistance corps.[23] In the absence of some variation of the FOPI, Italy's ability rapidly to project forces beyond the NATO Treaty area is quite limited. According to some Western military analysts, up to three Italian marine battalions and an additional airborne brigade are available for possible extra-European combat duties. But the bulk of Italian land forces remain deployed in the northeastern sectors of the country (approximately twenty brigades organized into three army corps based in Milan, Bolzano, and Vittorio Veneto), as do the vast majority of Rome's armor and air force support resources.[24]

Italy has nonetheless undertaken some important force modernization initiatives in recent years—particularly in its naval development program. During the period between 1960 and 1976, budgetary pressures led successive Italian governments to reduce the size of the Italian navy by approximately 40 percent.[25] Since the late 1970s, however, Rome has been revitalizing portions of the Italian navy. The cornerstone of this program is a major frigate modernization program, but the launching of the helicopter carrier *Giuseppe Garibaldi* in September 1983 and the addition of two new amphibious warfare units are also significant developments in this regard.[26]

During the 1980s, Italy had two opportunities to demonstrate the results of its naval modernization program, while at the same time demonstrating its solidarity with other NATO allies. The first instance was during August–October 1984, when Italian minesweepers accompanied American, British, Dutch, and French units to the Red Sea at the request of the Egyptian government, to search for and clear mines laid between the Suez Canal and the Gulf of Aden.[27] A second example of Italian out-of-area naval activity was the participation of three Italian frigates, three minesweepers, and two support vessels in minesweeping and escort activities in the Persian Gulf in 1987. In the latter case, Rome officially explained its presence in the gulf as support for UN efforts to achieve a cease-fire in the Iran-Iraq War. But the fact that the Italian decision to show the flag followed shortly after an attack (presumably by Iran) on an Italian freighter in the gulf demonstrates Rome's recognition of the fact that peacekeeping operations can make a contribution at a number of levels simultaneously—to national security, regional security, and the goals of the United Nations.

As Italy continues to improve its forces in the Mediterranean region, it will become increasingly important for Rome to coordinate its plans and actions with other NATO members in general and with the southern allies in particular. As we have occasion to discuss in the next two chapters, however, the prospects of defense policy coordination in the southern region are in fact declining, as key regional allies continue to develop distinct, and in some cases directly conflicting, visions of national security.

CONCLUSION

Italy finds itself today in the difficult position of reassessing its status and identity within NATO as one component of a more general process of foreign policy reassessment. After three decades of letting NATO and Washington shape Italian defense, Rome is now reconsidering the implications of its unique status within the alliance—"peripheral with respect to the center, but central within the southern NATO periphery."[28]

During the early 1980s, Rome enjoyed being singled out for special praise by Washington for its willingness to play a more ambitious role in the Mediterranean area, for its commitment to defense modernization, and for its support for the U.S.-sponsored INF deployment program. Over time, however, it has become increasingly obvious to both Rome and Washington that Italy's "Mediterranean vocation" reflects certain interests and concerns that are unrelated to—and, in some cases, in competition with—U.S. security interests in the southern region. Under these circumstances, Rome will continue to improve its ability to take unilateral action in the Mediterranean and to contribute to multilateral initiatives in the southern region. But Rome will not permit its allies—in particular, the alliance leader—to depict these improvements as an adjunct of the RDF, or as some NATO variant of the RDF. Nor will Rome be willing to stand quietly on the sidelines while NATO allies undertake actions in the Mediterranean for which Italy will be forced to pay the price.

CHAPTER 22

THE AEGEAN ALLIES

TURKEY

THE ISSUE of how best to protect Turkey and the eastern approaches to the Mediterranean preoccupied many Western security planners in the immediate postwar period. By the end of 1945, American and British policy makers agreed that Western security required active support for Turkey in its resistance to Soviet diplomatic and politico-military pressure. The Soviet pressure campaign included territorial claims to Eastern Anatolia, troop build-ups along the Bulgarian and Caucasian frontiers, retention of Soviet troops in Iran, support for Armenian nationalist claims against Turkey, and, most importantly, demands for renegotiation of the Montreaux Convention (to end what Stalin described as "a situation in which Turkey had a hand on Russia's throat").[1] Washington's commitment to Turkish security was confirmed as early as April 1946 when the U.S. battleship *Missouri* anchored at Istanbul. But, as discussed in Chapter 1, neither the United States nor any of the other participants in the Washington Preparatory Talks of 1948/49 were willing to accede to Ankara's request for membership in the North Atlantic Alliance. Consequently, Turkey itself was an out-of-area problem for allied defense planners during the first three years of NATO's existence.

Ankara was frustrated but not discouraged by the rejection of its request for membership in NATO. By this time, the Turks had concluded that compromise with the East was impossible and a geostrategically and politically exposed position between East and West was untenable. The only viable policy was to continue to press for full integration into the Western defense community at the earliest possible date. In order to accomplish this, Turkey had to overcome two prejudices held by many Western leaders: that Turkey was an unreliable ally, as demonstrated by its policy of neutrality during World War II, and that Turkey was of limited value to the allies in terms of the direct contributions which it could make to NATO's defense or to out-of-area contingencies.

Certain U.S. policy makers, such as the ambassador to Ankara, George Wadsworth, supported Turkey's efforts to join NATO during 1949 and 1950.[2] Other factions, including the U.S. Joint Chiefs, were sympathetic to Turkey's concerns but still reluctant to support Ankara's requests for a quick decision in favor of NATO membership. The JCS contended that the NATO central front was still not adequately built up and that any extension of the alliance into the Eastern Mediterranean risked further delays in achieving NATO force goals for Central Europe. With the "Year of Maximum Danger" (1954) rapidly approaching, the Joint Chiefs considered the addition of Turkey and Greece to be a misallocation of scarce resources.[3] Other NATO governments concurred with the JCS. Turkish security was recognized as a common Western concern, but the European NATO members were reluctant to risk cuts in their respective portions of the MDAP allotment by adding a large, poor ally that was geographically and culturally on the margin of Europe. The NATO Council of Ministers met during September 1950 to reconsider Turkey's request for membership, and Ankara was once again rebuffed.

The Korean War provided the opportunity for Turkey to demonstrate its reliability as an ally and its commitment to containing communism. Ankara was quick to volunteer its forces for duty under the UN banner, sending a fifty-two-hundred-man brigade. Turkish forces made an important contribution to the military effort in Korea and suffered severe losses—most notably during the November 1950 "Home by Christmas" offensive. The Turkish government also played upon the growing tendency among U.S. policy makers in 1950 to see the communist threat as a single entity, global in character and centrally controlled from Moscow. Ankara argued—along the lines of France's *guerre révolutionnaire* thesis—that only a globally active Western alliance could cope with the worldwide communist offensive. The Turkish government stated that it was prepared to contribute to this effort in such far-flung locales as Korea, but it required status and support from the Western allies in return. A global anticommunist campaign stood the best chance of succeeding if it was anchored in a strong Atlantic Alliance; and in order for Ankara to be an effective Western ally in the Third World, it had to be a full and equal member of that alliance.[4]

Turkey's strategy of gaining access to NATO through Korea was a success. Six months after the September 1950 rejection of Turkish membership by the NATO Council of Ministers, Washington was reconsidering its global security policy in light of growing domestic concern about the Soviet threat and public frustration over the Korean entanglement. A key document was prepared by the Policy Planning Staff in February 1951, warning about the risks of encouraging insecurity and a sense of isolation in Turkey by continuing to refuse Ankara's requests for NATO membership.[5] By the spring of 1951, even the JCS had become more sensitive to Turkish and Greek solicitations, in spite of the risk of "spreading the butter too thin" within NATO, since the Aegean nations represented a combined manpower contribution of twenty-five new divisions to NATO.[6] Concurrent with—and contributing to—this change in U.S. policy, British and American attempts to create an alternative institutional framework for Mediterranean defense (MEDO, as discussed in Chapter 10) were foundering. By the fall of 1951, the United States had committed itself to obtaining quick approval of Greek and Turkish membership from the NATO Council of Ministers. The approval was duly obtained in October of that year, and Greece and Turkey became full members of the alliance early in 1952.

After Turkey achieved its goal of NATO membership, it continued to pursue policies aimed at convincing Washington of its value as an ally. Ankara played upon what one scholar has recently described as a "common understanding between the United States and Turkey on the indivisibility of different fronts and the interdependence of different types of confrontations occurring at different but interrelated strategic levels."[7]

During the 1950s, Ankara sought to reinforce the good ally image by actively supporting U.S. policy in the Middle East. Turkey played an especially important role during the 1958 U.S. intervention in Lebanon, by permitting U.S. aircraft to utilize the Incirlik base for resupply and refueling. Ankara also sent its own direct offer of military assistance to the U.S.-supported regime of Camille Chamoun in Beirut, but Turkish forces were not called upon during the subsequent crisis.[8]

Turkey further enhanced its good ally image during the 1950s by becoming a founding member of the Baghdad Pact (subsequently CENTO). By doing so, Turkey established itself as the strategic bridge linking NATO to the Middle East and Southwest Asia in U.S. global security planning. This role was more symbolic than real, however, owing to the fundamental weakness of the Baghdad Pact and CENTO and the reluctance of the United States to encourage transregional security links.

If Ankara had become a very supportive ally, it had also become a special source of concern because of the growth of Greek-Turkish tension over Cyprus. Britain sought to resolve the escalating conflict by the Zurich and London agreements of 1959—designed to establish the guidelines for power sharing on the island and to clarify the rights and duties of Ankara, Athens, and London vis-à-vis Cyprus. But the constitutional framework established in 1959 was effectively stillborn. By the time that the Republic of Cyprus was declared (August 1960), neither the Greek nor the Turkish Cypriot community was satisfied with the governmental system. When intercommunal fighting finally broke out on the island in December 1963, the United States and NATO were drawn in.[9] "Britain requested that a peacekeeping force, comprised of NATO member-states' personnel, be formed."[10] It was probably a no-win situation for the United States from the start, but Lyndon Johnson's handling of the crisis did not help. Johnson sought to discourage Turkey from intervening militarily on behalf of the Turkish Cypriot minority. Toward this end, he dispatched a strongly worded letter to Turkish premier Ismet Inonu warning Ankara against taking military action in the Cyprus situation. Johnson advised Inonu that U.S. military equipment allocated to Turkey under NATO auspices could not be used in Cyprus. He also took the extraordinary step of warning Ankara that in the event that Turkish actions precipitated a military response from Moscow, Ankara could not be certain of NATO support. From the point of view of the Turkish government, the Johnson letter was the most serious foreign policy setback of the postwar era, because it demonstrated the fragility of the good ally strategy which Ankara had been following for fifteen years.[11]

The incident was especially upsetting to Turkish policy makers because it occurred at a time when Turkish-American relations had not yet recovered from disputes that had arisen during and after the Cuban Missile Crisis. As mentioned in Chapter 1, the missile crisis illustrated the difficulty involved in insulating NATO from out-of-area crises involving the superpowers. Considering the circumstances, the Kennedy administration did a good job of advising its allies and taking allied concerns into account during the crisis. The one exception, however, was Turkey, which was wedded to the Dulles-type cold war policy that Kennedy disdained. When U.S. Jupiter missiles based in Turkey became a stumbling block during the crisis, Kennedy demonstrated little sympathy for Turkish sensibilities. Recently released transcripts of Executive Committee deliberations during the crisis indicate that JFK was more interested than any of his advisers in working out some sort of trade—missiles in Cuba for missiles in Turkey. He nonetheless accepted the advice of his assistants to the effect that such a trade would establish a dangerous precedent, one that might encourage further Soviet challenges to the status quo. The important point, from Turkey's perspective, was that the United States paid scant attention to Turkish wishes or concerns as it considered the option of a missile swap.[12]

As a result of these and other developments, the Turkish government had begun to adjust its overall foreign and security policy by the mid–1960s. The cold war/good ally strategy was gradually modified to permit greater foreign policy flexibility. Ankara began to lay the groundwork for its own form of *Ostpolitik* toward the Soviet Union.

A point of special relevance for this book is that the Turkish government began to be more restrictive regarding U.S. access to Turkish bases for out-of-area contingencies. Since the late 1960s, Ankara has maintained a policy of treating U.S. requests for base use and overflights on a case-by-case basis. During the 1970 internal crisis in Jordan, Turkey permitted U.S. aircraft to fly supplies from Adana to Amman to assist King Hussein in his crackdown on Palestinian dissidents.[13] But Ankara rejected Washington's requests for basing and overflight rights during the 1973 Arab-Israeli War, while granting over-flight rights and naval transit rights through the Dardanelles to the Soviet Union so that Moscow could resupply Egypt and Syria. The paramount concern of Turkish leaders in this case was to avoid any action that might trigger Soviet diplomatic or military retaliation. This consideration was also at the forefront of Turkey's decision in 1979 to require prior Soviet authorization for future American U-2 flights from Turkey for purposes of monitoring Moscow's compliance with SALT II.[14]

At least as important as Turkish concerns about the Soviet Union, however, has been Turkey's interest since the early 1970s in enhancing its status and influence among the Arab states in the Middle East.[15] This consideration was probably the most important determinant of Turkey's decision to abrogate the 1954 U.S.-Turkish Military Facilities Agreement in 1969 and to require a new Defense Cooperation Agreement (DCA), which was more restrictive of U.S. base utilization and overflight rights for out-of-area contingencies. Subsequent defense cooperation agreements (in 1976 and 1980) have maintained this policy. According to Article 5, Paragraph 4 of the 1980 agreement (still in effect), "The extent of the defense cooperation envisioned in this agreement shall be limited to obligations arising out of the North Atlantic Treaty."[16]

U.S.-Turkish relations regarding base access reached their worst point following the 1974 crisis on Cyprus. The United States once again found itself in the no-win situation of being caught between two Aegean allies. In this case, the executive branch sought to preserve good relations with both parties. But following the Turkish invasion of Cyprus in July, the administration came under strong pressure from Congress publicly to condemn and sanction Ankara. The Staff Report of the Senate Judiciary Committee concerning the Cyprus situation reflects the stridency of many members of Congress regarding the Turkish role in the crisis. It described U.S. efforts to present an "even-handed" picture of Greek and Turkish roles in the crisis as "an incredible move of bad timing, if not bad policy" and attacked Turkey for using NATO areas and materiel for its "invasion" and "occupation" of Cyprus, asserting "that Turkey violated the relevant laws is not in doubt." The report also claimed that "the combination of nationalist fervor and government instability in Ankara has resulted in the Turks not really wanting a settlement . . . even if the Greek majority wallows in despair."[17]

The White House initially resisted this type of congressional pressure but ultimately agreed to an arms embargo at the end of 1974. Turkey retaliated seven months later, after repeatedly failing in its efforts to convince Congress to lift the embargo, by nationalizing the twenty-five U.S.-Turkish bases that were maintained under a 1969 bilateral agreement. Ankara nonetheless permitted those facilities under NATO control to remain open and continued to permit U.S. military units to use them.[18]

Turkish-American relations finally began to improve in 1978, after the Carter administration succeeded in convincing Congress to lift the arms embargo. Prime Minister Bulent Ecevit applauded the action as the first step in a new era of Turkish-American cooperation. But Turkish policy makers also complained about the damage that the four-year embargo had done to the armed forces. One

Western journalist reported that by 1978, Turkey's air force was only "50% operational." He also quoted a confidential U.S. report on the situation which concluded that "Turkey, at this point, manages to feed and clothe its armed forces but hardly more."[19] In a well-known speech delivered to the International Institute for Strategic Studies, Prime Minister Ecevit directly linked the future American use of Turkish bases to increased levels of long-term U.S. economic assistance extended to Ankara.[20] He later offered the aforementioned qualification that American U-2 surveillance flights over the Soviet Union could occur only with Soviet approval.[21]

During the 1980s, Turkey's relations with the Arab world improved, as reflected in the growth of Turkish trade with the Middle East/gulf region.[22] At the same time, however, Turkish-American relations have improved considerably since the U.S. Congress lifted the arms embargo against Turkey. The context of U.S.-Turkish defense cooperation also changed after the 1979 invasion of Afghanistan, which both Washington and Ankara saw as a possible first step in a Soviet push into the Persian Gulf region.

Since the early 1980s, then, Turkey has been attempting to walk a tightrope between its commitment to security cooperation with the United States and the high priority that it accords to diplomatic and economic cooperation with the Arab states in an environment of continuing Arab-Israeli and inter-Arab conflict. Ankara is also highly critical of some aspects of U.S. policy in the Middle East. In the words of Seyfi Tashan, director of Turkey's Foreign Policy Institute, in 1984: "The problem is that we don't agree with American policy in the Middle East. We are allies against a common Soviet threat, but not for Israeli aggression."[23]

The tensions inherent in this situation are reflected in Ankara's handling of Washington's request for facilities to support the multinational force in Lebanon during 1983. Turkey initially rejected U.S. solicitations. Ankara then reversed itself in October 1983 and permitted U.S. forces to use the Incirlik facility for storing nonmilitary supplies and for refueling in support of the MLF operation. One important factor that contributed to Turkey's policy reversal was ongoing American basing negotiations with the Greek Cypriot government, at a time when Ankara was soliciting U.S. support for the Turkish Cypriot regime in Northern Cyprus.[24] But Ankara's decision was widely criticized within Turkey. An editorial appearing in Istanbul's *Cumhuriyet* in mid-December complained, "Why must it be Incirlik air base? The ink of the 'strategic agreement' signed with Israel is not even dry yet. Aren't the Israeli ports and airfields right under Lebanon's nose? Isn't the Mediterranean sun just as bright over the Israeli roads for the 'rest and recuperation' needs of the U.S. troops?"[25] Part of the point was, of course, that the sun was just as bright over the Greek Cypriot facility at Larnaca.

Turkey continues to permit the United States to improve existing basing facilities and to open new facilities for forward defense, prepositioning of materiel, and intelligence gathering and electronic surveillance. In particular, Ankara has permitted Washington to improve its defense infrastructure in eastern Turkey, where forward-deployed U.S. strike aircraft contribute significantly to the West's ability to oppose any Soviet attempt to invade Iran and the Gulf region. But the 1982 Memorandum of Understanding governing these facilities permits their utilization only for *NATO missions*.[26] As Thomas McNaugher has observed, "The question of whether a Soviet threat to Iran constitutes a NATO contingency will be answered only when events demand an answer."[27]

Ankara has also been consistent in disassociating itself from U.S. contingency planning for the USCENTCOM. It prefers regional solutions to problems of Middle East and gulf security and has pursued a low-key policy of contributing to regional conflict reduction where and when opportunities arise. For instance, Turkey made a special effort to maintain links with both sides in the Iran-Iraq War—a difficult trick in view of the intensity of the conflict. Indeed, the difficulty of preserving diplomatic and trade links with both sides is illustrated by the fact that Turkish vessels in the gulf were attacked by both Iraq (in 1984) and Iran (in 1986).

Turkey is a unique and highly valued NATO partner with special cultural, historical, and geostrategic links to the Arab region. Only a very shortsighted Western policy maker would seek to press Ankara back into the 1950s mold of good (read "obedient") ally. In spite of the fact that Turkey is no longer willing to provide the United States and NATO with unconditional access to its bases for out-of-area contingencies, it still plays a vital role in helping to discourage the Soviet Union from intervening militarily in the Middle East/gulf region. The assessment found in a 1975 congressional study still holds true: "As long as Turkey remains aligned with the United States, the Kremlin would find large-scale, sustained military operations difficult in the Mediterranean or Middle East."[28] The same conclusion applies to Soviet military operations against Iran or through northwestern Iran into the gulf region. While the United States would like to obtain a more firm and explicit assurance of Turkish support for American operations in the region, such an assurance would not significantly increase Turkey's deterrent capability vis-à-vis the USSR. This is because the most important elements in the deterrence equation are Turkey's geostrategic placement (controlling the straits, facing the USSR across the Black Sea, and bordering northern Iran) and a clear and reliable Turkish commitment to NATO and to Western values. A U.S. campaign of pressure for a more explicit assurance of support could in fact work to undermine Turkey's deterrent value, if it encouraged factions within Turkey to reassess the benefits of the Western security commitment in light of Turkey's geostrategically exposed situation.

With regard to other Middle East/gulf contingencies—not directly involving the Soviet Union—a prior assurance of base access and overflight rights would certainly simplify USCENTCOM planning. But at what cost? As the only predominantly Moslem ally in the Western alliance, as the only NATO ally sharing a land border with an Arab nation (in fact, three Arab nations), Turkey is uniquely qualified to represent Western interests in the Middle East/gulf region and to mediate between the Atlantic allies and selected Arab governments. To attempt to force Turkey to jeopardize this extremely advantageous political position in order to reassure USCENTCOM planners would be short-sighted, to say the least. A campaign of pressure would fail in any event, and might create widespread resentment in Turkey against the United States.

GREECE

Much of what has been said about the early postwar history of Turkey applies to Greece as well—the frustrated desire to become a founding member of NATO, the subsequent allied reconsideration of membership as cold war fears intensified, and participation in the Korean War as a means of softening up the United States on the issue of NATO membership. Greece, like Turkey, also performed a "good ally" support function for U.S. and U.K. forces involved in out-of-area actions during the 1950s.[29]

The most significant difference between Greece and Turkey in their relations with NATO in general and the alliance leader in particular has been in the way in which each nation has moved from the good ally policy toward a more diversified and balanced foreign and security posture. As discussed in the previous section, Turkey's abandonment of the good ally role was part of a fairly gradual process of political maturation through the 1960s. In the case of Greece, however, the process of maturation, which was clearly under way in the late 1950s and early 1960s, was abruptly interrupted in 1967 by the coup that brought a military junta to power in Athens. The colonels shored up the decaying good ally policy toward NATO and the United States, providing Washington with base access during the 1967 Arab-Israeli War and the 1970 crisis in Jordan and opening new ports to U.S. naval vessels. In return, the United States and various NATO allies helped to legitimize the junta by providing official forms of recognition, including visits to Athens by such officials as NATO Supreme Allied Commander General Andrew Goodpaster, U.S. Secretary of Defense Melvin Laird, and Secretary of State William Rogers.[30] These initiatives virtually assured that NATO in general and Washington in particular would face a "guilt by association" problem in their dealing with any democratic successor to the military regime in Athens.

When the junta fell from power in 1974, Western governments were hopeful that Greek-NATO reconciliation could be managed gradually, as part of the process of foreign policy maturation in Greece. But any hope of such a development disappeared in the same year, when, in the wake of the Turkish invasion of Cyprus, Greek prime minister Constantine Karamanlis announced his intentions to quit NATO. The decision was widely supported by the Greek public, which blamed NATO in general, and the United States in particular, for not restraining Ankara.

The process of Greek-NATO reconciliation has been under way only since October 1980, when Athens agreed to return to the alliance. Most of the period of reconciliation has been dominated by one man—Prime Minister Andreas Papandreou—leader of the Panhellenic Socialist Movement (PASOK), who held office from 1981 until 1989. In his campaign to develop an independent and diversified foreign and security policy for Greece, Papandreou often played to the anti-American, anti-NATO, and pro-neutralist elements in his party and in the Greek public. He was most successful in this strategy when he linked his criticisms of the West to criticisms of Turkey, which is considered by the vast majority of the population to be the principal threat to Greek sovereignty and security.

Papandreou referred to the threat posed by Turkey as "our special problem, which unfortunately has not been recognized even within the Atlantic Alliance."[31] Athens' response to this perceived threat was announced in January of 1985—a ten-year, $2.8-billion-dollar defense modernization program designed to reorient the major part of Greece's army, navy, and air force away from their NATO-designated positions (facing Bulgaria) toward the "constant, continuing and growing threat" from Turkey.[32]

At the same time that Greece was adjusting its defense plans, it began to experiment with a variety of formulas for escaping from, or at least loosening, the constraints that it associated with a Western-oriented foreign policy. At times this experimentation took the form of a Hellenic *Ostpolitik* (the Soviet Union was "struggling for détente," while the United States sought to "extend its sovereignty" around the world).[33] At other times it took the form of a new Middle Eastern policy (PASOK is reported to have concluded an agreement with the Syrian Ba'athist party jointly to oppose "world imperialism and racist Zionism").[34] At still other times it was aimed at a Balkan role for Greece (in particular, Papandreou's efforts to sponsor a Balkan nuclear-free zone with Yugoslavia, Albania, Rumania, and Bulgaria and a February 1983 joint communiqué issued with Nikolai Tikhonov, chairman of the USSR's Council of Ministers, supporting the concept).[35]

It is worth reiterating that Greece's efforts to establish links to the Soviet Union, the Middle East, and the Balkan subregion were a natural manifestation of a sensible quest for a more diversified foreign policy. Furthermore, widespread anti-American and anti-NATO feelings in Greece were entirely understandable in light of recent Greek history. The Papandreou regime was nonetheless more frenetic than necessary in its foreign policies and more strident than necessary in its criticisms of its Western allies.

Most of the time Papandreou's flailing foreign policy behavior was a response to developments in Greek domestic politics. Papandreou frequently resorted to anti-Western, neutralist, or pro-Arab foreign policy initiatives to divert public attention from economic problems or to placate the left wing within PASOK.[36] These initiatives were usually rhetorical rather than substantive, and most Western governments treated such statements correctly—as sound and fury, signifying nothing. It is worth reiterating, however, that Papandreou was playing to widely held resentments within the Greek public— against NATO in general and Washington in particular. These resentments did not disappear in June 1989 when Constantin Mitsotakis replaced Papandreou as prime minister.

Serious issues of dispute remain to be addressed between Greece and NATO in the 1990s. In particular, NATO cannot remain indifferent to the steady erosion of its southeastern flank, as Greek forces are redeployed against Turkey during the next few years. NATO governments must make it clear to Athens that a fundamental reorientation of the Greek armed forces would represent a threat to the alliance as a whole and an abdication of responsibilities embodied in the 1980 agreement by which Athens was reintegrated into NATO.

But an assertive NATO policy will either stall or backfire unless the allies help to address the root of the problem—Greek fear of a Turkish invasion. This, in turn, requires NATO governments to play a more active role in assisting Athens and Ankara to reduce the level of bilateral tension over Cyprus and resolve the territorial disputes in the region. A first step in this regard is for NATO as a whole to adopt a more ambitious and a more balanced policy of aid to Greece and Turkey. At present, fully 95 percent of the military aid and the bulk of the economic aid provided to Athens and Ankara comes from Washington and Bonn. A more diversified program of NATO support would help to depoliticize the aid issue and enhance the leverage of the Council of Ministers and the NATO secretary general. NATO's influence would likewise be increased if the size of the multilateral aid package was raised. The groundwork for such a program of coordinated, increased aid to Greece and Turkey was laid in 1978 when the NATO Council of Ministers empowered the secretary general to submit a biannual report on economic problems in the southern region of the alliance and to make recommendations for cooperative aid programs.[37]

A coordinated NATO program of aid to Greece and Turkey would be especially useful to Washington, because it would shift the focus of attention away from America's bilateral aid to Athens and Ankara and reduce one of the most persistent sources of dispute between Washington and the Aegean allies—the 7 : 10 ratio. Since 1976 the United States has employed a proportional aid formula, according to which Athens is allocated 70 percent of the Security Assistance provided to Turkey. The formula is unsatisfactory from the point of view of both Athens and Ankara. Greece claims that the 7 : 10 ratio does not include U.S. Foreign Military Sales (FMS) to Turkey, which it contends are a form of hidden assistance. The Turkish government, meanwhile, claims that the 7 : 10 formula holds down U.S. assistance to Turkey and does not accurately reflect the much greater contribution that Ankara makes to Western security, as reflected in the size of its military force and by its geostrategic placement.[38] Any amelioration of the Greek-Turkish dispute, and any improvement in Greek-American relations on the question of Security Assistance, will make it easier for Washington to negotiate with Papandreou's successors on the issue of basing. Papandreou's decision to sign the 1983 bilateral agreement represented an important retreat from his earlier commitment to shut the bases down.[39] Washington continues to be optimistic about the prospects for a new basing accord. But the United States is under no illusions about the possibility of USCENTCOM's using the bases in Greece for any future intervention in the Middle East/gulf region. Papandreou repeatedly made this point during the Multilateral Force operation in Lebanon, when he refused U.S. and Italian requests for refueling rights at facilities in Greece. In fact, in the event of a crisis in the Middle East/gulf area, Washington would probably be naive even to make informal inquiries to Athens about base access or overflight rights. But a crisis in the Middle East/gulf region could sour U.S.-Greek relations, even if America did not solicit the support of the Greek government, if Athens felt compelled by its commitments to certain Arab nations to take action against Washington for its intervention in the region. Such responses could take the form of public criticism inside or outside of the NATO forum, or they could involve Greek pressure on the U.S. bases.

CONCLUSION

Greece will continue to present the Western alliance with special diplomatic and military problems for the foreseeable future. The departure of Papandreou may have removed a difficult personality factor from the Greek-NATO relationship, but many of Papandreou's themes of foriegn policy independence and suspicion of U.S. and allied activities continue to enjoy widespread support among the mass and elite publics in Greece. Some problems can be ameliorated by coordinated NATO action; others will be impossible to control or avoid. Greece is likely to represent special difficulties for the United States as Washington continues to develop plans for USCENTCOM operations in the Middle East/gulf region. When possible, the U.S. administration should follow Lyndon Johnson's policy toward de Gaulle in response to Greek criticisms. ("When de Gaulle gets up to pitch, I step out of the box.") But the limits of U.S. tolerance are established by the priority that Washington accords to Athens as a diplomatic and military ally. In this regard, Washington has been fairly consistent since 1945 in recognizing that Turkey is far more important than Greece. This assessment is likely to be increased in Turkey's favor in the future, in spite of the fact that neither Aegean ally will be very attracted to the idea of helping Washington to carry out contingencies beyond the NATO Treaty area.[40]

298

CHAPTER 23

THE IBERIAN ALLIES

SPAIN

L IKE I TALY , Spain has been in the process of reassessing its security needs since the 1970s. But Italy was a member of the alliance for almost thirty years before it began the process of strategic reassessment, while Spain was an outsider during this entire period. Indeed, the most important security issue for Madrid during the first half of the 1980s was whether to join NATO at all—for what benefit, and at what cost.

As long as Franco was in power, Spanish membership in NATO proved to be out of the question, and the defense of Spain was an out-of-area problem for the alliance. The anomalous status of Madrid—a pariah government that was nonetheless an ally of the United States (following the bilateral basing accord of 1953) and an integral component of postwar allied plans for Western European defense—represented a persistent diplomatic problem for Western defense planners.[1] Postwar plans called for the utilization of Spanish territory as a strategic redout and invasion route in the event that a Western counteroffensive was necessary after Soviet troops had succeeded in breaking through NATO's defense line along the central front. The fact that such plans made more sense, and could be better developed, if Spain were a member of the alliance did not seem to the allies a sufficient justification for overlooking Spain's history and politics (as they had done for Portugal) and inviting Madrid to join NATO. Franco, for his part, was content to remain outside of the alliance rather than open his country to European and North American meddling through the NATO consultative mechanism. He understood that he could obtain a better deal, with less risk of interference from abroad, by negotiating directly with the United States. These bilateral basing arrangements initially gave the United States broad latitude regarding the administration of the bases and the purposes for which they were used. By the late 1960s, however, Franco had become far more restrictive in his handling of basing arrangements, emphasizing Spanish national control and specifically stipulating that the bases were to be used only for Western European contingencies unless otherwise authorized by Madrid.

Following the death of Franco, the leading political parties in Spain began the long-delayed debate on the issue of Spanish accession to NATO. The debate occurred in the context of a more wide-ranging discussion of foreign and security choices for Spain which included such issues as détente, North-South relations, a new Iberian policy, and a new role in Latin and Central America. The debate about NATO membership tended to focus on five points:

1. Did Spanish security require closer affiliation with the Atlantic Alliance? What were the principal threats to Spain, and could NATO be relied upon to deter them or actively defend against them?
2. Would NATO membership make it easier for Spain to achieve two more important foreign policy goals—accession to the EEC on favorable terms and the return of Gibraltar to Spain?
3. Could Spanish membership in NATO be used to advance the transition to democracy?
4. Would membership in NATO make it easier or harder for Spain to pursue other foreign policy goals, including the improvement of ties with the Arab world and Latin and Central America?
5. Would NATO membership provide other NATO allies with new opportunities for meddling in Spanish domestic affairs?

Related questions were being asked by members of the NATO alliance at the time: How much of a contribution could Spain make to NATO in terms of geostrategic depth, an improved Mediterranean and Atlantic reach, manpower, and logistical assistance? What would Spanish accession cost the alliance in terms of intra-alliance burden sharing? What would be the costs and benefits of adding another southern member to the NATO Council of Ministers? Would NATO membership make it easier for Madrid to control its army, address its problems of internal security, and encourage the process of democratization?

Since the issues were potentially divisive in Spain, the coalition government of Leopoldo Calvo Sotelo pursued a strategy designed to limit public debate on the NATO membership question. Following discussions with the United States and other NATO governments, Calvo Sotelo announced plans for Spanish accession to the alliance in 1981 and successfully pressed for quick endorsement of his decision by the Cortes.

In an effort to win support for NATO membership, some conservative politicians in Spain sought to inject an out-of-area element into the debate by arguing that NATO affiliation would enhance the security of Ceuta and Melilla, Spain's two possessions on the North African coast. The two cities have been a periodic point of dispute between Spain and Morocco since Morocco's King Hassan raised the issue in 1963. Both sides continue to express a commitment to a peaceful solution to the issue of Ceuta and Melilla, but many commentators in Spain have warned of the risk of riots escalating into direct military confrontations if the Moroccan people become frustrated with the continued Spanish presence. Another scenario envisions Hassan increasing pressure on Spain regarding the two Spanish communities in order to divert Moroccan attention from other economic or political problems.

Since the vote on NATO membership was pushed through during the last months of the Calvo Sotelo government's term of office, the successor Socialist (PSOE) government under Felipe González Márquez claimed that Spain had been railroaded into the alliance and called for a national referendum on the issue of NATO membership. Since public opinion polls at the time were showing widespread opposition to alliance membership (only about 13 percent of the Spanish public favored Spanish participation in NATO during 1981–1983), it was easy for the Socialists to bind themselves to the outcome of a referendum.[2]

During the referendum debate, all parties in Spain agreed that the issue of defending Ceuto and Melilla was a problem of Spanish sovereignty that would not be turned over to NATO. Indeed, discussions at the time of the Spanish accession agreement made it clear that Ceuta and Melilla would not be included in the NATO Treaty area. It was nonetheless contended by the supporters of NATO membership that Spanish affiliation with the alliance would enhance the security of the two North African cities by the deterrent effect that it would have on the calculations of any potential aggressor. At the very least, it was claimed, NATO would provide Madrid with an additional institutional forum for registering complaints and soliciting diplomatic support in the event of a crisis on the North African coast.[3]

The history of the referendum debate between 1981 and 1986 is complex, and beyond the scope of this volume. It is sufficient to note that Prime Minister González gradually adjusted his personal views on NATO membership during his first three years in office and ultimately chose to support a pro-NATO vote in the referendum. This decision antagonized not only the Spanish communists but a large portion of the left wing of his own party as well.

A key component of González' strategy to gain public support for a "yes" vote on the referendum was to distinguish his government's support for NATO from support for the United States. Indeed, NATO membership was presented to the electorate as a means for Spain to move away from its former dependence on the bilateral basing relationship with the United States. This proved to be an effective strategy, in view of the widespread anti-Americanism in Spain as a result of Washington's association with the Franco regime. The actual wording of the referendum is instructive:

The government considers it appropriate for the national interest that Spain stay in the Atlantic Alliance according to the following terms:
1. Spain's participation in the Atlantic Alliance shall not include its incorporation into the military command.

2. The installation, storage or introduction of new nuclear arms in Spain will continue to be forbidden.
3. There will be a progressive reduction of U.S. military presence in Spain.
   Do you think it appropriate for Spain to remain in NATO under these conditions?[4]

The government succeeded in winning the March 1986 referendum by a vote of 52.5 percent in favor of alliance membership to 39.8 percent opposed, although the abstention rate for the referendum was over 40 percent—by far the largest abstention since Spain's return to democracy.[5] As the wording of the referendum makes clear, however, Spain's "yes" to the alliance was very conditional and grudging. Madrid does not participate in the military structure of the alliance, although Spain has retained its observer status in the Nuclear Planning Group (NPG) and participates in the Defense Planning Committee. Spain's participation in the Defense Planning Committee and its observer status in the NPG are two important differences between the Spanish and French roles in the alliance.[6]

But the question of Spain's legal status within the alliance is not as important to the topic of this book as the more general questions of what Spain expects from NATO and what it is prepared to give the alliance in return. On the issue of out-of-area cooperation, we have already mentioned that Spain did not formally request that the NATO guarantee be extended to the North African coast, nor would the NATO allies have been prepared to make such a commitment. This does not mean, however, that Madrid would not refer to its NATO affiliation, implicitly or explicitly, to discourage any threatening initiatives by King Hassan. Indeed, the Spanish citizens of Ceuto and Melilla demonstrated their faith in the deterrent value of NATO by being the two provinces of Spain that registered the highest proportion of "yes" votes in the 1986 referendum (68 percent and 74 percent, respectively).[7]

Spain's concern about Ceuta and Melilla has increased since fall 1984, when Morocco signed a mutual defense treaty with Libya. According to one Spanish defense planner, Major Fernando Ripoll, this action tipped the military balance in favor of Morocco. The most direct means of reestablishing that balance, according to Ripoll, was "transferring the problem to the Atlantic Alliance, whose Mediterranean strategy has been based on dominating the [Gibraltar] strait, which now may be compromised."[8] Hassan, meanwhile, has used Spain's decision to stay in NATO as a new lever in his own campaign to edge the Spanish out, arguing that the Soviet Union will never allow Spain, as a member of the NATO alliance, to control both sides of the strategic strait between Gibraltar and Ceuta. Thus, he asserts that when Spain finally succeeds in reacquiring sovereign control over Gibraltar from its NATO ally, Great Britain, Spain should immediately abandon its claim to the two North African enclaves.[9]

NATO would have great difficulty in staying out of any crisis that develops in the Mediterranean or North Africa which threatens Spanish control over the Balearic/Strait/Canary Axis—which one defense expert recently described as the "hinge around which the Spanish defense effort swings."[10] The axis describes an area stretching approximately fifteen hundred miles from the Atlantic coast of northwest Africa into the Western Mediterranean. Spain argues that neither the United States nor NATO will be permitted to dominate security planning for the Balearic/Strait/Canary Axis, but this area is nonetheless recognized (by the 1976 and 1983 U.S.-Spain security agreements) as a "zone of common interest" where "the activities of American and Spanish Forces are coordinated and planned by the combined organs."[11] NATO defense experts recognize the potential value of this area as a component of any strategy involving large-scale deployments of men and materiel from North America to continental Europe. In general, however, NATO planners accord greater strategic importance to the security of the Azores/Madeira/Portugal triangle off the Atlantic coast of continental Europe.

The principal questions in the minds of U.S. defense planners are how the Spanish decision to enter NATO will affect Madrid's position on the basing issue and whether Spain will be more or less willing to provide base access and overflight privileges for any future U.S. contingencies in the Middle East/gulf region. Regarding both of these concerns, U.S. policy makers are likely to find the Spanish government difficult to work with for some time to come. González expended a great deal of his political capital to convince members of the left wing of the PSOE to support his pro-NATO position in the referendum. Since that time, he has been attempting to rebuild his bridges to the left, and one of his strategies has been to reassure critics that Spanish membership in the alliance will result in a reduced U.S. presence in Spain—both militarily and politically. As one highly placed Spanish government spokesman recently observed, "Spanish public opinion does not wish to see an eventual permanent Spanish presence in the alliance which is merely a translation on the multilateral level of our bilateral defensive relationship with the U.S."[12] The PSOE has called for a reduction in U.S. manpower at the three major American facilities of Torrejon, Zaragoza, and Rota, in accordance with the wording of the 1986 referendum. The 401st Tactical Fighter Wing at Torrejon has already been ejected, and it remains to be seen if the government will be content with this significant action or treat it as a precedent for further base closings.[13] Madrid is also likely to attempt to extract clearer commitments from the United States regarding the security of the Balearic/Gibraltar/Canary Axis, as well as at least unofficial American support for Spain's claim to Gibraltar, on the grounds of improving command, control, communications, planning, and exercises in the region.

On the issue of out-of-area support, there is no reason to expect that the present government, or any likely future government, will be particularly responsive to requests from the United States or other allies. In this regard, the continuity of Spanish foreign policy from the Franco era to the present is informative:

–During the 1967 and 1973 Arab-Israeli wars, Franco refused American requests to permit U.S. aircraft to utilize Spanish bases in support of the Israeli war effort.

–In 1979, Madrid refused U.S. requests to use Spanish bases to refuel F-15s en route to Saudi Arabia.

–In 1982, literally one day after joining the NATO alliance, the UCD government under Calvo Sotelo announced its strong opposition to British policy in the Falklands. The statement was in response to an assertion by NATO secretary general Joseph Luns that "the countries of the alliance are unanimous in their support of Britain." As Spanish foreign minister José Pedro Perez Llorca put it at the time, "Spain is allied to England in the context of defending democracy, [but] it is absolutely not allied to England in the Malvinas."[14]

–During the 1986 U.S. confrontation with Libya, the PSOE government strongly criticized the U.S. actions and made it clear that it would not grant stopover or overflight rights to U.S. F-111s deployed from England against Tripoli and Bengasi.

Madrid was especially concerned about guilt by association during the 1982 Falklands War, because of its desire to establish itself as an intermediary between the Atlantic community on the one hand and the nations of Central and Latin America on the other. A dramatic step in this campaign was the González government's hosting of Fidel Castro in Spain in 1984—the Cuban leader's first visit to Western Europe. Madrid failed in its efforts to sponsor a full European tour for the Cuban leader (with proposed stops in France, Sweden, and Austria as well as Spain), but Castro's visit to Madrid was nonetheless a major diplomatic victory for the architects of Spain's new image in the Iberian world.[15]

The PSOE is also anxious to develop a more active and constructive foreign policy in the Maghreb and the Middle East. In doing so, however, it has confronted the same problems of balancing Mediterranean and Atlantic commitments as have Turkey, Italy, and Greece. Madrid has found it especially hard to manage these conflicting demands over the issue of state-sponsored terrorism. Spain joined Greece in opposing efforts by the foreign ministers of the European Community in 1986 to condemn Libya and Syria for supporting terrorism. The Assembly of the West European Union was uncharacteristically blunt in its criticism of Greece and Spain in this regard, as well as in its criticism of the European Community's value as an institution for the coordination of foreign and security policies.[16]

The West is likely to see more such *gestes* by Spain in the near future, as

Madrid continues to develop its post-Franco identity in the Mediterranean region and in the broader international system. Spain has made conditional participation in NATO an important—but certainly not the most important—element in that identity.

PORTUGAL

Portugal is unique among the European NATO allies in terms of the priority that it has traditionally accorded to security issues outside of the NATO Treaty area. Geography, economics, and history provide the explanation. Portugal is one of the smallest NATO allies in terms of territory and population. It is also the second poorest ally in terms of per capita GDP.[17] In spite of these limitations, Portugal was the last European NATO ally to abandon its commitment to empire. Indeed, the preservation of its colonial possessions in Africa was the overriding preoccupation—the obsession—of Portuguese foreign policy for nearly three decades after World War II.

Since extricating itself from the colonial obsession in the mid-1970s, Portugal has been attempting to establish a more balanced foreign policy while enhancing its status and influence in the Atlantic community. Ironically, however, Lisbon has had to rely heavily upon the vestiges of its imperial past—its ties to selected African governments and, in particular, its island possessions in the Atlantic—to provide Portugal with negotiating leverage in its dealings with NATO in general and the United States in particular.

As discussed in Part 1, the United States was clear about the importance that it accorded to Portuguese participation in the NATO alliance during the 1948–49 Washington Preparatory Talks. The U.S. delegation believed that Lisbon's control of the Azores made it an essential component of any defense arrangement that might require the transatlantic resupply of continental Europe in time of crisis. Under these circumstances, the United States opted for *realpolitik,* sweetened with a bit of hypocrisy and self-delusion, to justify its support for including the Salazar regime in an alliance committed to the preservation of democratic principles. Thus, Salazar was, according to Dean Acheson, "not a dictator in his own right as Stalin was, but a dictator-manager employed and maintained by the power of the army."[18] Somehow, this distinction was interpreted by Acheson as making cooperation with Lisbon more palatable.

For his part, Salazar was not inclined to make the Americans' job of managing the membership issue any easier. This was because he realized that Washington was the *demandeur* in this particular negotiation, and that there was consequently no need for Lisbon to bargain directly with other European governments on behalf of its desired goal of NATO membership. Salazar thus took a hard line in his discussions with various governmental representatives on the issue of NATO membership. The guiding premises of Salazar's hard line were, first, that the commitment to democratic principles—what Salazar described to the Portuguese Parliament as the "unfortunate definition of an ideology"—in the Preamble to the NATO Treaty would not be used as a device for meddling in Portuguese domestic politics. Second, the NATO forum would not be used as a platform for lecturing Lisbon on its policies toward its colonial possessions in Africa and Asia. Finally, NATO membership would not represent an extra financial burden for Lisbon. Rather, the alliance would be utilized by Portugal to obtain military assistance funds from the United States—the expenditure of which would be under the sovereign authority of the Portuguese government.[19] Since Britain shared America's interest in bringing Portugal into the alliance—London and Lisbon had been traditional allies since 1373—the issue of Portuguese membership proved manageable within the context of the Washington talks.

In return for U.S. support for Portuguese membership in NATO (and for Washington's grudging and unofficial acceptance of the above-mentioned Portuguese conditions), Salazar was prepared to provide Washington with relatively unrestricted base access in the Azores, in accordance with the terms of the U.S.-Portugal Defense Agreement of 1951.

The Portuguese bases did serve the interests of the United States and other NATO allies on a number of occasions during the ensuing three decades. For example:

−During the 1958 American intervention in Lebanon, the Lajes facility served as an important refueling point for U.S. aircraft.
−During the 1961 Congo Crisis, Washington routed its transport aircraft through the Azores, in a situation that was made especially difficult by the refusal of overflight privileges by France and its Francophone African allies.[20]
−During the 1973 Arab-Israeli War, the United States obtained "unconditional transit rights" at the Lajes base to resupply the Israeli war effort. Kissinger advises us, however, that in this case it was necessary to exert some pressure, in the form of threatening to cut off arms to the Caetano government in Lisbon and to "leave Portugal to its fate in a hostile world" in order to obtain access to the Lajes facility.[21]
−During the second Shaba crisis of 1978, Portugal provided access to its base in Porto Santo in the Madeira archipelago as a refueling point for Belgian aircraft.

Salazar had initially hoped that he could trade base access for active NATO support for his colonial policies. There is little doubt that he personally believed that colonialism was essential to the recovery of European influence in the postwar era. As he explained in a public address in May 1944, "Europe is irremediably dividing itself and impoverished, losing positions and weakening by the sole fact of the war. The problem now is that it must not continue carelessly wasting the conditions within its grasp for the sake of western life.

Fortunately, the whole of Africa is a Western European dependence, the two making, face to American and from pole to pole, the material basis for the role it ought to continue playing in the world."[22] As the cold war developed, however, Salazar tended to shift his emphasis from the theme of the enduring European *mission civilisatrice* to the theme of the *guerre révolutionnaire,* stressing the contribution that Portugal was making to world order and anticommunist containment by its continued presence in Africa. He also lowered his expectations regarding NATO, abandoning hope for active allied support and settling for noninterference.

The Truman and Eisenhower administrations were for the most part quietly sympathetic to Salazar's arguments and grateful for the fact that Portugal was neither a very obstreperous nor a very expensive ally at the time.[23] Salazar had been relatively successful in managing the postwar economic recovery of Portugal, and the African and Asian colonies did not as yet represent a massive drain on Portuguese manpower or U.S. military assistance funds.[24] Washington therefore encouraged other allies not to make too much of either the domestic politics of Portugal or Lisbon's colonialist policies during the first fifteen years of the postwar era.

One of JFK's principal advisers, George Ball, described the foreign policy approaches of Truman and Eisenhower as based upon "the assumption that the United States . . . was a status quo power. . . . If stability could be assured for a reasonable period through colonial structures, such as Portugal's, there was no reason for America to rock the boat." The Kennedy administration, according to Ball, "frontally challenged this approach."[25]

The Kennedy administration attempted to reverse the hands-off U.S. policy toward Portugal during its first months in office, in accordance with JFK's campaign commitment to "get things moving" in America's relations with the Third World. But Salazar proved to be a far tougher opponent than Kennedy had envisioned. When the first large-scale rioting began to occur in Angola in early 1961—at precisely the same time that Kennedy and the "Africanist" faction within his administration began publicly to criticize Lisbon in the UN— Salazar responded quickly and forcefully. Within three years, the size of the Portuguese military presence in Africa grew from "a few thousand garrison troops and police" to 125,000 men.[26] Salazar's diplomatic offensive against Washington was no less impressive. Within NATO, Salazar worked to convince other European colonial governments that Kennedy was using Portugal as a stalking horse for a major campaign of criticism and interference against each of them. Belgium proved to be especially sensitive to this argument after the "Stevenson plan" for the management of Congolese independence was presented by the United States in the UN in February of 1961.

At the same time that Salazar was acquiring allies of convenience within NATO he was also increasing the pressure on Washington directly, through his traditional "Europeanist" supporters within the State Department and the U.S.

Joint Chiefs of Staff. The most effective pressure point was, of course, the Azores basing agreement, which was due to expire at the end of 1962. By this time, fully 80 percent of U.S. air transport traffic to continental Europe was being funneled through the Azores. This fact was driven home to the new president by members of the JCS in the context of growing East-West tension over Berlin and the adminstration's expressed goal of enhancing the conventional response capability of the alliance.[27] From the Joint Chiefs' point of view, there was no alternative to the Azores, at least in the short term.

By the end of the year, Salazar's campaign had succeeded. Washington backed away from its criticisms of Lisbon for its colonialist policies, in exchange for what John Kenneth Galbraith bitterly described as "a few acres of asphalt in the Atlantic."[28] Kennedy abandoned his initial policy of restricting military assistance and commercial sales to Portugal, and the United States subsequently backed a $69 million Export-Import Bank loan to Lisbon. He nonetheless held firm in his embargo against the use of U.S. arms and materiel in Portuguese Africa. In the wake of the confrontation, the Lajes base remained under U.S. control, but Salazar refused to continue the policy of negotiating five-year access agreements and demanded instead that the agreements be renegotiated yearly—with each side being entitled to abrogate the treaty with six months' notice.[29] The Kennedy administration had, in the words of S. J. Bosgra and C. van Krimpen, "re-joined the NATO club."[30]

During the next decade, U.S. policy makers either avoided the issue of Portuguese colonialism (under Johnson) or quietly supported the Portuguese war effort within the NATO forum (under Nixon). It was the Nixon administration that succeeded in returning to the earlier five-year basing arrangement in 1971 by providing a $436 million "package deal" to Lisbon.[31] Nixon nonetheless continued the embargo, which had been in effect since 1961 against the use of U.S. arms and military equipment in the Portuguese colonial wars.

In spite of the more positive attitude of the Nixon administration toward Portuguese colonialism, Lisbon was finding it increasingly harder to deal with other NATO allies by the early 1970s. Several members of the NATO club—in particular, the Scandinavian countries—were beginning to argue that the diplomatic costs of "guilt by association" with the Salazar regime were simply not worth the benefits that Portugal provided to the alliance. In fact, from the military perspective, Lisbon's negotiating leverage within NATO had declined somewhat by the end of the 1960s, since improvements in U.S. airlift capability and changes in NATO doctrine (prepositioning, etc.) had resulted in a considerable reduction in NATO's reliance on the Azores facility (from 80 percent of all military flights between the United States and continental Europe in 1962 to about 20 percent by 1968).[32]

Under these circumstances, we are led to inquire why the Nixon administration was inclined to increase U.S. support for Portugal in spite of its reduced importance for NATO. The answer may be that the Nixon-Kissinger team was guided by an expectation that over the long term the action would be shifting to Africa and the Middle East in a post-Vietnam world, and that this reorientation of U.S. strategic thinking would mean a new importance for the Azores. Whether or not this long-term geostrategic calculation was guiding Nixon and Kissinger's policies, the United States was prepared to resist pressure against Portugal within the NATO councils in the beginning of the 1970s.

But the issue never came to a head within NATO. Domestic instability within Portugal—precipitated in large part by the fact that nearly 40 percent of the Portuguese budget was being spent in the African campaigns by the 1970s—culminated in the "Revolution of the Carnations" in April 1974 and the subsequent collapse of the Portuguese colonial empire. For the time being, NATO was spared another out-of-area crisis.

After a turbulent transitional period, Portuguese domestic politics settled down enough to permit policy makers and defense experts in Lisbon to begin to lay the groundwork for a postimperial defense policy. But the colonial wars had been going on for so long that a fundamental restructuring of Portugal's defense establishment was required. The armed forces, trained and equipped for jungle warfare and riot control in Africa, had to be fit into a new role in NATO. A first obvious and essential step was a radical reduction in the size of the military from 280,000 at the end of the colonial wars to 80,000 by 1979 (in accordance with NATO force requirements).[33] New equipment was financed through direct aid from Washington and Bonn, while the World Bank, the IMF, and the EC contributed to the stabilization and resuscitation of the post—revolutionary economy in Portugal.[34]

The streamlining and reorientation of the Portuguese military took place against the backdrop of an internal debate about Lisbon's status within Europe and the Atlantic community in the early 1980s. A special concern of Lisbon was that post-Franco Spain was positioning itself to dominate post-Salazar Portugal in both of these areas—fulfilling Salazar's warning that "Portugal without the Empire will become a colony of Spain."[35] Thus, Lisbon watched closely as Spain negotiated its position in the alliance, alert for any deals between NATO and Madrid which would result in the creation of an Iberian military command under Spanish control. U.S. sensitivity to Portugal's concern is reflected in the fact that former U.S. secretary of state Alexander Haig made a point of detouring through Lisbon in January of 1982 after attending a CSCE follow-on conference in Madrid, in order to reassure Portuguese leaders that they had not been sold out by Washington during the secretary's visit.[36] Since that time, both Spain and Portugal have made it clear on numerous occasions that neither country will permit their armed forces to be under the control of the other's military—particularly in those areas (such as the Canaries for Spain and the Madeira and Azores archipelagos for Portugal) that are considered to be of special geostrategic importance by either side.[37]

Ironically, Lisbon will have to continue to stress out-of-area issues, even in a postimperial era, as a means of enhancing Portugese leverage within the alliance. Specifically, Portugal will continue to encourage Washington to view it, not as a small and poor ally on the periphery of Europe, but as a geostrategically important ally located in a central position between Africa, the Middle East, and Europe. Yet this Portuguese policy is constrained by a desire to avoid being viewed by others—in particular in the Middle East—as merely an American *point d'appui*.

Portugal is also actively pursuing closer relations with its former colonies in southern Africa. In the case of Angola, Portugal is providing nonmilitary assistance only, in consideration of Washington's support for the antigovernment forces in that country. As one Portuguese official put it, it would be awkward for "two NATO allies to militarily support two different sides there." [38] But the United States can expect no help, and some active opposition, from Lisbon, if it chooses to become more directly involved in the Angolan situation.

Lisbon has reiterated on numerous occasions that its basing arrangements with the United States do not provide prior authorization for use in out-of-NATO contingencies. The United States and Portugal renewed the Lajes basing agreement at the end of 1983. To obtain the new agreement, which will be in effect for seven years, the United States approved a package of financial aid agreements for Portugal totaling $145 million per year.[39] But the United States was not able to obtain any public assurance that the Azores base will be available during future out-of-area crises. For its part, Lisbon assured various Arab representatives that it will not permit its territory to be used by the United States in any replay of the 1973 Arab-Israeli confrontation. Former Portuguese foreign minister Jaime Gama went out of his way to reassure concerned Arab governments during a visit to Iraq one month after the Azores deal was completed, stating, "Portugal will never be used against the Arab countries."[40]

The same restrictions apply to Portuguese facilities in the Madeira archipelago (the southwestern limit of the NATO Treaty area), which have been undergoing modernization. The military base at Porto Santo in the Madeiras has received extensive improvements, including construction of a deep-water jetty and expansion of the airstrip so that it can accommodate the largest military transport aircraft. Inevitably, some Western press accounts compared these improvements to the U.S. program to develop the facilities in Diego Garcia. The comparison is misleading, however, since Washington cannot assume that either the Azores or the Madeira facilities will be accessible in the event of a crisis beyond the NATO Treaty area.[41] Indeed, Western defense planners remember that during the turbulent postrevolutionary period in Portugal, when the Portuguese Communist party exercised a strong influence within the provisional government, Lisbon permitted Cuban troop transports to stop at the Santa Maria air base in the Azores on their way to Angola.[42]

But where does this leave Portugal? There is a real possibility that Lisbon is painting itself into a corner by its attempt to stress the geostrategic importance of its Atlantic islands in negotiations with Washington while at the same time reassuring Arab and African governments that it will not permit itself to be used as a staging area for USCENTCOM operations. Sooner or later, Lisbon's bluff will be called. The current chief of staff of the Portuguese armed forces has argued that "in spite of its small physical dimensions, Portugal cannot . . . accommodate itself to a situation that could be defined as similar to that of Iceland."[43] This is certainly true—particularly in view of Portugal's historical experience and its fear of domination by Spain. The question is how to avoid it, with the limited assets that it has available.

CONCLUSION TO PART IV

Part 4 has provided a brief survey of the security interests and concerns of NATO allies in the Northern, Central, and Southern European regions. In some cases, we have attempted to relate these interests and concerns to the positions taken by these allies on out-of-area issues. In other cases, we have attempted to explain the role played by out-of-area disputes themselves in shaping the overall defense postures of these NATO allies. In every case, we have attempted to speculate on the general position that each of these NATO allies is likely to take in response to out-of-area problems in the medium-term future.

A common thread throughout Part 4 is the theme of European concern about guilt by association with recent Third World initiatives by the alliance leader. The concern is reflected in the attempts by all of the allies to distinguish themselves from the United States in one way or another—through Scandinavian efforts to preserve a policy of simultaneously deterring and reassuring the Soviet Union, through the increased Central European interest in an almost exclusively European defense orientation, and through the separate "Mediterranean vocations" of the Southern European allies.

The relative decline of U.S. power in the international system has both permitted and encouraged these European allies to establish their own economic and political ties with the East bloc and in the Third World. These new linkages are the most visible and vulnerable stakes that the European allies have in North-South and East-West cooperation. As a consequence, allied interest in supporting U.S. foreign policy beyond the NATO Treaty area has been relativized in the calculations of European governments as they develop more multifaceted and independent foreign policies.

CONCLUSION

In the midst of all of the changes in the international system over the last four decades, NATO has endured. The Atlantic Alliance has outlasted SEATO, CENTO, the Baghdad Pact, and ANZUS.[1] The question, of course, is why? What are the characteristics of the NATO Treaty which have made it so much more resilient than these other cold war experiments in multilateral defense cooperation?

We believe that the most important reason for NATO's persistence is the clarity and specificity of the perceived threat from the Soviet Union. Thirty years of revisionist writing about NATO have not impugned the fact that the alliance was built upon a strong Atlantic consensus on the need for a deterrent to Soviet aggressive intentions. This was the point of NATO secretary general Spaak's observation that Joseph Stalin was the "true father" of the alliance. The debates within SEATO, CENTO, the Baghdad Pact, and ANZUS simply do not reflect the same unifying consensus about the nature and degree of the Soviet threat. Too many other issues—regional power struggles; ethnic, political, and economic disputes; nationalism; nonalignment; and antinuclearism— intervened to undermine the initial consensus about the anti-Soviet purpose of these alliances.

In our Introduction, we noted Glenn Snyder's distinction between *general* security interests (the structurally determined security concerns that encourage nations to enter into alliance) and *particular* interests (the distinct national concerns that each signatory government brings to an alliance).[2] Snyder actually chose the NATO alliance to illustrate the binding force of an overriding and commonly agreed-upon general interest in the face of competing particular interests. Most of the other Western alliances cited above (ANZUS being the exception) were never as tightly integrated into the East-West bipolar framework, and consequently they never exhibited the degree of unifying general interest that characterized the Atlantic Alliance. In the absence of such a powerful common interest, these extra-European alliances either collapsed under the weight of competing particular concerns or died of neglect.

If we apply Snyder's arguments to our study of the history of NATO out-of-area disputes, we can conclude that the NATO allies have been guided by a

313

clear sense of priorities. They have not permitted their disagreements over particular out-of-area interests to jeopardize their commonly held interest in preserving a strong deterrent to Soviet aggression against Western Europe. Farther on, we will relate this general finding to developments in the 1980s.

Article 6 of the NATO Treaty, which established the geographic boundaries of the alliance, helped NATO governments to develop and maintain consensus about the threat posed by Moscow. It is a tribute to the foresight of such men as Robert Lovett, Charles Bohlen, and Dean Acheson that they argued for a limited alliance membership and a clearly delimited treaty area during the discussions that led up to the creation of NATO. Geographic delimitation encouraged all members to focus their attention on the Soviet/Warsaw Pact threat to the central front, thereby simplifying the public debate about security and making it possible for NATO to evolve into a "social institution" (George Liska's term) based on a shared democratic and anti-Soviet ideology.[3]

Geographic delimitation also helped NATO to skirt potentially divisive disputes over developments in the Third World. If the founding members of the alliance had opted for some variant of George Kennan's "three circles" concept of global security cooperation rather than the region-specific arrangement approved in 1949, it is unlikely that the alliance would be around in any form today. This is because a more ambitious, globalist alliance would probably have torn itself apart over events in the Third World. Nor would a less regionally focused alliance have been as successful at developing and maintaining the aforementioned consensus about the core issue—the threat posed by the Soviet Union.

As we have seen, even the precise wording of Article 6 could not completely insulate the alliance from events occurring beyond the treaty area. But the fact that the borders of NATO are explicitly defined by the treaty has served in two ways to defuse or ameliorate many out-of-area disputes over the last forty years. First, Article 6 has provided various allies with precisely that "legalistic argument" which so infuriated Kissinger when he sought the support of NATO for U.S. resupply efforts during the 1973 Arab-Israeli War. On numerous occasions since 1949, these "legalisms" have performed the function of a circuit breaker—permitting allies to terminate discussion of divisive out-of-area issues before they reached the point of destroying NATO from within. John F. Kennedy's efforts to use the NATO forum to raise the issues of Portuguese and Belgian colonialism were rebuffed in this way. So were the solicitations of support by France and then the United States in Vietnam.

The second way in which the geographic boundaries of the alliance have served the interests of alliance cohesion is as a point of reference for assessing what is, and what is not, a reasonable issue for discussion within the NATO forum. Frequently this has been enough to convince allies not to bother to bring an out-of-area issue to the attention of the alliance. British policy (as illustrated in Brunei, Aden, etc.) has tended to be guided by this rule. In those cases in which an out-of-area dispute has surfaced within the alliance (Malaysia, Irian Jaya), Article 6 has encouraged governments not to invest too much energy or credit in an issue that was, by definition, beyond the clearly established purview of the alliance.

Geographic delimitation of the alliance was particularly beneficial during the first twenty years of NATO—the era of European decolonization. During this period, most NATO out-of-area disputes were of two types: European solicitations of support from the United States in order to maintain control over residual colonial possessions, and European complaints about American meddling in Third World *domaines réservés*. For its part, Washington was generally concerned about guilt by association with the colonial policies of its allies and suspicious of their ability to manage the challenges of the Third World. On a few occasions during this period, European colonial powers were moderately successful at convincing U.S. policy makers that a particular Third World issue was, in fact, an issue of containing communism. France, the indirect beneficiary of the Korean War and the Red Scare in the United States, was able to use this strategy to obtain conditional NATO support in Indochina from 1950 to 1954. In general, however, if American policy makers felt that a certain Third World country was especially vulnerable to communist or communist cum nationalist pressures during this period, they would question the wisdom of trusting European allies to cope with the complexities of the situation. This logic would lead to a subtle, or sometimes not too subtle, American campaign to supplant the European ally.

The disputes over guilt by association and *domaine réservé* which characterized the first twenty years of NATO's history would probably have been uncontrollable if NATO had been a more globalist alliance in which Third World events were understood to be legitimate issues for common response. Even with Article 6 as a guide, alliance rhetoric, which stressed the themes of "common security interests" and shared values, misled NATO members from time to time, by encouraging unrealistic expectations of out-of-area support. British and French policy makers certainly exhibited this type of wishful thinking during the discussions that led up to the 1956 Suez crisis. In the wake of Suez, however, all parties developed a healthy cynicism regarding the prospects for out-of-area cooperation, which on balance served NATO's interests well during the rest of this twenty-year period.

By the end of the 1960s, the situation was reversed. Washington had become the *demandeur* within NATO, soliciting allied support for out-of-area responsibilities and pressing the case for de jure or de facto extension of the treaty area. The frequent refrains of the European colonialists in the 1950s—the *guerre révolutionnaire* argument, the claims that Atlantic and global security were indivisible, the warnings about the vulnerability of Western resource lifelines to Soviet bloc disruption—had become the favorite themes of American defense analysts. By this time, however, European retrenchment from abroad was almost complete, and Washington's allies had resigned themselves to concentrating their energies at home. Consequently, the European NATO members began to rebuff Washington's solicitations of support and to express a new concern about the risks of guilt by association with American interventionism in the Third World.

If we are correct in our general assessment of the value of Article 6 of the NATO Treaty, then the direction that the NATO out-of-area debate took during the period from the late 1960s to the mid-1980s was seriously misguided. During this period, a growing number of policy makers and defense experts came to accept as a given that Article 6 of the treaty had to be abandoned. This trend developed largely at the urging of the United States, in response to a number of out-of-area challenges, including the 1973 Arab-Israeli War, the Arab oil boycott, the "loss" of Iran to Islamic fundamentalism, the Soviet intervention in Afghanistan, and the increase in the incidence and severity of international terrorism. American pressure succeeded in eliciting modest statements of sympathy and support from the NATO Council of Ministers, but these statements fell far short of what Washington sought. During its second term, the Reagan administration moderated its public demands for a new out-of-area role for the alliance. But another crisis beyond the established treaty area could lead to a new round of proposals for revision or abandonment of Article 6.

We believe that this would be a mistake. Our survey of the history of NATO out-of-area disputes convinces us of the fundamental wisdom of keeping NATO as a regionally focused alliance. Blurring the boundaries of the NATO Treaty will only encourage the kind of unrealistic expectations which preceded the Suez crisis more than thirty years ago. It will also run counter to the principles accepted by all signatory governments at the time that the alliance was established, which distinguish the right of regional collective defense without prior UN authorization (under Article 51 of the UN Charter) from the need for Security Council approval for any extraregional "enforcement actions" by the participants in a regional defense pact.

Those who recommend revising or renegoting the NATO Treaty in order to make the alliance more elastic must also explain how they would manage the problem of legitimizing this transformed alliance for the Western European and North American publics. A more elastic NATO would be a less ideologically coherent NATO—more like a SEATO or CENTO, and just as vaporous.

DEFINITION OF THREAT: NATO's CHALLENGE FOR THE 1990s

Just as geographic delimitation helped NATO governments to finesse guilt by association and *domaine réservé* disagreements during the 1950s, it is likely to prove invaluable in helping NATO governments to manage burden sharing, guilt by association, and, in particular, definition of threat disputes in the

1990s. We see these kinds of out-of-area disagreements as the wave of the future for the alliance, and we assume, based on our survey of the historical record, that NATO members will continue to utilize Article 6 as a convenient instrument for skirting destructive confrontations over these issues.

The growth of definition of threat disputes during the last decade deserves special mention in our Conclusion, since these disputes go to the core of the alliance's rationale for existence. We have already observed that NATO was formed around a commonly held perception of Soviet aggressive intentions. But intra-alliance disputes during the last decade (over Afghanistan, the Yamal pipeline, events in Poland) reflect growing disagreement between and within key allied governments regarding the nature and degree of the threat posed by Moscow. Thus, it is ironic but altogether understandable that Soviet misbehavior (such as the Afghanistan intervention of 1979) and Soviet good behavior (such as the removal of Soviet forces from Afghanistan in 1988–89) had the same effect on the alliance. Both types of actions precipitated intra-alliance disagreements about what the Soviets were doing, why the Soviets were doing it, and how the West should respond.

We should not be surprised to find that questions about the nature and degree of the threat posed by the USSR have become an increasingly important part of the alliance out-of-area debate after forty years. In fact, the problems of alliance self-definition and self-justification have been evident since 1967, when NATO issued the Harmel Report, which formally designated the pursuit of détente as an essential alliance responsibility. NATO is a victim of its own success. The fact that there has been no direct military challenge to NATO by the Soviet Union or the Warsaw Pact for forty years is the principal reason for the ongoing, and growing, debate about the threat posed by the USSR. We expect this trend to continue. Indeed, the Soviet leadership in the late 1980s made it clear that it intends to make East-West détente politics a cornerstone of its foreign policy. And NATO Secretary General Manfred Wörner has recently asserted his continued "faith in the Harmel Doctrine" as one of the most important elements of the NATO commitment.[4] Under these circumstances, it is not inconceivable that the alliance could break up over some future out-of-area issue that precipitates a snowballing internal disagreement about the threat posed by the Soviet Union or the meaning and importance of détente.

PROSPECTS FOR OUT-OF-AREA COOPERATION
IN THE 1990s

One recent development that we have identified provides reason to be somewhat optimistic about the prospects for out-of-area cooperation. We refer to the fact that since 1985, transatlantic discussions about out-of-area issues have been more moderate, pragmatic, and productive than in the past. Washington has been gratified by the more assertive positions taken by most European

NATO allies regarding state-sponsored terrorism and by the collaboration of seven European governments in support of the Persian Gulf task force. For their part, Washington's allies have appreciated the change in tone of the Reagan and Bush administrations since about 1984. The United States still presses its case for shifting more of the NATO defense burden to the allies, and it continues to seek at least diplomatic backing for its out-of-area initiatives in the name of alliance solidarity. But the haranguing and the public condemnations have effectively stopped.

Recent studies relating to the theory of collective goods may give us some guidance about why we are seeing greater transatlantic accommodation on out-of-area issues at present, and why this may be the beginning of a trend. According to Mancur Olson and Richard Zeckhauser's classic formulation of the theory of collective action, a nation's particular out-of-area interests represent private goods, and out-of-area cooperation takes the form of a side payment by one ally to another (unless the allies have parallel or complementary interests in the out-of-area issue—as was the case in Indochina when America chose to provide conditional support for France).[5] In a situation of "pure" collective goods in which there are identifiable suppliers and consumers of the common good, it should be in no ally's interest voluntarily to assist another ally beyond the established treaty area. From the provider's point of view, such a side payment is unnecessary, since it does not have to give the other allies anything more to convince them to accept the collective good. Likewise from the point of view of the consumer, support for another ally's out-of-area interest would be gratuitous, since the alliance already provides the consumer with the good for which the alliance was established, and this good can be neither increased nor reduced as a result of actions taken beyond the treaty area. This was arguably the situation within NATO at the time when the United States was the provider of a pure collective good in the form of a reliable extended nuclear deterrent guarantee.[6]

Since the mid-1960's, however, NATO has been moving away from this situation of pure extended deterrence and toward a mixed situation of defense and deterrence as enshrined in the doctrine of flexible response. As NATO has moved closer to the defense pole, the pure theory of collective goods has become increasingly less relevant to the realities of intra-alliance bargaining. The dichotomy between public and private goods has diminished, and the possibilities for "free riding" have declined. Furthermore, as NATO has moved from a posture of pure deterrence to a defense/deterrence mix, the specific size and type of defense contribution that the United States makes to the European theater is much more significant than in the past. Washington's allies must now consider the possibility that the former provider of the common good may be unable or unwilling to make this defense contribution in the future. Under these circumstances, out-of-area cooperation that previously took the form of a gratuitous and unrewarded side payment may now take the form of a *barter item—*

given to the alliance leader in exchange for some increment of help in shoring up the common good for which the alliance was created.[7] And in a situation in which Washington's allies still accord a high priority to the preservation of the NATO alliance, conditional accommodation on a particular out-of-area issue is a way for some European governments to respond to American demands for greater burden sharing while skirting the more difficult issues of defense budget increases or manpower contributions.

The case of allied support for U.S. policy in the Persian Gulf is illustrative. Charles Kupchan and Janice Gross Stein have each written an excellent study of the intra-alliance negotiations that led to the European decision to provide at least conditional support for U.S. policy in the gulf. Both authors conclude that the allies did so not because they agreed with the U.S. policy per se but because, as Kupchan puts it, "if the Europeans did not show at least some support for America's efforts outside the area, then the strength of America's military commitment to Europe could well be diminished." Kupchan also notes that many Europeans feared that the United States "might move toward an isolationist posture" if it felt itself overextended and unsupported.[8]

The literature relating to hegemonic decline and regime maintenance offers a slightly different explanation for increased out-of-area cooperation in the late 1980s. In his influential book *After Hegemony,* Robert Keohane argues that the recognition of a common problem that can no longer be resolved by a dominant hegemonic actor can encourage constructive action by junior members of a community: "The prospect of discord creates incentives for cooperation."[9] Duncan Snidal has developed these arguments further, by recourse to formal models. Snidal has observed that "secondary powers will be willing to participate in collective action provided that they have incentives to avoid the collapse of the regime. . . . This changed strategic situation may even lead to higher levels of cooperation."[10] Viewed from this perspective, modest European accommodation of U.S. requests for out-of-area burden sharing represents cooperation on the margin (literally) as a small adjustment to the problems posed by the relative decline of U.S. power.

It is worth noting that Washington undertook policies during the 1980s which were specifically designed to discourage speculation about America's decline. Under the Reagan administration, the United States made a concerted effort to engage in the politics of nostalgia, by seeking to convince itself and its allies that it was capable of resuscitating the U.S.-sponsored global containment network of the 1950s.[11] If we are correct that key European allies have begun to demonstrate greater sensitivity to the risks involved in encouraging U.S. unilateralism over out-of-area issues, the reason may be that these allies began to recognize that the politics of nostalgia could not be preserved for long, and that American efforts to preserve it were detrimental to the entire Western community.

The exchange/barter explanation for out-of-area cooperation tends to focus on transatlantic struggle, while the regime maintenance explanation presents a more positive picture of U.S.-European relations. But both theories point to increased American leverage in intra-alliance relations, in matters of out-of-area cooperation, and in the more general issue of burden sharing.

There is a caveat, however. The reader will note that two of the trends mentioned above are at least potentially in conflict. On the one hand, we have identified a tendency toward intra-NATO disagreements over the nature of the threat posed by the Soviet Union and have predicted that this tendency is likely to continue. On the other hand, we have observed that transatlantic discussions about out-of-area issues have been characterized by moderation and greater mutual accommodation since the mid-1980s, and we have attributed this latter development to a new sensitivity among leading Western European governments to the implications of declining U.S. hegemony. But the willingness of Western European governments to carry the political and economic costs involved in a new campaign of transatlantic security cooperation will be contingent upon the extent to which these governments continue to share America's view that the Soviet Union represents the paramount threat to their survival. During the late 1980s, Soviet leader Mikhail Gorbachev began a impressive and very successful campaign to convince Western European publics that the threat had disappeared and that continued spending on NATO defense would be unnecessary and counterproductive.

Washington will have a great deal of control over the evolution of this situation in the 1990s. The way in which the United States manages its relations with the USSR during the next few years will be crucial. The United States will have to offer its allies in Europe more than Dulles-style containment arguments if the Soviet Union continues its "peace offensive" in the West. Washington will also have to manage its out-of-area initiatives and its decisions about defense budget reductions in ways that do not drive wedges between the United States and the rest of NATO.

We are also convinced that the United States should encourage the trend toward greater European responsibility in defense affairs which began to develop quietly and incrementally during the 1980s. Some extremely positive developments in this regard include the creation of a Franco-German Brigade, the adjustment of French strategy to link the security of West Germany explicitly to the security of France, and the growth in prestige and influence of the Western European Union (WEU). It is in the interest of all NATO governments, including the alliance leader, to move this process in the direction of a European "second pillar," for the sake of European security and for the protection of the West's common security interests within and beyond the Continent. It is difficult to predict the effect that the upcoming integration of the internal market of the European Communities in 1992 will have on the debate about European defense cooperation. On the one hand, it could encourage further defense efforts by contributing to a mood of regional self-reliance and responsibility among European publics. Alternatively, EC integration could resuscitate the chimera of a "civilian-power Europe," which diverted European governments from considerations of their military needs and responsibilities and exacerbated transatlantic tensions during the 1970s. It is in the interest of all allies for the United States to help steer this debate in the direction of the former possibility.

We also appreciate the kinds of pressures which led the United States to encourage NATO allies to accept a broader interpretation of alliance boundaries during the late 1970s and early 1980s. For it is certainly true (as Washington has stressed) that some developments beyond the treaty area have security implications for all of the nations of the Atlantic community. Consequently, we support the loose, informal, and voluntary arrangements that were worked out within NATO during the late 1980s for dealing with out-of-area challenges. These boil down to a three-step procedure for responding to an out-of-area crisis:

1. *Analysis* within the NATO alliance. The NATO Political Directorate facilitates such analysis by hosting twice-yearly meetings of defense experts whose discussions span the globe to identify likely security threats and consider their possible implications for NATO.

2. *Consultation* among concerned allies within the NATO institutional framework. Such consultations have generally been between two or three allies. On occasion, however, the alliance has provided the institutional umbrella for multilateral consultations involving most of the NATO governments (for example, discussions relating to Persian Gulf security).

3. *Compensation* as a "solidarity obligation" in the event that a NATO member feels compelled to reduce temporarily its NATO manpower or equipment contribution in response to an out-of-area crisis. Allied assistance to Britain during the Falklands crisis is the best example of this arrangement.[12]

To the extent that these in-house arrangements can be kept informal and voluntary, they serve a very useful purpose. Indeed, we believe that NATO could go a step farther and establish a separate directorate within its International Staff with responsibility for analyzing ongoing extraregional developments from a NATO perspective. Studies done by this directorate would be provided to the secretary general and, through him, to member governments. The directorate would look at out-of-area issues from the point of view of NATO's institutional history and would comment upon political, security, and legal aspects of extraregional developments. Legal advice on out-of-area issues is likely to become especially important in the future, as changes in technology and disputes over freedom of the seas make it more difficult to delineate NATO boundaries clearly (see in particular Chapter 19).

A new NATO directorate for out-of-area issues would be a useful bureaucratic initiative. But it should not (and need not) be a further step in the direction of abandoning Article 6 of the treaty. Indeed, we would expect that over time the new directorate would come to serve as an institutional memory, and that in this capacity it would represent a further check on the tendency to elevate particular out-of-area challenges to the status of alliance-wide crises.

Such bureaucratic arrangements will not satisfy the demands of those scholars and policy makers who see a regionally restricted NATO as an anachronism. These individuals will continue to argue that more is needed in order to defend common Western interests throughout the world. But this argument was also pressed in 1949, when various Western leaders questioned the logic of a NATO that was to be "merely Atlantic." It was in the mind of George Kennan, for example, when he dabbled with the aforementioned idea of three circles of alliance membership. But Kennan ultimately realized the fundamental flaws in his own proposal, and he backed away from it. His reasons for abandoning the globalist approach are as valid today as they were then: "The only sound standard for membership . . . was indeed the geographic one; this was the only one that was without ambiguity and could clearly be shown to have only defensive connotations."[13]

NOTES

INTRODUCTION

1. See, for example, Marc Bentinck, *NATO's Out-of-Area Problem,* Adelphi Papers, no. 211 (London: International Institute for Strategic Studies, Autumn 1986); Peter Foot, *Beyond the North Atlantic: The European Contribution,* Aberdeen Studies in Defense Economics, no. 21 (Aberdeen University, 1982); Karl Kaiser et al., *Western Security: What Has Changed? What Should Be Done?* (New York: Council on Foreign Relations, 1981); Charles Kupchan, *The Persian Gulf and the West* (Boston: Allen and Unwin, 1987); Elizabeth Sherwood, *The Out-of-Area Debate: The Atlantic Alliance and the Challenges beyond Europe,* RAND Note, no. N-2268-USDP (May 1985); Steven Spiegel, ed., *The Middle East and the Western Alliance* (Boston: Allen and Unwin, 1982); Gregory Treverton, "Global Threats and Trans-Atlantic Allies," *International Security* (Fall 1980).

2. An important exception is the recent study by Joseph Coffey and Gianni Bonvicini, eds., *The Atlantic Alliance and the Middle East* (Pittsburgh: University of Pittsburgh Press, 1989), which provides interesting historical analyses of aspects of the out-of-area question. The works by Bentinck, Sherwood, and Foot cited in note 1 also furnish useful historical information.

3. Robert Jervis, "Hypotheses on Misperception," *World Politics* (Summer 1968): 463. See also Ole Holsti, Terrence Hopmann, and J. D. Sullivan, *Unity and Disintegration in International Alliances: Comparative Studies* (New York: Wiley, 1973), p. 144.

4. Glenn Snyder, "The Security Dilemma in Alliance Politics," *World Politics* 36, no. 4 (1984): 464.

5. Stephen Walt argues that the term *balance of threat* is preferable to the more well-known *balance of power* because the former more accurately describes the combination of geographic location, perceived intention, and perceived capabilities which determines a state's decision to seek alliance. See *The Origins of Alliances* (Ithaca: Cornell University Press, 1987), p. 5. We have also opted to employ Walt's broad definition of an alliance: "a formal or informal relationship of security cooperation between two or more sovereign states" (p. 1).

6. Snyder, "Security Dilemma," p. 5.

7. Ibid., esp. pp. 484–85, 494.

8. See Walt on the general concept of balancing as a motivation for alliance formation (*Origins of Alliances,* pp. 21–32). See also Kenneth Waltz, *Theory of International Politics* (Reading, Mass.: Addison-Wesley, 1979), pp. 168–69.

9. Hans Morgenthau, "The Containment Policy and the Rationale of the Alliance System," in *American Diplomacy in a New Era,* ed. Stephen Kertesz (Notre Dame: University of Notre Dame Press, 1961) p. 71.

10. See, for example, Winston Churchill's "Three Circles Doctrine," which is discussed in Wolfram Hanrieder and Graeme Auton, *The Foreign Policies of West Germany, France, and Britain* (Englewood Cliffs, N.J.: Prentice-Hall, 1980), pp. 177–79. George Kennan's interest in

"gradations" of membership is recounted in Alan Henrikson, "The Creation of the North Atlantic Alliance," in *American Defense Policy*, 5th ed., ed. John Reichart and Steven Sturm (Baltimore: Johns Hopkins University Press, 1982), p. 307. Kennan also expresses interest in a "dumbbell" arrangement in his *Memoirs: 1925–1950* (Boston: Little, Brown, 1967), pp. 406–7.

11. "Memorandum by the Participants in the Washington Security Talks, July 6 to September 9, Submitted to Their Respective Governments for Study and Comment," in *Foreign Relations of the United States* (hereafter cited as *FRUS*), vol. 3, *Western Europe, 1948* (Washington, D.C.: Government Printing Office, 1974), p. 240.

12. "Minutes of the Fifth Meeting of the Washington Exploratory Talks on Security" (July 9, 1948, 10 A.M.), in *FRUS 1948*, vol. 3, *Western Europe*, p. 181.

13. Alfred Grosser, *The Western Alliance* (New York: Continuum, 1980), pp. 131–32. See also Michael Harrison, *The Reluctant Ally: France and Atlantic Security* (Baltimore: Johns Hopkins University Press, 1981).

14. Dwight D. Eisenhower, *Waging Peace, 1956–1961* (New York: Doubleday, 1965), p. 83.

15. "Spain Distances Itself from Britain's Action," *Financial Times*, June 1, 1982, p. 2.

16. For a survey of U.S.-British relations and the Monroe Doctrine, see Cecil Crabb, *The Doctrines of American Foreign Policy: Their Meaning, Role, and Future* (Baton Rouge: Louisiana State University Press, 1982), pp. 9–45.

17. Malcolm Rutherford, "End of the Special Relationship," *Financial Times*, October 28, 1983, p. 15. See also "American Indifference to Outcry in Britain," *Financial Times*, October 27, 1983, p. 4, and "Licensed to Kill?" *Economist*, November 5, 1983, pp. 13–15.

18. According to a 1985 Rand study prepared for the Office of the Undersecretary of Defense for Policy, "Since the deployment of intermediate-range nuclear missiles in Europe appears to have passed its critical phase, out-of-area problems may pose the greatest threat to alliance cohesion." Sherwood, *The Out-of-Area Debate*, p. 1.

19. Readers will note that one important issue, the French Algerian war, is not included in table 1. This is because Algeria was in fact within the NATO Treaty area until independence was achieved in 1963. Algeria is nonetheless discussed in Part 3 of this book because of its implications for allied thinking about NATO's proper boundaries and because of its effect on U.S.-French security relations. Readers will also notice that certain issues (Malaysia, Irian Jaya, Laos, Vietnam) were primarily SEATO-related disputes. To the extent, however, that each of these events affected intra-NATO relations in some way, we have included them in table 1.

20. Janice Gross Stein has discussed this European concern for guilt by association in "The Wrong Strategy in the Right Place: The United States and the Gulf," *International Security* 13 (Winter 1988/89): 159–61.

21. Report to the Senate Committee on Foreign Relations, *NATO Today: The Alliance in Evolution*, 97th Cong., 2d sess., April 1982, pp. 34–35.

1: SIX SCHOOLS OF THOUGHT ON AMERICAN POSTWAR SECURITY

1. John Lewis Gaddis, *Strategies of Containment* (New York: Oxford University Press, 1982), esp. pp. 27–29.

2. See "Minutes of the Thirty-first Meeting of the United States Delegation, Held at San Francisco" (May 7, 1945), in *FRUS 1945*, vol. 1, *General: The United Nations* (1967), pp. 615–26. Consult "Minutes of the Third Five-Power Informal Consultative Meeting on Proposed Amendments (Part I), Held at San Francisco" (May 12, 1945), in ibid., pp. 691–704; "Record of First Informal Consultative Meeting with Chairmen of Delegations of Certain American Republics, Held at San Francisco" (May 14, 1945), in ibid., esp. pp. 716–17; and "The Acting Secretary of State to Diplomatic Representatives in the American Republics" (May 21, 1945), in ibid., pp. 831–37.

3. See Thomas M. Campbell, Jr., "NATO and the United Nations in American Foreign Policy: Building a Framework for Power," in *NATO after Thirty Years*, ed. Lawrence S. Kaplan and Robert W. Clawson (Wilmington, Del.: Scholarly Resources, 1981), p. 138.

4. Arnold Wolfers, "Collective Defense Versus Collective Security," in *Alliance Policy in the Cold War*, ed. Wolfers (Baltimore: Johns Hopkins Press, 1959), pp. 4–5.

5. For background, see Foster Rhea Dulles and Gerald E. Ridinger, "The Anti-Colonial Policies of Franklin D. Roosevelt," *Political Science Quarterly* 70, no. 1 (1955): 1–18.

6. See "Document 473 [Roosevelt to Churchill, December 5, 1944]," in Francis L. Lowenheim, Harold D. Langley, and Manfred Jonas, eds., *Roosevelt and Churchill: Their Secret Wartime Correspondence* (New York: Saturday Review Press, Dutton, 1975), pp. 615–16. See also A. W. Deporte, *Europe between the Superpowers* (New Haven: Yale University Press, 1979), pp. 83–84.

7. Scott L. Bills, "The United States, NATO, and the Colonial World," in *NATO and the Mediterranean*, ed. Lawrence S. Kaplan, Robert W. Clawson, and Raimondo Luraghi (Wilmington, Del.: Scholarly Resources, 1985), p. 154.

8. An eloquent defense of the European point of view was offered by Lord Hailey, "British Colonial Policy," in *Colonial Administration by European Powers*, ed. Royal Institute of International Affairs (London: Chatham House, 1947), pp. 83–87.

9. Raymond Aron, *The Imperial Republic* (Englewood Cliffs, N.J.: Prentice-Hall, 1974), pp. 259–60, expands on this point.

10. Melvin P. Leffler, "The American Conception of National Security and the Beginnings of the Cold War, 1945–1948," *American Historical Review* 89, no. 2 (1984), esp. pp. 349–50.

11. The JCS calculations are analyzed in depth by Robert C. Good, "The United States and the Colonial Debate," in *The Lion and the Eagle: British and Anglo-American Strategy, 1900–1950*, ed. Arnold Wolfers (New York: Putnam, 1972), pp. 376–77; and James F. Schnabel, *The Joint Chiefs of Staff and National Policy, 1945–1947*, vol. 1 of *The History of the Joint Chiefs of Staff* (Wilmington, Del.: Michael Glazier, 1979), pp. 214, 219–20, 324–26.

12. William W. Kaufmann, *Planning Conventional Forces, 1950–1980* (Washington, D.C.: Brookings Institution, 1982), p. 2.

13. The JCS also communicated their concern about overcommitment to European security in discussions with British and Canadian representatives at the end of World War II. Cited in Bills, "The U.S., NATO, and the Colonial World," p. 154.

14. JCS 1868/6 (May 19, 1948), "Report by the Joint Strategic Survey Committee (JSSC) on the Position of the United States with Respect to Support for Western Union and Other Related Free Countries," in *Records of the Joint Chiefs of Staff*, pt. 2, *Europe and NATO, 1946–1953*, (Washington, D.C.: University Publications of America, 1980), reel 4, 0102.

15. JCS 1868/40 (January 5, 1949) includes the "Report by the Joint Strategic Survey Committee (JSSC) on the North Atlantic Pact," in *Records of the JCS*, pt. 2, reel 5, 00234 onward. See also "Memorandum of the Joint Chiefs of Staff to the Secretary of Defense (Forrestal)" (January 5, 1949), in *FRUS 1949*, vol. 4, *Western Europe* (1975), p. 12.

16. The U.S. auxiliary affiliation issue is examined in depth by Timothy P. Ireland, *Creating the Entangled Alliance: The Origins of the North Atlantic Treaty Organization* (Westport, Conn.: Greenwood Press, 1981), pp. 162–63, and by Stephen Kirby, "Britain, NATO, and European Security: The Irreducible Commitment," in *British Defense Policy in a Changing World*, ed. John Baylis (London: Croom Helm, 1977), p. 99.

17. Leffler, "American Conception of National Security," pp. 363–64, and Kenneth W. Condit, *The History of the Joint Chiefs of Staff* (Wilmington, Del.: Michael Glazier, 1979), vol. 2, *The Joint Chiefs of Staff and National Policy, 1947–1949*, pp. 26–27.

18. E. Timothy Smith, "The Fear of Subversion: The United States and the Inclusion of Italy in the North Atlantic Treaty," *Diplomatic History* 7, no. 1 (1983): 153. See also Condit, *JCS 1947–49*, pp. 69–73, where a February 1948 JCS memorandum to the secretary of defense is cited noting that it was "unrealistic to conclude that the United States should . . . nevertheless make full use of

its military power to prevent Italy from falling under the domination of the USSR, unless the United States has available sufficient military forces to accomplish this objective."

19. For example, see the JSPC's and Joint Intelligence Committee's "World-Wide Military Situation Report" (J.I.C. 558/38), August 30, 1951, in *Records of the JCS*, pt. 2, reel 6, 00572–80.

20. Acheson's executive session testimony, in Hearings before the Senate Foreign Relations Committee, U.S. Senate, *Reviews of the World Situation*, 81st Cong., 2d sess., May 1, 1950, p. 292, is cited in Gaddis, *Strategies of Containment*, p. 114.

21. Acheson outlines his "self-defense" vs. "enforcement action" formulas in *Present at the Creation: My Years in the State Department* (New York: Norton, 1969), pp. 280–81, 283; see also "Memorandum of Conversation by the Assistant Secretary of State for United Nations Affairs (Hickerson)" (July 25, 1950), in *FRUS 1950*, vol. 1, *National Security Affairs: Foreign Economic Policy* (1977), pp. 349–60.

22. "Arguments Against/For Inclusion of Italy in the North Atlantic Pact—Annex of Memorandum of the Secretary of State" (March 2, 1949), in *FRUS 1949*, vol. 4, *Western Europe*, pp. 142–45; see also Sir Nicholas Henderson, *The Birth of NATO* (Boulder, Colo.: Westview Press, 1983), pp. 24–25.

23. See, for example, Acheson's "Private Conversations with Senator Bourke B. Hickenlooper of Iowa, Member of the Senate Foreign Relations Committee" (December 27, 1950), in *FRUS 1950*, vol. 1, *National Security Affairs: Foreign Economic Policy*, pp. 487–88. Both Western Europe and the Eastern Mediterranean were characterized as "platforms" from which U.S. forces could operate against the USSR.

24. Rosemary Foot, *The Wrong War: American Policy and the Dimensions of the Korean Conflict* (Ithaca: Cornell University Press, 1985), pp. 99–101.

25. Lawrence Kaplan, "The Korean War and U.S. Foreign Relations: The Case of NATO," in *The Korean War: A Twenty-five-year Perspective*, ed. Francis Heller (Lawrence, Kans.: Regents Press of Kansas, 1977), pp. 36–97.

26. "Letter to the Honorable Tom Connally, Chairman of the Foreign Relations Committee, United States Senate, by G. C. Marshall, Secretary of Defense, in *Executive Sessions of the Senate Foreign Relations Committee* (Historical Series) 3, pt. 1, 92nd Cong., 1st sess., February 28, 1951, 195, pp. 78–80.

27. Acheson testimony before the Senate Foreign Relations Committee, July 24, 1950, quoted in Gaddis, *Strategies of Containment*, p. 110.

28. George Kennan, *Memoirs: 1925–1950* (Boston: Little, Brown, 1967), p. 402.

29. Gaddis, *Strategies of Containment*, p. 58. The analysis found in this paragraph is largely taken from pp. 58–65.

30. "Minutes of the Fourth Meeting of the Washington Exploratory Talks on Security" (July 8, 1948, 10 A.M.), in *FRUS 1948*, vol. 3, *Western Europe*, pp. 165, 168; Alan Henrikson, "The Creation of the North Atlantic Alliance," in *American Defense Policy*, 5th ed., ed. John Reichart and Steven Sturm (Baltimore: Johns Hopkins University Press, 1982), pp. 307–8.

31. "Memorandum by the Director of the Policy Planning Staff [addressed to the Secretary and Under Secretary of State]" (November 24, 1948; also known as Policy Planning Staff Paper PPS 43), in *FRUS 1948*, vol. 3, *Western Europe*, p. 286. See also "Memorandum by the Director of the Policy Planning Staff (Kennan) to the Under Secretary of State (Lovett)" (August 31, 1948), in ibid., p. 225, and Kennan, *Memoirs*, pp. 411–13.

32. Henrikson, "Creation of NATO," pp. 307–8.

33. Lovett's comment is cited in ibid., pp. 307–8.

34. Kennan, *Memoirs*, p. 411.

35. Henrikson, "Creation of NATO," p. 308.

36. See Samuel Wells, from whom much of our chronology of the formulation of NSC 68 has

e3s

been drawn, "Sounding the Tocsin: NSC 68 and the Soviet Threat," *International Security* 4, no. 2 (1979): 126.

37. Nicholas John Spykman, *The Geography of the Peace,* ed. Helen R. Nicholl (New York: Harcourt, Brace, 1944), p. 45. See also David Wilkinson, "Spykman and Geopolitics," in *On Geopolitics: Classical and Nuclear,* ed. Ciro E. Zoppo and Charles Zorgbibe (Dordrecht, Netherlands: Martinus Nijhoff, 1985), pp. 81, 108–9.

38. Gaddis, *Strategies of Containment,* esp. pp. 352–53.

39. Ibid., p. 113.

40. Wells, "Sounding the Tocsin," p. 139.

41. "Memorandum by the Central Intelligence Agency: National Intelligence Estimates—The Strategic Importance of the Far East to the USSR" (November 13, 1951), in *FRUS 1951,* vol. 6, pt. 1, *Asia and the Pacific* (1977), pp. 107, 114–15. Emphasis is ours.

42. JCS Memo 1924 (July 14, 1950) cited by Daniel Calingaert, "Nuclear Weapons and the Korean War," *Journal of Strategic Studies* 11, no. 2 (1988): 181.

43. Walter S. Poole, *The Joint Chiefs of Staff and National Policy, 1950–1952,* vol. 4 of *The History of the Joint Chiefs of Staff* (Wilmington, Del.: Michael Glazier, 1980), p. 244, and Hearings before the Committee on Foreign Relations and the Committee on Armed Services, U.S. Senate, *Assignment of Ground Forces of the United States to Duty in the European Area,* 82d Congress, 1st sess., February 15, 1980, p. 45, where Marshall contended that six U.S. divisions constituted a "hard core" of Western European defense capability and represented "the smallest number of U.S. troops which could be perceived as reasonable support" to General Eisenhower's mission as NATO's first SACEUR.

44. Quoted in John C. Donovan, *The Cold Warriors: A Policy-making Elite* (Lexington, Mass.: Heath, 1974), p. 88.

45. Consult the definitive "Memorandum by the Central Intelligence Agency (NEI 25)" (August 2, 1951), in *FRUS 1951,* vol. 1, *National Security Affairs: Foreign Economic Policy* (1979), pp. 120–57, and the equally important "Memorandum by the Central Intelligence Agency: The Strategic Importance of the Far East to the USSR (NIE 43)" (November 13, 1951), in *FRUS 1951,* vol. 6, pt. 1, *Asia and the Pacific,* pp. 107, 114–15. See also "Report by the Joint Survey to the Joint Chiefs of Staff on Combat Operations in Indochina" (JCS 1992/1112, November 10, 1951), in *Records of the JCS,* pt. 2, reel 14, pp. 915–18. But the JCS still adhered to its "Resource/ Geographic Constraints" perspective by refusing to use the December 1951 NATO Military Committee meetings in Rome to fashion joint strategy with the British and French concerning Indochina, arguing that a single global military organization superimposing its authority over NATO would be an inappropriate use of the European alliance mechanisms. "Memorandum for the Secretary of Defense: Proposed Tripartite Discussion on the Defense of Southeast Asia" (JCS 1992/113, November 9, 1981), in ibid., pp. 919–22.

46. For a reprint of the Clifford Memorandum's text, see Arthur Krock, *Memoirs: Sixty Years on the Firing Line* (New York: Funk and Wagnalls, 1968), pp. 419–82. Evaluation of the document is found in Robert Messer, *The End of an Alliance* (Chapel Hill: University of North Carolina Press, 1982), pp. 208–9, 477–78, 480–81.

47. John L. Gaddis, *The Long Peace: Inquiries into the History of the Cold War* (New York: Oxford University Press, 1987), p. 33.

48. Marc Trachtenberg, "A 'Wasting Asset': American Nuclear Strategy and the Shifting Nuclear Balance, 1949–1954," *International Security* 13, no. 3 (1988/89): 8–11.

49. Poole, *JCS 1950–52,* pp. 164, 168.

50. Ibid.

51. Vandenberg speculated that even if SAC were adequately supported by ground and naval power in a European defense, the Soviet Union would prevail "despite the great losses that would be inflicted upon it by strategic bombing." Hearings, *Assignment of Ground Forces,* p. 222, and Poole, *JCS 1950–52,* p. 224.

52. David A. Rosenberg, "American Atomic Strategy and the Hydrogen Bomb Decision," *Journal of American History* 66, no. 1 (1979): 70–71; Trachtenberg, "Wasting Asset," esp. pp. 26, 29–30 (nn. 101, 102); Calingaert, "Nuclear Weapons and the Korean War," pp. 182–84; and Gaddis, *Long Peace,* pp. 111–12.

53. John Foster Dulles, "Where Are We? A Five Year Record of America's Response to the Challenge of the Community" (Address Delivered before the American Association for the United Nations, December 29, 1950), *Department of State Bulletin* 24, no. 602, January 15, 1951, pp. 87–88, and especially his remarks concerning the "fallacies of area defense."

54. The Eisenhower-Dulles approach to containment is discussed by Gaddis, *Long Peace,* esp. pp. 121–22.

55. Dwight D. Eisenhower, *The White House Years,* vol. 2, *Waging Peace, 1956–1961* (Garden City, N.Y.: Doubleday, 1965), pp. 290–91.

56. Roger Dingman, "Atomic Diplomacy during the Korean War," *International Security* 13, no. 3 (1988/89): 57. See also Robert M. Blum, *Drawing The Line: The Origin of the American Containment Policy in East Asia* (New York: Norton, 1982), pp. 133–35.

57. See Norman Graebner, *The New Isolationism: A Study in Politics and Foreign Policy since 1950* (New York: Ronald Press, 1956), esp. p. 24.

2: Defining the Alliance's Flanks and Balancing Its Center

1. Escott Reid, *Time of Fear and Hope* (Toronto: McClelland and Stewart, 1977), p. 195. Western intelligence sources were also expressing concern about the possibility that the Arctic might become a passageway for Soviet submarines. See Willy Ostreng, "Strategic Developments in the Norwegian and Polar Seas," *Bulletin of Peace Proposals* 13, no. 2 (1982): 106–7.

2. As noted by Herman de Fraye, "Denmark, Norway, and Iceland in the Postwar World," in *Small Powers in Alignment,* ed. Omer de Raeymaeker et al. (Leuven, Belgium: University of Leuven, 1974), p. 216.

3. Background on political developments leading to Norway's accession is provided by de Fraye, "Denmark, Norway, and Iceland," pp. 200–201, 207, and Krister Wahlback, "The Nordic Region in Twentieth Century Politics," in *Foreign Policies of Northern Europe,* ed. Bengt Sundelius (Boulder, Colo.: Westview Press, 1982), p. 16. See also Olav Riste, "Norway and the Western Powers, 1947–1950: Was 1949 a Turning Point?" in *Western Security: The Formative Years,* ed. O. Riste (New York: Columbia University Press, 1985), p. 134; Sir Nicholas Henderson, *The Birth of NATO* (Boulder, Colo.: Westview Press, 1983), pp. 85–89; Dean Acheson, *Present at the Creation: My Years in the State Department* (New York: Norton, 1969), p. 278; Sven Henningsen, "Denmark and the Road to NATO," *NATO Review* 27, no. 7 (1979): 18–22; Henningsen, "Denmark and the Road to NATO, Part 2," *NATO Review* 28, no. 1 (February 1980): 14–16; Eric S. Einhorn, "The Reluctant Ally: Danish Security Policy, 1945–1949," *Journal of Contemporary History* 10, no. 3 (1975): 493–512.

4. "Policy Statement of the Department of State: Relations of the United States with Denmark" (Washington, October 1, 1949), in *FRUS 1949,* vol. 4, *Western Europe,* pp. 618–25; and "The Ambassador in Norway (Bay) to the Acting Secretary of State" (January 17, 1949), in ibid., p. 35.

5. See the key preamble of the treaty as cited by Bjørn Bjarnson, "The Security of Iceland," in *Five Roads to Nordic Security,* ed. Johan Jorgen Holst (Oslo: Universitetsforlaget, 1973), p. 64.

6. "Statement of General Omar Bradley, Chairman of the Joint Chiefs of Staff, Accompanied by Major General L. I. Lemnitzer, Director of Military Assistance, Office of the Secretary, Department of Defense, June 6, 1950," in *Executive Sessions of the Senate Foreign Relations Committee (Historical Series),* vol. 2, 81st Cong., 1st and 2d sess., 1949–1950, pp. 418–19.

7. JCS 1868/6 (May 19, 1948), "Report by the Joint Strategic Survey Committee (JSSC) on the Position of the United States with Respect to Support for Western Union and Other Related Free

Countries," in *Records of the Joint Chiefs of Staff*, pt. 2, *Europe and NATO, 1946–1953*, reel 4, at 0102.

8. George Kennan, *Memoirs: 1925–1950* (Boston: Little, Brown, 1967), p. 150.

9. See Lawrence Kaplan, *The United States and NATO: The Formative Years* (Lexington: University Press of Kentucky), pp. 108–10.

10. "Hickerson to McVeagh," in *FRUS 1948*, vol. 3, *Western Europe*, p. 999.

11. "The Ambassador in Greece (MacVeagh) to the Secretary of State" (February 11, 1947), in *FRUS 1947*, vol. 5, *The Near East and Africa* (1971), p. 17.

12. For comments on the applicability of "interdependent security" to the politics of the Truman Doctrine, see Stanley Hoffman, "Revisionism Revisited," in *Reflections on the Cold War*, ed. Lynn H. Miller and Ronald W. Pruessen (Philadelphia: Temple University Press, 1974), p. 19.

13. "Joint Chiefs of Staff on MEDO, 24–77," June 1952 [Revised British Middle East Command Proposals] (JCS 1868/395, July 3, 1952), in *Records of the JCS*, pt. 2, reel 7, pp. 944–47.

14. Peter C. Hahn, "Containment and Egyptian Nationalism: The Unsuccessful Effort to Establish the Middle East Command, 1950–1953," *Diplomatic History* 11, no. 1 (1987): 26–27.

15. JCS perceptions of the British problem with Middle Eastern nationalism in the postwar era are well documented by Walter S. Poole, *The Joint Chiefs of Staff and National Policy, 1950–1952*, vol. 4 of *The History of the Joint Chiefs of Staff* (Wilmington, Del.: Michael Glazier, 1980), pp. 338–39.

16. "First Meeting of the Foreign Ministers of the United States and the United Kingdom" (July 11, 1953, 2:45 P.M.), in *FRUS 1952–1954*, vol. 5, *Western European Security* (1983), p. 1638, and Hahn, "Containment and Egyptian Nationalism," p. 39.

17. For analysis of U.S. military assistance to the Northern Tier's regional actors during this time, see Harold A. Hovey, *United States Military Assistance: A Study of Policy and Practices* (New York: Praeger, 1968), pp. 95–100.

18. "Statement of George V. Allen, on Mutual Security Program (Middle East)," in *Executive Sessions of the Senate Foreign Relations Committee (Historical Series)*, 84th Cong., 2d sess., May 8, 1956, pp. 217–19.

19. Quoted in Donald Neff, *Warriors at Suez* (New York: Simon and Schuster, 1981), p. 153.

20. Graebner, *New Isolationism*, p. 256.

21. "Strategic Concept for the Defense of the North Atlantic Seas" (December 1, 1949), in *FRUS 1949*, vol. 4, *Western Europe*, pp. 353–56; "The Secretary of State to the President" (January 3, 1950), in *FRUS 1950*, vol. 3, *Western Europe* (1977), pp. 1–3; Christopher Rau, *American Military in Europe: Controversy over NATO Burden-Sharing* (New Delhi: Raj Choudhry for ABC Publishing House, 1983), p. 15; Allan Bullock, *Ernest Bevin: Foreign Secretary, 1945–1951* (London: Heinemann, 1983), pp. 776–77.

22. Peter Foot, *Defense Burden-Sharing in the Atlantic Community, 1945–1954*, Aberdeen Studies in Defense Economics, no. 20 (Aberdeen, Scotland: Center for Defense Studies, Summer 1981), p. 19.

23. "Statement by the President upon Approving an Increase in U.S. Forces in Western Europe" (September 9, 1950), *Public Papers of the Presidents of the United States: Harry S Truman—1950* (Washington, D.C.: Government Printing Office, 1981), pp. 396–401.

24. Richard Barnet, *The Alliance* (New York: Simon and Schuster, 1983), p. 136. See also "Memorandum Prepared in the Department of State for the President Outlining Secretary Acheson's Presentation of North Atlantic Treaty Problems to General Eisenhower" (January 4, 1951), in *FRUS 1951*, vol. 3, *European Security and the German Question* (1981), pp. 396–401.

25. Norbert Wiggershaus, "The Decision for a West German Defense Contribution," in Riste, *Western Security*, p. 202.

26. Statement cited in Edward Furdson, *The European Defense Community: A History* (New York: St. Martin's Press, 1980), p. 68.

27. Cited in Grosser, *Western Alliance*, p. 126.

28. Anthony Eden, *Full Circle: The Memoirs of Anthony Eden* (Boston: Houghton Mifflin, 1960), pp. 188–89.

29. For Mendès-France's remarks at the Nine-Power Conference, see "Telegraphic Summary by the United States Delegation of the Second Plenary Meeting of the Nine Power Conference" (September 29, 1954), in *FRUS 1952–1954*, vol. 5, *Western European Security*, pt. 2, p. 1303. For the EDC stipulations, consult Royal Institute of International Affairs, *Survey of International Affairs, 1952* (London: Oxford University Press, 1955), p. 84.

3: THE SUEZ CRISIS

1. Richard Neustadt's *Alliance Politics* (New York: Columbia University Press, 1970) is one of the earliest, and still one of the best, attempts to focus on the misperceptions that exacerbated U.S.-British tensions during the crisis See also Robert Jervis's references to Suez misperceptions in *Perception and Misperception in International Politics* (Princeton, N.J.: Princeton University Press, 1976), passim.

2. See Royal Institute of International Affairs, *Survey of International Affairs, 1955–1956* (London: Oxford University Press, 1960), pp. 298–300.

3. Dwight D. Eisenhower, *The White House Years*, vol. 2, *Waging Peace, 1956–1961* (Garden City, N.Y.: Doubleday, 1965), p. 28.

4. See "Telegram from the United States Delegation at the North Atlantic Council Ministerial Meeting to the Department of State" (May 5, 1956), in *FRUS 1955–1957*, vol. 4, *Western European Security and Integration* (1986), pp. 61–62, and "Telegram from the United States Delegation at the North Atlantic Council Ministerial Meeting to the Department of State," in ibid., p. 60.

5. "Verbatim Minutes of the Western European Chiefs of Missions Conference" (Paris, May 6, 1957), in *FRUS 1955–1957*, vol. 4, *Western European Security and Integration*, p. 584.

6. Anthony Eden, *Full Circle: The Memoirs of Anthony Eden* (Boston: Houghton Mifflin, 1960), p. 5.

7. Quoted in Donald Neff, *Warriors at Suez* (New York: Simon and Schuster, 1981), p. 214.

8. The Northern European disillusionment with Anglo-French behavior in the Suez crisis became especially apparent during the December 1956 NATO Ministerial Meeting. See "Telegram from the United States Delegation at the North Atlantic Council Ministerial Meeting to the Department of State" (December 11, 1956), in *FRUS 1955–1957*, vol. 4, *Western European Security and Integration*, p. 107, for Norway's position and "Telegram from the United States Delegation at the North Atlantic Council Ministerial Meeting to the Department of State" (December 12, 1956), in ibid., p. 119, for Denmark's position.

9. Royal Institute of International Affairs, *Survey of International Affairs, 1956–1958* (London: Oxford University Press, 1962), p. 13.

10. Ibid., p. 28.

11. A. J. Barker, *Suez, the Seven Day War* (New York: Praeger, 1965), pp. 27–28.

12. Richard Rosecrance, *Defense of the Realm* (New York: Columbia University Press, 1986), p. 229.

13. Neff, *Warriors at Suez*, p. 409.

14. Alistair Horne, *A Savage War of Peace* (New York: Viking Press, 1978), p. 163.

15. Cited in Alfred Grosser, *The Western Alliance* (New York: Continuum, 1980), p. 145.

16. Neustadt, *Alliance Politics*, p. 136.

17. Eden, *Full Circle*, p. 512.

18. This remark was cited in Eisenhower, *Waging Peace*, p. 77. See also *Manchester Guardian*, December 10, 1960, as cited in Royal Institute of International Affairs, *Survey 1956–58*, p. 50; Michael Harrison, *The Reluctant Ally: France and Atlantic Security* (Baltimore: Johns Hopkins University Press, 1981), p. 42.

19. Anthony Adamthwaite, "Suez Revisited," *International Affairs* 64, no. 3 (1988): 464.

20. See Robert Jordan, *The NATO International Staff/Secretariat, 1952–1957* (London: Oxford University Press, 1967), pp. 71–72, and Roger Hill, *Political Consultation in NATO,* Wellesley Papers, no. 6 (Toronto: Canadian Institute of International Affairs, 1978), p. 18.

21. See Jordan, *NATO International Staff,* p. 71.

22. The text of the "Wise Men"'s recommendations is in the Ministerial Sessions of the North Atlantic Council, the Defense Planning Committee, and the Nuclear Planning Group, *Text of Final [NATO] Communiqués, 1949–1974* (Brussels: NATO Information Service, 1975), pp. 101–4.

23. "Telegram from the United States Delegation at the North Atlantic Council Ministerial Meeting to the Department of State" (December 13, 1956), in *FRUS 1955–1957,* vol. 4, *Western European Security and Integration,* pp. 132–45.

24. Ibid., p. 143.

25. Ibid., p. 141.

26. See the contemplations of Dulles in his talks with the West German foreign minister, Dr. Heinrich von Brentano, as summarized in "Memorandum of a Conversation, Department of State" (Washington, November 21, 1957), in ibid., p. 204.

27. The Eisenhower Doctrine's basic precepts and implications are analyzed by Alexander George and Richard Smoke, *Deterrence in American Foreign Policy: Theory and Practice* (New York: Columbia University Press, 1974), pp. 309–62.

28. "Enclosure by the Chief of Naval Operations for the Joint Chiefs of Staff on Middle East Policy" (JCS 1887/414, November 7, 1957), in *Declassified Documents Reference System,* vol. 8, 1982 (Microfilm Series), item 2335.

4: The Issue of Decolonization from 1949 to 1964

1. "The Secretary of State to the Embassy in the United Kingdom" (March 4, 1949), in *FRUS 1949,* vol. 4, *Western Europe,* p. 163, and "Memorandum of Conversation by Mr. John Foster Dulles of the United States Delegation to the U.N. General Assembly" (April 13, 1949), in ibid., pp. 549–50. General background is provided by Gary R. Hess, *The United States: Emergence as a Southeast Asian Power, 1940–1950* (New York: Columbia University Press, 1987), pp. 275–309.

2. "Study Prepared by the Joint Chiefs of Staff" (n.d.), in *FRUS 1949,* vol. 1, *National Security Affairs: Foreign Economic Policy* (1976), p. 304, and "Report by the Policy Planning Staff" (n.d.), in ibid., pp. 371–72.

3. The text of NSC 124/2 is reprinted in *The Senator Gravel Edition: The Pentagon Papers,* ed. Mike Gravel, vol. 1 (Boston: Beacon Press, 1971–72), pp. 385–90.

4. For records of discussions between Dulles, Admiral Radford, chairman of the U.S. Joint Chiefs of Staff, and Eden on possible British military collaboration with U.S. strategic interests in the Far East at the time, see "Memorandum of Conversation April 26, 1954," reprinted in *Declassified Documents Reference System,* vol. 8, 1983 (Microfilm Series), item 1870 onward.

5. The U.S. funding level is cited in Alfred Grosser, *The Western Alliance* (New York: Continuum, 1980), pp. 131–32. Documentation of the "united action" approach is contained in Department of Defense, *United States-Vietnam Relations, 1945–1967* (Washington, D.C.: Government Printing Office, 1971), bk. 1, B.1, pp. B-11/B-12, and B.2, pp. B-24/B-27. This version of the *Pentagon Papers* was released by the House Armed Services Committee.

6. The French reaction to JFK's speech is discussed by Arthur Schlesinger, *A Thousand Days: John F. Kennedy in the White House* (New York: Houghton Mifflin, 1965), pp. 510–12. See also Chester Bowles's study, *Africa's Challenge to America* (Berkeley: University of California Press, 1956).

7. George Ball, *The Past Has Another Pattern* (New York: Norton, 1982), p. 181.

8. Schlesinger, *A Thousand Days,* p. 517.

9. Cited in Luc Crollen, *Portugal, the U.S., and NATO* (Leuven: Leuven University Press, 1973), p. 127.

10. See Royal Institute of International Affairs, *Survey of International Affairs, 1961* (London: Oxford University Press, 1965), pp. 478–79.

5: U.S. MILITARY INVOLVEMENT IN ASIA

1. See the exchange between J.-B. Duroselle and Eugene V. Rostow in Atlantic Institute, *The Atlantic Papers,* by Alistair Buchan and others (New York: Dunellen, 1967), esp. pp. 64, 73–74. The quote is from Rostow, p. 74.

2. Cleveland World Affairs Council address on March 6, 1965, cited in ibid., and "Rusk Here Urges Close NATO Ties," *New York Times,* December 3, 1967, p. 13, reporting on speech he delivered in New York City the previous day. See also "Secretary Rusk Discusses Vietnam in Interview to Foreign Television" [USIA Transcript], *Department of State Bulletin* 57, no. 1480, November 6, 1967, pp. 598–99.

3. Sulzberger, "Foreign Affairs: The Western Flank—III," *New York Times,* January 8, 1967, pt. 4, p. 12. See also his "Foreign Affairs: The Western Flank—I," ibid., January 4, 1967, p. 42, and "Foreign Affairs: A New Look at NATO," ibid., January 24, 1968, p. 44.

4. Sulzberger, "Foreign Affairs: The Western Flank—II," *New York Times,* January 6, 1967, p. 34.

5. In fact, two such meetings did occur, on March 31 and July 13, 1965.

6. George Ball, *The Discipline of Power* (Boston: Little, Brown, 1968), pp. 64–65.

7. Paul-Henri Spaak, *The Crisis of the Atlantic Alliance,* Mershon Center Pamphlet no. 5 (Columbus, Ohio: Ohio State University Press, March 1967), p. 19.

8. Memorandum for the President from George Ball, "A Compromise Solution in South Vietnam," July 1, 1965, in *The Senator Gravel Edition: The Pentagon Papers,* ed. Mike Gravel, vol. 4 (Boston: Beacon Press, 1971–72), p. 619.

9. See, for example, Brandt's statements reproduced in his memoirs, *People and Politics: The Years 1960–1975* (Boston: Little, Brown, 1976), p. 322.

10. Gravel, *Pentagon Papers,* vol. 3, pp. 249–57.

11. Regarding Chancellor Erhard's rejection of Johnson's request, see Catherine Kelleher, "The Defense Policy of the Federal Republic of Germany," in *The Defense Policies of Nations,* ed. Douglas Murray and Paul Viotti (Baltimore: Johns Hopkins University Press, 1982), p. 283. For an assessment of the general European position, see Robert Hunter and Philip Windsor, "Vietnam and the United States Policy in Asia," *International Affairs* (London) 44, no. 2 (1968): 213.

12. Report of the Special Subcommittee on National Defense Posture of The Committee on Armed Services, U.S. House of Representatives, *Review of the Vietnam Conflict and Its Impact on U.S. Military Commitments Abroad,* 90th Cong., 2d sess., August 24, 1968, pp. 64–65.

13. David Watt, Introduction to *The "Special Relationship": Anglo-American Relations since 1945,* ed. William Roger Louis and Hedley Bull (Oxford: Clarendon Press, 1986), p. 6.

14. Brosio, "Address to the Eleventh NATO Parliamentarians' Conference," reprinted in a committee print prepared by the Subcommittee on National Security and International Operations, U.S. Senate, *The Atlantic Alliance: Allied Comment,* 89th Cong., 2d sess., January 1966, p. 56.

15. The secretary of the army's statement is found in *U.S. Department of Defense Annual Report, Fiscal Year 1966* (Washington, D.C.: Government Printing Office, 1967), p. 126.

16. "U.S. Temporarily Cutting Back Its Troop Commitment to NATO," *New York Times,* October 11, 1967, pp. 1, 2; *U.S. Department of Defense Annual Report, Fiscal Year 1968* (Washington, D.C.: Government Printing Office, 1971), pp. 26–27.

17. The statistical data are extracted from Secretary of Defense Harold Brown, *U.S. Department of Defense Annual Report, Fiscal Year 1981* (Washington, D.C.: Government Printing Office, January 29, 1980), p. 20.

18. Westmoreland's testimony is in Hearings before the Subcommittee of the Committee on Appropriations, U.S. Senate, *Department of Defense Appropriations for Fiscal Year 1971*, 91st Cong., 2d sess., p. 175.

19. James Schlesinger, "The Eagle and the Bear," *Foreign Affairs* 63, no. 5 (1985): 945.

20. Jane Stromseth has written an interesting history of Washington's campaign to sell flexible response to its allies: *The Origins of Flexible Response: NATO's Debate over Strategy in the 1960s* (London: Macmillan, 1988).

21. Seyom Brown, *The Crises of Power* (New York: Columbia University Press, 1979), p. 8.

22. See Robert S. Litwak, *Detente and the Nixon Doctrine* (Cambridge: Cambridge University Press, 1984).

6: NATO AND GLOBAL BURDEN SHARING

1. Report to the Congress by Richard M. Nixon, President of the United States, *U.S. Foreign Policy for the 1970s: Building for Peace* (Washington, D.C.: Government Printing Office, February 28, 1971), pp. 35-36.

2. Seyom Brown, *The Crises of Power* (New York: Columbia University Press, 1979), pp. 392-93. See also Lawrence S. Kaplan, "NATO and the Nixon Doctrine Ten Years Later," *Orbis* 24, no. 1 (1980), esp. p. 155, and Robert S. Litwak, *Detente and the Nixon Doctrine* (Cambridge: Cambridge University Press, 1984), p. 195.

3. Henry Kissinger, *The White House Years* (London: Weidenfeld and Nicolson, 1979), pp. 392-93.

4. In fact, 28,000 troops comprising two-thirds of a mechanized division, one armored cavalry regiment, and related logistical support units were withdrawn from West Germany to the United States. See William P. Mako, *U.S. Ground Forces and the Defense of Central Europe* (Washington, D.C.: Brookings Institution, 1983), pp. 23-27. See also Robert P. Haffa, Jr., *The Half War: Planning U.S. Rapid Deployment Forces to Meet a Limited Contingency* (Boulder, Colo.: Westview Press, 1984), pp. 38-51.

5. Cecil V. Crabb, Jr., *The Doctrines of American Foreign Policy: Their Meaning, Roles, and Future* (Baton Rouge: Louisiana State University Press, 1982), pp. 294-95.

6. Kissinger's speech, "A New Atlantic Charter," is reprinted in *Keesing's Contemporary Archives* (Keynsham, Bristol: Keesing's Publications, 1973), 19: 25933-34.

7. The logistical impediments are well covered by Lawrence L. Whetten, *The Canal War* (Cambridge, Mass.: MIT Press, 1974), pp. 430-31, and by Jeffrey Record, *The Rapid Deployment Force and U.S. Military Intervention in the Persian Gulf* (Cambridge, Mass.: Institute for Foreign Policy Analysis, February 1981), esp. pp. 6, 26-27.

8. Kissinger, *White House Years*, p. 711.

9. Henry Kissinger, *Years of Upheaval* (Boston: Little, Brown, 1982), p. 713.

10. Elmo Zumwalt, former U.S. Naval Chief of Operations, in "The Lessons for NATO of Recent Military Experience," *Atlantic Community Quarterly* 12, no. 4 (1974/75): 481.

11. Article 2 of the Atlantic Declaration, 1974, Ottawa, Canada, June 18-19, 1974. A full text of the declaration can be found in Roger Hill, *Political Consultation in NATO*, Wellesley Papers no. 6 (Toronto: Canadian Institute of International Affairs, 1978), pp. 131-34.

12. Sir Peter Hill-Norton, Lecture delivered to the Royal United Services Institute, London, November 28, 1974, reprinted as "Military Development in NATO," *RUSI* 120, no. 1 (1975): 18-19. See also his analysis in Admiral of the Fleet Sir Peter Hill-Norton, *No Soft Options: The Politico-Military Realities of NATO* (London: Hurst, 1978), pp. 152-54.

13. For background, see especially Phil Williams, *The Senate and U.S. Troops In Europe* (New York: St. Martin's Press, 1985), pp. 169-234. See also testimony by Jeffrey Record, Hearings before the Senate Armed Services Committee, *National Security Strategy*, 100th Cong., 1st sess., January 12-April 3, 1987 (Washington, D.C.: Government Printing Office, 1987), p. 714.

14. Report to the Congress by Richard M. Nixon, President of the United States, *U.S. Foreign Policy for the 1970s: The Emerging Structure of Peace* (Washington, D.C.: Government Printing Office, February 9, 1972), p. 44.

15. "NATO and the New Soviet Threat" [also referred to as the Nunn-Bartlett Report], *Congressional Record* (Senate), January 25, 1977, pp. 2192–98, at p. 2193. See also "NATO and the New Soviet Threat," quoted in Alexander Haig and staff of the Foreign Policy Research Institute, *The Three Percent Solution and the Future of NATO* (Philadelphia: Foreign Policy Research Institute, 1981), p. 17.

16. Haig, *Three Percent Solution*, pp. 48–51; James R. Golden, *The Dynamics of Change in NATO: A Burden-sharing Perspective* (New York: Praeger, 1983), pp. 82–88; and Simon Lunn, *Burden-Sharing in NATO*, Chatham House Paper no. 18 (London: Royal Institute of International Affairs, with Routledge and Kegan Paul, 1983), pp. 16–18.

17. Haig, *Three Percent Solution*, p. 20.

18. Ibid., p. 29.

19. Ibid., pp. 75–77, and Golden, *Change in NATO*, p. 84.

20. "General Report on the Economics of Atlantic Security, presented by Lord Avon (U.K.), Rapporteur," in Senate Committee on Foreign Relations, Committee Print, *Twenty-fifth Meeting of the North Atlantic Assembly Held at Ottawa, Canada, October 22–29, 1979*, 96th Cong., 2d sess., February 1980, pp. 260, 263.

21. David Calleo, *Beyond American Hegemony* (New York: Basic Books, 1987), p. 79.

22. Quoted in Irving Janis, *Groupthink* (Boston: Houghton Mifflin, 1983), p. 261.

23. Lunn, *Burden-Sharing in NATO*, p. 30, and Bernard Burrows and Geoffrey Edwards, *The Defense of Western Europe* (London: Butterworth, 1982), pp. 122–23.

24. See, for example, U.S. Department of Defense, *Report on Allied Contributions to the Common Defense* (Washington, D.C.: Government Printing Office, March 1983), pp. 50–51.

7: SOUTHWEST ASIA AND THE PERSIAN GULF

1. Fred Tanner, "NATO and the Persian Gulf: A New Concept of Burden-Sharing," *Fletcher Forum* 6, no. 1 (1982): 181.

2. See the comments on the French and German responses to the Carter Doctrine offered by Richard J. Barnet, *The Alliance* (New York: Simon and Schuster, 1983), p. 408, and Stanley Hoffman, *Dead Ends* (Cambridge, Mass.: Ballinger, 1983), pp. 235–36.

3. Foreign Affairs and National Defense Division, Congressional Research Service, Library of Congress, *Crisis in the Atlantic Alliance: Origins and Implications*, Committee Print, Senate Foreign Relations Committee, 97th Cong., 2d sess., March 1982, p. 3.

4. Jimmy Carter, "State of the Union" (January 23, 1980), in *Vital Speeches of the Day* 46 (February 1, 1980): 226–29.

5. For background, see Samuel F. Wells, Jr., "A Question of Priorities: A Comparison of the Carter and Reagan Defense Programs," *Orbis* 27, no. 3 (1983): 641–43.

6. Report to the Senate Committee on Foreign Relations, *NATO Today: The Alliance in Evolution*, 98th Cong., 2d sess., April 1982, p. 3.

7. See Undersecretary of Defense Robert W. Komer's testimony in Hearings before the Senate Committee on Armed Services, *Department of Defense Authorization for Appropriations for Fiscal Year 1981*, pt. 1, 96th Cong., 2d sess., February 21, 1980, p. 437.

8. Joshua M. Epstein, *Strategy and Force Planning: The Case of the Persian Gulf* (Washington, D.C.: Brookings, 1987), p. 5; Congressional Budget Office, *Rapid Deployment Forces: Policy and Budgetary Implications* (Washington, D.C.: Government Printing Office, 1983), passim, and Charles A. Kupchan, *The Persian Gulf and the West: The Dilemmas of Security* (Boston: Allen and Unwin 1987), pp. 190–91.

9. Hearings before the Senate Appropriations Committee, *Department of Defense Appropriations for Fiscal Year 1981*, pt. 1, 96th Cong., 2d sess., March 12, 1980, p. 429.

10. Interesting information regarding the SAIS is provided by Geoffrey Edwards, "Multilaterial Coordination of Out-of-Area Activities," in *The Atlantic Alliance and the Middle East*, ed. Joseph Coffey and Gianni Bonvicini (Pittsburgh: University of Pittsburgh Press, 1989), pp. 247–49.

11. See Kupchan, "Regional Security and the Out-of-Area Problem," in *Securing Europe's Future*, ed. Stephen J. Flanagan and Fen Osler Hampson (Dover, Mass.: Auburn House, 1986), p. 288; see also his *Persian Gulf*, pp. 194–95. In the former analysis, Kupchan extracts much of his data from the *New York Times*, April 4, 1980, and "An Interview with U.S. Secretary of Defense Harold Brown," U.S. International Communications Agency Dispatch, October 8, 1980.

12. See Joseph Fitchett, "NATO Seeks New Strategy," *International Herald Tribune*, July 18, 1980, p. 1, and Gregory Treverton, "Defense beyond Europe," *Survival* 25, no. 5 (1983): 222–23.

13. Simon Lunn, *Burden-Sharing in NATO*, Chatham House Paper no. 18 (London: Royal Institute of International Affairs, with Routledge and Kegan Paul, 1983), p. 31.

14. For the text of the Venice Economic Summit Conference, June 23, 1980, consult *Public Papers of the Presidents of the United States: Jimmy Carter*, bk. 2, *May 24 to September 26, 1980* (Washington, D.C.: Government Printing Office, 1982), pp. 1186–91. See also Philip Geyelin, "Schism among Allies on Security in Gulf," *International Herald Tribune*, July 15, 1980, p. 4. For an assessment of Schmidt's statement to the Bundestag, see Hans Reiser, "Schmidt Rejects Demands for Wider NATO Role," *Suddeutshe Zeitung*, January 18, 1980, reprinted in the *German Tribune*, no. 295 (January 27, 1980), p. 1.

15. Geoffrey Williams, *Global Defense: Motivation and Policy in a Nuclear Age* (New Delhi: Vikas, 1983), p. 55.

16. Irving Kristol, writing for the *International Herald Tribune*, January 8, 1980, cited in Bernard Burrows and Geoffrey Edwards, *The Defense of Western Europe* (London: Butterworth, 1982), p. 123.

17. Jimmy Carter, *Keeping Faith: Memoirs of a President* (Toronto: Bantam Books, 1982), pp. 587–88.

18. The formula was developed at the DPC meetings in Brussels during May and at the Bonn Summit, attended by the sixteen NATO heads of state and government the following month. See Kupchan, "Regional Security," p. 280; North Atlantic Assembly (NAA) Political Committee, *Final Report of the Subcommittee on Out-of-Area Security Challenges to the Alliance* (Brussels, International Secretariat, May 1986), pp. 9–12, 43–44; and Marc Bentinck, *NATO's Out-of-Area Problem*, Adelphi Papers, no. 211 (London: International Institute for Strategic Studies, Autumn 1986), p. 82, n. 57.

19. NAA, *Final Report*, pp. 11–12, and "The Meetings on Events on Regions Outside NATO's Zones," *Atlantic News*, no. 1497 (February 24, 1983), p. 4.

20. Bentinck, *NATO's Problem*, p. 82, n. 57.

21. Caspar W. Weinberger, Secretary of Defense, *Annual Report to the Congress, Fiscal Year 1983* (Washington, D.C.: Government Printing Office, February 8, 1982), pp. I-29, I-30. For background, see Robert P. Haffa, Jr., *The Half War: Planning U.S. Rapid Deployment Forces to Meet a Limited Contingency* (Boulder, Colo.: Westview Press, 1984), pp. 249–50; Richard B. Remneck, *Constraints on U.S. Military Power in Southwest Asia* (New York: Praeger, 1982), esp. pp. 71–73; and Dieter Braun, *The Indian Ocean: Region of Conflict or "Zone of Peace"* (London: Hurst, 1983), pp. 45–47.

22. Zbigniew Brzezinski, *Power and Principle* (New York: Farrar, Straus and Giroux, 1983), p. 445.

23. Weinberger, *Annual Report, FY 83*, pp. I-5, I-6. For in-depth analyses of horizontal escalation's global strategic implications, see Wells, "A Question of Priorities," pp. 653–55, Joshua M. Epstein, "Horizontal Escalation: Sour Notes of a Recurrent Theme," *International Security* 8, no. 3 (1983–84): 3–18, esp. pp. 4–7; and Epstein, *Strategy and Force Planning*, pp. 30–43.

24. See, for example, Epstein, "Horizontal Escalation."

25. Bernard Gwertzman, "Haig Expects Little Support from Allies," *International Herald Tribune*, December 11, 1981, p. 1.

26. "Allies Using Quiet Links in the Gulf War," *International Herald Tribune*, December 11, 1981, p. 1.

27. Department of Defense, *Report on Allied Contributions to the Common Defense: A Report to United States Congress* (Washington, D.C.: Government Printing Office, March 1985), p. 12.

28. Ibid., p. 18.

29. Joint Chiefs of Staff, *United States Military Posture, Fiscal Year 1987* (Washington, D.C.: Government Printing Office, 1986), p. 93.

30. See, for example, R. William Thornes, "Alliance Burden-Sharing: A Review of the Data," Staff Working Paper prepared for the Subcommittee on Conventional Forces and Alliance Defense, Senate Armed Services Committee, 100th Cong., 1st sess., June 1987.

31. Hearings before the Subcommittee on European Affairs of the Senate Committee on Foreign Relations, *A NATO Strategy for the 1990s*, pt. 5, 99th Cong., 1st sess., October 3, 1985, pp. 144–46.

32. Kenneth A. Oye, "Constrained Confidence and the Evolution of Reagan Foreign Policy," in *The Eagle Resurgent: The Reagan Era in American Foreign Policy*, ed. Kenneth A. Oye, Robert J. Lieber, and Donald Rothchild (Boston: Little, Brown, 1987), pp. 18–19.

33. Stanley Sloan, "The Political Dynamics of Defense Burden-Sharing in NATO," in *Evolving European Defense Policies*, ed. Catherine M. Kelleher and Gail A. Mattox (Lexington, Mass.: Lexington Books, 1987), pp. 86–87.

34. Ibid., pp. 87–90; *Congressional Record* (Daily Edition), June 20, 1984, p. 57721; and Phil Williams, "The Nunn Amendment in Europe," *Survival* 27, no. 1 (1985): 2–3.

35. Sam Nunn, "Improving NATO's Conventional Defenses," *USA Today Magazine* 113, no. 2480, May 1985, p. 21.

36. "North Atlantic Council Communique," *NATO Review* 29, no. 3 (1981): 27.

37. Derek Arnould, "The Institutional Implications of NATO in a Global Mileau," in *The Future of European Alliance Systems: NATO and the Warsaw Pact*, ed. Arlene Broadhurst (Boulder, Colo.: Westview Press, 1982), pp. 121–29.

38. Uwe Nerlich, "The Role of Western Europe in Peripheral Contingencies," Paper, 1982. Compare German foreign minister Hans-Dietrich Genscher's statements reprinted in Foreign Broadcast Information Service (FBIS), *West Europe (Daily Report)*, November 27, 1978, p. J-1, to his address to the Carl Shurz Society, April 10, 1984, reproduced, in part, in ibid., April 11, 1984, p. J-1.

39. Prepared Statements by Rear Admiral Jonathan T. Howe, director of Politico-Military Affairs, U.S. Department of State, in Hearings before the Senate Committee on Armed Services, *International Security Issues*, 98th Cong., 1st sess., April 25, 1983, p. 23. Further details on the 5th Infantry Brigade are found in an address by Michael Heseltine, U.K. Secretary of State for Defense, "The United Kingdom's Strategic Interests and Priorities," *RUSI* 128, no. 4 (1983): 4, and in Drew Middleton, "Britain Planning Intervention Force for Worldwide Deployment in Crisis," *International Herald Tribune*, November 14, 1983, p. 5. The revised French program is covered by General René Imbot, chief of staff of the French army, "The French Rapid Action Force," *NATO's Sixteen Nations* 28, Special Issue (1983): 34–35; see also an address delivered by French premier Pierre Mauroy as it appeared in *Défense nationale* (Paris) and translated/reprinted in Joint Publications Research Service (JPRS) 84909, *West Europe Report*, no. 2243 (December 8, 1983), pp. 53–60; and "The French Army: Shield and Sword for Europe?" *Economist* 291, no. 7347, June 23, 1984, pp. 37–40. U.S. Department of Defense out-of-region burden-sharing assessments are contained in U.S. Department of Defense, *Report on Allied Contributions to the Common Defense* (Washington, D.C.: Government Printing Office, March 1983), pp. 60–61. For Japanese Diet statements clarifying conditions of American use and transit of RDJTF elements, see

FBIS, *Asia and Pacific (Daily Report)*, February 1, 1980, p. C-1.

40. For a survey of recent developments, see John Chipman, "European Responses Outside Europe," in *Europe in the Western Alliance,* ed. Jonathan Alford and Kenneth Hunt (London: Macmillan, 1988), pp. 109–54.

41. Hearings before the House Subcommittee on Europe and the Middle East of the Committee on Foreign Affairs, *Developments in Europe, June 1987,* 100th Cong., 1st sess., June 29, 1987, pp. 21–22.

42. Ibid., p. 55.

43. See George Wilson, "Budget Goal Reaffirmed by NATO," *Washington Post,* June 9, 1989, p. 34A, and Melissa Healy, "Cheney Urges NATO to Boost Defense Spending," *Los Angeles Times,* June 9, 1989, p. 26.

44. The consultation and concertation formula is summarized in a report by NATO's Defense Planning Committee entitled *Enhancing Alliance Collective Security: Shared Roles, Risks, and Responsibilities* (Brussels, December 1988), pp. 60–61.

CONCLUSION: PART I

1. Measures of decline are discussed in Samuel P. Huntington, "The U.S.—Decline or Renewal," *Foreign Affairs* (Winter 1988–89), pp. 78–85; Paul Kennedy, *The Rise and Fall of the Great Powers* (New York: Random House, 1987), pp. 347–437; and the Trilaterial Commission, *Sharing International Responsibilities among the Trilateral Countries* (New York: Trilateral Commission, 1983), pp. 7–9.

INTRODUCTION: PART II

1. Among the best are C. J. Bartlett, *The Long Retreat* (London: Macmillan, 1972); Phillip Darby, *British Defense Policy East of Suez, 1947–1968* (London: Oxford University Press, 1973); and Lawrence W. Martin, *British Defense Policy: The Long Recessional,* Adelphi Papers, no. 61 (London: International Institute for Strategic Studies, November 1969).

2. Geoffrey Warner, "The British Labour Government and the Atlantic Alliance, 1949–1951," in *Western Security: The Formative Years,* ed. Olav Riste (New York: Columbia University Press, 1985), p. 249.

3. See, for example, D. Cameron Watt, *Succeeding John Bull: America in Britain's Place* (Cambridge: Cambridge University Press, 1984), esp. pp. 250–52, and the summary of British "revisionist historian" arguments by Lawrence S. Kaplan, "The Cold War and European Revisionism," *Diplomatic History* 2, no. 2 (1987): 154.

4. British Public Record Office, "NATO 'General Papers' Folder: 1949–1953, Part I," DEFE 7/743 [Secret], July 31, 1953.

5. John Baylis, "The Anglo-American Relationship and Alliance Theory," *International Relations* 8, no. 4 (1985): 369–70.

6. Robert O'Neill, "Challenges Outside the NATO Area," in *The Future of British Sea Power,* ed. Geoffrey Till (Annapolis, Md.: Naval Institute Press, 1984), p. 108.

8: POSTWAR BRITISH SECURITY POLICIES

1. Cited by Geoffrey Goodwin, "British Foreign Policy since 1945: The Long Odyssey to Europe," in *Constraints and Adjustments in British Foreign Policy,* ed. Michael Leifer (London: Allen and Unwin, 1972), pp. 35–36.

2. "C-68, Draft A, Not Sent," in *Churchill and Roosevelt: The Complete Correspondence,* ed. Warren F. Kimball, vol. 1, *Alliance Emerging* (Princeton: Princeton University Press, 1984), pp. 447–48.

3. Robert Murphy has outlined Allied frustrations with U.S. policy toward the Russians in *Diplomat among Warriors* (Garden City, N.Y.: Doubleday, 1964), pp. 177, 210–11.

4. Tony Allen-Mills, "Churchill Kept Secret His Intentions with Roosevelt," *Daily Telegram* (London), August 17, 1984, p. 17.

5. Document 520 [Churchill to Roosevelt, March 17, 1945], in Kimball, *Churchill and Roosevelt*, vol. 2, *Alliance Forged*, p. 678.

6. Regarding Bevin's proposals for a European bloc, see Alan Bullock, *Ernest Bevin: Foreign Secretary, 1945–1951* (London: Heinemann, 1983), p. 37.

7. See Geoffrey Warner, "The British Labor Government and the Atlantic Alliance, 1949–1951," in *Western Security: The Formative Years*, ed. Olav Riste (New York: Columbia University Press, 1985), pp. 247–66, and Bradford Perkins, "Unequal Partners: The Truman Administration and Great Britain," in *The "Special Relationship": Anglo-American Relations since 1945*, ed. William Roger Louis and Hedley Bull (Oxford: Clarendon Press, 1986), pp. 53–58. See also Bullock, *Ernest Bevin*, pp. 449, 517.

8. For information on US policy toward the "sterling bloc," see Richard Barnet, *The Alliance* (New York: Simon and Schuster, 1983), pp. 100–102.

9. Bullock, *Ernest Bevin*, p. 424, and Perkins, "Unequal Partners," p. 53.

10. Bullock, *Ernest Bevin*, p. 114, and Elisabeth Barker, *The British between the Superpowers, 1945–1950* (London: Macmillan, 1983), pp. 112–20.

11. "Budget Message by President Truman" (January 21, 1952), and "Message from President Truman to the Congress on the Mutual Security Program (March 5, 1952), in *The Dynamics of World Power: A Documentary History of United States Foreign Policy, 1945–1973*, Arthur M. Schlesinger, gen. ed., vol. 1, ed. Robert Dallek (New York: McGraw-Hill, 1971), pp. 183, 196. Emphasis is ours.

12. "Talks at Washington between the United States and the United Kingdom on Political and Economic Subjects Concerning the Near East," *FRUS 1949*, vol. 6, *The Far East and Australasia*, pp. 50–52.

13. U.S. misconceptions of actual British economic strength following World War II are cogently discussed by Perkins, "Unequal Partners," pp. 52–53.

14. Such British frustrations are particularly well chronicled by Ritchie Ovendale, "Britain, the United States, and the Cold War in Southeast Asia, 1949–1950," *International Affairs* 58, no. 3 (1982): 451–57, and Habibur Rahman, "British Post-Second World War Military Planning for the Middle East," *Journal of Strategic Studies* 5, no. 4 (1982), esp. pp. 512–20.

15. Barker, *British between the Superpowers*, p. 59.

16. For a sophisticated assessment of the Global Strategy Paper, see Lawrence Freedman, *Britain and Nuclear Weapons* (London: Macmillan, 1980), p. 304. See also Julian Lider, *Towards a Nuclear Doctrine: The 1950s*, Research Report no. 7 (Stockholm: Swedish Institute of International Affairs, 1981), pp. 104–7, and Trevor C. Salmon, "Britain's Nuclear Deterrent Force: Changing Environment," in *The Defense Equation: British Military Systems—Policy, Planning, and Performance since 1945*, ed. Martin Edmonds (London: Brassey's, 1986), p. 46.

17. Cited in Barnet, *Alliance*, p. 130.

18. Malcolm Mackintosh, *Juggernaut* (New York: Macmillan, 1967), pp. 271–74, provides extensive data on Soviet deployments in Europe between 1945 and 1953.

19. Geoffrey Williams, *Natural Alliance for the West: Flexibility and Global Security* (London: Atlantic Trade Study Policy Research Center, June 1969), p. 13.

20. John Groom compares American and British approaches to massive retaliation in *British Thinking about Nuclear Weapons* (London: Pinter, 1974), pp. 60–65. See also Lawrence Freedman, *The Evolution of Nuclear Strategy* (New York: St. Martin's Press, 1981), pp. 75, 80; Minister of Defense, *Statement on Defense, 1952*, Cmnd. 8475 (London: HMSO, February 1952), p. 2; Minister of Defense, *Statement on Defense, 1953*, Cmnd. 8768 (London: HMSO, February 1953), esp. pp. 3–4; Darby, *British Defense Policy*, pp. 47–48; and William P. Snyder, *The Politics of*

NOTES TO PAGES 113–19

British Defense Policy, 1945–1962 (Columbus, Ohio: Ohio State University Press, 1964), pp. 34–35.

21. Andrew Pierre, *Nuclear Politics* (London: Oxford University Press, 1972), p. 173.

22. Minutes by Sir Ivone Kirkpatrick, July 26, 1954, FO 371 1108424, as cited by William Roger Louis, "American Anti-colonialism and the Dissolution of the British Empire, in Louis and Bull, *"Special Relationship,"* p. 275.

9: AFTER SUEZ

1. Minister of Defense, *Defense: Outline of Future Policy*, Cmnd. 124 (London: HMSO, April 1957). See also Martin Edmonds, "The Higher Organization of Defense in Britain, 1945–1985: The Federal-Unification Debate," in Edmonds, ed., *The Defense Equation: British Military Systems—Policy, Planning, and Performance since 1945* (London: Brassey's, 1986), pp. 64–65, and esp. John Groom, *British Thinking about Nuclear Weapons* (London: Pinter, 1974), pp. 207–23, for comprehensive assessments of the Sandys White Paper.

2. Quoted in Phillip Darby, *British Defense Policy East of Suez, 1947–1968* (London: Oxford University Press, 1973), p. 118.

3. Anthony Verrier, *Through the Looking Glass* (New York: Norton, 1983), p. 94.

4. Stockholm International Peace Research Institute (SIPRI), *Tactical Nuclear Weapons: European Perspectives* (New York: Crane, Russak, 1978), p. 69.

5. John Bullock, "The Shifting Patterns of Alliance in the Eastern Mediterranean," *Brassey's Defense Yearbook, 1978/1979* (London: Brassey's, 1978), p. 19, and Jessie W. Lewis, Jr., *The Strategic Balance in the Mediterranean* (Washington, D.C.: American Enterprise Institute, 1975), pp. 114–15.

6. C. H. Bartlett, *The Long Retreat* (London: Macmillan, 1972), p. 41.

7. See Malcolm Yapp, "British Policy in the Persian Gulf," in Alvin J. Cottrell, gen. ed., *The Persian Gulf States: A General Survey*, ed. C. Edmund Bosworth et al. (Baltimore: Johns Hopkins University Press, 1980), p. 97. See also Jacob Abadi, *Britain's Withdrawal from the Middle East, 1947–1971: The Economic and Strategic Imperatives* (Princeton, N.J.: Kingston Press, 1982), p. 209, for cost figures on the intertheater airlift operations, and Anthony Verrier, *An Army for the Sixties* (London: Secker and Warburg, 1966), pp. 225–27, for an inventory of specific British units involved in the action.

8. Bartlett, *Long Retreat*, pp. 166–67, and Verrier, *Through the Looking Glass*, p. 190.

9. George W. Ball, *The Discipline of Power* (Boston: Little, Brown, 1968), pp. 101, 107. Emphasis is ours.

10. "Saturation Point in Destructive Weapons Approaching," *Times* (London), May 20, 1983, p. 9, and Andrew Pierre, *Nuclear Politics* (London: Oxford University Press, 1972), pp. 184, 237.

11. Author's (Stuart) interview with Kenneth Hunt, director of the British Atlantic Committee, November 1983.

12. Minister of Defense, *Statement on the Defense Estimates*, Cmnd. 3540 (London: HMSO, February 1968), p. 2.

13. Cited in Michael Chichester and John Wilkinson, *The Uncertain Ally: British Defense Policy, 1960–1990* (Aldershot, Hampshire: Gower, 1982), p. 26.

14. The contention of the British government's 1981 Defense White Paper is illustrative: "The Government has considered with special care the future of the large proportion of our land and air forces we maintain permanently in the Federal Republic of Germany. . . . the Government has decided that this contribution is so important to the Alliance's military posture and its political cohesion that it must be maintained. . . . the forward defence of the Federal Republic is the forward defence of Britain itself." Great Britain, Parliament, *The United Kingdom Defense Program: The Way Forward*, Cmnd. 8288 (London: HMSO), p. 6.

339

15. For more detailed comments on the British navy's frustrations, see Eric Grove, "The Royal Navy: The Fleet Comes Home," in Edmonds, *Defense Equation*, pp. 93–94.

16. Wilson's statement is cited and analyzed by Lawrence W. Martin, "British Policy in the Indian Ocean," in *The Indian Ocean: Its Political, Economic, and Military Importance*, ed. Alvin J. Cottrell and R. M. Burrell (New York: Praeger, 1972), p. 409. Other assessments of declining British military power in the Indian Ocean during this time are B. Vivekanandan, "Naval Power in the Indian Ocean: A Problem in Indo-British Relations," *Round Table* 65, no. 257 (1975), esp. pp. 64–65, and Vivekanandan, "Britain and the Indian Ocean," in *Indian Ocean Power Rivalry*, ed. T. T. Poulouse (New Delhi: Young Asian Publications, 1974), pp. 24–31.

17. *Daily Express* commentary, quoted in Harold Wilson, *A Personal Record: The Labor Government, 1964–1970* (Boston: Little, Brown, 1971), p. 56.

18. Ibid., pp. 55–57. Wilson's comments notwithstanding, Geoffrey Kemp in 1974 called attention to the extra-European character of Britain's NATO-designated nuclear deterrent (i.e., British reliance on SSBNs located in the Arctic or Eastern Mediterranean). Kemp speculated on the possibility that these forces could at some future date be deployed in the Southern Arabian Sea to cover "Middle Eastern, African and Asian . . . [except Chinese] targets as well." Kemp, *Nuclear Forces of Medium Powers*, pt. 1, *Targets and Weapons Systems*, Adelphi Papers, no. 106 (London: International Institute for Strategic Studies, 1974), p. 40.

19. Lawrence Freedman, "British Nuclear Targeting," in *Strategic Nuclear Targeting*, ed. Desmond Ball and Jeffrey Richelson (Ithaca: Cornell University Press, 1986), p. 125.

20. *Times* (London), October 19, 1976, p. 1.

21. Minister of Defense, *Statement on the Defense Estimates, 1972*, Cmnd. 4891 (London: HMSO, February 1972); Minister of Defense, *Statement on the Defense Estimates*, Cmnd. 5231 (London: HMSO, February 1973); John Groom, *British Thinking about Nuclear Weapons* (London: Pinter, 1974), pp. 592–93.

22. Secretary of State for Defense, *Statement on the Defense Estimates*, Cmnd. 6735 (London: HMSO, February 1977), p. 11.

23. Quoted in Lawrence Freedman, *Britain and Nuclear Weapons* (London: Macmillan, 1980), pp. 83–84.

10: British Security Policy
in the Middle East/Gulf Region

1. Bevin believed that if the Middle East could be developed into a prosperous producing area, it could "help the British economy and take the place of India as a market." John Bullock, "The Shifting Patterns of Alliance in the Eastern Mediterranean," *Brassey's Defense Yearbook, 1978/1979* (London: Brassey's, 1978), pp. 34–35, 350.

2. "Bevin to Atlee and Atlee's Reply" (April 3 and April 10, 1947), FO/800/451/5–6, cited in ibid., p. 471.

3. Habibur Rahman, "British Post-Second World War Military Planning for the Middle East," *Journal of Strategic Studies* 5, no. 4 (1982): 514.

4. "Bevin's Reply to the PM" (January 9, 1947), FO/800/476/ME/47/2, cited in Bullock, "Shifting Patterns," p. 351. For Atlee's memorandum of January 5, 1947, see FO/800/476/47/1, cited in ibid., pp. 348–49.

5. William Roger Louis, *The British Empire in the Middle East, 1945–1951* (Oxford: Clarendon Press, 1978), p. 70, and Jacob Abadi, *Britain's Withdrawal from the Middle East, 1947–1971: The Economic and Strategic Imperatives* (Princeton, N.J.: Kingston Press, 1982), p. 70.

6. One significant indication of a shift away from the bilateral approach was the Tripartite Declaration, signed by the United States, the United Kingdom, and France in May of 1950. This document is found in British Public Record Office, FO 371, 89190, E/1023/86, May 6, 1950.

7. Louis, *British Empire,* is the best work on London's Middle Eastern policy during the early postwar era. See esp. pp. 122–27.

8. Ibid., p. 601, citing "Minutes by A. A. Dudgeon" (May 29, 1951), FO/371/91185/E1024/29/6. Emphasis is in cited source.

9. Ibid., p. 710, and Bullock, "Shifting Patterns," p. 751.

10. British Public Record Office, "Record of Meeting between U.S. and British Chiefs of Staff [Top Secret]" (January 16, 1952, Washington, D.C.); C.O.S. (52) 43, esp. pp. 7–8.

11. British Public Record Office, "Allied Command in the Mediterranean Sea" [Secret] (May 7, 1952), C.O.S. (52) 253.

12. These forces had originally been deployed to the area for use as an interventionary instrument in the event that Mohammad Mossadegh nationalized the Anglo-Iranian Oil Company.

13. See, for example, analysis by Richard Barnet, *The Alliance* (New York: Simon and Schuster, 1983), pp. 154–55, 166–67.

14. Anthony Eden, *Full Circle: The Memoirs of Anthony Eden* (Boston: Houghton Mifflin, 1960), p. 247.

15. Discussed in Guy Hadley, *CENTO: The Forgotten Alliance* (Sussex: University of Sussex Institute for the Study of International Organization, 1971), p. 3. See also Harold Macmillan, *Tides of Fortune, 1945–1955* (New York: Harper and Row, 1956), pp. 631, 633, 642, 653.

16. For further details of the military assistance arrangements, see Minister of Defense, *Statement on Defense, 1955,* Cmnd. 9391 (London: HMSO, February 1955), pp. 6, 14, 20–21. The United States also placed contracts worth about $200 million in 1954 alone, for the purchase of British military equipment for resale to other NATO countries (including the Hunter, Javelin, and Sea Hawk aircraft, in addition to ammunition, armor, and electronic equipment). For a background appraisal of U.S. functions on specific British bases, consult Robert E. Harkavy, *Great Power Competition for Overseas Bases* (New York: Pergamon, 1982), pp. 123–28.

17. Richard Neustadt, *Alliance Politics* (New York: Columbia University Press, 1970), p. 8.

18. See ibid., esp. pp. 8–11, and Robert F. Randle, *Geneva 1954: The Settlement of the Indochinese War* (Princeton, N.J.: Princeton University Press, 1969), pp. 172–73.

19. Eden, *Full Circle,* p. 276.

20. Ibid. p. 288. See also the analysis by Abadi, *Britain's Withdrawal,* pp. 149–72.

21. Eden, *Full Circle,* p. 474.

22. Ibid., pp. 492, 502–6. See also his remarks before Parliament in *Hansard's Parliamentary Debates* (Commons), September 12, 1956, cols. 2–3, 15, and October 31, 1956, cols. 1452–53.

23. *Hansard's Parliamentary Debates* (Commons), August 2, 1956, col. 1622.

24. Consult Verrier, *Looking Glass,* pp. 138–39.

25. Chatham House Study Group, *British Interests in the Mediterranean and Middle East* (London: Oxford University Press, 1958), esp. pp. 92, 118.

26. See Neustadt, *Alliance Politics,* pp. 30–36.

27. Discussed in Baylis, *Anglo-American Defense Relations, 1939–1984: The Special Relationship* (London: Macmillan, 1984), pp. 94–95.

28. Cited in "The Balance Sheet of Intervention," *Economist* 188, no. 5995, July 19, 1958, p. 183.

29. "Adenauer Raises Mideast Doubts," *New York Times,* July 19, 1958, p. 3.

30. C. J. Bartlett, "The Military Instrument in British Foreign Policy," in *British Defense Policy in a Changing World,* ed. John Baylis (London: Croom Helm, 1977), pp. 165–66; Phillip Darby, *British Defense Policy East of Suez, 1947–1968* (London: Oxford University Press, 1973), p. 174.

31. Barry M. Blechman and Stephen S. Kaplan, *Force without War: U.S. Armed Forces as a Political Instrument* (Washington, D.C.: Brookings Institution, 1978), pp. 231–32. See also selected introductory comments by Steven Spiegel, ed., *The Middle East and the Western Alliance* (Boston: Allen and Unwin, 1982), pp. 1–5.

32. *Hansard's Parliamentary Debates* (Commons), July 17, 1957, cols. 1519, 1522.

33. William B. Quandt, "The Western Alliance in the Middle East: Problems for U.S. Foreign Policy," in Spiegel, *Middle East and Western Alliance*, p. 10. See also John Marlowe, *Arab Nationalism and British Imperialism* (New York: Praeger, 1961), pp. 173–76.

34. "Secretary Dulles' News Conference of July 31," *Department of State Bulletin* 34, no. 999, August 18, 1958, pp. 265–72.

35. Congressional authorization backing the declaration "was considered to insure U.S. military support for the [Baghdad Pact] powers as fully as would U.S. membership in the Treaty." For the Dulles statement and for the above citation, see *U.S. and Soviet Policy in the Middle East*, ed. John Donovan (New York: Facts on File, 1974), pp. 134–35; "Baghdad Pact," *International Organization* 12, no. 4 (1968): 548–49; and Royal Institute of International Affairs, *Survey of International Affairs: 1956–1958* (London: Oxford University Press, 1962), p. 38.

36. "Statement by [Department of] Defense of the Reasons for U.S. Adherence to the Baghdad Pact at This Time" [Top Secret], *Declassified Documents Reference System*, vol. 9, 1958 (Woodbridge, Conn.: Research Publications, Microfilm Series, 1983), item 5156-602335.

37. "Statement by State of the Reasons against U.S. Adherence to the Baghdad Pact at This Time" [Top Secret], ibid.

38. *Hansard's Parliamentary Debates* (Commons), February 11, 1959, cols. 1177–78.

39. See especially the statement by Francis T. F. Plimpton, deputy U.S. representative to the Security Council, reprinted as "Security Council Considers Situation in Kuwait," *Department of State Bulletin* 45, no. 1152, July 24, 1962, pp. 165–66. See also Elisabeth Munroe, "British Bases in the Middle East," *International Affairs* 42, no. 1 (1966): 30.

40. Harold Macmillan, *At the End of the Day: 1961–1963* (New York: Harper and Row, 1973), p. 268.

41. For background, see Darby, *British Defense Policy*, pp. 142–25, 175, and Julian Paget, *Last Post: Aden, 1964–1967* (London: Faber and Faber, 1969), p. 29.

42. The most comprehensive background analyses of the Aden conflicts include Paget, *Last Post*, and Michael Carver, *War since 1945* (New York: Putnam, 1981), pp. 62–82.

43. See Wilson's rationales accompanying the policy announcement in *Hansard's Parliamentary Debates* (Commons), January 16, 1968, cols. 1580–85. See also Darby, *British Defense Policy*, pp. 323–25.

44. James Wyllie, *The Influence of British Arms: An Analysis of British Military Intervention since 1956* (London: Allen and Unwin, 1984), esp. pp. 81–88.

45. Paget, *Last Post*, p. 87.

46. James Brown, "The NATO Challenge in the Middle East," in Royal United Services Institute (RUSI), *RUSI and Brassey's Defense Yearbook, 1987*, no. 2 (London: Brassey's, 1987), pp. 253–54, 260.

47. For the British government's position, see in particular U.K., Parliament (Commons), Fifth Report from the Foreign Affairs Committee, *Afghanistan: The Soviet Invasion and Its Consequences for British Policy, Session 1979–1980* (London: HMSO, July 30, 1980), p. xxv.

48. See excerpts of Defense Minister John Nott's remarks in Parliament concerning the unit designations for a British RDF contribution in "Britain Ready to Help Friends Outside NATO Area," *Times* (London), March 18, 1981, p. 9. The national restraints on any British RDF activities that would be undertaken are covered by David Tonge, "Nation's Military Capacity to Act Outside of NATO 'Only Limited,'" *Financial Times*, March 5, 1981, p. 6, and David K. Willis, "Rapid Deployment for NATO Approval Is Not So Rapid," *Christian Science Monitor* (Weekly International Edition), March 23, 1981, p. 4.

49. *Hansard's Parliamentary Debates* (Lords), January 24, 1980, cols. 540–42.

50. Carrington's February 6, 1980, remarks to the House of Lords are reprinted in "A World Changed by the Soviet Invasion of Afghanistan," *Atlantic Community Quarterly* 18, no. 1 (1980): 20–26.

51. Carrington argued that it was neither possible nor desirable to extend NATO to the Persian

Gulf because the alliance would lose its unique meaning. See "Lord Carrington Hopes Britain Will Join in U.S. Military Action if Needed to Protect Gulf," *Times* (London), February 7, 1980, p. 6, and "Afghanistan Crisis: Time for Brave Hearts and Cool Heads," in ibid., p. 5.

52. Nick Cook, "UK's £10 Bn. Record Deal," *Jane's Defense Weekly* 10, no. 2 (July 16, 1988), p. 59; Robert Hazo, "British-Saudi Arms Deal," *Washington Report on Middle East Affairs* 8, no. 4 (1988): 7–9.

53. Julian Langdon, "Diego Garcia Base Rent-Free for U.S.," *Sydney Morning Herald,* August 10, 1983, p. 6.

54. Desmond Wettern, "Britain Sends Three Carriers to Med," *Daily Telegraph,* September 17, 1983, p. 1.

55. See the remarks of British foreign secretary Sir Geoffrey Howe in a BBC interview given on August 25, 1987, and reprinted in British Information Service (BIS), "Shipping in the Gulf: Re-Registration of Kuwaiti Tankers and the Role of the Armilla Patrol," *Policy Background Paper* 18/87 (August 26, 1987), p. 1. For assessments of British naval strength in the area, consult University of Bradford School of Peace Studies, *A Further Note on U.S. Military Options in the Gulf,* Report no. 35 (September 10, 1987), pp. 4–5; Dov S. Zakheim, "Of Allies and Access," *Washington Quarterly* 4 (Winter 1981): 97–105; Zakheim, "Towards a Western Approach to the Indian Ocean," *Survival* 22, no. 1 (1980): 7–14; and Major-General T. A. Boam, "Defending Western Interests Outside NATO: The United Kingdom's Contribution," *Armed Forces Journal International* 122, no. 3 (1984): 116–20. The most comprehensive official description of the Armilla patrol is found in Minister of Defense, *Statement on the Defense Estimates, 1988,* Cmnd. 344-I (London: HMSO, 1988), pp. 35–36.

56. Boam, "Defending Western Interests," p. 118, provides specific details.

57. Hugh Hanning, "Britain's Military Ambassadors," *Daily Telegraph,* January 5, 1985, p. 18. See also, for general background on such British activities in the Persian Gulf, Jonathan Bloch and Pat Fitzsimmons, "An Air Force Made to Measure," *Middle East,* no. 89 (March 1982): 28–29, and Pat Fitzsimmons with Duncan Campbell, "Thatcher Sets Her Sights on the Gulf," *Middle East,* no. 96 (October 1982): 25–26. In addition, information was gained from author (Tow) background interview with MOD Defense Sales Office officials in London, September 22, 1981. The British concept of preserving geopolitical influence through "horizon-stretching" was raised during that interview and has been confirmed since that time by aggressive MOD arms sales tactics in the Middle East and East Asia.

11: BRITISH SECURITY POLICY IN THE FAR EAST

1. See Christopher Thorn's excellent study, *Allies of a Kind: The United States, Britain, and the War against Japan, 1941–1945* (London: Hamish Hamilton, 1978), and his equally useful sequel, *The Issue of War* (New York: Oxford University Press, 1985). See also William Roger Louis, *Imperialism at Bay* (New York: Oxford University Press, 1978) and J.D.B. Miller, "The 'Special Relationship' in the Pacific," in *The "Special Relationship": Anglo-American Relations since 1945,* ed. William Roger Louis and Hedley Bull (Oxford: Clarendon Press, 1986), pp. 379–80.

2. See Peter Lowe, *Britain in the Far East: A Survey from 1819 to the Present* (London: Longman, 1981), pp. 199–200, and John Vaizey, *The Squandered Peace: The World, 1945–1975* (London: Hodder and Stoughton, 1983), p. 260.

3. Admiral Sir James Eberley, "The Military Relationship," in Louis and Bull, *"Special Relationship,"* p. 155.

4. The relevant documents are British Public Record Office, F0 371, 83019, F1027/6G (Copy no. 8), Foreign Office Distribution [Top Secret], December 2, 1950; "Record of a Meeting of the Prime Minister and Minister of Foreign Affairs," p. B-O; and F0 371, 83018, FC/1022/318G—Annex 2/Min/UKUS, "Memo to Secretary of State/Talks with Acheson on SE Asia and Bipartite Agreed Minutes on China and Japan," May 6, 1950.

5. British concerns about avoiding possible Far Eastern conflicts and uncertainty over American management of Asian security issues are well covered by Elisabeth Barker, *The British between the Superpowers* (London: Macmillan, 1983), pp. 216–18.

6. See Douglas Stuart, "Prospects for Sino-European Security Cooperation," *Orbis* 26, no. 3 (1982): 730–31.

7. *FRUS 1950*, vol. 3, *Western Europe*, pp. 1707–87, cited in John Baylis, *Anglo-American Defense Relations, 1939–1984: The Special Relationship* (London: Macmillan, 1984), p. 60.

8. Percy Spender, *Exercise in Diplomacy* (Melbourne: Melbourne University Press, 1965), pp. 13–14, and T. B. Millar, *Australia In Peace and War* (Canberra: Australian National University Press, 1978), p. 205.

9. See "Memorandum by the Regional Planning Advisor in the Bureau of Far Eastern Affairs (Ogburn) to the Assistant Secretary of State for Far Eastern Affairs (Allison)" (Washington, January 21, 1953), in *FRUS 1952–1954*, vol. 12, pt. 1, *East Asia and the Pacific*, p. 260, where the dangers are emphasized about America's "appearing to join with other Western powers behind the backs of Asians in organizations for the defense of the Far East." A good overview of the U.S.-U.K. ANZUS dispute as it developed throughout 1951–52 remains Dean E. McHenry and Richard N. Rosecrance, "The 'Exclusion' of the United Kingdom from the ANZUS Pact," *International Organization* 12, no. 3 (1958): 320–29.

10. "The Secretary of State to the United States Political Advisor to SCAP" (February 8, 1951), in *FRUS 1951*, vol. 6, pt. 1, *Asia and the Pacific*, p. 150; and "Memorandum by the Special Assistant to the Consultant" (January 12, 1951), in ibid., pp. 139–40.

11. British Public Record Office, "Letter, Dated June 18, 1953, from the [British] Foreign Office to the Secretary, Chief of Staff," C.O.S. (53) 286, Annex 2 [Top Secret], June 19, 1953, esp. pp. 5–6. See also "United Kingdom Attitude toward a Pacific Pact," C.O.S. (52) 244 [Top Secret], April 30, 1952.

12. "The Acting Secretary of State (David K. G. Bruce) to the Embassy in Australia" (Washington, May 24, 1952), in *FRUS 1952–54*, vol. 12, pt. 1, *Asia and the Pacific*, pp. 93–94. The authors have incorporated a full text in lieu of the telegraphic shorthand prose that actually constituted the language of dispatch.

13. Secretary of State Acheson's remarks delivered at the first ANZUS council meeting in August 1952 directly related to differences in U.S.-U.K. defense interests in this context. See "United States Minutes of the First Meeting, ANZUS Council: Second Session" (Kaneohe, Territory of Hawaii, August 4, 1952), in *FRUS 1951*, vol. 6, pt. 1, *Asia and the Pacific*, pp. 179, 192.

14. Recounted in Robert S. Jordan, *Political Leadership in NATO: A Study in Multinational Diplomacy* (Boulder, Colo.: Westview Press, 1979), pp. 45–46. In his farewell address to the English Speaking Union on June 4, 1957, in London, Ismay implored the NATO membership to formulate and abide by common policy in extra-European areas. See Francis A. Beer, *Integration and Disintegration in NATO* (Columbus, Ohio: Ohio State University Press, 1969), p. 32.

15. *Hansard's Parliamentary Debates* (Commons), February 25, 1953, cols. 2096–97. See also David Langsam, "Britain Wanted a Say in ANZUS," *Sydney Morning Herald*, January 1, 1987, p. 13. Foreign Secretary Eden and the Chiefs of Staff, according to documents released by the British Public Record Office in late December 1986, were concerned that ANZUS could result in diverting Australian/New Zealand security interests from the defense of the Middle East to the Pacific.

16. See P.L.W. Wood, "The ANZAC Dilemma," *International Affairs* (London) 29, no. 2 (1953): 192. By September 1953, Prime Minister Churchill's position had evolved to one of "distaste" for ANZUS, and "accepting the situation with the best possible grace." *Times*, September 17, 1953, p. 9. For a recent analysis of Article 5 of the ANZUS Treaty, see Campbell McLachlan, "ANZUS: The Treaty Reappraised," *New Zealand Law Journal* (August 1985): 275.

17. For example, consult British Public Record Office, N. Pritchard, "Comments by the Commonwealth Foreign Relations Office," C.O.S. (53) 291, June 22, 1953. See also "ANZUS [Report of Chief of Staffs Committee]," C.O.S. (52) 641 [Secret], November 24, 1952. Emphasis is theirs.

18. British Public Record Office, "Indochina," British Cabinet Memoranda [hereafter noted as "C"] (54) 108 [Secret], March 18, 1954; "Discussions on the Situation in Southeast Asia, March 29-May 22, 1954," Memo by Eden to Sir Roger Makins, Washington, C (54), 196 [Secret], June 14, 1954; Richard Norton-Taylor, "Notion of Nuclear Attack Rejected," *Guardian*, January 2, 1985, p. 3; Seamus Milne, "U.K. Feared Atomic War," ibid.

19. The best account of Dulles' three-week odyssey in Europe, culminating with the London meetings, is by George C. Herring and Richard H. Immerman, "Eisenhower, Dulles, and Dien Bien Phu: 'The Day We Didn't Go to War' Revisited," *Journal of American History* 71, no. 2 (1984), esp. pp. 355–60. See also Leszek Buszynski, *SEATO: The Failure of an Alliance Strategy* (Singapore: Singapore University Press, 1983), pp. 4–5.

20. British Public Record Office, "Note by the Cabinet Secretary [Norman Brook] of the Cabinet Meeting," C (54) 155 [Top Secret], April 27, 1954, and Milne, "U.K. Feared Atomic War."

21. British strategic objectives were defined in official terms at the time in "Report by the Committee on Defense Policy—Memorandum by Lord President of the Council, Lord Salisbury," C (54) 250 [Top Secret], July 24, 1954 (British Public Record Office), which reiterated the arguments of the far more comprehensive document "British Overseas Obligations—Memorandum by Secretary of State for Foreign Affairs," C (52) 202 [Top Secret], June 18, 1952. The key planning document prepared by the British Chiefs of Staff for cabinet deliberations on the interrelationship of defense planning with Indochina and other Third World crises (C [54] 249) is still classified under Britain's fifty-year rule for document declassification and will be closed until 2005.

22. Buszynski, *SEATO*, p. 16.

23. British Public Record Office, Cabinet Meeting (hereafter cited as CC) (54) 26th, Conclusions [Secret], April 2, 1954, pp. 4–5, and CC (54) 29th, Conclusions, April 15, 1984. See also "Discussion on Dulles SEATO Proposals," CC (54) 29th, Conclusions [Secret], April 15, 1984, p. 4.

24. "The Ambassador in the United Kingdom (Aldrich) to the Department of State" (April 26, 1954), in *FRUS 1952–1954*, vol. 13, pt. 2, *Indochina*, p. 1416. For further accounts of Dulles' military requests made to the British while he was in Paris just prior to the Geneva Conference, see footnote 1 in "Memorandum of Conversation by the Assistant Secretary of State for European Affairs" (April 26, 1954), in ibid., pt. 1, p. 1196.

25. "Memorandum by Charles C. Stelle to Director of the Policy Planning Staff (Bowie)" (March 31, 1954), in ibid., pt. 1, p. 1196.

26. For Churchill's views on SEATO as an "extended ANZUS," see the top secret cablegram from Secretary of State Dulles to President Eisenhower, April 13, 1954 in *FRUS 1952–1954*, vol. 13, *Indochina*, pp. 1323–24.

27. *Hansard's Parliamentary Debates* (Commons), 526, no. 95, April 13, 1954, col. 463.

28. "Memorandum of Conversation by the Counselor with Participants Including Secretary Dulles, Ambassador Aldrich, Mr. Eden, and Mr. Dennis Allen (British Under Secretary of State for Foreign Affairs)" [Secret] (April 11, 1954), in *FRUS 1952–1954*, vol. 13, *Indochina*, pt. 1, p. 1309.

29. David K. Hall, "The Laos Crisis, 1960–61," in *The Limits of Coercive Diplomacy*, ed. Alexander L. George, David K. Hall, and William E. Simons (Boston: Little, Brown, 1971), pp. 50, 63, and "Laos Disputed," *Round Table* 51, no. 203 (1961): 248–49.

30. Phillip Darby, *British Defense Policy East of Suez, 1947–1968* (London: Oxford University Press, 1973), pp. 233–34.

31. T. B. Millar, *Australia in Peace and War*, p. 86.

32. For example, Richard Barnet notes that British policies in Malaysia served as the model for the U.S. strategic hamlets program in Vietnam. *Intervention and Revolution* (New York: Mentor, 1972), p. 236.

33. See Julian Lider, *Military Thought of a Medium Power*, Research Report 8 (Stockholm: Swedish Institute of International Affairs, 1983), pp. 286–87.

34. Darby, *British Defense Policy*, p. 234.
35. Secretary of State for Defense, *Statement on the Defense Estimates, 1967*, Cmnd. 3203 (London: HMSO, February 6, 1967), p. 7.
36. Harold Wilson, *A Personal Record: The Labor Government, 1964–1970* (Boston: Little, Brown, 1971), pp. 39, 187.
37. "U.S. Concern over British Role East of Suez," *Times* (London), June 18, 1965, p. 12; Darby, *British Defense Policy*, pp. 294–95.
38. Wilson, *Personal Record*, p. 264.
39. Ibid., p. 187.
40. See the Statement of the British representative to a SEATO meeting in British Information Services, *Survey of British and Commonwealth Affairs* 1, no. 10 (May 12, 1967), p. 4887.
41. Wilson speech delivered to the Labor party, June 17, 1966, as quoted in Alistair Buchan, "British East of Suez: Part 1—The Problem of Power," *RUSI* 62, no. 647 (1967): 210.
42. *Guardian*, January 4, 1964, quoted in Darby, *British Defense Policy*, p. 239.
43. Buchan, "British East of Suez," p. 210.
44. Peter Foot, *Improving Capabilities for Extra-European Contingencies: The British Contribution*, Aberdeen Studies in Defense Economics, no. 18 (Aberdeen, Scotland: Center for Defense Studies, Spring 1981), p. 28.
45. Stewart Menaul, "British Defense Perspectives after the Falklands War," *Strategic Review* 12, no. 1 (1984): 48. For comparative British force development-level data pertaining to the entire Far East in 1966 and 1978, see Catherine Kelleher, "The Conflict Without: European Powers and Nonnuclear Conflict outside of Europe," in *Nonnuclear Conflicts in the Nuclear Age*, ed. Sam C. Sarkesian (New York: Praeger, 1980), p. 277, and Wyllie, *Influence of British Arms*, p. 95. The January 1987 Gurkha reduction is covered in detail by Nick Steadman, "Hong Kong: Whitehall to Sack Fifth Battalion," *Armed Forces* 5, no. 2 (1986): 82–83.
46. See S. Bilveer, "Threat Containment in Singapore," *Asian Defense Journal* 17, no. 1 (1987): 37.
47. Secretary of State for Defense, *The United Kingdom Defense Program: The Way Forward*, Cmnd. 8288 (June 1981), p. 11.
48. Minister of Defense, *Statement on the Defense Estimates, 1987*, Cmnd. 101-I (London: HMSO, May 6, 1987), pp. 22–23.
49. Authorative accounts of U.K. arms sales to Southeast Asian nations are found in *International Defense Review* 19, no. 2 (1986): 232, and Stockholm International Peace Research Institute (SIPRI), *SIPRI Yearbook, 1985* (London: Taylor and Frances, 1985), p. 407.
50. Steve Hoadley, "Malaysia's Military Build-Up: A Political Assessment," *New Zealand International Review* 13, no. 6 (1988): 2–5; Nick Seaward, "Buying British Again," *Far Eastern Economic Review* 142, no. 40, October 6, 1988, p. 20; Tai Ming Cheung, "Enemy Spotting," *Far Eastern Economic Review* 142, no. 47, November 24, 1988, pp. 23–24; and Denis Warner, "Britain's Big Malaysian Deal," *Pacific Defense Reporter* 15, no. 4 (1988): 30.
51. "Global 86," *Armed Forces* 5, no. 5 (1986): 228–35. On the British role in the RIMPAC exercise, consult Fleet Lt. Ian Pearson, "RIMPAC 86," *Armed Forces International* 5, no. 10 (1986): 474–75.
52. R. S. Sasheen, "Exercise *Lima Bersatu*," *Asian Defense Journal* (October 1988): 14.
53. Lord Chalfont, "Britain Thirty Years after Suez," *Defense and Foreign Affairs* 14, no. 10 (1986): 11.

12: BRITISH DEFENSE POLICIES IN
THE CARIBBEAN AND LATIN AMERICA

1. In F. S. Northridge, "Britain as a Second Rank Power," *International Affairs* 46, no. 1 (1970): 43.

2. Anthony Eden, *Memoirs: Full Circle* (Boston: Houghton Mifflin, 1960), pp. 151-55, and Alfred Grosser, *The Western Alliance* (New York: Continuum, 1980), p. 137.

3. Richard Rosecrance, *Defense of the Realm* (New York: Columbia University Press, 1986), p. 13; John Mander, *Great Britain or Little England?* (London: Penguin Books, 1963), passim.

4. Harold Macmillan, *At the End of the Day: 1961-1963* (New York: Harper and Row, 1973), p. 216.

5. See Geoffrey Warner's analysis in Royal Institute of International Affairs, *Survey of International Affairs, 1959-1960* (London: Oxford University Press, 1964), p. 480.

6. Macmillan, *At the End of the Day*, p. 181.

7. Cited in a report to the Senate Committee on Foreign Relations, *NATO Today: The Alliance in Evolution*, 97th Cong., 2d sess., April 1982, p. 41.

8. Harold Wilson, *A Personal Record: The Labor Government, 1964-1970* (Boston: Little, Brown, 1971), pp. 625-26; "The Meteor Flag," *Economist* 230, no. 6552, March 22, 1969, pp. 25-26, and "The Party's Over," ibid. 230, no. 6553, March 29, 1969, pp. 29-30.

9. Ian Mather, "British Troops Stay in Belize," *Observer*, March 5, 1985, p. 13. FY 1985 U.S. security funding was $575,000—$75,000 above the half-million dollar figure cited by Mather. See House Committee on Armed Services, *Report on the Delegation to Latin America*, 99th Cong., 1st sess., April 1985, pp. 44-45.

10. "The modest U.S. military assistance program in Belize is designed to complement the United Kingdom's efforts at training the Belize Defense Force." *Report of the Delegation to Latin America*, p. 44.

11. Quoted in Abraham Lowenthal, ed., *Latin American and Caribbean Contemporary Record*, vol. 6,*1986-1987* (New York: Holmes and Meier, 1988), pp. B253-B254.

12. As quoted in Anthony Payne, "The Grenada Crisis in British Politics," *Round Table*, no. 292 (October 1984): 407-8.

13. House of Commons, Second Report from the Foreign Affairs Committee, Session 1983-84, *Grenada* (London: HMSO, March 15, 1984), p. xl.

14. As assessed in Payne, "Grenada Crisis," pp. 403-4.

15. Malcolm Rutherford, "The End of the Special Relationship," *Financial Times*, October 28, 1983, p. 15.

16. Quoted in Michael Tatu, "A Nest of Misunderstandings," in *Central America and the Western Alliance*, ed. Joseph Cirincione (New York: Holmes and Meier, 1985), p. 117.

17. Ibid.

18. Before 1979, the United States provided no military assistance to the Eastern Caribbean; in 1980, it allocated $4 million toward that region; in 1983, $13.3 million; in 1985, $25 million. Background on the RSS is provided by Jack Child, "Issues for U.S. Policy in the Caribbean Basin in the 1980s," Security Report of Atlantic Council's Working Group on the Caribbean Basin, in *Western Interests and U.S. Policy Options in the Caribbean Basin* (Boston: Oelgeschlager, Gunn and Hain, 1984), p. 168; Hugh O'Shaughnessy, "A Mini-NATO in the Caribbean," *Observer*, February 5, 1984, p. 7; "A Historic Step," Editorial in the Bridgetown *Sunday Advocate News*, October 31, 1982, reprinted in Foreign Broadcast Information Services (FBIS), *Latin America (Daily Report)*, November 5, 1982, p. S-4.

19. See Michael Desch, "Turning the Caribbean Flank: Sea-lane Vulnerability during a European War," *Survival* 19, no. 6 (1987): 528-52.

20. North Atlantic Assembly, *Official Report—Twenty-Eighth Annual Session* [Z310 SA/CR 2 82 16 rev. 11] (London: NAA, November 17, 1982). Emphasis is ours. In a previous address delivered in New York, however, Thatcher seemed to advocate a greater NATO-wide role in regions beyond Europe. See William Tuchy, "Thatcher Says NATO Must Enlarge Scope," *International Herald Tribune*, March 2, 1981, p. 1.

21. "America's Falkland War," *Economist* 290, no. 7331, March 3, 1984, p. 24.

22. Richard N. Lebow, "Miscalculation in the South Atlantic: The Origins of the Falklands

War," in *Psychology and Deterrence*, ed. Robert Jervis, Richard N. Lebow, and Janice Gross Stein (Baltimore: Johns Hopkins University Press, 1985), pp. 111–12. See also the analysis of Lawrence Freedman, "The War of the Falkland Islands, 1982," *Foreign Affairs* 61, no. 1 (1982), esp. p. 199.

23. Joseph G. Dibullo, "The Falklands: A Stern Lesson for NATO Planners," *Defense and Foreign Affairs* 10, no. 9 (1982): 29; Andrew Hurrell, "The Politics of South Atlantic Security: A Survey of Proposals for a South Atlantic Treaty Organization," *International Affairs* 59, no. 2 (1983): 189–90; John Nott, "The Falklands Campaign," *U.S. Naval Institute Proceedings* 109/5/963 (May 1983), esp. pp. 136–39.

24. Frederick Bonnart, "HQ Copes and Keeps Calm," *Times* (London), June 2, 1982, p. 6.

25. *The United Kingdom Defense Program: The Way Forward*, Cmnd. 8288 (London: HMSO), p. 11.

26. Secretary of State for Defense, *Statement on the Defense Estimates, 1984*, Cmnd. 9227-I, p. 29, and Desmond Wettern, "Falklands Navy Role Reduced," *Daily Telegraph*, January 10, 1985, p. 5.

27. International Institute for Strategic Studies, *The Military Balance, 1984–1985* (London: IISS, Autumn 1984), pp. 35, 39, 45; William T. Tow, "NATO's Out-of-Region Challenges and Extended Containment," *Orbis* 28, no. 4 (1985): 842–43.

28. House of Commons, Fifth Report from the Foreign Affairs Committee, *Falkland Islands*, vol. 1, sess. 1983–1984 (London: HMSO, October 25, 1984), p. xxiv.

29. Philip Windsor, "Diplomatic Dimensions of the Falklands Crisis," *Millennium: Journal of International Studies* 12, no. 1 (1983): 91–94. See also Peter Calvert, "Latin America and the United States during and after the Falklands Crisis," ibid., pp. 69–77.

30. Quoted in Insight Team, *The Falklands War: The Full Story* (London: Sphere Books, 1982), p. 137.

31. See "America's Falklands War," *Economist* 290, no. 7331, March 3, 1984, p. 29.

32. For specifics, see the *Observer*, "No Going It Alone in the Big Lesson of Falklands," June 20, 1982, p. 11.

33. Insight Team, *Falklands War*, p. 194.

34. Air Cdre. G. S. Cooper, "French Mock Attacks Helped Task Force," *Daily Telegraph*, July 27, 1982, p. 4, and Ian Murray, "NATO 'Battles' Helped Harrier Pilots," *Times* (London), July 29, 1982, p. 2.

35. W. F. Deedes, "A Hard Fought Battle That Has Concentrated NATO Minds," *Daily Telegraph*, June 22, 1982, p. 8. See also Ken Perkins, "Bloodied in Battle—An Assessment of British Defense Equipment in the Falklands Campaign," in Royal United Services Institute for Defense Studies (RUSI), *RUSI and Brassey's Defense Yearbook, 1984* (London: Brassey's, 1984), p. 137.

36. Secretary of State for Defense, *The Falklands Campaign: The Lessons*, Cmnd. 8758 (London: HMSO, December 1982), p. 15.

37. Ibid., p. 35. As observed at a Kings College Department of War Conference on the Future of British Sea Power in November 1983, "The Falklands Operation, in fact, was just the sort of war the Navy had been told it need not prepare for." Maj. Gen. J. A. Thompson, "The Amphibious Side of the Falklands Campaign," in *The Future of British Sea Power*, ed. Geoffrey Till (Annapolis, Md.: Naval Institute Press, 1984), pp. 166–67.

38. Lawrence Freedman, "British Defense Policy after the Falklands," *World Today* 38, no. 9 (1982): 339.

39. Air Cdre. G. S. Cooper, "Falkland Air Defense Still NATO-Assigned," *Daily Telegraph*, February 23, 1983, p. 6.

40. "Overdoing the Falklands," *Financial Times*, December 15, 1982, p. 20.

41. See "Cost of Retaking and Holding Falklands Put at 2,500 Million Pounds," *Times* (London), November 10, 1982, p. 1, and Ivor Owen, "Defence Budget Not Under Strain, Minister Insists," *Financial Times*, December 22, 1982, p. 4. See also David Watt, "In the End It's Down to America," *Times* (London), April 23, 1982, p. 14.

CONCLUSION: PART II

1. The concepts of "prefect" and "headmaster" are developed by Geoffrey Warner, "British Labor Government and the Atlantic Alliance," p. 249.

2. British Public Record Office, "Chiefs of Staff Committee on the 1952 Defense Program," C.O.S. (52) 618 [Top Secret], November 17, 1952. Regarding Churchill's tendency to "continue living with illusions" during the period 1951–55, see Anthony Adamthwaite, "Overstretched and Overstrung: Eden, the Foreign Office, and the Making of Policy, 1951–1955," *International Affairs* (Spring 1988): 241–59.

3. General Sir Edwin Barmall, "British Land Forces: The Future," *RUSI* 127, no. 2 (1982): 19, 26.

4. House of Commons, Second Report from the Defense Committee, *Statement on the Defense Estimates, 1981* (London: HMSO, April 28, 1981), p. 5.

5. The Thatcher government's rationales are perhaps most clearly expressed in *Parliamentary Papers*, Cmnd. 8212-I (April 1981), *Statement on the Defense Estimates, 1981*, p. 10 [of the report].

6. Statements by Pattie at the annual Verkunde defense conference in Munich during February 1981 as reported by David Fairhall, "Britain Backs 'Global' NATO Force," *Guardian*, February 23, 1981, p. 1; see also a later article by Pattie, "Western Security beyond the NATO Area," *Strategic Review* 12, no. 2 (1984): 39–43.

7. "Interview with Michael Heseltine," *NATO's Sixteen Nations*, 30, no. 2 (1985): 87.

8. Frederick Bonnart, "Rhine Army 'Vital for Balance of Forces,'" *Times* (London), December 13, 1982, p. 6, and Bonnart, "Troops Are Needed to Maintain Credibility," ibid., December 14, 1982, p. 8.

9. R. W. Apple, Jr., "Bush Wins Backing for His Arms Plan from Most Allies," *New York Times*, May 30, 1989, pp. 1–2.

10. Peter Foot, *Problems of Equity in Alliance Arrangements*, Aberdeen Studies in Defense Economics, no. 23 (Aberdeen, Scotland: Center for Defense Studies, Summer 1982), p. 40.

11. See Reference Services, British Information Service, "Britain's Defense Policy," no. 243/87 (June 1987), and Dov S. Zakheim, "Aftermath of the Thatcher Victory: Britain's Defense Budget Dilemma," *Armed Forces Journal International* (September 1987): 88, where a BAOR expenditure of 16.2 percent of the total British defense budget is cited.

12. "Britain and NATO—Forty Years of Security," Extracts from the full text of the *Statement on the Defense Estimates*, British Information Service, Policy Statement 31/89(B), May 3, 1989, par. 503.

13. 1987 Defense White Paper and BIS, "Britain's Defense Policy," p. 6.

14. Report by NATO's Defense Planning Committee, *Enhancing Alliance Collective Security* (Brussels: NATO, December 1988), pp. 68–70. See also Gen. John R. Galvin, SACEUR, "Getting Better: Improving Capabilities for Deterrence and Defense," *NATO Review* 37, no. 2 (1989): 11–16.

13: EMERGING FROM OCCUPATION

1. Charles de Gaulle, *The Complete War Memoirs*, vol. 3, *Salvation* (New York: Simon and Schuster, 1964), p. 186.

2. Cited in Alfred Grosser, *The Western Alliance* (New York: Continuum, 1980), p. 30. See also Grosser's insightful analysis of French foreign policy, *Affaires extérieures: La politique de la France, 1944–1984* (Paris: Flammarion, 1984).

3. The literature relating to the underlying premises of French imperialism is extensive. See in particular Jean Bouvier, René Girault, and Jacques Thobie, *L'impérialisme à la Française, 1914–1960* (Paris: Editions La Decouverte, 1986); Christopher Andrew and A. S. Kanya-Forstner, *The*

Climax of French Imperial Expansion, 1914–1924 (Stanford: Stanford University Press, 1981); Charles-Robert Ageron, *France: Idée coloniale ou parti coloniale?* (Paris: Puf, 1978); Henri Grimal, *Decolonization: The British, French, Dutch, and Belgian Empires, 1919–1963* (London: Routledge and Kegan Paul, 1978); Miles Kahler, *Decolonization in Britain and France: The Domestic Consequences of International Relations* (Princeton: Princeton University Press, 1984); and, especially, Raoul Girardet, *L'idée coloniale en France, 1871–1962* (Paris: Table Ronde, 1972).

4. De Gaulle, *The Complete War Memoirs*, vol. 1, *The Call to Honor* (New York: Simon and Schuster, 1964), p. 196.

5. Ibid., p. 914.

6. François Kersaudy, *Churchill and de Gaulle* (New York: Atheneum, 1981), p. 217.

7. Quoted in Guy de Carmoy, *The Foreign Policies of France, 1944–1968* (Chicago: University of Chicago Press, 1970), p. 19.

8. Regarding the Brazzaville Conference, see in particular Henri Grimal, *Decolonization*, pp. 125–26, 171–73.

9. See Stanley Karnow, *Vietnam: A History* (New York: Viking Press, 1983), pp. 2–89.

10. Brian Crozier, *De Gaulle*, vol. 2, *The Statesman* (London: Eyre, Methuen, 1973), pp. 364–66, and Grosser, *Affaires extérieures*, pp. 17–71.

11. The recently opened Indochina files of the French archives of the Service historique de l'armée de terre (SHAT) provide an in-depth analysis of the French military situation in Indochina during the second half of the 1940s. See in particular files 10H599 ("Indochine, Situation 1945"), 10H5898 5/9 ("Etude sur la guerre, 1946–1954"), 10H5920 1 ("Zone frontière"), 10H5926 1 ("Mission militaire du Nord Vietnam"), and 10H5938 1 ("Operations en Cochinchine").

12. Discussed in Douglas Stuart, "Paris and London between Washington and Beijing," in *Mainland China: Politics, Economics and Reform*, ed. Yu-ming Shaw (Boulder, Colo.: Westview Press, 1986), p. 565.

13. De Gaulle, *Complete War Memoirs*, vol. 3, p. 194.

14. Jean Fremaux and Henri Martel, "French Defense Policy, 1947–1949," in *Western Security: The Formative Years*, ed. O. Riste (New York: Columbia University Press, 1985), pp. 92–106.

15. De Carmoy, *Foreign Policies of France*, pp. 136–40.

16. J. R. Tournoux, *Secrets d'état* (Paris: Plon, 1960), p. 4.

17. See the summary analysis of the material and human costs of the French war effort in the wake of the fall of Dien Bien Phu in *Le Monde*, July 21, 1954, p. 3.

18. See "National Intelligence Estimate: Indochina, Current Situation and Probable Developments," Memorandum by the Central Intelligence Agency (December 29, 1950), in *FRUS 1950*, vol. 6, *East Asia and the Pacific*, p. 961.

19. Georgette Elgey, *Histoire de la IV République: La république des contradictions, 1951–1954* (Paris: Fayard, 1968), p. 139.

20. Office of the Secretary of Defense, Vietnam Task Force, *United States-Vietnam Relations, 1945–1967* (bk. 1 of 12), p. A–45.

14: THE WASHINGTON PREPARATORY TALKS OF 1948–1949

1. "Memorandum by J. D. Hickerson, Director of the Office of European Affairs, to Dean Acheson, Secretary of State" (February 17, 1949), in *FRUS 1949*, vol. 4, *Western Europe*, p. 121.

2. See, for example, "Memorandum of Conversation by the Secretary of State" (February 14, 1949), in ibid., pp. 107–8.

3. "Memorandum by Charles E. Bohlen, Counselor of the Department of State, to Dean Acheson, Secretary of State" (March 31, 1949), in ibid., p. 256.

4. "Memorandum Conversation, by the Secretary of State" (February 14, 1949), in ibid., pp. 107–8. "Memorandum by the Counselor of the Department of State (Bohlen) to the Secretary of State" (March 31, 1949), in ibid., p. 256. For a French analysis of the value of the Standing Group, see General Paul Vallery, *Se défendre? Contre qui? Pour qui? Et comment?* (Paris: Plan, 1960), pp. 182–86.

5. "Minutes of the Tenth Meeting of the Washington Exploratory Talks" (December 22, 1948), in *FRUS 1948*, vol. 3, *Western Europe*, pp. 325–26.

6. Ibid., p. 325.

7. "Minutes of the Twelfth Meeting of the Washington Exploratory Talks on Security" (February 8, 1949), *FRUS 1949*, vol. 4, *Western Europe*, p. 86. For allied responses to this argument, see Sir Nicholas Henderson, *The Birth of NATO* (Boulder, Colo.: Westview Press, 1983), p. 81.

8. "Minutes of the Twelfth Meeting of the Washington Exploratory Talks on Security" (February 8, 1949), in *FRUS 1949*, vol. 4, *Western Europe*, pp. 86–87.

9. Henderson, *Birth of NATO*, p. 58.

10. Dean Acheson, *Present at the Creation: My Years in the State Department* (New York: Norton, 1969, p. 278. See also "Minutes of the Tenth Meeting of the Washington Exploratory Talks" (December 22, 1948), *FRUS 1948*, vol. 3, *Western Europe*, pp. 86–87, where Bonnet specifically draws the parallel between the U.S. situation with Congress and the French government's situation with its constituents.

11. See the informative article by Cees Wiebes, "The Dutch Do Not Seem to Keep the Timetables Handy: The National Security Policy of the Netherlands, 1940–1949," in *The Origins of NATO*, edited by Joseph Smith (Exeter: University of Exeter Press, 1990).

12. Jacques Soustelle, "France, Europe, and Peace," *Foreign Affairs* 26, no. 3 (1948): 503.

13. "Memorandum on French North Africa by Policy Planning Staff" (March 22, 1948), *FRUS 1948*, vol. 3, *Western Europe*, pp. 683–84.

14. Ibid., p. 687.

15. Ibid., p. 684.

16. Acheson, *Present at the Creation*, p. 638.

17. "Minutes of the Fourteenth Meeting of the Washington Exploratory Talks on Security" (March 1, 1949), *FRUS 1949*, vol. 4, *Western Europe*, p. 128.

15: THE INTERNATIONALIZATION OF THE WAR IN
INDOCHINA AND THE FAILURE OF THE EDC

1. *The China White Paper, August 1949*, a compilation of documents produced by the U.S. Department of State (Stanford, Calif.: Stanford University Press, 1967), remains one of the most important background sources for a study of the evolution of U.S. policy toward the P.R.C. Following the victory of the Chinese Communist Party (CCP) forces, the United States undertook a series of important top-secret assessments of the threat posed by Beijing. See, for example, a memorandum from the Central Intelligence Agency, "Probable Developments in the World Situation through Mid-1953" (September 24, 1951), *FRUS 1951*, vol. 1, *Asia and the Pacific*, pp. 193–207.

2. Douglas Stuart, "Paris and London between Washington and Beijing," in *Mainland China: Politics, Economics, and Reform*, ed. Yu-ming Shaw (Boulder, Colo.: Westview Press, 1986), pp. 565–66.

3. Robert Boardman, *Britain and the People's Republic of China, 1949–1974* (New York: Barnes and Noble, 1976), p. 53.

4. See especially the secret summary report of the Comite mixte du renseignement en extreme orient, Annex A, "Aide chinoise aux Viet-Minh et voise de communications dans la région frontalière sino-tonkinoise" (SHAT, file 10-H-164, April 27, 1951) and the top-secret report by

General Salan to General de Lattre de Tassigny (SHAT, file 10-H-164, December 12,1951).

5. See Georgette Elgey, *Histoire de la IV République: La république des illusions, 1945–1951* (Paris: Fayard, 1965), pp. 498–99; see also Pierre Rocalle, *Pourquoi Dien Bien Phu?* (Paris: Flammarion, 1968), passim.

6. Neil Sheehan, Hendrick Smith, E. W. Kenworthy, and Fox Butterfield, *The Pentagon Papers, as Published by the New York Times* (New York: Quadrangle Books, 1971), p. 10.

7. "Message from John H. Ohly, Deputy Director of the Mutual Defense Assistance Program, to Dean Rusk, Assistant Secretary of State for Far Eastern Affairs" (November 20, 1950), in *FRUS 1950*, vol. 6, *East Asia and the Pacific*, pp. 924–25.

8. Memorandum from the Central Intelligence Agency, "National Intelligence Estimate on Indochina: Current Situation and Probable Developments" (December 29, 1950), in ibid., p. 961.

9. Ohly to Rusk, pp. 927–28.

10. Ibid., p. 930.

11. Dean Acheson, *Present at the Creation: My Years in the State Department* (New York: Norton, 1969), pp. 674, 678.

12. See "Memorandum by General Omar N. Bradley from the Joint Chiefs of Staff to the Secretary of Defense (Marshall)" (November 28, 1948); "Analysis Prepared for Joint Chiefs of Staff by Joint Strategic Survey Committee" (November 17, 1950); and especially "Memorandum by the Central Intelligence Agency on Indochina" (December 29, 1950), in *FRUS 1950*, vol. 6, *East Asia and the Pacific*, pp. 949–54, 945–48, and 958–63, respectively.

13. Acheson, *Present at the Creation*, p. 674.

14. Bradley to Marshall, p. 947.

15. Quoted in Stanley Karnow, *Vietnam: A History* (New York: Viking Press, 1983), p. 177.

16. "Departmental Discussions with General de Lattre de Tassigny" (SHAT, file 10-H-164, September 17, 1951), p. 3.

17. Statement by Marshal Juin at the Pentagon conference of U.S./U.K. and French defense experts (SHAT, file 10-H-164, January 11, 1952), p. 5.

18. See statements by General de Lattre de Tassigny (SHAT, file 10-14-164, September 17, 1951) and the previously cited report by General Salan to General de Lattre (SHAT, file 10-H-164, December 12, 1951).

19. "Minister of Saigon (Heath) to the Secretary of State" (Telegram, January 1, 1951), in *FRUS 1951*, vol. 6, pt. 1, *Asia and the Pacific*, pp. 335–36.

20. See especially "Memorandum by the Joint Chiefs of Staff to the Secretary of Defense: Proposed Military Talks Regarding Defense of Indochina" (January 10, 1951), in ibid., pp. 347–48.

21. "Telegram from David K. E. Bruce, Acting Secretary to the Embassy in France" (December 12, 1952), in *FRUS 1952–1954*, vol. 5, pt. 1, *Western European Security*, pp. 347–48.

22. Lord Ismay, *NATO: The First Five Years, 1949–1954* (Paris: North Atlantic Treaty Organization, 1954), p. 194.

23. Pierre Melandri, "France and the Atlantic Alliance from 1950–1953: Between Big Power Policy and European Integration," in *Western Security: The Formative Years*, ed. O. Riste (New York: Columbia University Press, 1985), p. 277.

24. "Telegram from Secretary of State (Acheson) to President (Truman)" (December 17, 1952), in *FRUS 1952–1954*, vol. 5, pt. 1, *Western European Security*, p. 352.

25. "The Acting Secretary of State to the Embassy in France" (December 12, 1952), in ibid., pp. 346–47.

26. The top-secret French document relating to the U.S. contingency plan for a joint invasion of China was obtained from the recently opened SHAT files (file 10-H-164, February 19, 1953).

27. Melandri, "France and the Atlantic Alliance," pp. 278–79.

28. See excerpts from "Truman/Pleven Meeting" (January 29, 1951), in *FRUS 1951*, vol. 6, pt. 1, *Asia and the Pacific*, pp. 366–67. See also "Synthèse des conversations de Washington," annex

D, "Aide militaire des Etats-Unis à l'Indochine," for a French assessment of U.S. naval support for the Indochina war in 1950–51 (SHAT, file 10-H-164, April 27, 1951), p. 2.

29. George C. Herring, *American's Longest War: The United States and Vietnam, 1950–1975* (New York: Wiley, 1979), pp. 15–25.

30. Dwight D. Eisenhower, *The White House Years*, vol. 1, *Mandate for Change, 1953–1956* (Garden City, N.Y.: Doubleday, 1963), pp. 338–44.

31. See the account of Operation Vulture in Karnow, *Vietnam*, pp. 196–97, and in George C. Herring and Richard H. Immerman, "Eisenhower, Dulles, and Dien Bien Phu, 'The Day We Didn't Go to War' Revisited," *Journal of American History* 71, no. 2 (1984): 347–48. Admiral Radford encouraged Ely to believe that the United States might be prepared to use three tactical nuclear weapons to destroy Vietminh forces surrounding the French contingent at Dien Bien Phu—a proposal that would never have been supported by the Eisenhower administration. In any event, French premier Laniel advised Eisenhower in a classified phone conversation that the use of U.S. nuclear weapons on what was still considered to be French territory would result in the collapse of the Fourth Republic government. He recommended instead that Washington consider using the nuclear weapons in southern China. (Based on Trumbull Higgins's interview with Laniel in Paris, June 11–12, 1971; Stuart conversation with Higgins, 1984.)

32. Lord Ismay, *NATO: The First Five Years* (Appendix), p. 200.

33. Eisenhower, *Mandate for Change*, pp. 349–51.

34. "Memorandum of Conversation, by the Counselor of the Department of State (Douglas MacArthur), with Prime Minister Laniel, M. Vidal, M. Bougenot, Mdme Laniel" (April 23, 1954), in *FRUS 1952–54*, vol. 5, pt. 1, *Western European Security*, p. 944.

35. Cited in Alfred Grosser, *The Western Alliance* (New York: Continuum, 1980), pp. 131–32. See the French interpretation of the U.S. contribution to the war effort, as reflected in *Le Monde*, July 21, 1954, p. 3.

36. Georgette Elgey, *Histoire de la IV République: La république des contradictions, 1951–1954* (Paris: Fayard, 1968), p. 149.

37. Jacques Soustelle, "France Looks at Her Alliances," *Foreign Affairs* 35, no. 1 (1956): 126.

38. Royal Institute of International Affairs, *Survey of International Affairs, 1957* (London: Oxford University Press, 1954), p. 26.

39. See "The United States Delegation to the Department of State" (February 21, 1952) and "The Secretary of State to the Department of State" (Telegram, February 21, 1952), in *FRUS 1952–1954*, vol. 5, pt. 1, *Western European Security*, pp. 120–24.

40. Grosser, *Western Alliance*, p. 126.

41. "Paper Prepared by Leon W. Fuller of the Policy Planning Staff on U.S. Policy toward Europe-Post EDC" [Secret] (September 10, 1954), in *FRUS 1952–1954*, vol. 5, pt. 2, *Western European Security*, pp. 1170–71. Emphasis is Fuller's.

42. "Memorandum of Conversation by Assistant Secretary of State for European Affairs (Merchant)" (August 30, 1954), in ibid., p. 1117. Dulles' public condemnation of French nationalism is found in "Statement by the Secretary of State" (August 31, 1954), in ibid., pp. 1120–22.

16: "LACHONS L'ASIE, PRENONS L'AFRIQUE"

1. Discussed by Alistair Horne, *A Savage War of Peace: Algeria, 1952–1954* (New York: Penguin, 1977), pp. 78–79.

2. Mitterrand's role in the Algerian War is discussed by Denis MacShane, *François Mitterrand: A Political Odyssey* (New York: Universe, 1982), pp. 60–64.

3. Michael Harrison, *The Reluctant Ally: France and Atlantic Security* (Baltimore: Johns Hopkins University Press, 1981), p. 35. Regarding the effect of the North African deployments on NATO readiness, see "Message" (Top Secret) from SACEUR General Gruenther, to Secretary of

Defense Anderson" (November 8, 1954), Declassified Documents Reference System, no. 353B, 1978.

4. Quoted in Horne, *Savage War of Peace*, p. 123.

5. "Policy Paper Prepared in the Department of State" (November 21, 1951), in *FRUS 1951*, vol. 5, *The Near East and Africa* (1982), pp. 1392–95: "If one takes into account the immediate objectives of NATO and the objectives of this government in Europe on the one hand, and our long term objectives and interests in the Moslem world on the other, the present situation . . . would appear to require that we continue to pursue a middle-of-the-road policy toward that area."

6. By 1955 the United States had invested $375 million in the bases in Morocco. See Council on Foreign Relations, *The United States in World Affairs, 1955* (New York: Harper Bros., 1957), p. 198.

7. "Telegram from US Ambassador to France (Douglas Dillon) to Department of State" (November 12, 1954), in *FRUS 1952–1954*, vol. 11, pt. 1, *Africa and South Asia* (1983), pp. 397–98. References to Tunisia relate to military actions in the Aures Mountain region bordering Algeria, where French forces were engaged in combat with an estimated three hundred to four hundred Fellahin.

8. Statement by the North Atlantic Council on the withdrawal of French forces assigned to NATO, March 27, 1956, reprinted in Royal Institute of International Affairs, *Documents on International Affairs, 1956* (London: Oxford University Press, 1959), pp. 677–78.

9. Jacques Soustelle, "France Looks at Her Alliances," *Foreign Affairs* 35, no. 1 (1956): 127. Mitterrand expressed a similar sense of frustration regarding the alliance as a whole: "To those allies that have not properly understood—perhaps because they have not been made to understand—the Mediterranean, and not the Rhine, is the very axis of our security, and therefore of our foreign policy." Quoted by Alfred Grosser, *Affaires extérieures: La politique de la France, 1944–1984* (Paris: Flammarion, 1984), p. 139.

10. Cited in Donald Neff, *Warriors at Suez* (New York: Simon and Schuster, 1981), p. 190.

11. Cited in Horne, *Savage War of Peace*, p. 85.

12. See Lord Hahn, "Algeria: The End of an Era," *Middle Eastern Affairs* 6, nos. 8–9 (1956): 286–93.

13. Quoted in Neff, *Warriors at Suez*, p. 390.

14. Ibid., p. 409.

15. Quoted in Grosser, *Affaires extérieures*, p. 149.

16. Arthur Schlesinger, *A Thousand Days: John F. Kennedy in the White House* (Boston: Houghton Mifflin, 1965), pp. 300–301.

17. Quoted in Lewis Paper, *The Promise and the Performance: The Leadership of John F. Kennedy* (New York: Crown, 1975), p. 52.

18. Russell Baker, "Kennedy Urges U.S. Back Independence for Algeria," *New York Times*, July 3, 1957, pp. 1, 5.

19. Arthur Schlesinger, *A Thousand Days*, pp. 510–11.

20. See Jacques Vernant, "France-Tunisie-Maroc," *Revue de défense nationale* 14, nos. 7–8 (1958): 1398–1405.

21. Grosser, *Affaires extérieures*, p. 150.

22. Quoted in Horne, *Savage War of Peace*, p. 243.

23. Council on Foreign Relations, *The United States in World Affairs, 1958* (New York: Harper, 1959), p. 245.

24. Charles De Gaulle, *The Complete War Memoirs*, vol. 3, *Salvation* (New York: Simon and Schuster, 1964), p. 187.

25. Ibid., p. 253.

26. According to Edgar Furniss, personnel costs increased from 40 percent to 47 percent of the French defense budget from 1954 to 1958, while spending on equipment declined from 30 percent

to 20 percent. Furniss, *De Gaulle and the French Army* (New York: Twentieth Century Fund, 1964), p. 182.

27. De Gaulle radio/TV speech, December 20, 1960, in *Discours et messages, 1958-1962*, vol. 3, *Vers la renouveau* (May 1958-July 1962), pp. 262–63.

28. Cyrus L. Sulzberger, *The Test: De Gaulle and Algeria* (New York: Harcourt, Brace and World, 1962), pp. 48–49.

17: POSTCOLONIAL FRANCE

1. Charles de Gaulle, *Discours et messages*, vol. 2, *Dans l'attente* (February 1946-April 1958) (Paris: Plon, 1970), pp. 274–75.

2. To date, the September memorandum has not been declassified, but an authoritative summary of its contents was offered by *Le Monde*, October 28, 1960, and translated into English by W. W. Kulski, *De Gaulle and the World: The Foreign Policy of the Fifth French Republic* (Syracuse, N.Y.: Syracuse University Press, 1966), pp. 164–65.

3. John Newhouse, *De Gaulle and the Anglo Saxons* (London: Deutsch, 1970), p. 7.

4. "Memorandum by the Joint Strategic Survey Council (JSSC) for the Joint Chiefs of Staff on [the] French Proposal for a Tripartite World-Wide Organization" (JCS 2278/5, October 17, 1958), reprinted in *Declassified Documents Reference System*, vol. 7, no. 3 (July-September 1981) (Woodbridge, Conn.: Research Publications Incorporated/Carrollton Press Microfiche Service, 1981), item 308A, pp. 23–25 of original document.

5. See Spaak's memoirs, *Combats inachevés*, vol. 2 (Paris: Fayard, 1969), p. 207.

6. See an illuminating December 16, 1957, telegram sent by Dulles to the American Embassy in Paris which reports on a meeting between Eisenhower and French prime minister Gaillard that month, in *Declassified Documents Reference System,*, vol. 13, 1986, fiche 145, 001942.

7. See "Memorandum For the President—Subject: Call on You by NATO Secretary General Spaak, [Dulles]" (September 24, 1958), in ibid., fiche 110, 001422; and Dulles' "Memorandum of Conversation with the President (October 13, 1958), in ibid., 1985, fiche 116, 001641.

8. Document reprinted in Bernard Ledwidge, *De Gaulle et les Américains: 1958–1964* (Paris, Flammarion, 1984), pp. 68–70. See also the "Telegram from American Embassy, Paris, to the Secretary of State" (February 24, 1959), *Declassified Documents Reference System*, vol. 13, 1986.

9. De Gaulle, *Discours*, pp. 247–50.

10. G. B. Noble, *The American Secretaries of State and Their Diplomacy*, vol. 18, *Christian A. Herter* (New York: Cooper Square, 1970), p. 250.

11. Newhouse, *De Gaulle and the Anglo Saxons*, p. 59.

12. Ibid., p. 82, and Wilfred L. Kohl, *French Nuclear Diplomacy* (Princeton: Princeton University Press, 1971), p. 80.

13. Bernard Montgomery, *The Memoirs of Field Marshal the Viscount Montgomery of Alamein, K.G.* (London: Collins, 1958), p. 520.

14. See "NATO Tackles the Problem of Political Cooperation," *Times* (London), December 19, 1958, p. 8.

15. Don Cook, *Charles de Gaulle: A Biography* (New York: Putnam, 1983), p. 337.

16. See "National Security Council, National Security Action Memorandum 64: Memorandum for the Secretary of State" (July 28, 1961), in *Declassified Documents Reference System*, vol. 12, 1985, fiche 93, item 1311.

17. Brian Crozier, *De Gaulle*, vol. 2, *The Statesman* (London: Eyre, Methuen, 1973), p. 514.

18. Arthur Schlesinger, *A Thousand Days: John F. Kennedy in the White House* (New York: Houghton Mifflin, 1965), p. 518.

19. Ledwidge, *De Gaulle et les Américains*, p. 87.

20. Alistair Horne, *A Savage War of Peace: Algeria, 1952–1954* (New York: Penguin Books, 1977), p. 312.

21. De Gaulle, *Discours et messages,* p. 413.

22. Ibid.

23. Jean-Luc Domenach, "Sino-French Relations: A French View, in *China's Foreign Relations: New Perspectives,* ed. Chun-Tu Hsueh (New York: Praeger, 1982), p. 89.

24. Quoted in Ledwidge, *De Gaulle et les Américains,* p. 105.

25. See, for example, the press conference with Prime Minister Pompidou on April 15, 1966, in *La Documentation française; Articles et documents,* no. 0.1795. See also de Gaulle's press conference of February 21, 1966, in *Discours et messages,* pp. 5-23.

26. Harold Wilson, *A Personal Record: The Labor Government, 1964-1970* (Boston: Little, Brown, 1971), pp. 404-6.

27. Quoted in Alfred Grosser, *The Western Alliance* (New York: Continuum, 1980), p. 215.

28. Newhouse, *De Gaulle and the Anglo-Saxons,* p. 285.

29. See *Discours et Messages,* January 8, 1959, pp. 72. See also de Gaulle's statements of February 9, 1959, discussed in *La politique africaine du Général de Gaulle: 1958-1969* (Paris: Pedone, 1980), pp. 233-35.

30. *La politique africaine,* p. 245.

31. Stockholm International Peace Research Institute (SIPRI), *The Arms Trade with the Third World* (Stockholm: SIPRI, 1971), pp. 263-70.

32. Ibid. p. 267.

33. Henry Tanner, "De Gaulle Declares Paris Uncommitted In Mideast Conflict," *New York Times,* June 3, 1967, pp. 1, 8.

18: THE OUT-OF-AREA QUESTION SINCE 1966

1. Edward Kolodziej, *French International Policy under de Gaulle and Pompidou* (Ithaca: Cornell University Press, 1974), p. 513.

2. Henry Kissinger, *Years of Upheaval* (Boston: Little, Brown, 1982), pp. 708-11.

3. See *Le Monde,* October 19, 1973, pp. 8-10. See also Maurice Delarue, "Ambiguïtés," ibid., p. 10; "M. Jobert et l'enthousiasme," *Le Monde,* November 14, 1983, p. 1; and Michel Schifres, "M. Michel Jobert souligne le progrès de la construction européen," ibid., pp. 12-14.

4. Kissinger, *Years of Upheaval,* p. 174.

5. Xavier De La Farnieux, *Giscard d'Estaing et nous* (Paris: Plon, 1976), p. xxx.

6. French strategist François de Rose has best captured Giscard's shift of emphasis concerning the French relationship to NATO. See *European Security and France* (Urbana: University of Illinois Press, 1983), pp. 51-52.

7. Kissinger, *Years of Upheaval,* p. 934.

8. "Les relations franco-zairoises de 1960 à 1978," *L'afrique et l'asie modernes,* no. 121 (1979): 30-40.

9. The Soviet presence in Angola included Soviet access to airfields and visits by Soviet vessels to Angolan ports, as agreed upon in the October 1979 Treaty of Friendship and Cooperation between the two countries. Moscow also provided much of the logistical support for the Cuban troop build-up in Angola, which by early 1976 had reached fifteen thousand and by 1977 had increased to twenty thousand. See David Albright, "Moscow's African Policy in the 1970s," and Edward Gonzales, "Cuba, the Soviet Union, and Africa," both in *Communism in Africa,* ed. Albright (Bloomington: Indiana University Press, 1980), pp. 35-66 and 145-67, respectively.

10. During the mid-1970s, France maintained bilateral defense treaties with five Francophone African states and military technical assistance agreements with six other states. The French security network in Africa was built around a system of thirty-seven garrisons (1974 figures) with the previously mentioned manpower total of around four thousand troops. For background, see Pierre Dabezies, "La politique militaire de la France en Afrique noire sous le général de Gaulle," in *La politique africaine du Général de Gaulle: 1958-1969* (Paris: Pedone, 1980), pp. 229-62. See

also Dominique Moisi and Pierre Lellouche, "French Policy in Africa: A Lonely Battle against Destabilization," *International Security* 3, no. 4 (1979): 108–33.

11. Special news conference reported in *Summary of World Broadcasts (SWB)*, April 14, 1977 (ME/5486/B/11). Also cited in Peter Mangold, "Shaba I and Shaba II," *Survival* 21, no. 3 (1979): 110.

12. Giscard chose not to press the case that France was acting in accordance with the 1974 military assistance agreements. The most thorough analysis of the 1978 election is in Howard Penniman, ed.,*The French National Assembly Elections of 1978* (Washington, D.C.: American Enterprise Institute, 1980). This collection unfortunately provides the reader with very little information regarding the impact of foreign policy on French voting patterns and makes no reference to the 1977 Shaba crisis.

13. According to one FLNC spokesman, "The only thing that we did not foresee was that the French response would be so strong." René Backmann, "Zaire: Les dessous de l'intervention," *Le nouvel observateur,* no. 707 (May 29, 1978): 37–38.

14. See Colin Legum, "Country-by-Country Review: Zaire," in *Africa Contemporary Record: Annual Survey and Documents, 1977–1978,* ed. Legum (New York: Africana, 1979), p. B-578. See also Zdenek Cervvanka and Colin Legum, "Cuba in Africa," in ibid., pp. A-58 through A-72.

15. Sixty Europeans were allegedly killed on the first day of attack, and another forty subsequently captured and executed. See Legum, "Country-by-Country Review: Zaire," in ibid., p. B-590.

16. Giscard delivered a major speech on the need for developing French mobile forces "to respond to the dangers which emerge from various areas of the world." See "Les déclarations de M. Giscard d' Estaing sur la défense satisfont les gaullistes et décoivant les centristes," *Le Monde,* March 27, 1985, pp. 1, 8.

17. Winriche Kuhne, "France's African Policy: Model of Problems for the Western Commitment in Africa" (mimeo), pp. 8–9.

18. Cyrus Vance, *Hard Choices: Critical Years in America's Foreign Policy* (New York: Simon and Shuster, 1983), p. 90.

_ 19. Richard Burt, "U.S. in Africa: What Are [the] Limit[s] of Congressional Curbs?" *New York Times,* May 31, 1978, p. 2.

20. Subcommittee on International Political and Military Affairs, House Committee on International Relations, *Congressional Oversight on War Powers Compliance: Zaire Airlift,* 95th Cong., 2d sess., August 10, 1978, pp. 16–17. See also Robert F. Turner, *The War Powers Resolution: Its Implementation in Theory and Practice* (Philadelphia: Foreign Policy Research Institute, 1983), pp. 68–69.

21. Vance, *Hard Choices,* p. 89.

22. "Text of President Carter's Speech at the Opening of NATO Parley," *New York Times,* May 31, 1978, p. 11.

23. Graham Hovey, "U.S. to Join Paris Parley on Southern Zaire Next Week," *New York Times,* May 31, 1978, p. 3. See also Legum, *Africa Contemporary Record, 1978–1979,* p. B-578.

24. Quoted in *L'anneé politique, 1978* (Paris: Etudes du grand siècle, 1978), p. 210.

25. F. Hernu, "France's Africa Policy from de Gaulle to Giscard," *Swiss Review of World Affairs* 28, no. 5 (1978): 11.

26. Cited in James Goldsborough, "Dateline Paris: Africa's Policeman," *Foreign Policy,* no. 72 (Winter 1978/1979): 179.

27. See Barry Cohen, "L'ébauche d'une strategie occidentale," *Le monde diplomatique,* no. 292 (July 1978): 5–7, and Christophe Batsch, "Le projet de force interafricaine," ibid., p. 8.

28. Goldsborough, "Dateline Paris," pp. 189–90.

29. See François Mitterrand, *L'abeille et l'architecte* (Paris: Flammarion, 1978), p. 367.

30. See "La France est assez seule du côté occidental, à proposer l'établissement d'un pacte de solidarité euro-africaine observe le général Mery," *Le Monde,* June 6, 1978, p. 5.

31. Jacques Isnald, "Des rebelles noirs du sud du pays constituaient l'essentiel des forces engagées contre l'armée franco-tchadienne," *Le Monde*, June 4–5, 1978, p. 3.

32. Christopher Coker, "The Western Alliance and Africa: 1949–1981," *African Affairs* 81, no. 324 (1982): 324.

33. Mangold, "Shaba I and Shaba II," p. 133.

34. See, in particular, Giscard's comments during a televised interview as reported in "M. Giscard d'Estaing peut persuader les français que la solidarité atlantique et l'indépendence national ne sont pas incompatibles," *Le Monde*, February 27, 1980, p. 42.

35. Giscard *did* attempt to insert casual references to the Zairian operation during the election, but Mitterrand generally resisted the temptation to rise to the bait. See, for example, "Les 2 candidats répondent aux 38 questions," *Le Point*, no. 450 (May 2–10, 1981): 68. See also de Rose, *European Security and France*, p. 43, who cogently analyzes the "ambiguity" of Mitterrand's campaign tactics.

36. Michel Tatu, "La position française: Des difficultes être un bon 'latino,'" *Politique étrangère* 47, no. 2 (1982): 319–24.

37. Ralph Uwechue, "Liberté, Egalité, Africanité," *Africa*, no. 119 (1981): 17.

38. Much of the French force was redeployed to Bouar in the Central African Republic near the Chadian border. The Bouar facility was expanded so that Transall and Jaguar aircraft could be flown in if a future crisis were to develop across the border. "Le remous en Afrique centrale," *Le Monde*, January 13, 1981, p. 1.

39. For background and analysis of developments in Chad, see David Yost, "French Policy in Chad and the Libyan Challenge," *Orbis* 26, no. 4 (1983): 965–99; John Chipman, *French Military Policy and African Security*, Adelphi Papers, no. 201 (London: International Institute for Strategic Studies, Summer 1985), pp. 13, 29–30; and Neil MacFarlane, *Intervention and Regional Security*, Adelphi Papers, no. 196 (London: International Institute for Strategic Studies, 1985), passim.

40. "'Ligne Verte' et 'Zone Rouge,'" *Le Monde*, January 28, 1984, p. 5. See also Jacques Isnard, "L'ouverture du feu sans préavis est autorisée contre toute intrusion dans la nouvelle 'zone rouge,'" ibid., p. 3, and Don Cook, "French Move Chad Defense Line 60 Miles North," *Los Angeles Times,* January 28, 1984, p. 3.

41. Julian C. Hollick, "Civil War in Chad, 1978–1982," *World Today* 38, nos. 7–8 (1982): 301.

42. See the chronology in *Africa South of the Sahara: 1983–1984* (London: Europa Publications, 1983), pp. 287–93.

43. Herbert Boyd, "Chad: A Civil War without End?" *Journal of African Studies* 10, no. 4 (1983–1984): 123.

44. Eric Rouleau, "Guerre et intoxification au Tchad," *Le monde diplomatique*, no. 354 (September 1983): 1, 8–9.

45. Monsour El-Kiklia, "Chad: The Same Old Story," *Journal of African Studies* 10, no. 4 (1983–84): 132.

46. Rouleau, "Guerre et intoxification," p. 1.

47. "Tchad: Le poker de Khadafi," *L'Express*, no. 1700, February 3–9, 1984, pp. 31–34.

48. René Lemarchand, "Chad: The Road to Partition," *Current History* 83, no. 491 (1984): 113.

49. "Chad: Now What?" *African Confidential* 24, no. 18 (1983): 7.

50. "Tchad: Le poker de Khadafi," pp. 45–48. See also François Heisbourg, "French Security Policy under Mitterrand," in *French Security Policy*, ed. Robin Laird (Boulder, Colo.: Westview Press, 1986), pp. 34–35.

51. "Can US Count on French to Stop Quadaffi?" *U.S. News and World Report* 95, no. 8 (August 22, 1983): 23.

52. See Jacques Amalric and Eric Rouleau, "Les explications du M. Mitterrand sur le crise su Tchad," *Le Monde*, August 26, 1983, p. 1.

53. Greg MacArthur, "France, Libya to Quit Chad," *International Herald Tribune*, September 18, 1984, p. 1, and Joseph Fitchett, "France's African Allies Uneasy," *International Herald*

Tribune, December 14, 1984, p. 5. See also Michael Field, "French and Libyan Troops to Quit Chad," *Daily Telegraph,* September 18, 1984, p. 5, who reports on French and Libyan joint determination to build good relations despite their continued tensions over Chad. Mitterrand also continued to distinguish French policies from the Reagan approach in other parts of Africa. Thus, France opposed what it viewed as U.S. attempts to polarize the OAU by its policy of support for Morocco in its struggles against the Polisario Front. See Paul Balta, "France Suspicious of Heightened US Activity in the Maghreb," *Guardian Weekly,* June 6, 1982, p. 12. See also E. J. Dionne, Jr., "Mitterrand Irked by US on Chad: Tries to Prod Quadaffi To Negotiate," *New York Times,* August 17, 1984, p. 1.

54. See Mitterrand's statement in *La défense de la France* (Dossier d'information no. 75, Ministers de la défense service d'information et ces relations publiques des armées), October 1984. See also Dominique Moisi, "Europe, The United States, and The Middle East Conundrum," *Atlantic Quarterly* 2, no. 2 (1984): 163–64. Even after fifty-three French soldiers were killed in the October 23, 1983, terrorist bombing attack against MLF forces, Mitterrand emphasized the need to counteract the "growth of neutralism and pacifism in Western Europe" by drawing lines against "aggression in the Middle East." Cited in John Vinocur, "French Public Swings Behind Lebanon Policy," *International Herald Tribune,* November 1, 1983, p. 2.

55. John Vinocur, "Nations in Lebanon Peace Force Are Reported to Discuss Reprisals," *New York Times,* October 28, 1983, pp. 1, 9.

56. Thomas Friedman, "French Jets Raid Bases of Militia Linked to Attacks," *New York Times,* November 18, 1983, pp. 1, 6, and Bernard Gwertzman, "U.S. Now Facing Lebanon Decision," ibid., pp. 1, 5.

57. Comment by Anthony Cordesman, quoted by Joseph Fitchett, "Gulf Armada Seen as a Quiet Plus for West," *International Herald Tribune,* November 18, 1987, p. 1.

58. See Robert Rudney, "Mitterrand's New Atlanticism: Evolving French Attitudes toward NATO," *Orbis* 28, no. 1 (1984): 83–101; Pierre Lellouche, *L'avenir de la guerre* (Paris: Editions Mazarine, 1985); and International Institute for Stategic Studies, *Stategic Survey, 1985–1986* (London: IISS, Spring 1986), pp. 90–92.

59. See Georges Vincent, "La loi de programmation militaire, 1984–1988: Continuité de la politique de dissuasion nucléaire et developpement des capacités d'action rapide—visite du président de la République Fédérale d'Allemagne aux FFA," *Défense nationale,* no. 39 (July 1983): 155–61. Regarding budget reductions, see "Less, Later," *Economist,* June 10–16, 1989, p. 46.

60. Discussed in David Yost, *France and Conventional Defense* (Boulder, Colo.: Westview Press, 1985), pp. 92–93.

61. Ibid., p. 91.

62. Aside from transport, French interventionary planning relies on prepositioned naval assets in place throughout selected Third World locales. See Vincent, "La loi du programmation militaire"; see also P. Buffotot, "Les forces politique et la défense: Le débat sur le réorientation stratégique," *ARES, Défense et sécurité* (Grenoble: University of Grenoble, 1983), pp. 167–79; Dominique David, "La FAR en Europe: Le dire des armes," *Défense nationale,* no. 40 (June 1984): 27–49; and an article published under the pseudonym "CRITIAS," entitled "Entre Europe et l'outre-mer," *Le Monde,* October 25, 1983, p. 8.

63. "La France ne réintegrera pas l'organisation militaire de l'OTAN souligne M. Charles Hernu," *Le Monde,* July 23, 1983, p. 6.

CONCLUSION: PART III

1. Philip Gordon, "France and European Security after the INF Treaty," *SAIS Review* (Summer-Fall 1988): 209.

INTRODUCTION: PART IV

1. Alan K. Henrikson, "The Creation of the North Atlantic Alliance," in *American Defense Policy*, 5th ed., ed. John Reichart and Steven Sturm (Baltimore: Johns Hopkins University Press), pp. 396–97.

2. Roger Hilsman, "NATO: The Developing Strategic Context," in *NATO and American Security*, ed. Klaus Knorr (Princeton, N.J.: Princeton University Press, 1959), p. 15.

3. These developments are surveyed by Douglas Stuart in the introductory chapter of Stuart, ed., *Politics and Security in the Southern Region of the Atlantic Alliance* (Baltimore: Johns Hopkins University Press, 1988), pp. 1–11. See also Lawrence S. Kaplan, Robert W. Clawson, and Raimondo Luraghi, eds., *NATO and the Mediterranean* (Wilmington, Del.: Scholarly Resources, 1985); John Chipman, ed., *NATO's Southern Allies: Internal and External Challenges* (Beckenham, Kent: Croom Helm, 1987); Stefano Silvestri and Maurizio Cremasco, eds., *Il fianco sud della NATO* (Milan: Feltrinelli, 1980); Curt Gasteyger, ed., *Forces militaires et conflits politiques en Méditerranée* (Paris: Atlantic Institute, 1970); and Charles Zorgbibe, *La Méditerranée sans les grands* (Paris: Presses universitaires de France, 1980).

19: NATO's NORTH

1. See especially remarks of U.S. State Department Policy Planning Staff Director George Kennan in "Memorandum of the Thirteenth Meeting of the Working Group Participating in the Washington Exploratory Talks on Security" (September 2, 1948), in *FRUS 1948*, vol. 3, *Western Europe*, pp. 226–27, and "Memorandum by the Participants in the Washington Security Talks, July 6 to September 9, Submitted to Their Respective Governments for Study and Comment [referred to in subsequent meetings and correspondence as 'the Washington Paper']: Territorial Scope of a North Atlantic Security Arrangement and Its Relationship to the Security of Other Nations" (September 9, 1948), in ibid., pp. 240–41. See also Geir Lundestad, *America, Scandinavia, and the Cold War, 1945–1949* (New York: Columbia University Press, 1980), p. 251.

2. See Eric S. Einhorn, "The Reluctant Ally: Danish Security Policy, 1945–1949," *Journal of Contemporary History* 10, no. 3 (1975): 507.

3. British Public Record Office, J.P. (50) 90 Final Draft, 6/14, quoted in Rolf Tammes, "Norway Struggle for the Northern Flanks, 1950–1952," in *Western Security: The Formative Years*, ed. O. Riste (New York: Columbia University Press, 1985), p. 218.

4. The National Security Council went no farther than calling for "supporting Norway in maintaining her sovereignty over these islands and preventing their use by a hostile military power." See "Report by the National Security Council, NSC 28/1—The Position of the United States with Respect to Scandinavia" (September 3, 1948), in *FRUS 1948*, vol. 3, *Western Europe*, p. 234. See also Lundestad, *America, Scandinavia, and the Cold War*, pp. 228–29. An earlier draft of recommendations for prospective NATO coverage drawn up by the U.S.-U.K.-Canadian Security Committee in April called for the NATO coverage to include Spitzbergen. This remained the minority position, however. See "Minutes of the Sixth Meeting of the United States-United Kingdom-Canada Security Conversations, Held at Washington" (April 1, 1948—Final Draft), *FRUS 1948*, vol. 3, *Western Europe*, p. 74.

5. "Report by the Joint Strategic Plans Committee to the Joint Chiefs of Staff on Force Requirements for the Defense of Island Bases in the Atlantic Command" (JCS 2073/551, April 7, 1953), in *Records of the Joint Chiefs of Staff*, pt. 2, *Europe and NATO, 1946–1953* (Frederick, Md.: University Publications of America, 1949), reel 8, frame 0639.

6. Nils Orvik, *NATO's Northern Cap and the Soviet Union*, Occasional Papers on International Affairs, no. 6 (Cambridge: Harvard University, September 1963), p. 45. Emphasis is his.

7. The strategy of balancing deterrence and reassurance is discussed by Johan Holst, "The Pattern of Nordic Security" (Oslo: Norwegian Institute of International Affairs, undated mono-

graph), and by Willy Ostreng, *The Soviet Union in Arctic Waters*, Study no. R:013/2 (Oslo: Fridtjof Nansen Institute, 1982).

8. "Memorandum of Conversation by the Assistant Secretary of State for European Affairs (Perkins)" (September 16, 1951), in *FRUS 1951*, vol. 3, pt. 1, *Europe Security and the German Question*, p. 659, and "Memorandum of Conversation by the Assistant Secretary of State for European Affairs (Perkins)" (September 16, 1951), in ibid., pp. 661-62.

9. Joe Wilkinson, "Denmark and NATO: The Problem of a Small State in a Collective Security System," *International Organization* 10, no. 3 (1956): 395.

10. Ole Bjørn Kraft, *Danish Parliamentary Debates* (Folketingets Forhadlinger), October 1951, as cited in ibid., p. 396.

11. Ingemar Dorfer, "Scandinavia and NATO: A la Carte," *Washington Quarterly* 9, no. 1 (1986): 21.

12. Christopher Coker, *NATO, The Warsaw Pact, and Africa* (New York: St. Martin's Press, 1985), esp. pp. 59-70, and John Major, "The Emergence of African Rivalries," in *Survey of International Affairs, 1961*, ed. D. C. Watt (London: Oxford University Press and the Royal Institute of International Affairs, 1965), p. 423. Major notes, however, that Scandinavian pressure on London finally resulted in the British Government's announcing (June 27, 1961) that "applications to supply military equipment to the Portuguese are in suspense."

13. For background, see "Danish Aid for Nationalists in Africa," *New York Times*, March 13, 1972, p. 22, and Coker, *NATO, Warsaw Pact, and Africa*, p. 68.

14. A Report by the Expert Subcommittee on the Government Committee on Danish Security Policy, *Problemer ourkving dansk sikkerhedspolitik [Problems of Danish Security Policy]* (Copenhagen, 1970), as cited in Nikolaj Peterson, "Danish Security Policy in the Seventies: Continuity or Change?" *Cooperation and Conflict* 6, nos. 3/4 (1972): 12. Regarding the risks of spillover from a Third World conflict, see Miroslav Nincic, *How War Might Spread to Europe* (London: Taylor and Francis for the Stockholm International Peace Research Institute), pp. 72-73.

15. Cited in Wolfram von Raven, "NATO's Biggest North Atlantic Maneuvers," *Aussenpolitik* [English Edition], no. 4 (1972): 409.

16. This thesis is particularly well developed by Willy Ostreng, "The Strategic Balance and the Arctic Ocean: Soviet Options," *Cooperation and Conflict* 12, no. 1 (1977): 41-62. See also J. Gelner, "The Military Task: Sovereignty and Security, Surveillance and Control in the Far North," in *The Arctic In Question*, ed. E. J. Dosman (Toronto: Oxford University Press, 1976), pp. 85-101; T. A. Hockin and P. A. Brennan, "Canada's Arctic and Its Strategic Importance," in ibid., pp. 102-20; G. R. Lindsey, "Strategic Aspects of the Polar Regions," *Behind the Headlines* 35, no. 6 (1977): 1-24; Anders C. Sjaastad, "The Changing Geopolitical Environment," in *Deterrence and Defense in the North*, ed. Johan Holst, Kenneth Hunt, and Anders C. Sjaastad (London: Universitetsforlaget, 1985), pp. 36-38; Anthony R. Wells, "The Soviet Navy in the Arctic and North Atlantic," *National Defense* 70, no. 415 (1986): 39-44; and Sverre Jervell and Kare Nyblom, eds., *The Military Buildup in the High North: American and Nordic Perspectives* (Harvard University, Center for International Affairs, 1986).

17. See Katrina Enberg, "The U.S. Maritime Strategy: A Scandinavian Perspective," Paper presented at the Second Harvard Nordic Conference, Hveragerd, Iceland, August 7, 1987.

18. Christian Muller, "Strategic Arctic Outposts," *Swiss Review of World Affairs* 29, no. 7 (October 1979): 10.

19. Background on the growing strategic importance of Spitzbergen over the past decade is provided by John C. Ausland, *Nordic Security and the Great Powers* (Boulder, Colo.: Westview Press, 1986), pp. 175-76; Ausland, "Spitzbergen: Who's in Control?" *U.S. Naval Institute Proceedings* 104, no. 11/909 (November 1978): 62-70; and Muller, "Strategic Arctic Outposts," pp. 8-12.

20. The concept of a "Mediterraneanized" north was introduced by G. R. Lindsey from a somewhat different context in "The Future of Anti-Submarine Warfare and Its Impact on Naval

Activities in the North Atlantic and Arctic Regions," in *New Strategic Factors in the North Atlantic*, ed. Christoph Bertram and Johan Holst (Oslo: Universitatsforlaget, 1977), esp. p. 172. Johan Holst also discusses Norwegian concerns about Mediterraneanization in "The Effect on Norway: Increased Caution," in Jervell and Nyblom, *Military Buildup in the High North*, p. 85.

21. Regarding Soviet submarine sightings, see Kirsten Amundsen, "Soviet Submarines in Scandinavian Waters," *Washington Quarterly*, 8, no. 3 (1985): 111–22.

22. Dorfer, "Scandinavia and NATO," p. 16.

23. Dov S, Zakheim, "NATO's Northern Front: Developments and Prospects," *Cooperation and Conflict* 17, no. 4 (1982): 194. For a recent survey of the military situation in the north, see H. F. Zeiner-Gundersen, "NATO's Northern Flank," in *NATO's Maritime Flanks: Problems and Prospects*, ed. Gundersen et al. (Washington, D.C.: Pergamon-Brassey's, 1987), pp. 1–26.

24. For information about U.S.-Norwegian agreements for prestocking, see Örjan Berner, *Soviet Policies toward the Nordic Countries* (New York: University Press of America, 1986), pp. 172–73.

25. Liv Hegna, "Lieutenant General Ulf Berg Says NATO Presence in Norwegian Sea Too Little," *Aftenposten*, January 31, 1986, p. 56, translated and reprinted in Joint Publications Research Service (JPRS), *West Europe Report* 86–023, March 4, 1986, pp. 90–91.

26. See Johan Jorgen Holst, "Norwegian Security Policy: The Strategic Dimension," in Holst, Hunt, and Sjaastad, *Deterrence and Defense*, pp. 110–18, and William T. Tow, "NATO's Out-of-Region Challenges and Extended Containment," *Orbis* 28, no. 4 (1985): 850–51. The Canadian Air-Sea Transportable (CAST) Brigade Group was withdrawn in early 1987 from Norway to Canada for budgetary reasons but is still designated to northern Norway in time of crisis.

27. The multinational composition of the ACE AMF is covered more thoroughly by Charles Messenger, "The ACE Mobile Force," in *Jane's Military Review, 1983–1984*, ed. Ian V. Hogg (London: Jane's, 1983), pp. 21–33.

28. Sharon Hobson, "Canadian Senate Salvo," *U.S. Naval Institute Proceedings* 110, no. 3/973 (1984): 147–48; "Canadian Military Faulted," *Los Angeles Times*, May 24, 1984, p. 2; and Tow, "NATO's Out-of-Region Challenges," p. 851.

29. Ministry of National Defense, *Challenge and Commitment: A Defense Policy for Canada* (Ottawa, June 1987), p. 61. The 1987 White Paper is analyzed by Ian Kemp, "The Canadian Defense White Paper," *Armed Forces* 6, no. 10 (1987): 464–68.

30. Ausland, *Nordic Security and the Great Powers*, pp. 137–38. See also Maj. Gen. Edward Fursdon, "Vital Role for Marines in Norway," *Daily Telegraph*, February 28, 1986, p. 5.

31. See Arne Olav Bruntland, "Norwegian Security Policy: Defense and Non-provocation in a Changing Context," in *NATO's Northern Allies*, ed. Gregory Flynn (Totowa, N.J.: Croom Helm, 1985), p. 220.

32. McDonald interview by Derek Wood, published in *Jane's Defense Weekly*, 3, no. 16 (April 20, 1985): 652–53. See also Vice Admiral H. C. Mustin, "The Role of the Navy and Marines in the Norwegian Sea," *Naval War College Review* 39, no. 2 (1986): 2–3, and Linton F. Brooks, "Naval Power and National Security: The Case for the Maritime Strategy," *International Security* 11, no. 2 (1986): 58–88.

33. "Statement of Adm. Lee Baggett, Jr., USN, Commander in Chief, U.S. Atlantic Command," Hearings before the Senate Armed Services Committee, 100th Cong., 2d sess., *Department of Defense Authorization for Appropriations for Fiscal Year 1989*, February 19, 1989, p. 402.

34. Ibid., p. 405.

35. Holst, "Pattern of Nordic Security," p. 11.

36. Discussed by Erling Bjøl, *Nordic Security*, Adelphi Papers, no. 181 (London: International Institute for Strategic Studies, 1983), pp. 25–26, and Dorfer, "Scandinavia and NATO," esp. p. 20.

37. According to Kirsten Amundsen, "Technically, of course, a seizure of Svalbard would be an attack on a member country of NATO. But here is the rub: Who among Norway's allies would want

to go to war with the Communist superpower over some remote islands in the Arctic, in waters already dominated by the Soviet Navy?" *Norway, NATO, and the Forgotten Soviet Challenge, Policy Papers on International Affairs*, no. 14 (Berkeley: University of California Press, 1981), p. 18.

38. Holst, "Pattern of Nordic Security," p. 15, and Barry Posen, "Inadvertent Nuclear War? Escalation and NATO's Northern Flank," *International Security* 7, no. 2 (1982): 28–54, esp. pp. 48–51. Recently, Mikhail Gorbachev has been engaged in a campaign to manipulate Scandinavian insecurities by his call for an "Arctic Peace Zone," which might include establishing a denuclearized zone in the north or banning all military activity in that region. See Martin Walker, "Russian Plan for Arctic Peace Zone," *Guardian*, October 2, 1987, p. 32, and John Burns, "Canada Catches a Cold War Chill," *New York Times*, July 3, 1988, p. E-2.

39. Nincic, *How War Might Spread to Europe*, p. 72.

40. Bjøl, *Nordic Security*, p. 26.

41. Oslo *Arbeiderbladt*, March 3, 1981, p. 1, reprinted in Foreign Broadcast Information Service (FBIS), *West Europe (Daily Report)*, March 5, 1981, p. P-1. See also Brundtland, "Norwegian Security Policy," pp. 218–20, and "Storting Committee to Central America and U.S.," *News of Norway* 41, no. 2 (February 3, 1984), p. 1.

42. North Atlantic Assembly, Political Committee, *General Report on Challenges for Alliance Northern Security—The Gorbachev Era* (Brussels: International Secretariat, September 1987), pp. 2–7.

43. See John Honderich, *Arctic Imperative: Is Canada Losing the North?* (Toronto: University of Toronto Press, 1987).

44. See "New Soviet Bomber Base Cited in Norwegian Report," *Los Angeles Times*, August 23, 1986, p. 4. Reports on the Greenland radar dispute include Michael R. Gordon, "U.S. Plan for a Greenland Radar Made a Public Issue in Denmark," *New York Times*, January 27, 1987, p. 5, and an editorial, "Radar Trap, and Opportunity," ibid., January 28, 1987, p. 26.

45. David Lamb, "Superpower Strategies Focus on Alaska," *Los Angeles Times*, September 25, 1987, p. 20.

46. "3 U.S. Nuclear Subs Surfaced at North Pole, Navy Discloses," *Los Angeles Times*, May 24, 1986, p. 30.

47. See Sharon Hobson, "Canada's New Defense Plans," *Jane's Defense Weekly* 7, no. 27 (1987): 1385–89; David Buchan, "Fortress Canada Toughens Up," *Financial Times*, August 5, 1987, p. 2; and the very useful in-depth analysis by David Cox, "Living Along the Flight Path: Canada's Defense Debate," *Washington Quarterly* 10, no. 4 (1987), esp. pp. 100–105. See also John F. Burns, "In the Arctic Tundra, Thunder of Ottawa's Military Buildup," *New York Times*, July 6, 1987, pp. 1–2, and *Challenge and Commitment: A Defense Policy for Canada*, pp. 51–55.

48. Report of the Sub-Committee on National Defense of the Standing Senate Committee on Foreign Affairs, *Canada's Maritime Defense* (Ottawa: Canadian Senate, May 1983), passim.

49. See Kenneth Freed, "Canada Plans Submarines for Arctic Claims," *Los Angeles Times*, June 6, 1987, pp. 1, 21.

50. Tariq Rauf and John Lamb, "Should Canada Bring the Boys Home?" *Bulletin of the Atomic Scientists* (September 1989): 37.

20: The Central European NATO Powers and the Out-of-Region Issue

1. See accounts of the French deployment in Robert C. Doty, "French Again Add to Algeria Force," *New York Times*, March 18, 1956, pp. 1, 2.

2. Benjamin Wells, "NATO Allies Chide London and Paris," *New York Times*, November 3, 1956, p. 4; Arthur J. Olsen, "Bonn May Speed Troops on Field," ibid., November 6, 1956, p. 2; and "Dr. Adenauer's Satisfaction," *Times* (London), November 8, 1956, p. 9. Adenauer returned

from a November 7 conference with French foreign minister Mollet convinced that "his advice had been a crucial factor in persuading the British and French . . . to agree to a cease-fire in Egypt" and had "pressed for an immediate cessation of hostilities," insisting that Western Europe would be "in great danger" if the Russians were to intervene on Egypt's behalf.

3. "West German Misgivings," *Economist* 188, no. 5996, July 26, 1958, p. 301.

4. Cited by Catherine Kelleher, "The Defense Policy of the Federal Republic of Germany", in *The Defense Policies of Nations: A Comparative Study,* ed. Douglas Murray and Paul Viotti (Baltimore: Johns Hopkins University Press, 1982), p. 293.

5. Willy Brandt, *People and Politics: The Years 1960–1975* (Boston: Little, Brown, 1976), p. 456.

6. See the summary of this incident in George Rosie, *The Dictionary of International Terrorism* (New York: Paragon House, 1986), pp. 181–82.

7. Brandt's diplomacy is ably covered by Michael Wolfsohn, *West Germany's Foreign Policy in the Era of Brandt and Schmidt, 1969–1982: An Introduction* (Frankfurt am Main: Verlag Peter Lang, 1986), pp. 18–24. A broader assessment is provided by Alexander L. George, "The Arab-Israeli War of October 1973: Origins and Impact," in *Managing U.S.-Soviet Rivalry,* ed. George (Boulder, Colo.: Westview Press, 1983), pp. 148–81.

8. See Hearings before Subcommittee on Military Construction Appropriations of the House Committee on Appropriations, *Military Construction Appropriations for 1982,* 97th Cong., 1st sess. January 15, 1981, p. 169. See also James R. Golden, *The Dynamics of Change in NATO: A Burden-sharing Perspective* (New York: Praeger, 1983), pp. 130–31.

9. The 1980 proposal was actually an outgrowth of discussions undertaken during the 1979 Long Term Defense Program (LTDP) negotiations "based on the possibility of a reallocation of NATO resources resulting from potential action in the Persian Gulf." Golden, *Dynamics of Change in NATO,* pp. 130–31.

10. Mainz ZDF Network broadcast, translated and reprinted in Foreign Broadcast Information Service (FBIS), *West Europe (Daily Report),* April 17, 1986. For a background analysis of "mainstream political leadership's views on the effects of the U.S. air strike on European diplomatic efforts in the Middle East", consult *NRC Handelsblad* (Rotterdam), April 16, 1986, translated and reprinted in FBIS, *West Europe (Daily Report),* April 22, 1986, p. J-1. See also "The Europeans: Tut Tut, Mostly," *Economist* 299, no. 7442 (April 19–25, 1986), p. 24.

11. U.S. conservatives still complained that the U.S. F-111s used to attack Libyan targets touched nowhere between England and Libya, "though most of the land involved was that of American's NATO allies." See Owen Harries, "The Line of Shame," *Los Angeles Times,* April 17, 1986, pt. 2, p. 7.

12. The speech is reprinted in Schmidt's *A Grand Strategy for the West* (New Haven: Yale University Press, 1985), pp. 95–96.

13. Ibid., p. 96.

14. See "Naval Task Force Being Sent to Mediterranean," Hamburg DPA Report, translated and reprinted in FBIS, *West Europe (Daily Report),* October 9, 1987, p. 1.

15. Kelleher, "Defense Policy of the FRG," p. 293.

16. Remarks delivered at the Verkunde Conference in Munich and reprinted in FBIS, *West Europe (Daily Report),* February 23, 1981, p. J-3. Apel's comments are also assessed in Report to the Senate Committee on Foreign Relations, *NATO Today: The Alliance in Evolution,* 89th Cong., 2d sess., April 1982, pp. 37–38.

17. Vice Adm. C.H.E. Brainich Von Felth, "Neglecting Maritime Defense Is Paid For Dearly," *NATO's Sixteen Nations* 31, no. 1 (1986): 75.

18. For background, see Henri Grimal, *Decolonization: The British, French, Dutch, and Belgian Empires, 1919–1963* (London: Routledge and Kegan Paul, 1978), pp. 192–213.

19. See Cees Weebes, "The Dutch Do Not Seem to Keep the Timetable Handy: The National Security Policy of the Netherlands, 1940–1949," in *The Origins of NATO,* ed. Joseph Smith

(Exeter: University of Exeter Press, 1990), and Franz Govaerts, "The Road toward Alignment," in *Small Powers in Alignment,* ed. Omer de Raeymaeker et al. (Leuven, Belgium: University of Leuven Press, 1974), pp. 320–22, 327.

20. S.I.P. van Campen, *The Quest for Security: Some Aspects of Netherlands Foreign Policy, 1945–1950* (The Hague: Martinus Nijhoff, 1958), pp. 110–11.

21. For background on the Irian Jaya dispute, consult Arend Lijphart, *The Trauma of Decolonization: The Dutch and West New Guinea* (New Haven: Yale University Press, 1966), esp. pp. 63–66. For a South Pacific perspective, see Sjirk Bajema, "West Irian: A Neo-Colonial Dilemma," *Pacific Perspective* 9, no. 2 (1980): 77–87, and for an updated account of the current political imbroglios in this unfortunate geographic region, see Ian Bell, Herb Freith, and Ron Hatley, "The West Papuan Challenge to Indonesian Authorities in Irian Jaya: Old Problems, New Possibilities," *Asian Survey* 26, no. 5 (1986): 539–56.

22. Henri Baudet, "The Netherlands after the Loss of Empire," *Journal of Contemporary History* 4, no. 1 (1969): 128.

23. Background on Dutch defense policy and capabilities is provided by Jan G. Siccama, "The Netherlands Depillarized: Security Policy in a New Domestic Context," in *NATO's Northern Allies,* ed. Gregory Flynn (Totawa, N.J.: Croom Helm, 1985), pp. 113–70; International Institute for Strategic Studies, *The Military Balance, 1985–1986* (London: IISS, 1985), pp. 54–55; Rose Kelly, "The Special Operations Forces of Belgium and the Netherlands," *Defense and Foreign Affairs Monthly* 13, no. 7 (July 1985): 33–34; and Ben J. Ullings, "Defensienota 1984," *Armed Forces Magazine* (April 1984): 153–56.

24. Gregory R. Copley, *Defense and Foreign Affairs Handbook, 1985* (Washington, D.C.: Perth Corp., 1985), p. 458. See also *Amigoe* (Willemstad), March 6, 1985, p. 3, translated and reprinted in *Joint Publications Record Service, Latin America,* 85–038, May 3, 1985, pp. 112–13.

25. Charles Kupchan, *The Persian Gulf and the West* (Boston: Allen and Unwin, 1987), p. 203.

26. "Allies Reported Dividing Task of Minesweeping," *Los Angeles Times,* September 23, 1987, p. 11; David Buchan and Richard Johns, "Too Many Guns in Crowded Waters," *Financial Times,* September 23, 1987, p. 6; and dispatches on both the Dutch and Belgium contingents in FBIS, *West Europe (Daily Report),* November 23, 1987, p. 3.

27. The *Sunday Telegraph* report was picked up by the Dutch press (*De Volkskrant,* December 1, 1987, p. 6) and translated and reprinted in FBIS, *West Europe (Daily Report),* December 8, 1987, p. 3.

28. Jonathan E. Helmreich, *Belgium and Europe: A Study in Small Power Diplomacy* (The Hague: Mouton, 1976), pp. 344–95; Thomas Kanza, *The Rise and Fall of Patrice Lumumba* (Boston: G. K. Hall, 1979), p. 175; and by far still the best account of the crisis, Ernest W. Lefever, *Crisis in the Congo* (Washington, D.C.: Brookings Institution, 1965), esp. pp. 11–12, 59.

29. Lefever, *Crisis in the Congo,* pp. 11–12.

30. G. Warner, "The Western Alliance," in *Survey of International Affairs, 1959–1960,* ed. G. Barraclough (London: Oxford University Press, 1964), p. 83.

31. Paul-Henri Spaak, *The Continuing Battle: Memoirs of a European, 1936–1966* (Boston: Little, Brown, 1971), pp. 221–22.

32. Department of State Cable (3), August 12, 1960 (Secret), *Declassified Document Reference System,* vol. 9, 1983 (Woodbridge, Conn.: Research Publications Incorporated/Carrollton Press, Microfiche Series, 1983), item 000903.

33. "But How Much of Africa Can Giscard Embrace?" *Economist* 267, no. 2030, May 22, 1978), p. 60.

34. A concise but thorough account of the French/Belgian troop deployments is in *Keesing's Contemporary Archives,* August 11, 1978, p. 29126. See also "Not by France Alone," *Economist* 267, no. 7030, May 22, 1978, pp. 13–14; and "One Dithered, One Acted," ibid., p. 60.

35. "But How Much of Africa Can Giscard Embrace?" p. 60.

36. Frederick Bonnart and Victor Neels, Interview with Belgian minister of defense Xavier-

François de Donnea, "Rationalizing the Defense Effort of Belgium," *NATO's Sixteen Nations* 32. no. 4 (1987): 51.

37. *Le Soir,* November 13, 1987, p. 8, translated and reprinted in FBIS, *West Europe (Daily Report),* November 27, 1987, p. 4.

21: ITALY

1. See, for example, Andrew Borowiec, "Craxi's Mediterranean Vocation," *Insight,* February 3, 1986, p. 32.

2. Regarding Italy's postwar status, see U.S. Department of State, *Postwar Foreign Policy Preparations: 1939–1945* (Washington, D.C.: Government Printing Office, 1949), pp. 343–44.

3. Scenarios for Italy's role in the defense of central Europe are discussed by Luigi Caligaris, "Italy," in *Politics and Security in the Southern Region of the Atlantic Alliance,* ed. Douglas Stuart (Baltimore: Johns Hopkins University Press, 1988), pp. 68–95, and Jed C. Snyder *Defending the Fringe: NATO, the Mediterranean, and the Persian Gulf,* SAIS Papers in International Affairs, no. 11 (Boulder, Colo.: Westview Press, 1987), p. 32.

4. Caligaris, "Italy."

5. On the evolution of the PCI's foreign and defense platform up to 1977, see Congressional Research Service, Library of Congress, Report submitted by Senator Edward Brooke to the Committee on Appropriations, U.S. Senate, "A Report on West European Communist Parties," 95th Cong., 2d sess., June 1977, esp. pp. 61–73.

6. See "PSI Role in World Detente, Disarmament Outline," July 6, 1982, report in *Avante,* translated and reprinted in FBIS, *West Europe (Daily Report),* July 7, 1982, p. L-2.

7. Quoted in Maurizio Cremasco, "An Italian Rapid Intervention Force: The Geopolitical Context," *International Spectator* 20, no. 2 (1985): 60.

8. Regarding this new Italian sense of responsibility, see Fabrizio Coisson and Vittorio Scutti, "Noi, i vigilantes del Mediterraneo," *L'Espresso,* October 30, 1983, pp. 20–23.

9. Snyder, *Defending the Fringe,* p. 32.

10. For Spadolini's comments, see Paul Lewis, "Italy Hints at Pullout of Its Contingents," *New York Times,* December 1983, p. 19.

11. The Italian MLF mission is discussed in the 1985 Defense White Book (Rome: Ministry of Defense, 1985). See the appendix, esp. pp. 162–68. See also Luigi Caligaris, "Western Peacekeeping in Lebanon: Lessons of the MLF," *Survival* 26, no. 6 (1984): 262–68.

12. Regarding Italian crisis management capabilities, see Stefano Silvestri, "E tutto fuori controllo," *Europeo,* April 26, 1986, pp. 10–14.

13. Based on interviews by one of the authors (Stuart) with Prof. Laura Forlati Picchio, who is currently doing research on the legal aspects of the Sigonella case. The U.S. government decided to take dramatic, unilateral action at Sigonella after it was disclosed that an American citizen had been executed by the terrorists on board the *Achille Lauro.*

14. Craxi also complained about the two U.S. aircraft that tracked the Egyptian airliner when Italian authorities flew the plane and its occupants (under Italian air escort) from Sigonella to Rome.

15. Andreotti came under special criticism for his pro-PLO posture. See, for example, "Giulio d'Arabia," *L'Espresso,* October 20, 1985, pp. 14–15.

16. See, for example, "La politica Di Rambo," *L'Espresso,* October 20, 1985, pp. 9–10.

17. Pertaining to Italian offshore oil exploration in the Gulf of Sidra, see Giacomo Luciani, *The Mediterranean and the Energy Picture,* Monograph no. A1/16/82, Instituto d'affari internazionale (Rome, 1982).

18. Quoted by Caligaris, "Italy," in Stuart, *Politics and Security,* p. 89.

19. Regarding Italy's handling of the Lampedusa attacks in the NATO forum, see Franco Papitto, "L'alleanza spera di restarne fouri," *La Republica,* April 18, 1986.

20. Giovanni Valentini, "Qualcosa e cambiato tra noi e gli USA," *L'Espresso*, May 4, 1986, p. 5.

21. 1985 Defense White Book, pt. 1, p. 7.

22. 1985 Defense White Book. See also excerpts from the Defense White Book cited in Assembly of Western European Union, Committee on Defense Questions and Armaments, *European Security and the Mediterranean*, doc. 1073 (Paris: WEU Assembly, October 14, 1986), pp. 16–17. For analysis, see Luigi Caligaris, "Possible Scenarios for an Italian Rapid Deployment Force," *International Spectator* 20, nos. 3/4 (1985): 64–87.

23. For background on the FOPI's civil defense/disaster functions, consult Andrea Lusa, "The FOPI (Ready Intervention Force) and National Disasters," *Rivista militaire* (March/April 1986): 16–23.

24. Italian land and air forces' national deployment patterns are assessed by Assembly of Western European Union, Committee on Defense Questions and Armaments, *European Security and the Mediterranean*, p. 17, and International Institute for Strategic Studies, *The Military Balance, 1987–1988* (London: IISS, Autumn 1987), p. 69. The June 1988 decision by Rome to host the 401st NATO Tactical Fighter Wing in southern Italy, after Spain insisted on its withdrawal from Torrejon, nevertheless represents a valuable step in the direction of a more balanced deployment pattern throughout Italy.

25. Geoffrey Till, "European Navies," *Naval Forces—International Forum for Maritime Power* 8, no. 2 (1987): 90.

26. See Catherine Kelleher, "Alternative Models for Middle Power Navies," in *The Future of British Sea Power*, ed. Geoffrey Till (Annapolis, Md.: Naval Institute Press, 1984), p. 245. Data on the *Garibaldi*'s missions and characteristics are offered by Sergio Mecchia, "'Garibaldi' Officially Joins the Italian Navy," *Military Technology*, no. 12 (1985): 88–90.

27. To date, no government has admitted laying the mines in the Red Sea in 1983.

28. Luigi Caligaris, "Italian Defense Policy: Problems and Prospects," *Survival* 25, no. 2 (1983): 70. See also the insightful analysis by Maurizio Cremasco, "NATO's Southern Flank and Italy's Role in It," *International Spectator* 2 (April–June 1988): 79–89.

22: THE AEGEAN ALLIES

1. Regarding Turkey's postwar security situation, see Duygu Sezer, *Turkey's Security Policies*, Adelphi Papers, no. 164 (London: International Institute for Strategic Studies, 1981); Bruce Kuniholm, "Turkey and NATO: Past, Present, and Future," *Orbis* 27, no. 2 (Summer 1983): 421–45; George S. Harris, *Troubled Alliance: Turkish-American Problems in Historical Perspective, 1955–1971* (Washington, D.C./Palo Alto, Calif.: American Enterprise Institute for Public Policy Research/Hoover Institution, 1972); Andrew Mango, *Turkey: A Delicately Poised Ally*, Washington Paper no. 28 (Washington, D.C.: Center for Strategic and International Studies, 1975); and Ali Karaosmanoğlu, "Turkey's Security Policy: Continuity and Change," in *Politics and Security in the Southern Region of the Atlantic Alliance*, ed. Douglas Stuart (Baltimore: Johns Hopkins University Press, 1988), pp. 157–80.

2. "The Ambassador in Turkey (Wadsworth) to the Secretary of State" (July 31, 1950), in *FRUS 1950*, vol. 5, *The Near East and Africa* (1978), pp. 1287–88.

3. Ibid.

4. See Yulug Tekin Kukat, "Turkey's Entry to the North Atlantic Treaty Organization," *Dis Politika* (*Foreign Policy*, Foreign Policy Institute, Ankara) 10, nos. 3–4 (1983): 50–77.

5. Memorandum by Henry S. Villard to the Director of Policy Planning (Nitze)" (February 5, 1951), in *FRUS 1951*, vol. 5, *The Near East and Africa* (1982), p. 1117.

6. Ibid., pp. 1145–46.

7. Karaosmanoğlu, "Turkey's Security Policy," p. 158.

8. Ibid., pp. 158–59.

NOTES TO PAGES 290-96

9. For background, see Robert McDonald, *The Problem of Cyprus*, Adelphi Papers, no. 234 (London: International Institute for Strategic Studies, Winter 1988/89), and Andrew Borowiec, *The Mediterranean Feud* (New York: Praeger, 1983).

10. Robert McDonald, *Problem of Cyprus,*, p. 12.

11. "Document: President Johnson and Prime Minister Inonu: Correspondence between President Johnson and Prime Minister Inonu, June 1964, as Released by the White House, January 15, 1966," *Middle East Journal* (Summer 1966): 386–89, and Jed C. Snyder, *Defending the Fringe: NATO, the Mediterranean, and the Persian Gulf*, SAIS Papers in International Affairs, no. 11 (Boulder, Colo.: Westview Press, 1987), p. 47.

12. For more recent information on Turkey, see James Blight and David Welch, *On the Brink* (New York: Hill and Wang, 1989).

13. Cited in *Greece and Turkey: Some Military Implications Related to NATO and the Middle East*, Committee Print, prepared by the Congressional Research Service, Library of Congress, for the Special Subcommittee on Investigations of the House Committee on Foreign Affairs, 94th Cong., 1st sess., February 28, 1975 (Washington, D.C.: Government Printing Office, 1975), pp. 16–17.

14. See Jed C. Snyder, "Strategic Bias and European Security: Recognizing the Threat to NATO's Southern Flank," Conference Paper, International Studies Association (Philadelphia, March 18–21, 1981), p. 29.

15. See Ali Karaosmanoğlu, "Turkey's Security and the Middle East," *Foreign Affairs* 62, no. 1 (1983): 157–75.

16. Quoted in ibid., p. 167.

17. Staff Report, "Crisis on Cyprus: 1975," Subcommittee to Investigate Problems Connected with Refugees and Escapees, Senate Judiciary Committee, 94th Cong., 1st sess., July 20, 1975, passim.

18. Discussed by Dankwart Rustow, "Turkey's Travails," *Foreign Affairs* 58, no. 1 (1979): 95.

19. Borowiec, *Mediterranean Feud*, p. 48.

20. Bulent Ecevit, "Turkey's Security Policies," *Survival* 20, no. 5 (1978): pp. 203–8.

21. Curt Gasteyger, "The Southern Flank: New Diversions for the Alliance," in *NATO: The Next Thirty Years*, ed. Kenneth Myers (Boulder, Colo.: Westview Press, 1980), p. 181, and Snyder, *Defending the Fringe*, p. 48.

22. Data provided by Karaosmanoğlu, "Turkey's Security Policy," pp. 164–65.

23. "Turks Turn Down U.S. Facility for Intervention Force," *International Herald Tribune*, April 17, 1984.

24. The Turkish Republic of Northern Cyprus issued a unilateral declaration of independence on November 15, 1983.

25. Hasan Cemal, "Politics and Business," quoted in FBIS, *West Europe (Daily Report)*, WEU–83–242, December 15, 1983, at T4.

26. The 1982 memorandum of Understanding is discussed by Ali Karaosmanoğlu, "Turkey's Security Policy," p. 248. Washington and Ankara reached agreement on renewal of U.S. basing access in 1986. This agreement will remain in effect until 1990, at which time a new round of basing talks will be required.

27. Thomas McNaugher, *Arms and Oil* (Washington, D.C.: Brookings Institution, 1985), p. 56.

28. House Foreign Affairs Committee, *Greece and Turkey*, p. 5.

29. Documents relating to U.S. relations with Greece and Turkey during the 1950s are provided in ibid., pp. 2–4.

30. Cited in Thanos Veremis, *Greek Security: Issues and Politics*, Adelphi Papers, no. 179 (London: International Institute for Strategic Studies, 1982), pp. 18–19.

31. Quoted in *Financial Times*, March 8, 1985, p. 20.

32. Ibid. See also Van Coufoudakis, "Greek-Turkish Relations, 1973–1983: The View from

Athens," *International Security* 9, no. 4 (1985): 185–99, and *International Herald Tribune,* January 9, 1985.

33. Papandreou is quoted in the *International Herald Tribune,* May 11, 1984.

34. Cited in John Loulis, "Papandreou's Foreign Policy," *Foreign Affairs* 63, no. 2 (1984–85): 388.

35. See, for example, reports relating to the Greek-sponsored Balkan Summit, *Times* (London), June 25, 1983, and Thanos Veremis, "An Overview of Greek Security Concerns in the Eastern Mediterranean and the Balkans," *International Spectator* 17, no. 4 (1982): 339–45. See also Snyder, *Defending the Fringe,* p. 60. On the Papandreou-Tikhonov talks, see "Reportage on Tikhonov's Official Visit to Greece," FBIS, *Soviet Union (Daily Report),* February 22, 1983, pp. G1–G7.

36. See Ronald Steel, "NATO's Bad Boy," *New Republic,* March 21, 1983, pp. 18–21. See also Loulis, "Papandreou's Foreign Policy," pp. 380–84.

37. To date, NATO has preferred to employ existing multilateral channels such as OECD and IMF to assist Greece and Turkey. In the future, however, the NATO International Secretariat could be utilized to manage aid programs. Aid information up through 1985 is provided by Rainer Rupp, "Burden Sharing and the Southern Region of the Alliance," in Stuart, *Politics and Security.* See in particular pp. 41–45.

38. Regarding Greek complaints against the 7 : 10 formula, see T. Veremis, "Greece," in Stuart, *Politics and Security,* p. 147. Turkish complaints are reported in Henry Kamm, "Turkey Seeking Changes in U.S. Aid," *New York Times,* August 4, 1985, p. 3. It is worth noting that the Reagan administration agreed with the Turkish argument and made a concentrated effort to convince Congress to drop the 7:10 formula so that a much more ambitious program of aid could be established for Ankara. The Turks nonetheless continued to feel that the U.S. Congress is strongly pro-Greek and anti-Turk. In the words of a 1987 congressional report, "Turks feel that when they present an argument the United States has a counterargument and that when Greece presents an argument the United States is accommodating." House Committee on Foreign Affairs, Report of a Staff Study Mission to Portugal, Spain, Greece, and Turkey, *United States Political-Military Relations with Allies in Southern Europe,* October 15–30, 1986 (Washington, D.C.: Government Printing Office, June 1987), p. 39.

39. See, for example, Stefano Malatesta, "Ora in caso Papandreou lo Yankee e Benvenuto," *La Republica,* January 31, 1986. A more pessimistic assessment is offered by Jim Mann, "Greece Typifies Problems of American Bases Abroad," *Los Angeles Times,* May 16, 1988, pp. 4/6–7.

40. An example is the aforementioned 1975 congressional study, which concluded that "Greece is of marginal importance to U.S. security interests in the Middle East, given current base rights and restrictions. Conversely, U.S. military influence in the Middle East (present and potential) would suffer substantially if Turkey were to turn her back on this country" (House Foreign Affairs Committee, *Greece and Turkey,* p. 18).

23: THE IBERIAN ALLIES

1. The most comprehensive history of the U.S.-Spain basing agreements is by Angel Viñas, *Los pactos secretos de Franco con Estados Unidos* (Barcelona: GRIJALBO, 1981).

2. Public opinion polls are summarized by Antonio Garrigues Walker, "The Constitutional and Political Implications of a Referendum on NATO," Conference report (Madrid, March 24, 1984), p. 9.

3. William L. Heiberg argues that "Spain would be within its rights to open those facilities [in Ceuta and Melilla] to other forces in the Alliance. . . . it is likely that the deterrent value of even such a minor NATO presence in the enclaves would dissuade Morocco from taking any sudden action against them." See Heiberg, *The Sixteenth Nation: Spain's Role in NATO* (Washington, D.C.: National Defense University Press, 1983), p. 46.

4. Translation by the author (Stuart). An analysis of the referendum is provided by Donald Share, "Four Years of Socialist Government in Spain," Conference paper, American Political Science Association (Washington, D.C., August 28–31, 1986), p. 15.

5. Voting results for Spain's 52 provinces are provided in *Cambio 16*, March 17, 1986, p. 26.

6. Spain's pre-referendum status is explained by Rafael Spottorno, "Status actual de la presencia de España en la Otan," Conference paper (Johns Hopkins University, Bologna, April 26, 1985). See also Glenn Snyder's analysis of Spain's "semialigned" status in NATO, "Spain and NATO: The Reluctant Partner," in *Spain's Entry into NATO: Conflicting Political and Strategic Perspectives*, ed. Federico G. Gil and Joseph S. Tulchin (Boulder, Colo.: Lynne Rienner, 1988), pp. 140–88.

7. *Cambio 16*, March 17, 1986, p. 26.

8. Edward Schumacher, "Spanish Concerned by Military Aspects of Libyan-Moroccan Pact," *New York Times*, September 5, 1984, p. 5.

9. Reported in Edward Schumacher, "Spanish Eyes Turn to a Second Pillar of Hercules," *New York Times*, February 18, 1985, p. 2.

10. Antonio Sánchez-Gijon, "On Spain, NATO, and Democracy," in *Politics and Security in the Southern Region of the Atlantic Alliance*, ed. Douglas Stuart (Baltimore: Johns Hopkins University Press, 1988), p. 102.

11. Portions of the text of the 1976 and 1983 treaties are provided by Allain E. Chegut, "Redeployment militaire dans la péninsule ibérique," *Le monde diplomatique* (February 1984): 4.

12. Carlos Miranda, "Perspectivas para los futura cooperación en materia de seguridad entre España y los Estados Unidos," Mimeo, Conference presentation (Johns Hopkins University, Bologna, April 26, 1985), pp. 21–22.

13. See John Broder, "Defense 'Hole' Seen in Loss of Jets from Spain," *Los Angeles Times*, January 16, 1988, p. 1.

14. Quoted in the *International Herald Tribune*, June 1, 1982.

15. The background of the Castro visit is discussed in the *International Herald Tribune*, February 17, 1984. The PSOE's desire to develop a more multifaced and more ambitious foreign policy is the subject of former Spanish foreign minister Fernando Morán's book, *Una política exterior para España* (Barcelona: Editorial planeta, 1980). See also Angel Viñas, "Coordenados de la política de seguridad española," *Leviatan: Revista de hechos e ideas*, no. 17 (1984).

16. See Assembly of the West European Union, "Security and Terrorism: The Implications for Europe of Crisis in Other Parts of the World," document no. 1057 (April 29, 1986), p. 15.

17. See the analysis by Rainer Rupp, "Burden Sharing and the Southern Region of the Alliance," in Stuart, *Politics and Security*, pp. 27–45.

18. Dean Acheson, *Present at the Creation: My Years in the State Department* (New York: Norton, 1969), p. 628.

19. See the analysis of Salazar's approach to NATO by Albano Nogueira, "Portugal's Special Relationship: Azores, British Connection," Paper presented at the Conference on NATO and the Mediterranean, n.d.

20. See Col. R. G. Ferreira, "The Portuguese Platform—Reflections about Its Usefulness in the Context of the East-West Confrontation," in *The Seaford House Papers, 1983*, ed. Giles Binney (London: Royal College of Defense Studies, 1983), p. 97.

21. Henry Kissinger, *Years of Upheaval* (Boston: Little, Brown, 1982), p. 520.

22. Quoted in Nogueira, "Portugal's Special Relationship," p. 9.

23. Between 1949 and 1961, U.S. economic and military aid to Portugal totaled $370 million, according to S. J. Bosgra and C. van Krimpen, "Origins of Portuguese Military Equipment: Portugal and NATO," in *Africa Contemporary Record, 1969–1970* (London: Rex Collings, 1970), p. C-131.

24. Discussed in Malyn Newitt, *Portugal in Africa* (London: Hurst, 1981), pp. 225–30.

25. George Ball, *The Past Has Another Pattern* (New York: Norton, 1982), p. 181.

26. See Arthur Schlesinger's account of the struggle between the "Africanists" and the "Europeanists" in 1961 in *A Thousand Days: John F. Kennedy in the White House* (New York: Houghton Mifflin, 1965), pp. 467–538.

27. Regarding the conventional emphasis of the Kennedy administration, see A. Enthoven and W. Smith, *How Much Is Enough?* (New York: Harper and Row, 1971).

28. Schlesinger, *A Thousand Days*, p. 519.

29. For further discussion, see Douglas Stuart, "Africa as an Out-of-Area Problem for NATO," in *The United States, Western Europe, and Military Intervention Overseas*, ed. Christopher Coker (London: Macmillan, 1987), pp. 97–98.

30. Bosgra and van Krimpen, "Portugal and NATO," p. C–131.

31. For specifics regarding the "package deal," see *Department of State Bulletin*, January 3, 1972, pp. 7–9, and February 28, 1972, p. 21, summarized in Melvin Gurtov, *The U.S. against the Third World* (New York: Praeger, 1974), p. 76.

32. William Minter, *Portuguese Africa and the West* (New York: Monthly Review Press, 1974), p. 109.

33. The demobilization is discussed in a North Atlantic Assembly report, "Information Report on Economic Situation and Portugal's Economic and Military Requirements," EC(79) 10, rev. 1 (October 1979), p. 19.

34. See the analysis of aid programs by Rupp, "Burden Sharing and the Southern Region of the Alliance," pp. 39–40. Regarding new equipment, see Desmond Wettern, "Madeira Base Is Planned for NATO Central Supply Route," *Daily Telegraph*, September 25, 1981.

35. Quoted in Alvaro Vasconcelos, "Portugal in Atlantic-Mediterranean Security," in Stuart, *Politics and Security*, p. 118.

36. See Richard Wigg, "Iberian Joint Command Versus History," *Times* (London), February 24, 1982, p. 16.

37. Regarding the issue of an Iberian joint command, see Gregory Treverton, "The Strategic Significance of the Iberian Peninsula," *NATO's Fifteen Nations* (June–July 1981): 30–33.

38. Quoted by Paul Delaney, "Portugal Woos Two Aggrieved Ex-Colonies," *New York Times*, February 18, 1988, p. 5.

39. *International Herald Tribune*, December 14, 1983, pp. 1, 4. One Lisbon newspaper displayed a photo of U.S. secretary of state George Shultz arriving to sign the basing agreement under the headline "Santa Claus Is Here!" The Portuguese government has nonetheless called for renegotiating the terms of the 1983 agreement and is seeking a $205 million annual aid package in compensation for access to the Lajes facility. See "Portugal, U.S. to Consult about Increased Aid," *Los Angeles Times*, February 25, 1988, p. 5.

40. Quoted by Vasconcelos, "Portugal in Atlantic-Mediterranean Security," p. 126.

41. See Mario Mesquito, "O valor estratégico dos Azores na perspectiva Africana," in *A Africa num mundo multipolar*, Estudos africanos, no. 1 (Lisbon: Instituto de estudos estrategicos e internacionais (IEEI), 1983).

42. See the analysis of the PCP prepared by the Congressional Research Service, Library of Congress, *A Report on West European Communist Parties*, submitted by Senator Edward Brooke to the Senate Appropriations Committee, June 1977, pp. 113–37. Regarding the issue of PCP access to NATO secrets, see Lawrence Whetten, *New International Communism* (Lexington, Mass.: Lexington Books, 1982), pp. 139–59.

43. Quoted in Vasconcelos, "Portugal in Atlantic-Mediterranean Security," p. 135.

CONCLUSION

1. The ANZUS situation is explained by Thomas-Durell Young: "While it is the case that the treaty itself remains in force, the United States formally ended its security commitments to New Zealand on 11 August 1986. This diplomatic 'divorce' was followed by an exchange of notes

between Washington and Canberra transforming the ANZUS alliance into a bilateral security arrangement." "Rethinking U.S. Foreign Policy and Strategy toward the South and Southwest Pacific Region," *Asian Survey* 28, no. 7 (1988): 775–88.

2. Glenn Snyder, "The Security Dilemma in Alliance Politics," *World Politics* 36, no. 4 (1984): 464.

3. George Liska, *Nations in Alliance: The Limits of Interdependence* (Baltimore: Johns Hopkins Press, 1968), p. 61.

4. Manfred Wörner, Speech, New Senate Office Building (Washington, D.C., September 13, 1988, attended by one of the authors).

5. The thesis is presented in Mancur Olson and Richard Zeckhauser, "An Economic Theory of Alliances," *Review of Economics and Statistics* 48 (1966): 266–79.

6. Janice Gross Stein relates the concept of extended deterrence to the issue of NATO out-of-area cooperation in "The Wrong Strategy in the Right Place: The United States in the Gulf," *International Security* (Winter 1988–89): 142–67.

7. For a discussion of pure and impure public goods, see Michael Ward, "Research Gaps in Alliance Dynamics," *Monograph Series in World Affairs,* vol. 19, bk. 1 (University of Denver, 1982), pp. 27–30. The concept of barter is analyzed by James Buchanan, *The Demand and Supply of Public Goods* (Chicago: Rand McNally, 1968). This concept is applied to NATO by Mark Boyer, "The Trading of Public Goods: The Case of the Western Alliance System," ISA Conference paper (St. Louis, Mo., March 29-April 2, 1988), pp. 11, 19.

8. Charles Kupchan, *The Persian Gulf and the West* (Boston: Allen and Unwin, 1987), p. 197. See also Stein, "Wrong Strategy," pp. 159–61.

9. Robert Keohane, *After Hegemony: Cooperation and Discord in the World Political Economy* (Princeton, N.J.: Princeton University Press, 1984), p. 215.

10. Duncan Snidal, "The Limits of Hegemonic Stability Theory," *International Organization* (Autumn 1985): 162. See also Boyer, "Trading of Public Goods."

11. See Stanley Hoffmann's analysis of U.S. "fundamentalism" in *Dead Ends* (Cambridge: Ballinger, 1983), pp. 123–29.

12. The three-step procedure was summarized by Henning Wegener, NATO Assistant Secretary General, Political Affairs, in a meeting with one of the authors (Stuart) on June 21, 1988.

13. George Kennan, *Memoirs: 1925–1950* (Boston: Little, Brown, 1967), p. 411.

INDEX

Federal Republic of Germany (*continued*)
  Korean War effects on, 267
  presence in NATO, 267
  security threatened, 267
  U.S. relations, 268
Finland
  Soviet defense treaty (1948), 47
FLN (Front de libération nationale), 59, 202,
    203, 205, 206–8, 217, 219
FLNC (Front de libération nationale con-
    golaise), 228, 231
FOPI (Forza Operativa di Pronto Intervento),
    285, 286
Forrestal, James, 37
FPDA (Five Power Defense Arrangements),
    149
France, 4, 6, 7, 19
  Algeria as colony of, 178, 185, 186
  Algerian War, 209, 210
  ally with Soviet Union, 241
  and Atlantic Alliance, 185
  attacks Iran, 242
  boycotts NATO, 208, 218, 220
  breaks with NATO, 213, 217
  British relations with, 195, 198, 200, 204
  Chadian crisis, 238
  and communism, 180, 190, 191, 232
  détente with Soviet Union, 227
  economic problems, 181
  and European Defense Community, 198,
    200, 201
  foreign policy, 219
  global influence, 223
  global security interest, 247
  global strategy, 184
  Indochina relations, 69, 70, 178, 179,
    180–82, 183, 190, 194, 198, 199, 201,
    209
  invasion of Tunisia, 217
  involvement
    in Chad, 239
    in Suez crisis, 206
    in Vietnam, 219
  and Korean War, 191
  leader in Europe, 222
  military
    forces in, 179, 229, 231
    forces of, 96, 181, 197, 276
    forces on African continent, 228, 234
    intervention in Zaire, 275–77
  NATO sanction, 7
  naval maneuvers in Persian Gulf, 242

  nuclear weapons in, 213, 214, 218, 242–
    43
  oil trade with Tripoli, 238
  peacekeeping efforts in Middle East, 241
  policies in Maghreb, 214
  reconciliation with NATO, 246
  relations
    with Africa, 221, 227
    with Belgium, 232–34, 275–77
    with Britain, 206, 246
    with Egypt, 205
    with P.R.C., 191, 219
    with Soviet Union, 176, 177
    with U.S., 70, 181, 182, 199, 212, 240
    with West Germany, 242
  role in NATO, 183
  solicits U.S. military assistance, 232
  support
    in Central America, 237
    for Habré, 240
    for Italy in NATO, 280
  Third World interests, 176, 194, 228
  troops in Beirut, 241
  U.S. relations with, 190, 192, 193, 196,
    197, 203, 204, 232
  war in Indochina, 192, 196, 197
  Western ally, 236
Franco-African summit, 232
Franco-German Brigade, 320
Franco-Soviet Treaty of Mutual Aid and As-
    sistance (1944), 176
Franks, Sir Oliver, 139
Fryden, Knut, 263

Gaddis, John, 35
Gaillard, Felix, 208, 209
Gama, Jaime, 310
Geneva
  collapse of disarmament talks in, 241
Geneva Conference (1954), 126
Germany, 6, 20
Giscard d'Estaing, Valéry, 88, 227, 228,
    232–34, 235, 238
  foreign policy of, 231
  and French defense policy, 227
  views of U.S. and USSR, 227
Gonzáles Márquez, Felipe, 301
Goodpaster, Andrew, 295
Gorbachev, Mikhail, 320
Gouvernement d'union nationale de transition
    (*GUNT*), 237
Great Debate, 36, 39

Composed by The Composing Room of Michigan
in Times Roman text and display
Printed by the Maple Press Company, Inc.
on 50-lb Glatfelter Eggshell Cream Offset paper
and bound in Holliston Roxite

Designed by Laury A. Egan